Environmental Humanities

ROWMAN AND LITTLEFIELD
INTERNATIONAL – INTERSECTIONS

The Rowman and Littlefield International – Intersections series presents an overview of the latest and emerging trends in some of the most dynamic areas of research in the Humanities and Social Sciences today. The texts explore emerging subdisciplines or topics or established subdisciplines that are evolving as interdisciplinary fields.

TITLES IN THE SERIES

Environmental Humanities

Voices from the Anthropocene

Edited by
Serpil Oppermann and Serenella Iovino

ROWMAN &
LITTLEFIELD
INTERNATIONAL
London • New York

Published by Rowman & Littlefield International Ltd
Unit A, Whitacre Mews, 26-34 Stannary Street, London SE11 4AB
www.rowmaninternational.com

Rowman & Littlefield International Ltd.is an affiliate of Rowman & Littlefield
4501 Forbes Boulevard, Suite 200, Lanham, Maryland 20706, USA
With additional offices in Boulder, New York, Toronto (Canada), and Plymouth (UK)
www.rowman.com

British Library Cataloguing in Publication Data
A catalogue record for this book is available from the British Library

ISBN: HB 978-178-348-938-1
      PB 978-178-348-939-8

Library of Congress Cataloguing in Publication Data is Available

ISBN 978-1-78348-938-1 (cloth: alk. paper)
ISBN 978-1-78348-939-8 (pbk: alk. paper)
ISBN 978-1-78348-940-4 (electronic)

The paper used in this publication meets the minimum requirements of American
National Standard for Information Sciences—Permanence of Paper for Printed Library
Materials, ANSI/NISO Z39.48-1992.

Printed in the United States of America

Table of Contents

List of Illustrations

Acknowledgements

Transdisciplinary and multiperspectival, the Environmental Humanities are, by definition, a research field based on teamwork. Faithful to this premise, this book also comes from the joint efforts of people and institutions whose support we are happy to recognise.

Sarah Campbell at Rowman & Littlefield International deserves heartfelt thanks for asking us to assemble this volume. Her invitation has given us another opportunity to work with so many important colleagues who share our scepticism about the 'Great Divide' between the sciences and the humanities, and whose work stimulates us to cross disciplinary boundaries and envision new productive forms of dialogue. To all of them, as 'our' authors on the pages of this book, goes therefore a deep gratitude: because their voices and ideas are the real strength of this project. In particular, we would like to thank Baird Callicott for his expert and patient feedback on our Introduction. The editorial team at Rowman & Littlefield International (Sinead Murphy, Isobel Cowper-Coles) added to our efforts its scrupulous and resourceful work on texts, illustrations, and captions.

For these many years of ecocultural debates, we owe thankfulness to the international and intersectional community of ASLE and EASLCE: projects like this book, among all the others we have pursued over the last decade, would be unthinkable apart from this collective atmosphere of sharing, thinking, and caring.

In addition, Serenella Iovino would like to thank the Alexander-von-Humboldt Foundation for yielding her a research grant at the Rachel Carson Center for Environment and Society of the Ludwig-Maximilians Universität, Munich. There, thanks to the welcoming, inclusive collegial atmosphere created by Christof Mauch and coordinated by Rob Emmett, she found an amazingly inspirational milieu, where cutting-edge cross-disciplinary inquiry goes hand in hand with Bavaria's legendary *Lebensgenuss*. Some of the contributions in this volume come from presentations and discussions held during the Thursday meetings in the Leopoldstrasse. Sincere gratitude also goes to her colleagues at the Turin International Group of Environmental Humanities Research, especially Daniela Fargione, Laura Bonato, and Alberto Baracco, and to the students and colleagues at the Elitestudienkolleg 'Ethik der Textkulturen' at the University of Augsburg, Germany, masterfully led by Hubert Zapf.

To our families, an inextinguishable debt of gratitude that words could never convey.

Ankara–Turin, May 2016

J. Baird Callicott's chapter previously appeared with the the title 'A NeoPreSocratic Manifesto' in *Environmental Humanities* 2 (2013): 169–186.

Stefan Helmreich's chapter is reproduced by permission of the American Anthropological Association from *American Anthropologist* 113.1 (March 2011): 132–144. Not for sale or further reproduction.

Thom van Dooren and Deborah Bird Rose's chapter was previously published in the special issue of *Environmental Humanities*, 'Multispecies Studies.' Ed. Thom van Dooren, Ursula Münster, Eben Kirksey, Deborah Bird Rose, Matthew Chrulew, Anna Tsing. 8.1 (Spring 2016).

Rob Nixon's chapter appeared in the special issue of *Perspectives*, 'The Edges of Environmental History: Honouring Jane Carruthers.' Ed. Christof Mauch and Libby Robin. 1 (Spring 2014): 101–109.

Rosi Braidotti and Cosetta Veronese's 'Can the Humanities Become Posthuman? A Conversation' appeared in Part I of the special double issue of *Relations: Beyond Anthropocentrism*, 'Past the Human: Narrative Ontologies and Ontological Stories.' Ed. Serenella Iovino, Roberto Marchesini, and Eleonora Adorni. June 2016: 95–102.

All these texts are reproduced in revised or expanded form with the kind permission of the previous publishers or of the authors as copyright owners.

Foreword

Richard Kerridge

Debate continues about whether the Anthropocene should be recognised as our current geological era and, if so, when that era began. But, in any case, what are the cultural, ethical, and personal implications of the concept? Is it much of a paradigm-changer?

The challenges it brings are paradoxical. Atmospheric chemist Paul J. Crutzen and biologist Eugene F. Stoermer, proposing the idea in 2000, declared that their purpose was to 'emphasize the central role of mankind in geology and ecology' (17). In the Holocene, the era that officially we still inhabit, 'mankind's activities' had gradually become 'a significant geological morphological force' (17). That force is ever more pervasive, due to the global nature of the climate system, the globalization of industrial capitalism, the continuing increase in the overall human population, and the accumulation of waste-matter such as CO_2 in the atmosphere and plastic in oceans and landfill sites. The geologist Jan Zalasiewicz, in his essay in this collection, uses the example of discarded plastic to illustrate several facets of the change made by human beings:

> Plastic in its various forms is essentially a post-WWII phenomenon, now being produced in hundreds of millions of tons per year and—hard-wearing, decay-resistant, light and easily transportable—is finding its way to the oceans. There, particularly in the almost invisible 'microplastic' form (the thousands of fibres, say, that come from your fleece after it has been through a wash cycle), it is transported by currents and within animal bodies to reach the most distant beaches and the deepest sea floors. . . To regard these phenomena as part of the fabric of geology is certainly novel — but is defensible, in that it does appear to reflect a genuine departure within the Earth system.

Zalasiewicz's description consists mainly of things we cannot see directly—things that challenge the human body's field of vision. They are either too small or too big: the fibres too small to notice, the vast oceanic sweep, the penetration into every deep corner. We are able to encounter the plastic waste at the two extremes of perspective, the panoramic zoom out and the microscopic zoom in, but not, it would seem, in the middle range, the range available to human vision without technological assistance. Yet this middle perspective is the one we need in order to visualise the actions of human individuals or communities. The difficulty of attaining it makes Filippo Bertoni, in his essay, ask '*how* to tell stories that won't easily fit together in the ways we are accustomed to?', and Lowell Duckert focus on unfilled gaps and lacunae, represented symbolically by the landscape forms known as lagoons:

> 'Lagoon' derives from the Latin word for 'pool', *lacūna*, which comes from *lacus* ('lake'). 'Lacuna'—meaning an unfilled space or interval, a gap—comes from *lacūna* as well, but in the additional sense of 'a hole, pit'.

In the case of plastic, there is also a mismatch between the global extent of the transformation and the short time it has taken ('essentially a post-WWII phenomenon'). Such are the 'derangements of scale', as the ecocritic Timothy Clark calls them (see Clark 2015, 71–137), that the Anthropocene brings.

For Bill McKibben, as early as 1989, the imminence of severe climate crisis had already brought about the fundamental category-change that he called 'the end of nature'. No longer could the damage done by human beings be regarded as merely local. 'Nature' was no longer the backdrop, the world outside human influence, the great beyond, limitless yet close at hand:

> We have changed the atmosphere, and thus we are changing the weather. By changing the weather, we make every spot on earth man-made and artificial. We have deprived nature of its independence, and that is fatal to its meaning. Nature's independence is its meaning; without it there is nothing but us. (54)

The concept of the Anthropocene is an extension and scientific substantiation of McKibben's idea, but although it makes obsolete certain traditional attributes of 'Nature', what the Anthropocene brings about is much more complex than a simple erasure of the distinction between nature and artifice, such as to transfer 'every spot on earth' into the latter category. As one binary distinction begins to fade, others emerge to replace it. Human activity has become a geomorphic force on a global scale, but this observation does not simply present us with an enlargement of the scope of human artifice and power, since the geomorphic changes are, for the most part, unintended and threatening. The Anthropocene is a duck-rabbit. Looked at one way, it calls on us to accept that there is now no alternative to a much more concerted effort to engineer the climate and other ecological processes. Humanity has to embrace its lonely role. There is no route of retreat to the old position of smallness in the face of mighty nature. But from another viewpoint, human capability is diminished by the spectacle of the sheer magnitude of the consequences we did not foresee. Even as the concept of the Anthropocene challenges us—collective humanity—to take greater and more exceptional responsibility, it also admonishes us for past hubris, and relegates us to the category of stumbling, floundering creatures whose plans go awry because we understand too little: in other words, natural creatures, caught up in forces beyond our understanding. This latter perception returns us to nature.

Similarly, McKibben's statement that now 'there is nothing but us' makes sense as a recognition of an exceptional and lonely responsibility, but is also provocatively misleading, since we are clearly embedded in ecosystems inhabited and constituted by numerous nonhuman creatures, some of them living inside our bodies. If we damage the systems, these creatures will suffer with us. Many already are. New Materialist ecocritics, with their analysis of forms of agency that are distributed between different species and entities across these ecosystems, confront the difficult task of combining this sense of shared agency in vastly complex systems with an acceptance of urgent and exceptional responsibility. Some of the leading voices are in this collection.

Crutzen and Stoermer expressed the hope that a general recognition of unintended consequences, and of the scale of responsibility involved, would prompt an era of deliberate collective responsibility, to counter-balance and counter-act the unintended responsibility: 'To develop a world-wide accepted strategy leading to sustainability of ecosystems against human-induced stresses will be one of the great future tasks of mankind' (2000, 18). Their hope is that an unprecedented form of deliberate collective human agency, on a global scale, will be brought into being by the new visibility of centuries of unintended agency. This is a major part of their purpose in proposing the Anthropocene era for official recognition. They suggest that 'mankind', in the sense of the collective subjectivity that this 'world-wide accepted' shared task would produce, would be a new product of the new era, and of the performative act of that era's official naming—though they should say 'humankind'. A positive Anthropocene would follow the negative Anthropocene that has developed so far.

The principal objection to the Anthropocene concept is that the human, '*Anthropos*', is presented, in classically Enlightenment-humanist fashion, as a single entity and agent. This all-inclusive personified 'humanity' is a construct that hides political questions about specific responsibility for environmental disasters. Is it not the rich, especially the rich in the wealthy industrialised countries, mainly in the West, who are more responsible than the poor, especially the poor in poor countries? Is it not those with access to

Western consumerist styles of life? If we think of institutions and systems rather than people, is it not industrial capitalism, or corporate capitalism, or industrial modernity? Joni Adamson, in this collection, makes the point thus:

> When employed unconsciously to mean 'aggregate *Anthropos*', or 'all humans', the word *anthropos* fails to account for unequal human agency or unequal human vulnerabilities . . . As Crutzen and Stoermer propose it, the steam engine is 'referred to as the one artefact that unlocked the potentials of fossil energy' and thereby catapulted *anthropos* to full-spectrum dominance . . . However, steam technology was not adopted by some 'natural-born deputies of the human species' but by a tiny minority in Britain, and this 'class of people comprised an infinitesimal fraction of the population of Homo sapiens in the early 19th century'. At no time did the species as a whole vote for a fossil fuel economy or exercise any shared authority over the destiny of Earth systems.

This objection cannot easily be answered, and some of the contributors to this collection reject the term 'Anthropocene', proposing alternatives. A unitary Anthropos sits uneasily alongside the emphasis in recent schools of ecocritical theory upon ecosystems in which all the diverse participants, human and nonhuman, are continuously engaged in the production and modification of the system and thus of each other. Wendy Wheeler, for example, observes that '[t]he most centrally important biosemiotic impetus, however, takes the form of a move away from a sole focus on an ontology of substances (and essences)' towards 'a much greater focus . . . upon an ontology of relations and processes'. Greta Gaard points to 'the clear intersections of queer theory, feminism, anticapitalist and environmental thought'. Kate Rigby adds certain kinds of religious thought and doctrine. Among the 'material-discursive' accounts of how the world works—accounts that bring together insights from ecological science and post-structuralism—are Deleuze and Guattari's rhizome-theory, Latourian actor-network theory, biosemiotics, New Materialist descriptions of 'distributed agency', Timothy Morton's 'mesh', Karen Barad's 'intra-actions', and Stacy Alaimo's 'trans-corporeality'.

Critics like these ask challenging questions about the usefulness of the Anthropocene concept, and how to identify different kinds of responsibility within it. But when it is considered in relation to these schools of theory, rather than on its own, the Anthropocene idea can serve as a provocation, challenging people to accept as much responsibility as possible, but also to see clearly the relationship between environmental responsibilities and the distribution of wealth and power. Again, it is a matter of zooming in and zooming out. The ecocritic Ursula Heise, in *Sense of Place and Sense of Planet* (2008), proposed the zooming facility of Google Earth as a suggestive model for ecocritical practice and for the literary and cinematic representation of environmental problems. J. Baird Callicott makes a similar connection, offering the zooming and world-wide roaming of the internet as a harbinger—both promising and alarming—of a new holistic culture in which the traditional distance between arts and sciences has disappeared:

> We are presently in the midst of another revolution in communications and information technology, from literacy to Googality—I'm sorry, but I cannot think of a better name. If these scholars are right about the transformation of human consciousness effected by the transition from orality to literacy, then another transformation of human consciousness may be forthcoming as we leave the linear world of letters and the privacy and intimacy of the one-way conversations we have with books, for the simultaneity, interconnectedness, and interactivity of the cyber 'cloud'.

From a feminist, postcolonial or more broadly Environmental Justice perspective, the necessary zooming involves withdrawing to the point from which humanity is visible as a single geomorphic force, and then zooming back in, perhaps further than before, to make necessary distinctions between rich and poor, privileged and oppressed. Crutzen and Stoermer's vision of a positive Anthropos—a humanity defined as such by its world-wide engagement with a recognised necessity—must be conceived in these terms if it is to meet the Environmental Justice objection. Such mobility of perspective is an essential aim for the new Environmental Humanities, to which this fine collection of essays makes an excellent introduction—an aim for interdisciplinary academic method and also for literary form. In bringing together perspectives from geology, literary criticism, philosophy, postcolonial studies, anthropology, sociology, biosemiotics, historical studies, studies of religion, medieval studies, animal studies and creative writing, Serpil Oppermann and Serenella Iovino have made this principle of mobility the energizing force of a fascinating book.

WORKS CITED

Clark, Timothy. *Ecocriticism at the Edge: The Anthropocene as a Threshold Concept*. London: Bloomsbury, 2015.

Crutzen, Paul J. and Eugene F. Stoermer. 'The Anthropocene'. *International Geosphere-Biosphere Programme Newsletter* 41 (May 2000): 17–18.

Heise, Ursula. *Sense of Place and Sense of Planet: The Environmental Imagination of the Global*. New York: Oxford University Press, 2008.

McKibben, Bill. *The End of Nature*. London: Penguin, 1990.

Introduction

The Environmental Humanities and the Challenges of the Anthropocene

Serpil Oppermann and Serenella Iovino

> The environmental humanities contextualises and complements environmental science and policy with a focus on narrative, critical thinking, history, cultural analysis, aesthetics and ethics.

These lines are from *The Environmental Humanities Newsletter*, published by University of Oregon's Environmental Studies Program in 2014. Such programs and centres now proliferate in universities from North America to Europe and Australia, indicating the growing influence of this burgeoning field of study. As concisely defined in the opening pages of the *Newsletter*, the field of the Environmental Humanities is interdisciplinary. It brings the social sciences, the humanities, and the natural sciences together in diverse ways to address the current ecological crises from closely knit ethical, cultural, philosophical, political, social, and biological perspectives. Engaging with the global reach of old and new environmental challenges, values, environmental justice issues, and theoretical conceptions of the human and nonhuman natures, the Environmental Humanities address the complexities of material networks that cross through local and global cultures, economic and social practices, and political discourses. As Andrew Pickering concedes, science studies and the humanities 'are mangled in practice' (1995, 23) in a common effort to develop a comprehensive approach to the multifaceted aspects of environmental crises. It is therefore not surprising to observe that the Environmental Humanities offer a rich array of scholarship with combined insights from many research fields. They forge reconfiguration and extension of the notions of nature, agency, and materiality, which are intertwined co-constitutively in formulating new theoretical models of environmentality that coalesce human and nonhuman ecologies.

1

We are called upon to understand our liberal engagements with whatever is not human in causing global environmental changes and to recognise our worldly embodiments within systems of massive exploitation of limited natural capital. The ways in which we are immersed in the more-than-human environments point to a 'vortex of shared precariousness and unchosen proximities' (Cohen 2015, 107). They can also be understood in terms of what Timothy Morton, in *The Ecological Thought*, calls 'coexistentialism' (2010, 47). These conceptual frameworks enable discussion of how we are also ethically entangled with the nonhuman, this 'strange stranger' at once unpredictable, intimate, and uncanny—whose presence prompts us to rethink the scope of our deeds and attitudes. The pivotal question here is: how will new modes of knowing and being, which the Environmental Humanities call for, enable environmentally just practices? They in fact limn the field with possible answers about how to relate to that which is beyond human dichotomies, which is both vulnerable and dangerous, distant and proximal, and which is risky and familiar at the same time. Such is the material world of nonhuman agencies, which is bound up with the human reality on many scales and levels, from viruses and bacteria to geological forces. The evidence emerging from research focused 'on the interface between social and biological systems' (Heise and Carruth 2010, 3) already epitomises how the human is always already enmeshed, to quote Stacy Alaimo, 'within the material flows, exchanges, and interactions of substances, habitats, places, and environments' (2011, 281). Therefore, we need 'complex modes of analysis that travel through [these] entangled territories' (282), conceptual patterns that allow us to follow the 'frictions' of natures and beings into a contaminated dimension of 'transformative encounters' (Tsing 2015, 28), so insightfully mapped by Anna Tsing. What is happening to the Earth's climate, for example, is also 'occurring on all levels of the material, social, and cultural fabric of the world, including the micro level of the individual and his or her life-style' (Rossini 2012). That is why environmental problems are not the concerns of Earth scientists only. They are also social and cultural, philosophical and political, as their insidious signals of precariousness and risks have long extended into the social sphere—a sphere where, after all, they are also rooted. As Uwe Lübken and Christof Mauch put it, 'environmental risk is not simply a phenomenon "out there" but the result of social, economic and cultural processes' (2011, 112). Food scarcity, poverty, water and air pollution, social injustices and gender inequalities, energy demands, and climate-related health challenges are only some of the conditions to rethink the social in ecological terms and vice versa. The geo- and biopolitical consequences of this discourse on a global scale are also expectable. As Kathleen McAfee writes,

The politics of nature cannot be neutral . . . [It] is ultimately about who is entitled to what, who owes what to whom, how such rights and entitlements are to be enforced, and who gets to decide. In a world of great geographic variety and vast social difference, decisions and actions by states and others, or inactions opting for the status quo inevitably have consequences that affect some people and places very differently than others. (2016, 65)

The fundamental argument, then, fuelling the research in the Environmental Humanities is that the urgent environmental problems that stretch from the geological to the biological are also essentially social and cultural issues deeply interwoven with economic and political agendas and thus demand solutions on many dimensions. These dimensions include building new environmental imaginaries, formulating new discursive practices, and making changes in economic and political structures. The ongoing anthropogenic process and their various combinations aggregate many levels not only of human wellbeing (Di Paola 2015, 184, 185) but also the wellbeing of all planetary life. Political scientist Marcello Di Paola is correct in claiming that we are all confronted with an ethical task 'when trying to live in a better integrated relationship with the dynamic systems that govern our changing planet' (185). Hence, the significance of ethical as well as critical reflection with regard to the wounded body of the planet by human activities. In the same vein, science studies scholars Eileen Crist and H. Bruce Rinker issue a stern warning: '[T]o rip into the planet's rhythms, cycles, and interconnections, as the civilization we have created is doing, signals human folly not mastery. For one, the Earth system is ultimately unpredictable and more powerful than humanity's actions' (2010, 13). Such warnings have invited intersectional academic responses to the injured habitats and beings. The spirit underlying these responses is lucidly expressed by what Stephanie LeMenager and Stephanie Foote have called 'the sustainable humanities': humanities that 'can also confront hyperindustrial modernity in the era of unconventional energy mining, of fracking, tar sands, and mountaintop removal, with the unfashionable but nonetheless ecological concept of civic responsibility' (2012, 574).

With their ethical-educational project of creating alliances between science, society, and cultural discourses, the Environmental Humanities are the very materialization of this vision. And 'materialization' is not a neutral word in this context. In fact, taking ecological relationships as their straightforward thematic referent, the Environmental Humanities veer off the idea of culture and education as 'spiritual' abstractions. At once they lay bare the production processes and impacts of their own means and media—be they books, archives, artworks, digital devices, or classroom teaching—and the costs of anthropocentric mindsets and practices for the health of the planet. The theoretical frameworks and reflections they articulate are de facto instrumental to *practices* meant to better interpret the matter and meanings of human interconnectedness with the nonhuman. This is why it is so important, in this context, to develop convincing and comprehensive epistemological tools.

Many subfields in the Environmental Humanities—ecocriticism, environmental philosophy and history, critical animal studies, queer ecologies, ecofeminisms, environmental sociology, political ecology, ecomaterialisms, and posthumanism, among others—hold the conviction that the wounds of the natural world are also social wounds and that the planetary ecological crisis is the material and historical consequence of an anthropocentric and dualistic worldview. Fraught with nature/culture, human/nonhuman, man/woman, East/West, North/South, and ecology/economy binary oppositions, this 'inflated anthropocentric credo' (Crist and Rinker 2010, 13) acts as the driving force behind economic growth, political strategies, and technological development—all to the detriment of the Earth's life support systems. At the root of all ecological crises, in other words, lie the divisive epistemologies that create an illusory sense of an ontological dissociation between the human and the nonhuman realms. The legacy of this dissociation explains why the planetary environment today is seen as 'a swirling biogeochemical *playground* whose elements combine to form patterns, cycles, and circulations of landscapes, species, and ecologies' (Thomashow 2001, 3; emphasis added), resulting in the relentless disruption of the Earth's rhythms, biocycles, species connections, and ecosytemic processes.

One of the daunting consequences of the dissociative thinking that we are currently experiencing is global climate change, which affects the Earth's living fabric with melting glaciers, ocean acidification, extreme heats, droughts, floods, increased tornado and hurricane activity and intensity. Other distressing events linked to climate change—such as water resource depletion, extinction of valuable species, climate-related diseases, and mutating viruses—have also resulted from the 'anthropocentric credo' in its long historical path. The social impact of this array of phenomena is clearly unequal. As Marco Armiero suggests, to repeat that 'we are all in the same boat . . . occludes at least as much as it reveals' (2015, 52): not all, in this boat, are first-class travellers, and not all will be saved if (or when) it will shipwreck. The impact that these phenomena have on cultural models and discourses, in turn, is ambivalent. On the one hand, ecological changes have triggered revolutionary ways of rethinking human relations to the more-than-human environments as indicated by the new materialist theories. On the other hand, however, the ideological, ethical, and social dimensions of global climate change have made environmentalism more complicated and fraught with controversy than ever before.

All this is mainly due to the fact that human relations with the planet at large and with local ecosystems on national and regional scales have so far been grounded in unsustainable practices that rely on systems of domination and 'hyperseparation', as explained by the ecofeminist analyses of thinkers such as Karen Warren and Val Plumwood. According to this vision, social as well as ecological relationships are framed within 'the logic of Othering' (Plumwood 2002, 117) that subjugates not only humans and sentient animals but also everything else that is exploitable. This radicalised 'hypersepara- tion', however, creates in the dominant subjects the illusion of their 'disem- deddedness', thus blocking their own survival. It is, therefore, imperative to seek new modes of thought that would shift our mindset towards a disanthro- pocentric discursive change, which in turn will create and implement more sustainable economic practices, social behaviors, and moral paradigms. The fundamental impediment in the way of this objective is the collective mind the majority of people share in relating to the world. And this anthropocentric mindset is a perfect example of resistance to change as it operates, in Claire Colebrook's words, as 'hyper-Cartesianism' (2015, 169)—an amplified ver- sion of the separation of the subject from the object, rewritten in terms of an ontological gulf dividing the social and the natural. When one considers the intersecting and often messy biophysical and social realities, however, human/nature dualisms lose their grounding. We begin to rethink the dynam- ics of life through the fundamental inseparability of the human and the non- human in their shared earthly rootedness. We come to recognise the fact that, against scientific (and cultural) paradigms that objectify and commodify all life, the Earth, as Bruno Latour contends, 'is no longer "objective"; it cannot be put at a distance and emptied of all its humans. Human action is visible everywhere—in the construction of knowledge *as well as* in the production of the phenomena those sciences are called to register' (2014, 6). And something that our sciences cannot help registering is that, radically and profoundly, we are trans-corporeal subjects, undeniably embroiled in the Earth's biophysical processes along with other species.

Like other biological entities, we all carry nature within us even if we think of members of our species as discrete beings unaffected by the punctured ecosystems and human-induced environmental stresses placed on the natu- ral world. As Anna Tsing puts it, '[t]he evolution of our "selves" is already polluted by histories of encounter; we are mixed up with others before we even begin any new collaboration' (Tsing 2015, 29). In other words, '[e] veryone carries a history of contamination; purity is not an option' (27). The human microbiome is alive with trillions of microbial cells—bacteria, fungi, archaea, sometimes viruses, and other swarming microscopic organisms that make us all interspecies beings. In his short essay 'The New You', Anthony Doerr compellingly writes that 'if you decided to name one organism every second (You're Barbara, You're Bob, You're Brenda), you'd likely need fifty lifetimes to name them all'. He is right in claiming that from the moment we are born, 'we are colonized, seized, and occupied by other entities', and '[t] o even write that you are "you" and the microbes are "them" is, perhaps, a failure of pronouns'.[1] The Environmental Humanities engage with this complicated *naturalcultural* landscape and transitive 'pronominality'. But they also engage with stories, discourses, and narratives that disclose the proximal relations among bodily natures and the environments within which they are inseparably enmeshed. As Donna Haraway insists, 'all earthlings are kin in the deepest sense . . . Kin is an assembling sort of word. All critters share a common "flesh", laterally, semiotically, and genealogically' (2015, 162). The main idea that is highlighted in this new understanding of natures and cultures, or *naturecultures* in Haraway's terms, is that—ecologically as well as evolutionarily—the body circulates through the environment and the environment circulates through the body. And whether it is a human or a nonhuman body, or whether it is a microscopic or a geological body, all bodies are inscribed with the flows and mutual transformations of material and discursive elements. One need only to remember here that ecological knowledge can never be disentangled from philosophical inquiries about the nature of nature, from political decisions about energy and resource use, and thus from the regimes of power and ethical concerns accompanying social complexities. Simply because, as Karen Barad explains, 'our knowledge-making practices are social-material enactments that contribute to, and are a part of, the phenomena we describe' (2007, 26).

Moreover, if 'human ideas, meanings and values shape and are shaped by, in some important way, the "environment out there"', as Astrida Neimanis, Cecilia Åsberg, and Johan Hedrén state, 'questions traditionally belonging to natural sciences and engineering domains are thus equally questions for the humanities' (2015, 71–72). Therefore, the solutions offered by natural scientists remain incomplete as they seem to neglect cultural values and social practices, but most importantly 'sociocultural imaginaries' (81) that influence ecological practices. 'Natural scientists', as the Swedish environmental historian Sverker Sörlin also writes, 'suggest solutions, aided by technology, economics, and policy' (2012, 788). Or they investigate the large-scale impacts of climate change on ecological systems, producing formidable data with reports of warning and serious risk scenarios on the destabilised Earth systems. The field of the Environmental Humanities, on the other hand, concentrates its energy on the ways in which such data is effectively translated into narratives and socio-cultural discourses that capture the public attention as well as political and economic agencies more arrestingly than scientific reports can do. As Donna Haraway contends, 'we need stories (and theories) that are just big enough to gather up the complexities and keep the edges open and greedy for surprising new and old connections' (2015, 160). Addressing the intersecting social and ecological problems from new ecological perspectives and perceptions, the Environmental Humanities bring attention to the significance of formulating 'stories (and theories)', narratives and discourses that would be accountable to ecologically sustainable social, economic, and political practices. This implies that, once human agency is set in a horizon of space-time-matter which is broad enough to encompass its innumerable ties, the discourse of the Environmental Humanities can also be instrumental in '[scaling] up our imagination of the human' (Chakrabarty 2009, 206), at the same time reinforcing the memory of our contact zones with the nonhuman world.

In 'Thinking through the Environment, Unsettling the Humanities', Deborah Bird Rose and her colleagues explain that in the Environmental Humanities

> we are able to articulate a 'thicker' notion of humanity, one that rejects reductionist accounts of self-contained, rational, decision making subjects. Rather, the environmental humanities positions us as participants in lively ecologies of meaning and value, entangled within rich patterns of cultural and historical diversity that shape who we are and the ways in which we are able to 'become with' others. (Rose et al. 2012, 2)

If we cohabit this trans-corporeal site of knotted agencies and encounters, and if it is impossible to get disengaged from this turbulent *oikos*, we can begin thinking of it as the site of unremitting becomings, meetings, transformations, representations, and narratives, which constitute the research objectives of the Environmental Humanities. Conceived this way, 'the whole world, at all scales, is a "contact zone". The deepening environmental and social crises of our time are unfolding in this zone where the nature/culture divide collapses and the possibilities of life and death for everyone are at stake' (2). It is thus important to reiterate that 'humanistic disciplines may help us understand and engage with global ecological problems by providing insight into human action, perceptions, and motivation', as expressed in 'Humanities for the Environment—A Manifesto for Research and Action' (Holm et al. 2015, 978). This 2015 Manifesto stresses the significance of the 'human factor' in investigating the 'biogeophysics of global change' (979) as it is not included in scientific calculations. In Sörlin's words, '[i]t seems this time that our hopes are tied to the humanities' (2012, 788). Or, espousing LeMenager and Foote's passionate claim, '[a]t the risk of sounding grandiose, Earth needs the humanities' (2012, 575).

It is in this framework that the Environmental Humanities seek to develop new convivial partnerships between the humanities, natural and social sciences, the fine arts, and other fields in order to devise and practice new critical humanisms. In producing 'sustainable artifacts and socialities' (Le

Menager and Foote 2012, 574), these transdisciplinary crossings are indeed a way to reaffirm critique 'as a kind of making'—almost an 'infrastructure' (574) for building inclusive forms of citizenship and projects of 'multispecies ecojustice' (Haraway 2015, 161). Offering new conceptualizations for the contact zones of human and more-than-human natures and environments, as well as new directions, posthumanisms, for example, are key modes of these critical forms of the Humanities. Rosi Braidotti's ground-breaking reflections on the role of the 'posthuman Humanities' are here a mandatory reference. Posthumanism, Braidotti argues, provides the humanities with 'a new set of narratives about the planetary dimension of globalised humanity; the evolutionary sources of morality; the future of our and other species; the semiotic systems of technological apparatus; . . . the role of gender and ethnicity as factors that index access to the posthuman predicament and the institutional implications of them all' (2013, 162–163). Developing on these insights, in 'Four Problems, Four Directions for Environmental Humanities: Toward Critical Posthumanities for the Anthropocene' (2015), Astrida Neimanis, Cecilia Åsberg, and Johan Hedrén present four specific directions to address what they delimit as four problems: 'alienation and intangibility; the post-political situation; negative framing of environmental change; and compartmentalization of "the environment" from other spheres of concern' (67). In order to tackle these problems, the authors suggest that we need to formulate 'diverse environmental imaginaries', rethink the field in terms of 'naturecultures and feminist posthumanisms', develop the field 'in a specifically transdisciplinary and postdisciplinarity vein', and create a 'citizen humanities' (70). All these spheres must be thought in terms of interconnected entanglements rather than homogenous connections that project a 'blanket humanity' (Vansintjan, 2016).[2]

Even if we perfectly know how distant it is from the grain of reality, such a universalizing conception of humanity traverses the accounts of the Anthropocene, too often reductively thought of as the epoch of the 'great homogenization' of terrestrial systems and fates under the geological layer of *the* human. Seeking less vague articulations, however, the Environmental Humanities not only conceptually challenge the Anthropocene's unilateral image of the human agency but also subvert its formulations that focus mostly on geological time scales. With their intersectional analyses, the Environmental Humanities reveal indeed that the Anthropocene concept involves 'much more than "just" geology' (Parikka, 'Introduction'). More precisely, filtering the Anthropocene through the lens of their disciplinary mergers is a way, as Jussi Parikka effectively puts it, to prove that geology itself 'does not refer exclusively to the ground under our feet. It is constitutive of social and technological relations as well as environmental and ecological realities' (Chapter 2). One of the primary goals of this collection is, therefore, to present different voices and conceptual models emerging from the sites of the Anthropocene discourses, such as those oriented in new feminist, spiritual, ecocultural, and nonhuman onto-epistemologies. As the subtitle of this volume indicates, the 'Voices from the Anthropocene' join the ongoing multidisciplinary conversations in the Environmental Humanities, mingling geological, biological, ecological, political, cultural, and social matters in working with 'questions of meaning, value, ethics, justice, and the politics of knowledge production' (Rose et al. 2012, 2). This approach of thinking through and with the more-than-human agencies corrects the scientific accounts of the Anthropocene and repudiates their image of an exceptional and universal human subject acting as an epoch-making geological force. The title of Will Steffen, Paul J. Crutzen, and John McNeill's article, for example, is: 'The Anthropocene: Are Humans Now Overwhelming the Great Forces of Nature?' In their conclusion, the authors claim that '[h]umans will remain a major geological force for many millennia, maybe millions of years, to come' (618). The idea of a 'blanket humanity' as an omnipresent planetary force, however, is due to the colossal scale of human impact on the planet's biogeochemical processes that make the scientists claim that the present interglacial era—the Holocene—should be called the Anthropocene, as the term signifies the profound 'chemical and biological effects of global human activity' (Zalasiewicz et al. 2010). In *The Earth after Us*, Jan Zalasiewicz observes that 'if we make enough of a mess of the world, we might compete with the Yucatan meteorite, or with the mysterious forces that, almost exactly a quarter of a billion years ago, suffocated most of the Earth's oceans and killed off an estimated 95 percent of the world's species' (2008, 156–157).

Originally coined by the atmospheric chemist Paul J. Crutzen and biologist Eugene Stoermer, the term Anthropocene came to signify 'the geology of humanity'. Considering the 'still growing impacts of human activities on earth and atmosphere' (17), in their famous essay 'The Anthropocene' (2000), Crutzen and Stoermer write:

> it seems to us more than appropriate to emphasise the central role of mankind in geology and ecology by proposing to use the term 'anthropocene' for the current geological epoch. The impacts of current human activities will continue over long periods. According to a study by Berger and Loutre . . . because of the anthropogenic emissions of CO_2, climate may depart significantly from natural behaviour over the next 50,000 years. (17)

Since the scientific accounts of the Anthropocene focus on the global scale of human impact on planetary systems, the depiction of the human as a geological force occasions what Andrew Revkin calls 'a hubristic overstatement of human powers' in his 2011 article in *The New York Times*. The popular accounts of the term reinforce this vision of 'man' as a geological force as well. The website called 'anthropocene.info', for example, announces that 'we're disrupting the grand cycles of biology, chemistry and geology . . . We're changing the way water moves around the globe as never before. Almost all the planet's ecosystems bear the marks of our presence' ('Welcome to the Anthropocene'). Also, the editorial on 'The Anthropocene', again in *The New York Times* on 27 February 2011, is similarly formulated: 'We are the only species to have defined a geological period by our activity—something usually performed by major glaciations, mass extinction and the colossal impact of objects from outer space'. To describe the human agency as a geophysical force is perhaps the major conceptual challenge the Anthropocene poses for the Environmental Humanities. One of the most discussed accounts of this challenge is found in postcolonial historian Dipesh Chakrabarty's article 'The Climate of History: Four Theses'. 'To call human beings as geological agents', writes Chakrabarty, 'is to scale up our imagination of the human. Humans are biological agents, both collectively and as individuals. But we can become geological agents only historically and collectively' (2009, 206). This can happen, Chakrabarty continues, if we invent technologies 'that are on a scale large enough to have an impact on the planet itself. To call ourselves geological agents is to attribute to us a force on the same scale as that released at other times when there has been a mass extinction of species' (207). However, this claim that—though conditionally—we can become geological agents is highly problematic as it involuntarily makes Chakrabarty's account subscribe to the same conceptual challenge that he attempts to critique. Furthermore, in his fourth thesis Chakrabarty also holds that '[e]ven if we were to emotionally identify with a word like *mankind*, we would not know what being a species is, for in species history, humans are only an instance of the concept species' (220). Certainly, the pronoun 'we' creates confusion about the categories of gender and sexual orientation—let alone ethnic identity and socio-economic status—by pushing all humans into the concept of 'mankind'. While pointing out humanity's dysfunctional relationship to the Earth's ecosystems, such statements underwrite an anthropocentric arrogance, which also conceals profound differences in the degree of responsibility attributable to distinct subsets of humanity. In this volume we have aimed to contest this hubristic formulation of the Anthropocene and discuss it in all its complexity, at once ecological, ontological, and socio-political.

Considering that issues of formulation and naming occupy a big part of the Anthropocene discourse, an analysis on terminology is also a necessary task. In fact, very much like Aristotle's being, the Anthropocene 'is said in many ways'. Some of these ways might sound ferociously ironical. Jussi Parikka, for example, calls it 'Anthrobscene', a term that explicitly qualifies the 'unsustainable, politically dubious, and ethically suspicious practices that maintain technological culture and its corporate networks' ('Introduction'). Kathleen Dean Moore goes further, proposing to name it 'the Unforgivable-crimescene' or simply 'the Obscene' (from the Latin *obs-*: against, onto; and *-coenum*: filth), a term that evokes 'the layers of rubble that will pile up during the extinction of most of the plants and animals of the Holocene—the ruined remains of so many of the living beings we grew up with, buried in human waste' ('Anthropocene'). In another key, those who emphasise the increasing standardization of global ecosystems, due to the massive intro-duction of alien species that drive to extinction the local and often unique ones, talk of the 'Homogenocene', a new biological epoch, inaugurated by Columbus' travels, characterised by 'mixing unlike substances to create a uniform blend' and where 'places that were once ecologically distinct have become more alike' (Mann, 'Introduction'). This resonates with Tsing's discussion of the plantation model in her *The Mushroom at the End of the World*. In its 'scalability', namely, in its total abstractedness from the con-texts and subjects it involves, the colonial plantation is indeed a model based not only on homogeneousness but also on alienation: it is an imported power structure that standardises production processes by disconnecting native spe-cies, isolating workers, exploiting labour, and radically transforming envi-ronments and bio-cultural relationships (Tsing 2015, 38–43). The colonial plantation opens an epoch in which, regardless of places and ecologies and unlike the 'dynamic multispecies diversity of the forest' (40), everything is 'interchangeable' (39). The idea that natural cycles are not impermeable to capital has inspired others to use the term 'Capitalocene', a definition—pro-posed somehow independently by Andreas Malm, Jason Moore, and Donna Haraway—to indicate an age in which 'capitalism is understood as a world-ecology, joining the accumulation of capital, the pursuit of power, and the co-production of nature in dialectical unity' (J. Moore 2014). To this term, Haraway adds two more: Plantationocene and Chthlucene. Whereas the first (collectively elaborated during a seminar in Aarhus) refers to 'the devastat-ing transformation of diverse kinds of human-tended farms, pastures, and forests into extractive and enclosed plantations, relying on slave labor and other forms of exploited, alienated, and usually spatially transported labor' (2015, 162), the second is in turn a 'trans-terran' collaborative vision: 'a name for the dynamic ongoing sym-chthonic forces and powers of which people are a part, within which ongoingness is at stake' (160). In fact, at a time when the Earth is 'full of refugees, human and not, without refuge' (160), the only way to exist 'as mortal critters . . . is to join forces to recon-stitute refuges, to make possible partial and robust biological-cultural-politi-cal-technological recuperation and recomposition' (160).

In light of such discussions, the Anthropocene forces us to rethink the human condition, climate, other species, and the Earth's biogeochemical processes, something which is reinforced as we think that, as Ben Dibley has stated, the Anthropocene can be defined as 'the folding of human into the air, into the sea, the soil and DNA' (2012, 139). When human and nonhuman bodies fold into one another in these processes, and when human beings are caught in the networks of earthly materiality and economic and political forces, moving through the Anthropocene becomes a precarious ontological performance in 'the world's differential becoming' (Barad 2007, 149), rather than an enactment of a grandiose narrative that emplots the human species as an epochal geo-force. This approach attempts to find alternative figurations. Donna Haraway and Karen Barad's views of life in terms of entangled agencies and converging forces are particularly useful in reconfiguring the subjects of the Anthropocene, the *anthropoi*, as human subjects (in the plural) with multiple corporeal, cultural, and social specificities, not an abstract male subject engaged in epoch-making planetary transformations. To challenge this problematic conception of the human subject, as well as the 'naturalization of social relationships' and the 'de-politicization' (Armiero 2015, 53) of the Anthropocene discourse in its hubristic versions, we need to think across humans, nonhumans, bodies, natures, cultures, classes, and the physical environments 'in ways that highlight their interactions' (Alaimo 2014). And this also entails a cross-species project, one of 'collaborative survival', as Anna Tsing also underlines: in fact, 'staying alive—for every species—requires livable collaborations. Collaboration means working across difference . . . Without collaborations, we all die' (Tsing 2015, 28). Consider, for example, the disappearance of bee colonies worldwide and how catastrophic the consequences would be for food production, not to mention the health of ecosystems.

Such a rethinking transforms the hyper-Cartesian dream of mastery into a disanthropocentric alliance of entangled subjects that ostensibly work with, through, and across material agencies that comprise the world. Moving through the Earth's innumerable agentic forces, we come to realise that being part of the Earth's physical systems we cannot perpetuate the image of a disembodied and petrified figure as the *anthropos* causing planetary alterations. This also suggests that even culture and its means can no longer afford such a self-deceptive dream. After all, the immense proportions of mineral extraction and chemical transformations that allow industrial development are also to be traced in the tools we use every day, our computers, our cell phones, our digital media. And so, issues of energy turn into issues of geophysics, and we find that 'the deep time of the planet is inside our machines, crystallised as parts of the contemporary political economy: material histories of labor and the planet are entangled in devices, which . . . unfold as part of planetary histories' (Parikka, 'Conclusion').

What underlies all these considerations is that the Anthropocene issues are also about imagining and visualizing the entanglements, the agencies, the connections, and their social and political consequences. In fact, if the human has become a geological force, the Anthropocene 'body politic' is not the same as it was before: it includes the built environment as well as forests, body cells as well as vegetation and fauna, domestic animals and melting glaciers; it entails issues of political freedoms and individual wellbeing, as well as energy democracy and global pollution. In the age of the Anthropocene, 'body politic' is a collective of agents and of processes, themselves resulting from collective agencies and dynamics. It is the Earth, in its geological, chemical, and biological cycles.

It must be clear by now that the Anthropocene is a contested and problematic term, and the intrinsic difficulty here is about conceiving of the immemorial plotting of geology and life as intermingled with human activities over time spans that transcend the limited scope of our mind's eye. At the same time, crucial to this endeavour is to question naturalizations and presumptions of innocence that perpetuate forms of injustice, both ecological and social. It is for this reason that we need more and more critical and imaginative tools to *comprehend* the Anthropocene. This is a point that Alexa Weik von Mossner has clearly made, by saying that '*all* stories about the Anthropocene keep pushing against the boundaries of what is currently imaginable' (2016, 85). With their extended critical imagination and theoretical tools, the Environmental Humanities challenge these very boundaries allowing us to visualise and voice these stories and their subjects. In other words, they 'fill in this deficit of the social imaginary and help us think the unthinkable' (Braidotti 2013, 160), thus proposing themselves as the 'Anthropocene Humanities' (159).

The chapters in this volume try to offer insightful ways to increase this imagination and sharpen our understanding of this biogeochemical network of agencies, which has surprisingly ended up bearing our name.

CHAPTERS OVERVIEW

Opening with a Foreword by the British writer and ecocritic Richard Kerridge, *Environmental Humanities: Voices from the Anthropocene* is divided into four sections. In the first section, 'Re-mapping the Humanities', our contributors, moving from the vantage point of their respective fields and orientations, reflect about the way to extend the disciplinary boundaries in order to create more fruitful connections that could shed light on the numerous (and unpredictable) objects that emerge from the layers of the Anthropocene. In the first chapter, 'Posthuman Environs', Jeffrey J. Cohen explores the connections between language and materiality. Overturning the picture of the Anthropocene as an epoch in which humans inscribe themselves into stone, becoming at last a part of the geological record, Cohen looks at how matter inscribes itself into the human record, becoming part of our linguistic archive. Three resonant words signal this Disanthropocene: *tsupu, woof,* and *fnorte th.* Each reverberates across cultures and time to open a story of matter's bustling agency, enduring companionships, and the limits of community. The second chapter, 'Environmental History between Institutionalization and Revolution: A Short Commentary with Two Sites and One Experiment' by Marco Armiero, investigates the contribution of environmental history in the shaping of the environmental humanities, in particular reflecting on the dialectic between adaptation to/transformation of the broader academic and disciplinary context. As he maintains, the challenge for an emerging field of studies seems always to be the choice between a transformative, or even revolutionary, project and the incorporation into the mainstream academic setting. Through 'one experiment' (the Anthropocene Cabinet of Curiosities Slam) and 'two sites' (the nation and the body), Armiero illustrates the decisive function of environmental history not only in complementing traditional historical discourses but also in consolidating the bases of the Environmental Humanities and making their themes more accessible to the general public. In the third chapter, Hubert Zapf's 'Cultural Ecology, the Environmental Humanities, and The Transdisciplinary Knowledge of Literature', literary topics enter the scene. From the angle of cultural ecology, Zapf investigates how the place and function of literature and literary studies can be newly assessed as a distinct form of transdisciplinary ecological knowledge within the Environmental Humanities. Discussing topics such as postcoloniality and ecoglobalism, metaphor and ecological knowledge, Zapf evinces a number of contexts in which cultural ecology can be used as a means to reinforce the ties between the cognitive experience of literature and the environmental humanities. The fourth chapter, 'Where Is Feminism in the Environmental Humanities?' by Greta Gaard, reflects on the apparent exclusion of feminism in the broad definitions of our field. The most worrying consequence of this absence is that it limits the reliability and utility of Environmental Humanities research and teaching. However, to uncover feminism in the field, Gaard claims, we can look not only at the presence of diversity in the perspectives of scholars or in Environmental Humanities curricula, but, more importantly, we can explore the topics chosen for research and study, considering how the research questions are defined and the methods for researching those questions. Gaard's chapter explores seven key features of feminist methodology, discussing how these features contribute to our understanding of human–human, human–animal, and human–environmental interactions, framing the challenges of climate change and our future on Earth. The fifth chapter, Scott Slovic's 'Seasick among the Waves of Ecocriticism: An Inquiry into Alternative Historiographic Metaphors', returns to the theme of literary studies, this time using the standpoint of ecocriticism. He first goes over the metaphors used to describe the trajectory of the discipline in the time of its academic 'canonization' and discusses their benefits and limits. Then, in this concise chapter, Slovic proposes alternative figures, insisting in particular on metaphors that highlight the interdisciplinary potential of ecocriticism as we enter the era of the Environmental Humanities.

The second section, 'Voicing the Anthropocene', comprises five chapters. Even if the Anthropocene appears regularly in most of the volume's essays, it is in this section that this notion is most specifically addressed. From their own fields of research and experience, the authors of this second part suggest visions and interpretations that use this new geological epoch as a prism to 'diffract' the various entanglements of our time. The first chapter, 'The Extraordinary Strata of the Anthropocene', is written by Jan Zalasiewicz. The rocks of the Earth, a vast and complex data storehouse, says Zalasiewicz, are the source of Earth history. Considering the characterization and potential formalization of the Anthropocene, he explains that, though geologically terribly brief, the Anthropocene is the latest phase of Earth history. It was first revealed more from observation of recent trends in properties of the atmosphere, oceans, ice masses, and biota than by analysis of strata. Its strata, from icecap to ocean floor to cityscape, are revealed as distinctive and geologically extraordinary and help place this new phase of our planet's history in the context of deep time. To understand the Anthropocene, he claims, one must understand the effect of the human drivers, but he also claims that this should not mean that the driving force should necessarily be ascribed to 'humanity per se'. The second chapter, J. Baird Callicott's 'Worldview Remediation in the First Century of the New Millennium', calls for an adjustment of our general perspectives concerning the Anthropocene problematics and suggests that new social ontologies should be more commensurate with the current political and environmental problems. In this discussion, Callicott focuses on 'interdisciplinarity' as the watchword of the Environmental Humanities, which for him signifies a disciplinary hybridity reintegrating the 'two cultures' lamented by C. P. Snow in the 1950s. He considers environmental philosophy as a case in point of the integration of the ecological sciences with the humanities as are conservation biology and ecological economics. In the third chapter, 'We Have Never Been "Anthropos": From Environmental Justice to Cosmopolitics', Joni Adamson, too, emphasis how problematic the term *anthropos* is as it has come to mean 'aggregate *Anthropos*', or 'all humans', which fails to account for unequal human vulnerabilities. Adamson's chapter discusses Alejandro González Iñárritu's 2006 film *Babel*. The film's title alludes to the story of the fall of the Tower of Babel, a story that has long served as a thought experiment for examining notions of cosmopolitanism in a world where modern nations are failing to communicate, cooperate, and make sense of each other. For Adamson, *Babel* presents opportunities to examine the 'babble' of confusion around the intellectual genealogy of 'American Studies'. She argues that what environmental humanists gain through a more precise use of the terms 'American Studies' and 'environmental justice' is a better understanding of the entangled debates over keywords central to both American Studies and the Environmental Humanities, including Anthropocene, *anthropos*, exceptionalism, nationalism, cosmopolitanism, multiculturalism, localism, globalism, and environmentalism. The fourth chapter in this section, 'Resources (Un)Ltd: Of Planets, Mining, and Biogeochemical Togetherness' by Filippo Bertoni, explores the metabolic transformativity of the earthly togetherness of microbes and its excesses—by-products, life forms, and forms of living. With its focus on the Iberian Pyrite Belt, this chapter explains how the ores of Río Tinto feed a complex and delicate underground microbial ecosystem with references to a team of astrobiologists from the Centro de Astrobiología in Madrid that studies these extremophiles as possible analogs for life under the surface of Mars. If we take the Iberian Pyrite Belt seriously as a Mars analog, Bertoni states, we can similarly think of the specific metabolic relationality of its chemolithotrophs and the planetary relationality of the sciences that shaped Earth and Mars as we know them as analogs to imagine extraction. The fifth and the last chapter of this section, 'Lacuna: Minding the Gaps of Place and Class' by Lowell Duckert, delves into the shallow bodies of water known as *lagoons*: fresh- or saltwater lakes separated from the sea or a nearby larger lake or river. 'Lagoon' derives from the Latin word for 'pool', *lacūna*, which comes from *lacus* ('lake'). 'Lacuna'—an unfilled space or interval, a gap—comes from *lacūna* as well, but in the additional sense of 'a hole, pit'. Although lagoons are often associated with desire (the 1980 film *The Blue Lagoon*), recreation (UC Santa Barbara's walking tour), and health (Iceland's famous geothermal spa), they also contain environmental refugees (Carteret Islanders) and indicate communities at risk (Venice). Emphasizing the ecological and etymological interrelationship between 'lacuna' and 'lagoon', Duckert argues that lagoons are precarious hydrological sites that allow us to address, at once, the political-economic lacunae (gaps) of class and the material lacunae (lakes) of place in order to promote more nonhuman modes of social justice.

The five chapters of the third section, 'Nature's Cultures and Creatures', explore different forms of nonhuman cultural ecologies from the perspectives of anthropology, ethography, religion, and biosemiotics. In the first chapter, 'Nature/Culture/Seawater: Theory Machines, Anthropology, Oceanization', Stefan Helmreich contends that seawater occupies an ambiguous place with respect to anthropological categories of nature and culture. Seawater as nature appears as potentiality of form and uncontainable flux; it moves faster than culture—with culture frequently figured through land-based metaphors—even as culture seeks to channel water/nature's flow. Seawater as culture manifests as a medium of pleasure, sustenance, travel, disaster. Tracking these associations historically, Helmreich argues that while the

qualities of seawater in early anthropology were portrayed impressionistically, today it is technical and scientific descriptions of the form of water
that have become prevalent in figuring social, political, and economic forces.
The second chapter, 'Revisiting the Anthropological Difference' by Matthew
Calarco, sets out to challenge the recent return to discourses that aim to
develop an 'anthropological difference', namely, a sharp distinction between
human beings and animals. According to Calarco, such a project is subject to
thoroughgoing objections not only on scientific-empirical grounds but also
in view of ethico-political concerns. Against a desire to establish distinctions
between human beings and animals, the author proposes that we consider
letting the distinction fall into indistinction. He points to two key upshots of
thinking in terms of indistinction: first, it allows us to catch sight of the ways
in which human beings come to see themselves as being profoundly and surprisingly like animals; second, it allows for a return to the ontological task
of rethinking relations beyond 'the human'. Calarco concludes by suggesting
that this conception of indistinction provides alternative grounds for linking
a variety of movements that seek to displace anthropocentrism. The third
chapter penned by Thom van Dooren and Deborah Bird Rose is titled 'Lively
Ethography: Storying Animist Worlds'. It explores the possibilities of a mode
of knowing, engaging and storytelling, here deemed 'lively ethography',
that aims to recognises the meaningful and entangled lives of diverse others—human and not—and that in so doing enlivens our capacity to respond
to them by singing up their character or ethos. Alternating between two types
of writing, the chapter offers both an exposition—laying out an analysis of
ethos, liveliness, storytelling, response-ability, and becoming-witness—and
a performative enactment through short ethographic vignettes that highlight
some of the qualities and approaches discussed, primarily with reference to
the authors' ongoing fieldwork in the Hawaiian islands. In the fourth chapter,
'Religion and Ecology: Towards the Communion of Creatures', Kate Rigby
considers the importance of religion and ecology in comprising a crucial
component of the wider work of the Environmental Humanities. Among the
world's many diverse religions, Rigby argues, Christianity remains a dominant force globally, not only in percentage terms but also because its texts and
traditions have informed the secular ethos and institutions of all Western societies. For this reason, this chapter revisits earlier critiques of Christianity's
environmental legacy, along with evidence for an ecological turn that is now
gathering momentum, in which she traces the lineaments of an emergent
'communion of all creatures'. This section concludes with the fifth chapter
by Wendy Wheeler, 'How the Earth Speaks Now: The Book of Nature and
Biosemiotics as Theoretical Resource for the Environmental Humanities in
the Twenty-First Century'. Wheeler's argument is based on the idea that we
participate in the world biosemiotically as one among all the other of Earth's

creatures. What we are, as humans, is an outcrop of Earth's evolutionary meanings. Our stories and poetry, technics and art, music and meaning belong to Earth and its plants and animals before they find expression in us. We are caught in a mesh of material beings made of codes and channels and also of an immaterial mesh of relations and meanings. This mesh is also what joins us to the planetary biome. By the same principle, the semiome joins us communicatively to each other and the planet. These are vital dialogic interrelationships and we should recognise biotic and semiotic communication and the interdependency of all Earth's many meanings. We are part of the text the planet writes—both writers and written.

The fourth and the final section of this book, 'EcoStories and Conversations', consists of three creative essays and a conversation with Rosi Braidotti. Whereas the creative pieces braid the fictional and the factual together to enhance ecological awareness, sensibility, and our fundamental kinship with nonhuman communities, the conversation insists on the new ethical, ecological, and cultural dimensions of the 'posthuman humanities'. Rob Nixon's autobiographically inflected essay, 'How to Read a Bridge', reflects on the variety of forces—historical, infrastructural, botanical, and ornithological—that shape the fate of a South African bridge. Against the backdrop of the widening inequities of the neoliberal order, Nixon considers the relationship between the abandoned rural poor, their severance from infrastructural service, and their dependence on exhausted ecologies. He also argues for a rapprochement between the concerns of animal studies and environmental justice. Bronislaw Szerszynski's 'The Martian Book of the Dead' introduces an imaginary future text, *Martian Book of the Dead*, which is used to prepare the dying for the experience of 'interval-being' and the possibility of liberation into the deep becoming of their planet, and thus of the cosmos. It is 2197. Mars has been settled and terraformed, and a new 'Mars-vehicle' Buddhism is established there. The Earth has entered the 'solar-system' geological period—the period in which the becoming of the planet is fully incorporated into that of a larger, evolving star system. Earth religions and cultures have embraced a radical new metaphysics of matter, time, and space. It is a new mythos of the relationship between Mars and Earth about the mutual gifting of life and animacy across billion-year time scales. This mythos spreads among the humans, artificial intelligences, and human–machine hybrids that work in the extractive industries and terraforming activities of Mars. The third essay in 'EcoStories' is by Juan Carlos Galeano, 'On Rivers', which is a personal contemplation of the author's childhood memories and stories connected to the Amazonian life. This sets him off to discover tales of riverine people and of rituals in rivers of the Peruvian Amazon—stories of 'Cobra Grande', the big anaconda, the mother of all rivers and serpents, the supernatural anaconda called 'Yakumama', and also stories of pink dolphins, of mermaids, and spirits. Galeano relates the tales of the Amazonian world as the realm of storied matter. The conversation with Rosi Braidotti, one of the leading figures of the Environmental Humanities debate, is titled 'Can the Humanities Become Posthuman?' In this interview, conducted by Cosetta Veronese, Braidotti touches on such topics as posthuman subjects, the future of humanism, models of trans-disciplinarity, human exceptionalism, and the new ethics of responsibility for the Anthropocene—one in which '[a]nimals, insects, plants and the environment, in fact the planet and the cosmos as a whole, are called into play'. Animal, insects, plants, humans, and the Earth's organic and inorganic presences: these are also the voices of the Anthropocene. Our volume was conceived as a way to heed them and reintroduce them in the narratives of our epoch. Might the narratives that this book provides be yet another step towards stronger more-than-human coalitions.

NOTES

1. *Orion Magazine* 35.1 (January/February 2014). See online at https://orionmaga-zine.org/article/the-new-you/.
2. Aaron Vansintjan, 'Going beyond the "Ecological Turn" in the Humanities'. 1 March 2016. See online at http://entitleblog.org/2016/03/01/going-beyond-the-ecological-turn-in-the-humanities/.

WORKS CITED

Alaimo, Stacy. 'New Materialisms, Old Humanisms, or Following the Submersible'. *NORA: Nordic Journal of Feminist and Gender Research* 19.4 (December 2011): 280–284.

Alaimo, Stacy. 'Your Shell on Acid: Material Immersion, Anthropocene Dissolves'. Keynote Speech. C21 Conference on 'Anthropocene Feminisms', Milwaukee, April 2014.

Armiero, Marco. 'Of the Titanic, the Bounty, and Other Shipwrecks'. *intervalla* 3 (2015): 50–54.

Barad, Karen. *Meeting the Universe Halfway: Quantum Physics and the Entanglement of Matter and Meaning.* Durham: Duke University Press, 2007.

Braidotti, Rosi. *The Posthuman.* Cambridge: Polity Press, 2013.

Chakrabarty, Dipesh. 'The Climate of History: Four Theses'. *Critical Inquiry* 35 (Winter 2009): 197–222.

Cohen, Jeffrey Jerome. 'The Sea Above'. *Elemental Ecocriticism: Thinking with Air, Water, and Fire.* Eds. Jeffrey J. Cohen and Lowell Duckert. Minneapolis: Minnesota University Press, 2015. 105–133.

Colebrook, Claire. 'Introduction. Anthropocene Feminisms: Rethinking the Unthinkable'. *philoSOPHIA* 5.2 (Summer 2015): 167–178.

Crist, Eileen and H. Bruce Rinker. 'One Grand Organic Whole'. *Gaia in Turmoil: Climate Change, Biodepletion, and Earth Ethics in an Age of Crisis*. Eds. Eileen Crist and H. Bruce Rinker. Hong Kong: Massachusetts Institute of Technology, 2010. 4–20.

Crutzen, Paul, and Eugene F. Stoermer. "The 'Anthropocene.'" *IGB Global Change NewsLetter*. 41 (May 2000): 17–18.

Dibley, Ben. '"The Shape of Things to Come": Seven Theses on the Anthropocene and Attachment'. *Australian Humanities Review* 52 (2012): 139–153. Web. 25 December 2015.

Di Paola, Marcello. 'Virtues of the Anthropocene'. *Environmental Values* 24 (2015): 183–207.

Doerr, Anthony. 'The New You'. *Orion Magazine* 35.1 (January/February 2014). Web. 15 January 2016.

Haraway, Donna. 'Anthropocene, Capitalocene, Plantationocene, Chthulucene: Making Kin'. *Environmental Humanities* 6 (2015): 159–165.

Heise, Ursula K. and Allison Carruth. 'Introduction to Focus: Environmental Humanities'. *American Book Review* 32.1 (November/December 2010): 3.

Holm, Poul, et al. 'Humanities for the Environment—A Manifesto for Research and Action'. *Humanities* 4 (2015): 977–992.

Latour, Bruno. 'Agency at the Time of the Anthropocene'. *New Literary History* 45 (2014): 1–18.

LeMenager, Stephanie and Stephanie Foote. 'The Sustainable Humanities'. *PMLA* 127.3 (2012): 272–278.

Lübken, Uwe and Christof Mauch. 'Introduction'. *Uncertain Environments: Natural Hazards, Risk and Insurance in Historical Perspective*. Eds. Uwe Lübken and Christof Mauch. Special issue of *Environment and History* 17 (2011): 1–12.

Mann, Charles C. *1493: Uncovering the New World Columbus Created*. New York: Vintage, 2011. Kindle edition.

McAfee, Kathleen. 'The Politics of Nature in the Anthropocene'. *Whose Anthropocene? Revisiting Dipesh Chakrabarty's 'Four Theses'*. Eds. Robert. Emmett and Thomas Lekan. Special issue of *Rachel Carson Center Perspectives: Transformations in Environment and Society* 2 (2016): 65–72.

Moore, Jason. 'The Capitalocene. Part I: On the Nature and Origins of Our Ecological Crisis'. March 2014. Web. 20 March 2016.

Moore, Kathleen D. 'Anthropocene Is the Wrong Word'. *Earth Island Journal* (Spring 2013). Web. 20 March 2016.

Morton, Timothy. *The Ecological Thought*. Cambridge: Harvard University Press, 2010.

Neimanis, Astrida, Cecilia Åsberg, Johan Hedrén. 'Four Problems, Four Directions for Environmental Humanities: Toward Critical Posthumanities for the Anthropocene'. *Ethics & the Environment* 20.1 (2015): 67–97.

Nixon, Rob. 'The Anthropocene: The Promise and Pitfalls of an Epochal Idea'. *Edge Effects*. 6 November 2014. Web. 20 March 2016.

Parikka, Jussi. *The Anthrobscene*. Minneapolis: University of Minnesota Press, 2014. Kindle edition.

Pickering, Andrew. *The Mangle of Practice: Time, Agency, and Science.* Chicago: University of Chicago Press, 1995.

Plumwood, Val. *Environmental Culture: The Ecological Crisis of Reason.* London: Routledge, 2002.

Revkin, Andrew. 'Confronting the Anthropocene'. *The New York Times*. 11 May 2011. Web. 10 January 2016.

Rose, Deborah Bird, Thom Van Doreen, Matthew Chrulew, Stuart Cooke, Matthew Kearnes, Emily O'Gorman. 'Thinking through the Environment, Unsettling the Humanities'. *Environmental Humanities* 1 (2012): 1–5. Web. 10 November 2015.

Rossini, Manuela. 'Introduction: Energy as a Nomadic Concept'. *Energy Connections: Living Forces in Creative Inter/Intra-Action.* Ed. Manuela Rossini. Living Books about Life. 14 October 2012. Web. 2 March 2016.

Sörlin, Sverker. 'Environmental Humanities: Why Should Biologists Interested in the Environment Take the Humanities Seriously'. *BioScience* 62.9 (September 2012): 788–789.

Steffen, Will, Paul Crutzen, John R. McNeill. 'The Anthropocene: Are Humans Now Overwhelming the Great Forces of Nature?' *Ambio* 36.8 (December 2007): 614–621. Web. 27 February 2016.

'The Anthropocene'. Editorial. The Opinion Pages. *The New York Times*. 27 February 2011. Web. 4 February 2016.

Thomashow, Mitchell. *Bringing the Biosphere Home: Learning to Perceive Global Environmental Change.* Cambridge: MIT Press, 2001.

The Environmental Humanities Newsletter. University of Oregon, 2014.

Tsing, Anna Lowenhaupt. *The Mushroom at the End of the World: On the Possibility of Life in Capitalist Ruins.* Princeton: Princeton University Press, 2015.

Vansintjan, Aaron. 'Going beyond the "Ecological Turn" in the Humanities'. Entitle Blog: A Collaborative Writing Project on Political Ecology. 1 March 2016. Web. 4 March 2016.

Weik von Mossner, Alexa. 'Imagining Geological Agency: Storytelling in the Anthropocene'. *Whose Anthropocene? Revisiting Dipesh Chakrabarty's 'Four Theses'.* Eds. Robert Emmett and Thomas Lekan. Special issue of *Rachel Carson Center Perspectives: Transformations in Environment and Society* 2 (2016): 83–87.

'Welcome to the Anthropocene'. Anthropocene.info. Web. 2 January 2016.

Zalasiewicz, Jan. *The Earth after Us: What Legacy Will Humans Leave in the Rocks.* Oxford: Oxford University Press, 2008.

Zalasiewicz, Jan, Mark Williams, Will Steffen, Paul Crutzen. 'The New World of the Anthropocene'. *Environmental Science & Technology* 44 (2010): 2228–2231.

Part I

RE-MAPPING THE HUMANITIES

Chapter One

Posthuman Environs

Jeffrey Jerome Cohen

Sovereign Is He Who Declares the Anthropocene Carbon embedded in geological strata is our newest mode of autobiography, the latest means through which we fashion an enduring ode to our dwelling on earth. We have crafted the word 'Anthropocene' to name this lithic record of our domination over time and matter, to demarcate an era immutably altered through our bustle. But the term also conveys the human love of making things with rocks and words. We imbue stone and language with meaning, both thereby becoming signifiers in the grandiloquent stories we tell about ourselves. Yet what if neither word nor world is so passive? What if language is an ecological interface, resounding with nonhuman activity? What if rock refuses the stillness of being rendered a recording device, makes its own impress, exerts its own force? Serpil Oppermann and Serenella Iovino write that all matter is *storied*, 'a material mesh of meanings, properties, and processes, in which human and nonhuman players are interlocked in networks that produce undeniable signifying forces', rich in inhuman agency and ceaselessly productive of narrative (Iovino and Oppermann 2014, 2). Let us push this insight farther and wonder: Might ecomateriality enter word as well as plot? Might 'storied matter' pulse in fundamental units—nouns, verbs, syllables, morphemes? What if the nonhuman implants lingering presences deep within 'our' linguistic archives, traces that never become inert? What if language, supposedly the most human of tools, sometimes pulses with environmentality, even as we incise our stories into substances like stone? Might matter be inscribing us, rendering humans the record of a Disanthropocene that unfolds regardless of what epochs we declare?

As far as stories go, the Anthropocene is not all that well plotted. Perilous assumptions attend its formulation.[1] Our melancholic exultation in having become geological derives from imagining the Human as unified and solitary, an incorporeal force powerful enough to imprint foundational matter. To universalise and abstract the human, however, is to reinscribe a historically specific vision that declares itself unbeholden to time and place, to the misery of those who find themselves on the margins of this white, European, masculine entity that will not speak its originary exclusions. Not all humans are allotted an equal share of humanity. As Stacy Alaimo has shown, the Anthropocene narrative of men and rocks neglects the creatures and things obliterated as we herald this epoch of our own production, an era in which the seas are acidifying and becoming desolate (Alaimo forthcoming). To figure the human as a disembodied force is to forget the lessons of feminism, posthumanism, and environmental justice, and thereby to fail to consider the heterogeneous, unevenly distributed violence (swift and slow) that climate change engenders.[2] We suppose all things a resource for use, abuse, and transformation—and thereby blind ourselves to matter's vibrancy.[3] Yet we remain corporeal beings within a shared world that at every level exceeds us. Offering a counter-narrative to our lonely petric tales, stories arrive from posthuman environs (nonhuman spaces that seem at once beyond, adjacent to and intimate with the human, spaces without which that category of being cannot come into existence).[4] These placebound tales of interdependence and unlooked-for relation disperse the human without disembodying, a change of climate for thinking ecological terms.

Catastrophe's archive brims with narratives that unfold along timescales far exceeding the familiar, long arcs of impress and translation, generation and grapple. These stories are often glimpsed through etymology, the geology of language. We inherit in the strata of our words histories of composition and companionship that exceed the human, an epochal *poiesis*. Although it will become in English the word 'poetry', *poiesis* in classical Greek is quite simply a *making*, as when humans build a boat and climb aboard with animal companions to weather a flood. Or when a rock or pig enters water and the sound ripples into a word: swash, slosh, plash. As these sonorous examples suggest, I am especially interesting in following an intensely environmental form of *poiesis* with disanthropocentric force. Literally a 'name-making', onomatopoeia is a movement into language of acoustical vibrations from inhuman realms. The material world has always imprinted itself upon us, with us, despite us. If we tarry for a moment over longer histories we might recognise they already inhabit us, sometimes as narratives, sometimes in strangely communicative sounds that intermix matter and meaning. Language sometimes carries within its sonority inhuman presence and force.[5] Onomatopoeia and its allied modes of wordsmithing thrum with an impulse to mimesis, intensification and alliance; desires for capture and companionship; creative acts of environmental apprehension; communication with sound more than signification; an imprinting from a nonhuman elsewhere. Although typically associated with animal noise, onomatopoeia is also a transport of hissing wind, rumbling stone, grinding gears and crackling fire, a veering of ecology into language.

This essay attends to some onomatopoeic words that noisily transport beyond a singular Anthropocene, that suggest a path out of its hubris and anthropocentricity without losing sight of the specific violences that unfold along its fraught terrain. These words amplify and convey the elemental and the animal, no matter how imprecisely, no matter how mediated the form in which they arrive. Human collaboration with the nonhuman, onomatopoeia allies affective and material intensities.

My three eco-sonorous terms for posthuman environs are *tsupu*, *woof*, and *fnorteth*.

Tsupu (The World Is Wide)

Although you are likely never to have heard the lowland Ecuadorian Quichua word *tsupu*, according to the anthropologist Eduardo Kohn when you learn what the term conveys your reaction should be 'a sudden feel for its meaning', a recognition that its sound materially communicates (Kohn 2013, 27). So here goes. *Tsupu* designates 'an entity as it makes contact with and then penetrates a body of water' (27). *Tsupu* is the sonorous ripple into language of slap and swash, linguistic propulsion of the meeting of water and falling body. Kohn illustrates the word's signifying ambit with two examples: 'a big stone heaved into a pond or the compact mass of a wounded peccary plunging into a river's pool' (27). Something slips into water. *Tsupu*. Does that word feel wet, like spray from a rippled spring, the splash of pig in pond? Does *tsupu* echo in your ears and cling to your skin? Does it slip into cognition like pebble or peccary into liquid depths?

Building upon the material semiology of Charles Peirce, Kohn argues that 'iconic' words like *tsupu* carry a palpable impress of thing and event. As 'sonic images' that 'sound like what they mean', such words re-present what they designate (Kohn 2013, 30). Like Peirce before him, Kohn discerns a power in onomatopoeia that critics of a poststructuralist bent often deny. Hugh Bredin influentially argued that an onomatopoeic word is inevitably a failure of mimesis. The number of phonemes available within a given language offer formal constraints, and human vocalizations can only approximate natural sounds. Onomatopoeia must therefore be as conventional as any other kind of language. According to Bredin we learn to associate certain words with animal or industrial sounds and only thereafter believe we sense inherent relation. Because 'we *want* language to be onomatopoeic', he writes, we imagine that we hear within some words sounds that suggest movement, a retroactive positing rather than a recognition deriving from something the word conveys (Bredin 1996, 560). Yet neither Kohn nor Peirce would argue that iconic or onomatopoeic words are not highly mediated.[6] Neither would they side with Plato's Cratylus to argue that language arises through finding the right sound for the right object, as if words had natural affinities to the things they designate, as if communication could ever be anything but fraught.[7] Kohn insists however that an iconic word signifies differently from others, forcefully conveying the phenomena for which it stands, bearing resonant traces of the nonhuman world that cannot be wholly eradicated by invoking the arbitrariness of linguistic signification, 'a sort of paralinguistic parasite on the language that somewhat indifferently bears it' (Kohn 2013, 28). In Kohn's example a rock or animal tumbling into water purls into a word that 'somehow feels like a pig plunging' (28), capturing as well as conveying the greater than human communicative web within which its action unfolds. A monkey may as easily as a human recognise that this sudden splash signals the nearing of danger or opportunity. *Tsupu* relays shared worldedness, a forest lost in thought, word and pig as transport devices that disperse signals, receptions and reactions across the wood wide web.[8] Human speakers and auditors are only some of the multifarious nodes in this meaning-making assemblage, this sonorous and material machine for climatic, localised, and communal cognition.

Kohn glosses *tsupu* as any entity entering water, the movement of rock or pig. Yet only the peccary is part of the sylvan community that he describes. Only the animal participates in how forests think. Stone in his account slips into the river and vanishes, surfacing again only to be excluded from what Kohn calls the 'ecology of selves' (2013, 78). Forming a biosemiotic web through which forests become sites of shared cognition, plants and animals possess an animacy that can alter human perspectives and disrupt the equation of being with being human. Rocks possess no such power. A capacious category for Kohn, life in a rain forest includes humans, dogs, jaguars, fish, birds, ghosts, trees: 'life thinks; stones don't' (100). His ecology of selves emerges as and through possibilities barred to stone. In Kohn's estimation the best inorganic matter can accomplish is to impede, and—despite Jane Bennett's insistence to the contrary—'resistance is not the same as agency', nor does materiality in itself confer vitality (92). Yet is not recalcitrance a kind of doing? Is it not also perspectival? The rock that to a human is impedimental may be to a tree an essential ally, an anchor to embrace so that a stream does not wash away its trunk. Nor should every scale of being remain implicitly human, so that actors are recognised as such only when they possess a size or tempo easily perceived. Jamie Lorimer has listed as eco-critical challenges to such perspectival bias the idea of supra-organisms (systems where humans and animals form actual parts of larger organisms), the flourishing of the microbiome, and 'the mineral foundations of all life and the ways in which the bio and geo are entangled throughout interdependent webs of biochemical exchange' (2015, 24).[9] Within its native temporality the geological is just as restless as the arboreal.[10]

Tsupu is the sound of a rock moving through the world. Stones plunk into water when pulled by gravity, pushed by human hands, discarded by otters, kicked by deer, or propelled by rainwashed landslide. To stone belongs a fleeting archive continually reconstituted, generating knots of matter and mattering. Semiotic materiality functions over varied time scales, arising as easily from the lithic as from porcine motion or human mouth. Rosi Braidotti has argued eloquently for a 'post-anthropocentric posthumanism' that attends to the 'possible ethics' (2013, 92) of a world in which familiar ontologies fail to hold.[11] The project of posthuman ecocriticism is to attend to animal, water, stone, forest, and world—and not to deny force, thought, agency, emergence or thriving to any of these entities, all of which act, all of which are story-producing. Attentiveness to nonorganic things like rocks, wind, water, and fire is not easy to cultivate.[12] Unlike peccaries or plants, the elements do not necessarily exist within a familiar tempo or easily apprehensible spatiality: too fast, slow, vast, minute. Their pressing upon human feeling, thinking, speaking and narrating, however, remains heavy even when unseen. *Tsupu* is the plunge of rock into water into language into thought, the coming into story of companionships we deny when we declare the solitary and anthropocentric Anthropocene.

Even as we engrave our presence onto geological strata, ecomateriality has already left resonant traces upon our bodies and our words. Posthuman environs open a wide world, excluding little. Ecotheorists are fond of pointing out that the *oikos* (οἶκος) in ecology is the Greek word for house. This noisy home swings its doors and windows open, bolt them as we may. A fire blazes and the roof leaks. Its hearth, foundation and lintel are fashioned of stone. A dog wanders in and out, woofing for companionship, barking to announce this human space a shared and co-created territory.

Or perhaps the dog bays at the new risen moon, a story indifferent to feeble human ears.

Woof (A Posthuman Ecology Transcends No Violence)

Follow the noise of the dogs, their howls that reverberate into language, the warp and woof of shelter and story.[13] To disgrace a neighbour who has given birth to twin sons, a noblewoman declares that no one becomes pregnant with two children without having had sex with two men. Not long thereafter the woman herself delivers twin girls. This is a story about telling stories and the communities these narratives enable or taint. Her slander redounding upon her, the new mother contemplates infanticide. To preserve the new life her maid offers to bear an infant away before the household realises the double birth. Departing at nightfall, the maid follows an unknown road through thick forest. At long last animal sounds announce the proximity of human settlement:

> Bien loinz sur destre aveit oi
> Chiens abaier e coks chanter;
> Iloc purrat vile trover.
> Cele part vet a grant espleit
> U la noise des chiens oieit.
>
> Then, far off to the right, she heard
> dogs barking and cocks crowing;
> she knew she would be able to find a town over there.
> Quickly she went in the direction
> of the barking.[14]

Roosters and baying dogs lead the young woman and the child she is saving to the edge of a village. She sees a great ash tree before an abbey and places the infant within its protective boughs. A porter discovers the abandoned bundle the next day and delivers the baby to fostering by the abbey's nuns, the community that planted the tree many years ago in the hope of future shade. In honour of the place of her discovery, the girl is christened *Fresne* ('Ash').

Thus the opening of a lay composed by the great Marie de France in the twelfth century. Fresne's twin sister, raised in an aristocratic household, is named after a valued tree: *cordre*, the hazelnut. Unremarkable, uncultivated, yielding neither fruit nor nuts, the ash nonetheless generates the story that bears its name. 'Le Fresne' bears nothing yet proves ceaselessly productive of shelter. The intertwining of the sylvan and the human (Fresne is like her namesake ceaselessly productive of shelter) underscores an ecology like the Ecuadorian rain forest described by Eduardo Kohn, always more than human. Dogs, roosters, silk, stories, households, twins, and trees are the agents through which the plot unfolds. This enmeshment is foregrounded by the shared name of the poem, its heroine, and a tree that seems below regard. Like most words, *fresne* is not onomatopoeic, sounding nothing like what a tree does. Signification is arbitrary. But not *wholly* arbitrary, for in French and English the tree possesses an etymology that encodes larger relations: 'ash' (Old English *æsc*) and 'fresne' (Latin *fraxinus*) derive from unrelated words for *spear*, transporting a story about the shape of leaves and the making of weapons into these nouns. Against this martial etymology, the lay 'Le Fresne' offers a counter-narrative of ecological tendering, a future forged in the midst of peril. The story enmeshes through the word *fresne* a woman nearly murdered as an infant who finds herself in danger of later narrative obliteration (Fresne becomes mistress to a young count, her life nearly erased when he accedes to his household's demand to marry Cordre and father legitimate heirs); a tree too much taken for granted that reveals itself as fecund in possibilities of sanctuary, altered trajectories, and compassionate conclusions; and the act of poetry making, the *poiesis* that results in the lay itself. 'Le Fresne' is a story about environmental webs, community making, and the altering of climates.

The mingling of dense forest, noisy dogs, stone for echoes and hearths, and a tree for refuge quietly opens an admixing of the organic and inorganic into soundscape and ecotone. In this poem that interleaves the lives of humans, trees, and animals, movement is aided by trans-species alliances. The maid who carries the unwanted infant through the woods knows that the baying dogs signal nearness of human settlement. Dogs, not wolves: intimates, creatures of settlement and habitation. *Wouaf* or *voff* or *bow-wow* bounce from buildings to announce a living together that is a general story of humans and hounds, community and commensality. Most languages have an onomatopoeic term for what a dog sounds like, capturing canine communication diversely: hau-hau (Arabic), haff-haff (Czech), voff-voff (Icelandic), amh-amh (Irish), wan-wan (Japanese), aw-aw (Tagalog). Some distinguish the noise of small dogs, or demarcate the purpose and tone of the growl, yelp, yip, grrrr, or howl. Every language hears dogs slightly differently, even if when aggregated these words hold some uncanny similarities. That *woof* may be passed along with such variation emphasises the differences and heterogeneity with the same animal impress, and the inherent imperfection of sonic capture and retransmittal.

Collating animal sounds also possesses a long history, suggesting the enduring human fascination with communication across species. The Latin genre of *voces variae animantium* ('Voices of Various Animated Things') stretches far back into manuscript history, with one of the most famous lists having been composed at St Gall between 760 and 797. This Latin compilation collates animal noises ('the sheep bleats, the dog barks') with the gurgling of brooks and the crackling of fire.[15] Jonathan Hsy describes such lists as mapping a 'human/animal interface' that offers a mode of trans-species translation or bilingualism. Whether the baying of the dog is caught in Latin, English or French, though, the sound become word is never exact, never wholly successful, unmediated, or completely transparent. Yet something of the animal (or the water or the fire) resonates within the onomatopoeic term. Linguistic devices of capture and conveyance vary, just as there is no singular of 'the animal', only differences collected into insufficient category. Derrida's animal-word (*l'animot*) emphasises a plurality that resists totalization or synthesis (*The Animal That Therefore I Am* 41). But what all these renderings of the noise dogs make as they howl their stories have in common is sonic communion embedded in a linguistic archive between dogs and humans, an inscription at the level of word that conveys shared environmentality.

Marie uses the verb *abaier* to capture this canine resonance. Intimate to our modern word *bay*, the Old French verb is mimetic, an attempt like *tsupu* to transmit a sonic event from the nonhuman world by making it vibrate anew. A dog bays and an unwanted child finds sanctuary. It is almost a medieval version of *Lassie*: follow the sound of the agitated hound and know dedication to human community. Or know, perhaps, that inhabitance comes about at least in part through human–canine relation. As Donna Haraway has pointed out, domestication has been a cross-species affair. The dogs that bark in the night must therefore not be rendered symbols (they do not exist for the maid, or the baby), but acknowledged as fully embodied creatures, even when they bay their way into a fictive narrative. Canines are companion species and mess mates, animals without which we could not have become ourselves. Haraway writes: 'Dogs, in their historical complexity, matter here. Dogs are not an alibi for other themes; dogs are fleshly material semiotic presences . . . Dogs are not surrogates for theory; they are not just here to think with. They are here to live with' (2003, 5). And, as Marie de France makes clear, they are animals here to follow. But not everywhere the animal leads is human, or humane. As poets have long known, onomatopoeia is an invitation to play. As hunters have long known, onomatopoeia can also be a trap, a lure, a weapon. Susan Crane has built upon the work of Haraway and Derrida to elaborate the trans-corporeal communication and cooperation upon which hunting in the Middle Ages depended. The aristocratic hunt is a 'human–hound partnership' that contains no room for 'egalitarian thinking about cross-species relations' (Crane 2012, 111). The hunt declares and consolidates human dominion over other animals. Dogs are scolded and whipped into submission just like servants, so that maintaining social and species difference are revealed as analogues of the same disciplinary system, a hierarchy enforced through blows. The aristocratic hunt unites dogs and humans into a machine of violence. Hunting is intimacy and companionship in the dispensing of bloody death: *tsupu* is after all in Kohn's example the noise a wounded peccary makes.[16]

The hunting assemblage as call to cross-species alliance within forceful domination is vividly materialised in a book now held in the Folger Shakespeare Library in Washington, DC, an edition of George Gascoigne's *Noble Arte of Venerie or Hunting*.[17] In the nineteenth century, the manual's owner rebound the book in stag fur and affixed decorative metal bucks with large antlers.

Figure 1.1.   Cover of George Gascoigne, *The noble arte of venerie or hunting. Wherein is handled and set out the vertues, nature, and properties of fiutene sundrie chaces togither, with the order and maner how to hunte and kill* (1575). Image reproduced by permission of the Folger Shakespeare Library, Washington.

The book is now clasped by the skin of the creature that its text instructs readers how to pursue, trap, and dismember. Depending on how you feel about hunting, the Folger's edition of Gascoigne's *Noble Arte of Venerie* will seem repulsive or beautiful (or, most likely, both). Hidebound in the product of its practice, the volume is anything but inert. When placed in front of you its cover offers rough brown fur impossible not to stroke—a summons to material encounter, a call to touch that arrives too late after the call to still. The book is dead plant matter (paper and ink) bound in dead animal matter (stag skin and leather), ornamented with inert metals. The language it holds is also dead, or at least moribund: Early Modern English is no doubt going the way of Old English and Middle English, receding from swift contemporary comprehension and becoming a specialty subject for the well-trained special-ist. Dead matter, dead language, dead binding: in the face of all this lifeless-ness, it is entirely possible that the desire to touch the book, like the desire to read its contents, is a wholly individual and eccentric experience that has nothing to do with its insistent materiality. Perhaps we have entered a realm where only psychology and human subjectivity hold explanatory force.

Yet I am not convinced the volume's invitation to touch can be fully captured through humanizing reference to fantasy and a frustrated desire to possess. I have seen the volume in action too many times, and have witnessed the community of contact its presence repeatedly triggers. The book makes tangible the violence against animals that is its subject matter and refuses to disentangle its allure from its love of domination. Jesse Oak Taylor has argued that hunting is frequently dismissed as an 'exercise in hyper-masculine domination and sadism in ways that gloss over the affective complexity, and even trauma, of killing'. The stories that reside in hunting are often entwined in difficult tales of conservation that resist domesticating animals into the cute and cuddly, resist extinguishing 'something much darker, fraught with terror', resist the impulse to disregard violence or tame wildness. As an object the book materially manifests a brutal-beautiful entwining of deer and hunter, not just as trophy but as complicated narrative. It also offers the possibility of animal communication beyond animal death. The regal buck that adorns its cover and the floral buttons that pin the fur in place announce in lasting silver the possibility (no matter how unlikely) of endurance and memorialization over ephemeral consumption and final endings. The book wants something more than filing away in the Folger Library vault, wants to be read and stroked, wants to reactivate the historical contexts from which it has become divorced, to touch with its stories and its matter, its worlds and lives now lost, an effusive ecology of affect and force and blood. Enclosed in an animal become art that remains all the same an animal, the book proffers a hazard, a chance, insistent because of the violence it materialises.[18] Perhaps the book wants to kill again. But maybe the object also activates an alternative story, a tale without so lethal or so final a denouement.

Gascoigne's hunting manual closes with two leaves containing musical notation for bugle calls. By transmitting set sounds in precise sequences, the bugle instructs a baying pack on their next course of action. Similar treatises, medieval and early modern, also contain hunting cries, like this one for assisting hounds who have gone off track to realise that another dog in the pack has picked up the proper scent: 'Ta ça ta ça ta ho ta ho!'[19] Words break into reverberating syllables, sonic particles that communicate through shape and force. Aristocratic hunting is a cross-ontological alliance that unites dogs, humans, horses, knives, whips, bugles, books, landscape, and sonic emissions into a fatal machine. Through horn blasts, the baying of dogs, and the transformation of language into intensities of sound this assemblage opens a temporary space of interpenetration and admixture, a hazardous intermezzo of enmeshed agency and interspecies alliance that contrasts starkly with its bloody culmination.

Not every story that unfolds within posthumanism environs ends well. Yet as Marie de France insists, violence that unfolds within more-than-human ecosystems deserves the same scrutiny as the happy endings that sometimes occur. Perhaps narratives are best read as if they were open ended, without regard to their endings, since closure is always provisional, a shifting of attention rather than true cessation of story. The aristocratic hunt both a space of duress and the precipitation of what Susan Crane calls 'persistent, intimate contact' with animals that demands critical attending (2012, 119). That the interminglings of the hunt in action should be limned by and culminate in animal brutality underscores that human identity is typically asserted at the expense of other creatures, even when they are companions. Karl Steel writes that 'human domination of what it calls animal' (2011, 24) is sustained through the exertion of force the separation of these fragile categories.[20] Yet domination seldom fully silences. Tobias Menely has recently focused on sensibility as way to move discussion of animal presence away from linguistic constructivism and the symbolic order, focusing instead on 'an unintegrated origin and never fully actualised surplus of meaning' conveyed by the 'impassioned voice' of human or animal, a voice that resonates even when 'vocal and bodily expression' finds itself captured into text, story, print (Menely 2015, 5–6). This creaturely community, Menely argues, is best captured by poetry, which imbues the experience of mortality, suffering and loss with 'collective meaning' and creates 'a common world out of the shared experience of corporeal finiteness' (16).[21]

Menely's work is a needed corrective to a long critical tendency to equate communication and meaning-making with linguistic signification: animals and humans alike are responsible to the signs and voices of others. Describing children's books that connect animals to their 'signature vocalizations' (*woof, meow, moo*), however, Menely observes that such 'echolalia' ushers young audiences into the symbolic order, 'the domain of customary meanings' (Menely 2015, 19). An animal voice that can sound with 'creaturely affinity' is to be sought elsewhere, in 'vocal and gestural expressions' that address the world but do not function linguistically. I wonder, though, if the spoken word of the human and the 'creaturely voice' are not already cohabitating in resonant juvenilia. Do not onomatopoeic terms like *meow, neigh, baa, cocorico, cackle, kerplunk, caw, boom, whippoorwill, trill, chitter, tweet*, and *bay* resound with such affinity while enlarging what we might group within the category 'creaturely'?

Posthumanism possesses a deeply utopian bent. Its practitioners sometimes proceed as if the breaching of ontological categories were in itself affirmative or transcendent. Yet violence is omnipresent, part of the world's fabric, the provenance of plants, animals and materiality itself. Storied matter possesses many genres, including horror. Ethics resides in the choice not

to be resigned to this violence, in the choice not to make another copy of
the stag-fur bound hunting manual by Gascoigne—and in the choice not to
consign that brutal-beautiful volume to the flame or to the vault. The book
binds together matter that solicits lingering. Perhaps in one of its tales the
baying of the hounds leads somewhere other than to the flaying of the deer.
Posthumanism must not be blind to terror and tumult, to the blood that flows
when some cyborgs and assemblages are composed. Wildness is not always
affirmative, and nature really can be red in tooth, in claw, in unwanted
enmeshments. Yet posthuman environs also offer those proximities that may
shelter possibilities for a more complicated world, for a future at once less
human and less natural (what could be more natural than hunting and eating?), for a refusal of denouements generated through an excess of suffering
and death.

Animal capture is noisy conveyance into story, and a sonic disruption
of the human that no incorporation into language or identity can still.
*Follow the noise of the dogs, their howls that reverberate into language,
follow too the bugle that blasts and the voice made instrument of sound not
words: warp and woof of shelter and story, even when difficult to hear above
the violence of its din.* Bugle blasts and hunting cries are haptic modes of
interspecies communication, mimetic and multisensory. To co-inhabit a
dog's world means heightening the senses of smell and sound, allowing
meagre human olfaction and hearing to be overwhelmed, reoriented. In an
essay on medieval compilations of animal sounds—lists that stage a kind
of 'animal–human bilingualism'—Jonathan Hsy notes that 'much interspecies communication is *non-verbal and also non-sonic*—facial expressions,
somatic mimicry, physical contact (aggressive or playful), biting, motion
(e.g., blocking one's path), sniffing (and emitting pheromones), leaving
excrement or other internal fluids'. The world is wide, and to a canine
nose its smells are precise messages. To the proper eyes the vibrancy of its
colours overwhelms, as does the radiance of objects at night. To attentive
ears a dog announcing community may be discerned in *abaier, wouaf*, bay.
Maybe now we should also notice that it is not just the howling hounds
that signalled in Marie de France's lay the approach to a place of communal dwelling. Roosters were singing (*chanter*) to announce the nearing
day: a song of animal communication, avian response, territorialization,
co-dwelling, and rising sun. A posthuman ecology is an interpenetrative
cacophony—and not every sound the human mouth emits amounts to language. Not every human body from which such sounds escape is equally
marked, valued, legible. The violence of the hunt: whip and words are
deployed to discipline dogs and servants. 'Human' is false universal, a
category that punishes and excludes.

A noisy tale inheres here as well.

Fnorteth (The Atmosphere Is Heavy but the Climate Might Lift)

Trouble the boundaries and enmesh the cosmos, but even a posthuman ecology remains housebound. The walls shift but all things, even gendered human bodies, are likely still to be rendered commodities for equivalency and exchange, for the forced transport of messages not theirs. Humans differenti-ate themselves from world, from other animals, from other humans through ceaseless overpowering. You may think that a posthuman environs promises material intimacy and peaceful community, but then you are turning your eyes from what enduringly supports a fleeting equanimity. Utopian and full of futurity, posthuman environs also carry a heavy atmosphere, violences that cannot be disowned.

Another medieval tale, this one from Geoffrey Chaucer.[22] Aleyn and John, two clerks from the north of England studying in Cambridge, lay awake in strange lodgings. Tricked by an unscrupulous miller, the young men have paid to endure a night under his roof, in his very bedroom. They are assailed by sound. From their shared bed the clerks listen to the drunken family's noc-turnal 'melodye', a 'rowtyng' from the miller's wife and 20-year-old daughter loud enough to be heard a quarter mile away (1.4166). For the two clerks rest is impossible during this sonic barrage. The resonant Middle English word 'rowtyng' derives from Old English *hrūtan*, a verb that sounds like the action it conveys, *snoring* (a term likewise originating in onomatopoeia).[23] But it gets worse. The noise that thunders from the miller's open mouth is so intense that only animal comparison can convey its force: 'as an hors he fnorteth in his sleep' ('like a horse he snores in his sleep' 1.4163). Within slumber and without precise language, humans sound pretty much the same as other large mammals. *Fnorteth* is reverberation oblivious to species difference, and a noise that travels with violence.

The 'Reeve's Tale' invites what Martin Foys has called a *sensual philology*, an attending to how 'language serves as a gateway for a largely unmapped network of words, sounds, senses, bodies and media' (2014, 457). Yet philol-ogy (literally, a love of words) here offers mostly a dark ecology. This fabliau is known for its grim ambience, the cloy of its air. Whereas the preceding 'Miller's Tale' is full of hymns, love songs, and musical instruments, this story offers a narrative ecosystem resounding with dissonant, nonverbal signifying: the rowtyng and fnortyng of the sleeping family; the 'wehee' of escaping stal-lions (a cry of freedom, transport and desire, since the horses have scented wild mares in the nearby fens); whistles and shouts ('Keep! Stand! Jossa!') that the clerks use to call their mounts back, realizing they have been tricked into spending the night. Every word John and Aleyn speak at the beginning of the tale threatens to break from linguistic signification into mere sonority, so thick are their Northern accents (e.g., 'Swa werkes ay the wanges in his heed'

1.4030). Sound is a vibration that travels through the air and implants itself
in the flesh. But its force ripples far beyond merely human environs. Sound
saturates the atmosphere and renders air heavy with story. In the *House of
Fame*, Chaucer describes 'soun' ('sound')—of which human speech is special
type—as 'eyr ybroken' ('broken air' 770), a reverberation that moves 'with
violence' (775), as when 'thow / Throwe on water now a stoon' ('you toss a
stone into water' 788–789). Sonic vibrations ripple and intensify, saturating
the atmosphere with 'speche . . . or voys, or noys, or word, or soun' ('speech
or voice or noise or word or sound' 818–819), a dense archive of story. With its
snores, cries, shouts, pleas, poems and prayers, the Reeve's Tale is reverberant,
a material ecology that noisily foregrounds the penetrability and porousness of
flesh within a surrounding and story-laden atmosphere.

The miller and his family snore because their bodies are humoral environments out of balance. Liquor makes evident corporeal liquidity. As Chaucer
explains in the Squire's Tale, excessive drinking engenders a superfluity
of blood, which in turn triggers a profound need for restorative sleep. The
slumber that follows inebriation is restless, though, since a drunken sleeper is
filled with 'fumositee' (5.358), with wine- or ale-induced fumes that burden
the mind with meaningless signification. The intoxicated body well illustrates
the trans-corporeality of medieval embodiment, both human and animal: the
four humours do their work within skin that offers a permeable membrane
rather than a barrier to the world.[24] The human body is revealed as a dynamic
ecology easily thrown into crisis, a 'conviviality of animate and inanimate
matters' that makes clear 'anthropocentrism has not always been an inevitable mode of self-understanding' (Mitchell 2014, xix, xviii).[25] The medieval
equivalent to a posthuman ecology is this open, fleshly system that through
the four humours materially enmeshes the gravity of the moon, the impress
of place, the agency of matter, the density and humidity of atmosphere.[26]
Such material entanglement holds as true of animals, plants, and stones as of
humans—and underscores that human embodiment is a specific (gendered,
racialised) phenomena, rather than an abstract universal. Within this *geohumoralism* no space exists for a mind/body divide. Psychology and subjectivity are substantial, material, a tenuous system easily disrupted by wine or
sunshine or snoring.[27] Geohumoralism insists that 'human' is not a category
separable from ecology or economy. Embodiment happens in place, propelled
and then limned by specific and enduring violences.

Tocsin of an unbalanced ecology, *fnorteth* is a vibratory mechanism, the
sound of a body transmitting meaning parasitically within language, as an
event inhabiting a sound, a disorder conveyed by a word in motion. This
vibration into language of sonorous realities demands the coining of words
to capture and convey: ale to snores to action. The problem, though, is that
the action that arises in the Reeve's Tale is in the end all too human, all too

masculine, and not at all humane: two acts of sexualised revenge, a message sent by the clerks to the miller through the bodies of his wife and daughter. Within this domestic economy, horses, cakes, wheat, beds, sex, blows are exchanged with little regard for the lived consequences such equivalence and reduction entail. Economology: *economy* and *ecology* share an etymology in *oikos*, the house and its range, signalling the difficulty of movement beyond the inhumane. Interpenetrability is subject to constant economic recapture. The Reeve's Tale is the story of a miller who fleeces his customers. John and Aleyn are forced to purchase from the miller a breakfast baked from the flour he stole from them. The clerks believe the proper payment for such abuse is to be made through the sexual enjoyment of the women in his household. Once they sleep with the wife and daughter, the tale becomes a disturbing account of what happens when all the world is reduced to an economy of sale, substitution, and revenge, wheat to pie to profits, every ecology transformed into an economy, all matter—even virginity—rendered vendible. No wonder the story ends with screams, blows, blood. The narrative economics of the Miller's Tale renders even rape a clever trick, a joke. Women's bodies are used by men to send messages to other men. That these women have their own stories is hinted at but never with much narrative attention explored. *Fnorteth* ties men to horses, animals that in the tale convey but also when unconstrained seek copulation. Thunderous snoring resounds with sexual violence as well as humoral ecologies and nonlinguistic noise.

I do not think Marie de France would have much liked Geoffrey Chaucer's Reeve's Tale. The world she envisions in poems like 'Le Fresne' shares little with his heavy fabliau atmosphere. Whereas the wheat in the Reeve's Tale exists only to be ground to flour and rendered a product that may be substituted for other commodities, in 'Le Fresne' the immense ash tree is an anchoring and unsubstitutable presence that intensifies human relation. Marie foregrounds throughout the poem how gender is articulated within a system of entrenched social inequality, returning repeatedly to the unevenness and heterogeneity of what it means to be an emplaced, embodied human. Peril haunts the spaces across which female bodies pass, giving the poem an atmosphere of constant hazard that hovers without saturating. 'Le Fresne' is a story of women and precarity: the slanderous mother, the good hearted maid (a familiar figure in Marie's stories: the helper or intermediary who is the sine qua non, yet also forgotten, left behind), the endangered infant, the porter's widowed daughter who breastfeeds the foundling, a nunnery built against a world that keeps finding its way within, sisters and mothers metaphorical as well as biological, a concubine, wives who when they do not realise their power as authors and agents cause lives to unravel. 'Le Fresne' is about creating a world with more and better stories, tales that do not succumb to heavy ambience but instead embrace the shared precariousness of mundane life.

'Le Fresne' burgeons with a Disanthropocene of barking dogs and the bark of trees, of women who carry vegetal trace (*cordre, fresne* / hazelnut, ash), stories that enmesh the human and the nonhuman so that neither stands alone. But the lay also attends to the particularities of violence within the human, and warns us that when we attempt to transcend that category by declaring the Anthropocene we do so at the peril of specificities that require precise accounting. Ethics inheres in the choice not to universalise, not to ignore the differences that found the category human and that have not been left behind in the posthuman. In stories we have long been telling opens a more complicated space.

Tsupu, bay, fnorteth. In these onomatopoeic terms may be discerned inhuman resonance, posthuman environs. A wounded pig plunges into water and into word. A stone plunges into water and into word. *Tsupu* slips from stone and pig and water into Ecuadorian Quichua, from indigenous Amazonian mouths into an anthropologist's cognition, into book, into theory, into essay, into your own mouth. Stories of race, culture, colony, climate, taxonomy, and environment continue to resound with it. Dogs meanwhile howl the nearness of shelter, woof the story of how they enable human habitation. A tree entwines itself with the fostering of human life, with the creation of poetry. Violence and suffering are unevenly distributed. Within posthuman environs gender still matters. So do class and race. The human body is a machine of sonority, as ecological in its signalling as animals and stones. Human bodies are also plural phenomena, specific and universalised at peril. Drawing boundaries and declaring epochs may be necessary, but such systems are fragile, insufficient. They inevitably exclude. The Anthropocene is no doubt real, but so is the Disanthropocene, the impress of posthuman environs upon our very bodies, the resounding of environmental impress within our stories and our words.

ACKNOWLEDGEMENT

This essay originated in a plenary address for the conference 'Approaching Posthumanism and the Posthuman' held at the University of Geneva (where it was haunted by Ferdinand de Saussure and Victor Frankenstein) in June 2015. I thank the audience and organisers.

NOTES

1. On this point, see especially Luciano (2015), Malm (2015) and Nixon (2014). ('The Anthropocene').

2. On the varied tempos of ecological violence and its intimacy to environmental justice, see Nixon (2011), *Slow Violence and the Environmentalism of the Poor*.

3. On matter as agentic—and thereby vibrant—see Jane Bennett (2010), *Vibrant Matter: A Political Ecology of Things*. Mick Smith aptly names the diminution of matter into mere material 'resourcism' in *Against Ecological Sovereignty: Ethics, Biopolitics, and Saving the Natural World*.

4. On posthumanism as that which 'comes before and after humanism', opposing 'fantasies of disembodiment and autonomy' (xv), see Cary Wolfe (2011).

5. I use the terms 'inhuman' and 'nonhuman' interchangeably in this essay but prefer the former, foregrounding as it does the ways in which the not-human is always already within the human, as material trace or incorporated (if repudiated) foundation.

6. On the vexed status of onomatopoeia as a 'slipping away' of language from and into imitation, as a kind of 'contamination' of the arbitrary with the mimetic, see, for example, Jacques Derrida ruminating over Ferdinand de Saussure in *Glas* (1986, 93).

7. On the long history of the naturalism versus conventionalism debate that Plato's *Cratylus* narrates, see Attridge (1984).

8. References to a 'wood wide web' of communication are commonplace in both the environmental humanities and scientific literature, where it typically designates the mycorrhizal net enabling forest communication; see, for example, Manuela Giovannetti et al (2006). I am using the term more generally to designate a forest as an open system of biosemiotic communication.

9. The quotation describes the work of Kathryn Yusoff. See also p. 27 on the challenge of the nonbiological to Actor Network Theory accounts of agency.

10. I have written a great deal about lithic temporality and agency in *Stone*.

11. For a pragmatic development of what the contours such posthuman ethics might assume, see Wolfe, *Before the Law* (2013, 92–105).

12. On the challenges posed by thinking the elements, see Cohen and Duckert (2015).

13. On dogs in the Middle Ages, see especially Crane (2012, 101–119); Steel; and the short compilation of manuscript illustrations by Walker-Meikle. More generally I am inspired in my thinking here by Laurie Shannon's work on the 'reduction of plenitude' that thinking the animal too often entails. Also useful is Kohn's chapter on canine–human entanglement and 'trans-species pidgins' in *How Forests Think* (2013, 131–150).

14. 'Le Fresne' (ll. 144–148); further references by line number. The best overview of the work of Marie de France is Kinoshita and McCracken (2012).

15. St. Gallen, Stiftsbibliothek, Cod. Sang. 225, f. 132. Viewable online at http://www.ecodices.unifr.ch/en/list/one/csg/0225

16. For the complexities of hunting—and the appearance of a peccary to be hunted in a dream by the author—see *How Forests Think* (Kohn 2013, 153–156).

17. Gascoigne's (1575) book translates and adapts Jacques du Fouilloux, *La Vénerie*.

18. Cf. Taylor: 'What I encounter in my leopard is not just history, but history as it becomes legible in death: history by way of animal sacrifice and history as it passes into my hands through inheritance, as part and parcel of the work of mourning. When

I touch my leopard, I am put in touch (literally) with the historical past as potentially lived experience, highlighting the weird incommensurability between historical time and the arc of a life' (Taylor, 2015 (*Edge Effects*)).

19. From *La Chace dou Cerf* 38, l. 324; cited in Crane (2012, 112).

20. On human identity as the product of animal domination, see Steel, *How to Make a Human* (2011, 24).

21. Menely writes that a 'poem internalises, within the word and the symbolic order it organises, the significance of voice and the creatural imaginary, the domain of correspondence and association, address and metamorphosis . . . the vitality of poetic language comes from its proximity to creaturely life and loss' (2015, 16).

22. All quotations from Chaucer's works are from *The Riverside Chaucer*, Gen. Ed. Larry D. Benson.

23. On the Middle English verb 'rŏuten' and its derivation, see its entry in the Middle English Dictionary. Chaucer loves these sound words: 'Hayt!' (giddap!) in the Friar's Tale (3.1542), 'buf' (the sound of a burp) in the Summoner's Tale (5.1934), 'fneseth' for a drunken sneeze (9.62), 'chuk' for the noise a rooster makes to call hens to grain (7.3172).

24. On transcorporeality as a modern phenomenon of dermal permeability and toxicity, see Alaimo (2010), *Bodily Natures: Science, Environment, and the Material Self*. For a thorough discussion of embodiment as a material process in the Middle Ages, see Cadden (1993).

25. Mitchell well demonstrates something that I can only hint at here, that 'complicated ecologies underpin even the tidiest of cosmologies' (2014, 175) and 'it is in the very grain of ordinary life that we can find knotted multiplicities' (176).

26. Akbari explicates the place-bound environmentality of the body well.

27. On the materiality of premodern, humoral psychology, see especially Paster (1993).

WORKS CITED

Akbari, Suzanne Conklin. *Idols in the East: European Representations of Islam and the Orient, 1100–1450*. Ithaca: Cornell University Press, 2009.

Alaimo, Stacy. *Bodily Natures: Science, Environment, and the Material Self*. Bloomington: Indiana University Press, 2010.

Alaimo, Stacy. 'Your Shell on Acid: Material Immersion, Anthropocene Dissolves'. *Anthropocene Feminism*. Eds. Richard Grusin and John Blum. Minneapolis: University of Minnesota Press, forthcoming.

Attridge, Derek. 'Language as Imitation: Jakobson, Joyce, and the Art of Onomatopoeia'. *Modern Language Notes* 99 (1984): 1116–1139.

Bennett, Jane. *Vibrant Matter: A Political Ecology of Things*. Durham: Duke University Press, 2010.

Braidotti, Rosi. *The Posthuman*. Cambridge: Polity Press, 2013.

Bredin, Hugh. 'Onomatopoeia as a Figure and a Linguistic Principle'. *New Literary History* 27 (1996): 555–569.

Cadden, Joan. *The Meanings of Sex Difference in the Middle Ages: Medicine, Science, and Culture.* Cambridge: Cambridge University Press, 1993.

Chaucer, Geoffrey. *The Riverside Chaucer.* Gen. Ed. Larry D. Benson. 3rd edn. New York: Houghton Mifflin, 1987.

Cohen, Jeffrey Jerome. *Stone: An Ecology of the Inhuman.* Minneapolis: University of Minnesota Press, 2015.

Cohen, Jeffrey Jerome and Lowell Duckert, eds. *Elemental Ecocriticism: Thinking Earth, Air, Fire and Water.* Minneapolis: University of Minnesota Press, 2015.

Crane, Susan. *Animal Encounters: Contacts and Concepts in Medieval Britain.* Philadelphia: University of Pennsylvania Press, 2012.

Derrida, Jacques. *Glas.* Trans. John P. Leavey Jr. and Richard Rand. Lincoln: University of Nebraska Press, 1986.

Derrida, Jacques. *The Animal That Therefore I Am.* Ed. Marie-Louise Mallet. Trans. David Wills. New York: Fordham University Press, 2008.

Foys, Martin. 'A Sensual Philology for Anglo-Saxon England'. *Postmedieval: A Journal of Medieval Cultural Studies* 5 (2014): 456–472.

Gascoigne, George. *The Noble Arte of Venerie or Hunting.* London: Imprinted by Henry Bynneman, for Christopher Barker, 1575.

Giovannetti, Manuela, Luciano Avio, Paola Fortuna, Elisa Pellegrino, Cristiana Sbrana, Patrizia Strani. 'At the Root of the Wood Wide Web: Self Recognition and Non-Self Incompatibility in Mycorrhizal Networks'. *Plant Signaling and Behavior* 1.1 (2006): 1–5.

Haraway, Donna. *The Companion Species Manifesto: Dogs, Species and Significant Otherness.* Chicago: Prickly Paradigm Press, 2003.

Hsy, Jonathan. 'Between Species: Animal-Human Bilingualism'. *In the Medieval Middle.* October 2012. Web. 10 December 2015.

Iovino, Serenella and Serpil Oppermann. 'Introduction: Stories Come to Matter'. *Material Ecocriticism.* Eds. Serpil Oppermann and Serenella Iovino. Bloomington: University of Indiana Press, 2014. 1–17.

Iovino, Serenella and Serpil Oppermann. 'Material Ecocriticism: Materiality, Agency, and Models of Narrativity'. *Ecozon@* 3 (2012): 75–91. Web. 3 November 2015.

Kinoshita, Sharon and Peggy McCracken. *Marie de France: A Critical Companion.* Cambridge: D. S. Brewer, 2012.

Kohn, Eduardo. *How Forests Think: Toward an Anthropology Beyond the Human.* Berkeley: University of California Press, 2013.

Lorimer, Jamie. *Wildlife in the Anthropocene: Conservation after Nature.* Minneapolis: University of Minnesota Press, 2015.

Luciano, Dana. 'The Inhuman Anthropocene'. *Los Angeles Review of Books.* 22 March 2015. Web. 7 May 2015.

Malm, Andrea. 'The Anthropocene Myth'. *Jacobin.* 23 March 2015. Web. 7 May 2015.

Marie de France. *Lais*, Ed. Alfred Ewert. London: Bristol Classics Press, 1995. (*The Lais of Marie de France.* Trans. Robert Hanning and Joan Ferrante. Durham: The Labyrinth Press, 1978.)

Menely, Tobias. *The Animal Claim: Sensibility and the Creaturely Voice.* Chicago: University of Chicago Press, 2015.

Middle English Dictionary. University of Michigan. Online Dictionary.

Mitchell, J. Allan. *Becoming Human: The Matter of the Medieval Child.* Minneapolis: University of Minnesota Press, 2014.

Nixon, Rob. *Slow Violence and the Environmentalism of the Poor.* Cambridge: Harvard University Press, 2011.

Nixon, Rob. 'The Anthropocene: The Promise and Pitfalls of an Epochal Idea'. *Edge Effects.* 4 November 2014. Web. 8 November 2015.

Paster, Gail Kern. *The Body Embarrassed: Drama and the Disciplines of Shame in Early Modern England.* Ithaca: Cornell University Press, 1993.

Shannon, Laurie. *The Accommodated Animal: Cosmopolity in Shakespearean Locales.* Chicago: University of Chicago Press, 2013.

Smith, Mick. *Against Ecological Sovereignty: Ethics, Biopolitics, and Saving the Natural World.* Minneapolis: University of Minnesota Press, 2011.

Steel, Karl. *How to Make a Human: Animals and Violence in the Middle Ages.* Columbus: Ohio State University Press, 2011.

Steel, Karl. 'Ridiculous Mourning: Dead Pets and Lost Humans'. *Studies in the Age of Chaucer* 34 (2012): 345–349.

Taylor, Jesse Oak. 'Leopard in a Box', *Edge Effects.* 12 May 2015. Web. 2 July 2015.

Walker-Meikle, Kathleen. *Medieval Dogs.* London: British Library, 2013.

Wolfe, Cary. *What Is Posthumanism?* Minneapolis: University of Minnesota Press, 2010.

Wolfe, Cary. *Before the Law: Humans and Other Animals in a Biopolitical Frame.* Chicago: University of Chicago Press, 2013.

Chapter Two

Environmental History between Institutionalization and Revolution

A Short Commentary with Two Sites and One Experiment

Marco Armiero

Environmental history was born with the promise to shift the focus of history from humans to nature. Indeed, it was a revolution for such a deeply 'human-centric' discipline as history. It is a matter of debate how much, or even whether, environmental historians have been able to place nature at the centre of their analysis. We have had several kinds of environmental history, each with different approaches, priorities, and narratives, thereby, with a different degree of 'anthropocentrism'. There is no doubt that, historically, environmental historians have pursued the ambitious project to overcome the great divide that separates hard sciences from humanities. Since the beginning, geologists, foresters, biologists, and ecologists were the primary interlocutors. Environmental historians were supposed to learn the 'foreign languages' of those disciplines—to use Donald Worster's words—if they wanted to understand the book of nature. The other side of the coin has been a rather frail relationship with history and, in general, with the humanities. In this chapter I aim to explore the contribution of environmental history in the shaping of the environmental humanities, in particular reflecting on the dialectic between adaptation to/transformation of the broader academic and disciplinary context.

The challenge for an emerging discipline— or also for an emerging field of studies— seems always to be the choice between a transformative, or even revolutionary, project and the incorporation into the mainstream, existing academic setting. I will offer some insights on this issue drawing from the environmental history experience in the broader and consolidate field of history as well as in the emerging area of the environmental humanities.

DEFINING, PATROLLING, CONTAMINATING

In 1999 I spent a short stint at the University of Kansas studying with Donald Worster. Indeed, that experience shaped my path forever into the field of environmental history. I was coming out from a rather complicated PhD in Economic History in Italy where I had struggled to make the basic point that nature—in my case forests—mattered in history. Of course, wood was a staple in economic history research but things became more problematic when I tried to shift the focus from quantitative data on prices, tons, and deforestation to the complex connections linking local communities, forests, and the state. My forests were made by an intricate network of ecological and social relations, in which property rights and goats, agronomic treaties and landslides, common uses and political reforms blended.[1] At that time, studying forests was weird enough for an Italian historian, but arguing that they were not just 'nature' but rather socio-ecological formations made things even more odd. Disciplines share with nations a sense of belonging and a passion for borders. Trespassing remains a risky business that must be controlled and organised. However, borders do not work only among disciplines, they also organise the objects of study. One should not see fascism for the forest, or capitalism for the lungs. Disciplines do not order only office space in the university buildings, but the very reality that they should help understand. The more established a discipline becomes, the stronger is its ambition to order reality and own the knowledge to access a fraction of it. In this sense, it might even become acceptable to research the history of the environment—in some academic cultures more than others—but the borders of the 'environment' must be clear. Let the forest be the forest and nothing else.

I believe that this has been, and may still be in some cases, a crucial turning point in environmental history. After the rebellious and precarious years of the pioneers, the field has finally acquired respectability, even if more in the United States than in other countries. Environmental history is taught in the most prestigious US universities, has two established scholarly journals, and academic presses publish books or even entire series dedicated to this discipline. What is wrong with this? Absolutely nothing. Looking at this progress from the periphery of the Anglo-Saxon world, I can only hope that soon some of it might also reach those academic communities where environmental history is still struggling to have the right to exist. Nonetheless, there might be side effects of the mainstreaming of the discipline. I see two divergent movements in environmental history: on one hand, the tension to reinforce the discipline, to make it stronger, therefore, to mark its borders and define its tenets. What I would call the institutional option. On the other, the ambition to infiltrate history, or even the humanities at large, aiming to change their constituencies and having an impact on current problems. Let us call it the revolutionary option. These are with no doubt simplifications, because more often the two tendencies have not been mutually exclusive; it might occur that in order to make changes a stronger institutional position can be helpful. It is also true that sometimes it has not been a matter of choices but rather of necessity; in academic communities where environmental history is extremely weak, infiltrating other fields looks more like camouflage than a deliberate offensive strategy. In Italy, for instance, the absence of PhD programmes and professorships in environmental history forces scholars to be something else—as my PhD in economic history loudly states—which is more the result of marginalization than a hegemonic strategy.

Although jealous of the communities that have been successful in the institutional option, building a strong environmental history field, I still argue for the revolutionary path. I believe that the institutional option can easily lead to a sidebar discipline. To explain what I mean with 'sidebar discipline', consider a possible new history textbook that may offer boxes on specific topics, including some environmental ones. In the chapter on the Industrial Revolution the reader may find a box on pollution or more likely on energy, or in the section on the Discovery of the Americas—indeed, in too many schools that is still a discovery instead of conquest—a box on potatoes, viruses, and horses may be rather popular nowadays, after the success of Jared Diamond's books (1997, 2005). Of course, this is an improvement; when I was a student, coal and viruses had nothing to do with history, they were not even confined in a side box. However, I argue that the final effect of the side-box style is to reinforce the irrelevance of environmental history, or, in a more optimistic sense, its narrow disciplinary specialisation. Coal or viruses are interesting topics, maybe rather curious, but they do not change the mainstream ways of looking at either the Industrial Revolution or the conquest of the Americas. They are 'environmental' themes that speak to and about the environment. In a highly specialised and compartmentalised organization of knowledge, there might even be room for environmental history; the green ghetto may look welcoming, but it is still a ghetto. A personal example could help in clarifying my argument. Once a department in Italy offered me to teach an environmental history course, probably one of the first in the country, but when I proposed to teach a course on imperialism several colleagues were rather disappointed. 'We thought you were an environmental historian', they kept repeating, in a way or another. Apparently, I was expected to teach something on national parks or on some other environmental topics; with imperialism I was trespassing the borders of my side-box territory. Of course, I argued that natural parks might also be connected to imperialism, as so many scholars have demonstrated (Grove 1995; MacKenzie 1997; Neumann 1998). More in general, choosing to offer a course on imperialism is per se a rejection of the sidebar approach; instead it goes in the direction of what I have called the

revolutionary approach because it aims to address the 'big' issues of history
aiming not to add some environmental themes to the mainstream narrative but
to build a new, alternative narrative.

I have tried to work in this direction for all my academic life. This was,
for instance, the main challenge in my book on Italian mountains (Armiero
2011). The Alps and forests, landslides and dams, mountain climbers and
tourists were the obvious subjects for a book like that; nonetheless, I wanted
to go beyond the borders of the environment and of what environmental history should be. Thereby, I have tried to demonstrate that fascism and racial
rhetorics, nation-state building, nationalism and war, capitalism and science
have to do with mountains—and by extension with nature at large—more
than historians are generally willing to recognise. And I am not speaking
only of the marginalization that environmental historians may have suffered,
but also of the self-ghettoization, the self-conviction that our themes do not
intertwine with the wider historical processes. I did not want to write a book
on mountains in modern Italy, rather I aimed to narrate the modern history of
Italy employing the environment as my lens. I am doing a similar operation
when I study the environmental history of modern mass migrations; the aim is
again to reflect on how environmental history can contribute in changing the
mainstream understanding of the history of migrations. Evidently, migration
is not at all a minor or particular topic in the history of modern world.

I speak of a revolutionary approach not in terms of contents—in general
the posterity defines what has been revolutionary in knowledge production—
but rather in terms of ambitions and practices. I want to stress the ambition
to change mainstream historical narratives, and the attempt here is to infiltrate other fields rather than being satisfied within ones' own community.
By default, a revolutionary mode is less inclined to obey to strict borders,
always looking for alliances that can mobilise more people and communities.
Sometimes, this means to work on the fringes of the discipline. I think, for
instance, of the connections enhanced between environmental historians and
political ecologists, especially those working on environmental justice. In
those cases a strong disciplinary identity abdicates to common research topics
and, often, to a shared radical stance. This has been the case of the European
Network of Political Ecology 'Entitle' where environmental historians have
joined forces with critical geographers, ecological economists, and political
scientists to work on environmental conflicts on a global scale.[2] Being an
international training network, this programme has offered the opportunity
to include environmental history in the toolkit of PhD students who were
not, at least in large majority, either environmental or any other kind of historians. It is hard to say how much this has actually worked; two recently
published textbooks in political ecology include at least one environmental
historian belonging to the Entitle network, apparently proving that at least

some infiltration did occur (Barca 2015a and 2015b). Obviously, infiltrations do not work as occupations; the revolutionary approach does not aim, in my vision, to take over others' disciplinary territories but rather to infiltrate them, creating new spaces, free zones where the 'weird things are'.[3] Precisely as in the Marxist metabolic relationship of humans–nature, also in this disciplinary relationship the change must be reciprocal: as humans are changed changing nature, so environmental history changes through its effort in transforming other disciplines and, hopefully, the world, or at least, our way of understanding it.

As I have argued earlier, the effect does not only shape disciplinary borders but has the ambition to affect the objects of study, in other words, the reality disciplines control and organise. The sharp separation between environmental and social or cultural becomes blurry, empires taste of coffee, dams are political manifestos, and stock markets flow into human bodies as cancer cells. Such an environmental history cannot be satisfied with the usual definition that states that the discipline studies the relationships between societies and nature through time. For all the beauty of its simplicity, this definition reinforces the dichotomy nature vs. society, implying the possibility to separate the two. Coming back to the Marxist metabolic relationship, my understanding of the classical definition of environmental history is that the very relationship produces a new body that is neither natural nor social. Trying to overcome the nature/society dichotomy, Richard White (1995) once wrote:

> In aiming for a relationship, I mean to do more than write a human history alongside a natural history and call it an environmental history. This would be like writing a biography of a wife, place it alongside the biography of a husband and calling it a history of a marriage. I want the history of the relationship itself. (x)

Following Richard White's metaphor, I would like to define environmental history as the study of socio-ecological formations in a historical perspective. I realise that speaking of 'socio-ecological formations' looks extremely academic, typical social science jargon; nonetheless, I could not find a better expression to communicate the message that the object of environmental history is the hybrid formation of human societies and the environment. Furthermore, hybridity is not a matter of academic jargon, rather it is the very essence of our world, the matter of which it is made of. Quoting Richard White, again, the quest for purity—pure natural separated from pure societal—will not help us to understand the messy and dirty world we are part of (White 1999). However, maybe the best would be to refrain from any definition and leave environmental history free to be reinvented each time, infiltrating and changing. Patrolling borders is not for revolutionaries.

TWO SITES AND ONE EXPERIMENT

Strangely enough, for someone with my convictions, I have never been very passionate about theories and abstractions. Maybe this has spared me from staying trapped in some orthodoxy, condemned to deliver always the same truth. As many fellow historians, I am in turn obsessed with stories, with the multiplicity of empirical cases on which our craft is built. For this reason in what follows I have decided to offer some glimpses of environmental history in its making, exploring two examples of where the (non)discipline should go and presenting an experiment of which I have been part.

Site #1—The Nation

Is not this the historical place par excellence? History was born to tell the histories of the nation. To be more accurate, historians were supposed to tell the singular History of the nation; the very idea that histories might have been many was not contemplated in those early days. For a long time historians have dealt mainly with the national past. Languages and sources conspired in trapping historians within the national borders; it could also be said that history still remains one of the disciplines in which scholars generally publish in their own languages. The staple question has often revolved around the nation-state building process: how Germany, Italy, Japan, or the United States, to mention a few examples, have become nations. In the old days, the focus on the nation went hand in hand with the exclusive attention to the elites: kings, generals, inventors, statesmen (and the masculine was actually the only gender in these narratives). However, also a history from below could be pretty national: in the seventies a politically engaged social history produced a rich account of the diverse working-class national organizations.

Environmental history was born with an anti-national ambition (Worster 1982). It was not so much a political stance, rather an ecological consideration. The environment hardly follows the political borders of states; rivers and air, viruses and climatic events do not need any passport to trespass. Many scholars have emphasised the significance of the 1968 Earthrise photograph, taken by the astronauts from Apollo 8, in the making of a global environmental awareness.[4] The image of the Earth emerging from dark space annulled all the national divisions among states; the frontiers were invisible, therefore, irrelevant when thinking of the planet from a global perspective. Hence, did environmental history produce a post-national history? Looking at the publications in the field it would be hard to sustain this claim. Most of the research has been done within the national borders; the history of a metropolis, a national park, a disaster, an environmental legislation are all well rooted in their national framework. Nonetheless, I argue that this might not be a failure for environmental historians. Let me put this clearly: the point is not to ignore or avoid the nation as a scale of observation but to be reflexive about the effects that the adopted scale has on the very issues we aim to address. I invoke an environmental history that thinks of the nation beyond national frontiers, because parks, metropolis, or industrial pollution are at the same time local, national and transnational facts. The stories we wish to tell are not contained into national frontiers but national frontiers are part of those stories. The environmental history of a US metropolis, or for what matters whatever metropolis in the global north, is intrinsically both national and global. The energy complex feeding the urban daily life connects national and international politics, the global networks of military and corporate power and the underworld network of technological fixes that innervates the urban space. The city per se is a microcosm where the stratification of immigrants' communities has reproduced global inequalities on the local level. The case of the city is only an example in order to explain what I mean for an environmental history, which reflects on the nation without being trapped in its borders. In this sense, I envision the eruption of environmental history into the history of the nation as a revolutionary intervention, meaning with this the attempt to change the usual way of thinking of the nation rather than just adding some environmental themes to the same-old narrative. The ambition to change the usual narrative of the nation is clear in Ted Steinberg's path-breaking *Down to Earth*. As he writes in the introduction:

> This book will try to change the way you think about American history. It deals with some familiar topics—colonization, the industrial revolution, slavery, the Civil War, consumerism—and some not so well-known—the Little Ice Age, horse manure, pig sties, fast food, lawns, SUVs, and garbage. I will argue that the natural world—defined here as plants and animals, climate and weather, soil and water—has profoundly shaped the American past. (2002, ix)

As he explained a few lines below, nature has begun to be part of several historical accounts; Theodore Roosevelt and the conservation movement or the raising of environmentalism in the 1960s are often mentioned in the national histories, but with Steinberg we should ask ourselves whether this is actually changing the stories we tell. The environment is intertwined with the histories of the nation, for instance, with the history of colonization, Civil War, capitalistic industrialisation and farming. Steinberg uses a powerful strata metaphor to describe the limits of the New Social History that, nonetheless, has been able to introduce so many invisible subjects into the historical narrative; as he wrote: 'by and large, the social historians put away their shovels when they reached the land and soil itself' (2002, ix). I criticise that metaphor because the strata vision implies again a separation as if the environment were underneath social formations or actors, while I argue that instead it is mixed with all of them. Rather than finally reaching the layer of the environment the challenge is to recognise the environment throughout the whole of the core sampling we are examining, precisely as Steinberg magisterially has done in this volume.

Introducing Mark Fiege's *The Republic of Nature*, William Cronon stressed precisely this aspiration to enter 'historiographical territories that were relatively unexplored by environmental historians' (Cronon 2012, xi). Fiege himself explained the origins of his book as the need to escape what I have early defined the 'green ghetto':

> Years ago, two young women in the class challenged my choice of subject matter. They appreciated the historical study of diseases, soil, animals drought, forests, conservation, national parks, irrigation and industrial pollution but they wondered if the course was what it purported to be. If it was American history, they asked, then why weren't we covering the usual American history topics? Why weren't we studying the nature of the American revolution, for example, or the nature of the civil war? (Fiege 2012, 9)

Starting from those questions, Fiege has designed a book that leads the reader through the US history following a selection of crucial episodes, from the Salem witch hunting to the 1970s' oil crisis.

My own book *A Rugged Nation* aims to rethink the nation in its mutual constituency with nature. Far away from any naturalization of nation, I have explored how imagined communities and constructed natures have interacted in Italian history. It is not by chance that I have largely employed in that book the category of landscape even more than that of 'environment'. As Thomas Lekan and Thomas Zeller have written in another extremely significant book in this reassessing of the nation in environmental history, landscape works well when one tries to conceptualise and narrate the connections between the environmental space and the political space of the nation (2005, 5). Ventriloquistly I can give the voice back to myself:

> I envisioned this project as an attempt to engage environmental history with political, cultural, and social history. Wolves and fascists, hydroelectric companies and mountain climbers, war memorials and Scolytid Coleoptera cohabited in the pages of this book. I know that this will seem odd to some colleagues. Never mind. Mountains have never been places for conformity. (Armiero 2011, 9)

Indeed, the manuscript of the book was rejected by several Italian publishers on the basis that it was neither disciplinary nor academic enough. In the end, it was published firstly in English and then translated into Italian, where it attracted attention beyond the scholarly community. Sometimes going against the grain pays off.

Site #2—The Body

> The body—at once human and animal—has emerged as arguably the most critical middle ground where fin de siècle relations between nature and culture have been actively remade as well as rethought. (Seller 1999, 487)

With this 1999 article, Christopher Seller pushed environmental historians to reflect more about one part of nature that they have generally overlooked. The body has stayed marginal in the field, probably because rubricated under other disciplines. After all, if environmental history is the study of the relationships between society and the environment, it might become problematic to place the body within this scheme. In order to occupy the body, environmental history has to trespass both disciplinary and conceptual borders. Sellers wrote the 1999 article coming from a consolidated research interest on industrial hazards; he arrived to the body passing through the capitalistic organization of labour and its unequal distribution of exposures and risks (Seller 1997). The body is an exemplar place for the kind of environmental history I am proposing in this essay; it is neither just social or cultural nor purely ecological. In the body flows of materials and energy merge with genetic and social history, the external environment penetrates into the cells. The body is power inscribed into ecology. Epigenetics has actually demonstrated that the stratification of power relations, the memories of injustice, stay within the body telling their stories through the genetic narratives of each individual. In the factory or in the mine, in the slum or in the working-class neighbourhood, the subaltern body meets an ecology that is never just natural. David Harvey once said that capitalism is not only producing an ecology but it is an ecology. Therefore, what the subaltern body meets is not just 'the external nature', but rather a specific arrangement of power and ecology, that is, a socio-ecological formation. Environmental justice scholars—and it is not by a chance that I am not mentioning any discipline—have been especially significant in thinking of the ecology of body, power, and the environment. Through a rich series of case studies they have shown how the body is bound into a network of socio-ecological relationships that often imprint injustice into the flesh and blood of subaltern people. In her book *Inescapable Ecologies*, Linda Nash has consciously proposed an environmental history that places the body at the centre of its analysis: 'By placing the human body at the center of an environmental history, this work challenges the modern dichotomy that separates human beings from the rest of nature, a dichotomy that underwrites the very discipline of history' (2006, 8). Her distinction between the ecological and the modern body[5] is crucial in order to understand not only the knowledge and perceptions about health and disease but also the concrete practices through which the ecologies of bodies and those of places mixed. However, this meeting was not random or natural, but it interlaced with the fault lines of class and race (198).

In his wonderful book on allergies in the US history, Gregg Mitman writes: 'the places where Americans have struggled to breathe, as well as the spaces they have created to breathe more freely . . . have been shaped not only by the ecology of animal, insect, plant, and man-made allergens, but also by the unequal distribution of wealth and health care in American society' (2007, 2). For Mitman it is clear that allergies are not only an interface between the body and the external nature, because, as he explained, the landscape of breathing is shaped by the unjust arrangements of the US society. Actually, even the nature of the body is socially determined, at least in the possibilities to cope with the stresses coming from the surroundings. Mitman's book is a great example of an environmental history that takes the body seriously, trespassing the borders of the discipline to enter in cognate fields, as, for instance, history of medicine or science and technology studies (STS). Throughout the volume, Mitman discusses how medicine has understood allergies and contributed in shaping the body in its reaction to them. As Mitman explains, the medical practice progressively shifted from an understanding of allergies as a place-based problem of relationships to an individual deficiency to be addressed through drugs. Ecology, instead, is the science of relationships, and relationships matter, Mitman reminds his readers in closing his volume (253).

The agency of scientists in the unpacking of body/environment relationships is key in most environmental justice stories. Recovering what she has labelled 'working class environmentalism', Stefania Barca has explicitly dedicated one essay to 'Work, Bodies, Militancy', in which she demonstrates that in 1970s' Italy a class-based science was able to address the crucial issue of industrial risks much more than unengaged science. Militancy was a tool rather than an obstacle towards a more accurate scientific knowledge. One basic assumption of a militant scientist is that the body knows best—to paraphrase the famous Barry Commoner saying—especially if that body is at the frontline of exploitation and class, race or gender discrimination. In her *Bodily Natures*, Stacy Alaimo writes:

> Casting racism as environmental exposes how sociopolitical forces generate landscapes that infiltrate human bodies. Similarly, the 'pancreas under capitalism' and the 'proletarian lung' testify to the penetrating physiological effects of class (and racial) oppression, demonstrating that the biological and the social cannot be considered separate spheres. . . . The proletarian lung illustrates my conception of trans-corporeality, in that the human body is never a rigidly

enclosed, protected entity, but is vulnerable to the substances and flows of its environments, which may include industrial environments and their social/economic forces. (2010, 28)

Following Stacy Alaimo's trans-corporeality, Serenella Iovino has recently written about the porosity of the human and urban body in Naples, Italy: 'Naples' bodies are texts, the city itself is a text, and its texture is its own narrative. It is a narrative populated by substances, choices, voices, human presences, illnesses, scars, … natural catastrophes, war, contamination, fear, death, and life' (2016, 38). Iovino is referring here to the long-lasting toxic waste contamination that has affected a large portion of the Neapolitan territory and, consequently, of its inhabitants. Working on toxic contamination in Naples I have coordinated a project of guerrilla narrative with a group of women; from that experience we published a book that testifies to the material embodiment of environmental injustice and the politicization of apolitical subjects through the politicization of the body (Armiero 2014).

An Experiment—A Slam with the Center for Culture, History, and Environment, and Rachel Carson

In February 2014 the Center for Culture, History, and Environment, in collaboration with the Rachel Carson Center and the KTH Environmental Humanities Laboratory, launched a rather peculiar call for submissions. It was not the usual call for papers that fills our email boxes because it did not belong to the literary genre of academic conference announcements. That call asked for objects rather than papers inviting people to imagine what an Anthropocene Cabinet of Curiosities would look like.[6] As the call stated:

> In the spirit of poetry/spoken word slams, contributors will be asked to pitch in a public fishbowl setting an object for the Anthropocene that asks us to rethink humanity's relationship to time, place, and the agency of things that shape planetary change. How is the appearance and impact of Homo sapiens as a geomorphic force registered in the sediments of history, the objects around us, and the things yet to be?

I believe that the Anthropocene Slam is an inspirational example of what a non-disciplinary environmental history might be. It mobilised scholars, writers, and artists far beyond any narrow disciplinary and even academic border. The Slam received 72 submissions from anthropologists, historians, artists, literary scholars, and cultural theorists (if one must really label the variety of people who were interested in participating in the event). Thinking at the Anthropocene through one single object unleashed the creativity of scholars, too often trapped into the usual mode of production and reproduction of knowledge. Actually, it might be interesting to mention that a few scholars did send in abstracts for papers as if the Slam were the usual academic conference; a rather sad demonstration that creativity and scientific work do not go always together. Of course, the scholarly interest for 'things' is anything but new, as Appadurai made clear in his *The Social Life of Things*. However, if it is true, as he argued, that things have a social life, the Slam proposed to use the thing as a metaphor for the wider socio-ecological relation many call nowadays the Anthropocene. The point was not to illustrate the history of the object but rather to let the object speak of its relationships with the larger Anthropocene. A trivial thermostat speaks of our detachment from the external nature as well as of geo-engineering ambition to control the planet; the maritime satellite tag embodies the cyborg nature of the Anthropocene; the monkey wrench reclaims the agency of work(ers) and the creative power of sabotage. I could go ahead with more examples but the message would be the same: at the Slam the object worked as a reference to the larger relationships of which it was a part. Although built around things, the Slam was the opposite of the reification of the Anthropocene, precisely because of its focus on relationships rather than on the individual 'thing'.

I was among the organisers and I was in Madison, Wisconsin, for the Slam. I have no doubt in saying that it has been the most exciting and funny academic event in which I have ever been involved. Each participant pitched the proposed object in a creative and playful way, dismissing the usual language of scholars. As Wilko Graf von Hardenberg has written:

> Presenters at the Slam treated the audiences to a variety of approaches to public speaking, both challenging and playing with the standards of academic communication. Great dramatic performances took us back and forth in time, from the 1950s stage for Michelle Mart and Cameron Muir's Flit pump, to the 2060 backdrop for Tom Bristow's Silene stenophylla seed. Julianne Lutz Warren, meanwhile, used audience participation to echo her performance, stressing themes of reproduction and simulation in her object—a human imitating the song of the extinct Huia bird. Partly in response to the theatrical setting of the Slam, Bethany Wiggin called for us to revolutionise the scholarship of the Anthropocene, to move it away from classical Aristotelian drama like Faust and towards a more experimental Brechtian approach. ('The Anthropocene Slam')

As in every slam, the audience had the final say and selected by voting for the objects that have been included in an actual exhibition at the Deutsches *Museum* as part of their larger 2015 exhibition *Welcome to the Anthropocene*.

I have decided to include the Slam because I believe it represents a concrete experiment of a different kind of environmental history. Evidently, it trespassed across disciplines to be openly an environmental humanities arena; it had the ambition to speak beyond the scholarly circle, experimenting with unusual languages and tools; it aims to intervene in the current debates, reclaiming the political of the humanities without renouncing poetry, playfulness, and humour. After all, as Michel Foucault once wrote 'Do not think that one has to be sad in order to be militant' (1983, 12).

CONCLUSION

I am well aware that I have not offered a comprehensive review on the state of environmental history. Rather, I have presented my vision of the discipline and a few ideas about the directions I believe it should take. I am pretty sure that this is only a minority report. The two main options I have described, institutionalization vs. revolution, are largely ideal-types; in the actual practice, they are often mixed. Although I have focused mainly on the approaches and, more specifically, on the connections to other disciplines, I do believe that in terms of content a less disciplinary and mainstream environmental history is more likely to assume radical stances and aim towards a politically engaged scholarship. However, I hope I did not give the impression that I am dictating some kind of offensive strategy to take over whatever academic Winter Palace. I would rather prefer to ignore the academic Winter Palace and Occupy reality! I still like the idea that scholars should not only aim to understand the world but contribute in changing it.

ACKNOWLEDGEMENT

I want to thank Anne Gough and Irma Kinga Allen who have discussed with me this chapter, also for helping to de-Italianise my English. Research for this chapter benefited from the People Programme: Program (Marie Curie Actions) of the European Union's Seventh Framework Programme, under REA agreement no. 289374—ENTITLE and MSCA-ITN-2014-ETN Marie Curie, agreement no. 642935 'ENHANCE'.

NOTES

1. Later I published my PhD dissertation with the title *Il territorio come risorsa. Comunità, economie, istituzioni nei boschi abruzzesi.* Napoli: Liguori, 1999.
2. For more information about Entile, see www.politicalecology.eu.

3. I must acknowledge here my debt to Marcus Hall who at the European Society for Environmental History Conference in Versailles (2015) evoked the power of weirdness, of experimenting new paths for the discipline.

4. For a review on this, see Armiero and Graf von Hardenberg.

5. 'Using contemporary terms, I label this earlier conception of the body "ecological", though it clearly antedated the modern science of ecology. Until the late nineteenth century, the concept of health typically referred to a state of balance, or harmony, between a person's body and the larger world. In contrast, for the modern body, "health" came to connote primarily the absence of disease; it implies both purity and the ability to fend off harmful organisms and substances. Above all, health became a quality possessed (or not) by an individual body rather than a dynamic relationship between a body and its environment' (Nash 12).

6. All the information about the Slam is available at http://nelson.wisc.edu/che/anthroslam/.

WORKS CITED

Alaimo, Stacy. *Bodily Natures: Science, Environment, and the Material Self*. Bloomington: Indiana University Press, 2010.

Appadurai, Arjun. *The Social Life of Things: Commodities in Cultural Perspective*. Cambridge: Cambridge University Press, 1986.

Armiero, Marco. *Il territorio come risorsa: Comunità, economie, istituzioni nei boschi abruzzesi*. Naples: Liguori, 1999.

Armiero, Marco. *A Rugged Nation: Mountains and the Making of Modern Italy*. Cambridge: White Horse Press, 2011.

Armiero, Marco. *Teresa e le altre: Storie di donne nella Terra dei Fuochi*. Milan: Jacabook, 2014.

Armiero, Marco and Wilko Graf von Hardenberg. 'Editorial introduction to special issue: Nature and Nation'. *Environment and History* 20.1 (2014): 1–8.

Barca, Stefania. 'Work, Bodies, Militancy. The "Class Ecology" Debate in the 1970s Italy'. *Powerless Science? Science and Politics in a Toxic World*. Eds. Soraya Boudia and Nathalie Jas. New York: Berghahn Books, 2014. 115–133.

Barca, Stefania. 'Greening the Job: Trade Unions, Climate Change and the Political Ecology of Labour'. *The International Handbook of Political Ecology*. Ed. Raymond L. Bryant. Cheltenham: Edward Elgar Press, 2015a. 387–400.

Barca, Stefania. 'Industrialization and Environmental Change'. *The Routledge Handbook of Political Ecology*. Eds. Thomas Albert Perreault, Gavin Bridge, and James McCarthy. New York: Routledge, 2015b. 366–377.

Cronon, William. 'Foreword. Environmental History Comes of Age'. *The Republic of Nature: An Environmental History of the United States*. Ed. Mark Fiege. Seattle: University of Washington Press, 2012.

Diamond, Jared. *Germs Guns Steel: The Fates of Human Societies*. New York: W. W. Norton, 1997.

Diamond, Jared. *Collapse: How Societies Choose to Fail or Succeed.* New York: Viking Press, 2005.

Fiege, Mark. *The Republic of Nature: An Environmental History of the United States.* Seattle: University of Washington Press, 2012.

Foucault, Michael. 'Preface'. *Anti-Oedipus: Capitalism and Schizophrenia.* Eds. Gilles Deleuze and Félix Guattari. Minneapolis: University of Minnesota Press, 1983.

Graf von Hardenberg, Wilko. 'The Anthropocene Slam: Mutiny, Play, and the Everyday'. *Edge Effects.* 13 November 2014. Web. 20 February 2016.

Grove, Richard. *Green Imperialism: Colonial Expansion, Tropical Island Edens, and the Origins of Environmentalism, 1600–1860.* New York: Cambridge University Press, 1995.

Iovino, Serenella. *Ecocriticism and Italy: Ecology, Resistance, and Liberation.* London: Bloomsbury, 2016.

Lekan, Thomas and Thomas Zeller. 'The Landscape of German Environmental History'. *Germany's Nature. Cultural Landscapes and Environmental History.* Eds. Thomas Lekan and Thomas Zeller. London: Rutgers University Press, 2005.

MacKenzie, John M. *The Empire of Nature: Hunting, Conservation and British Imperialism.* Manchester: Manchester University Press, 1997.

Mitman, Gregg. *Breathing Space: How Allergies Shape Our Lives and Landscapes.* New Haven: Yale University Press, 2007.

Nash, Linda. *Inescapable Ecologies: A History of Environment, Disease, and Knowledge.* Berkeley: University of California Press, 2006.

Neumann, Roderick P. *Imposing Wilderness: Struggles over Livelihood and Nature Preservation in Africa.* Berkeley: University of California Press, 1998.

Seller, Christopher. *Hazards of the Job: From Industrial Disease to Environmental Health Science.* Chapel Hill: University of North Carolina Press, 1997.

Seller, Christopher. 'Thoreau's Body: Towards an Embodied Environmental History'. *Environmental History* 4.4 (1999): 486–514.

Steinberg, Ted. *Down to Earth: Nature's Role in American History.* Oxford: Oxford University Press, 2002.

White, Richard. *The Organic Machine.* New York: Hill and Wang, 1995.

White, Richard. 'The Problem with Purity'. *The Tanner Lectures on Human Values Delivered at University of California,* Davis. 10 May 1999.

Worster, Donald. 'History without Borders: The Internationalizing of Environmental History'. *Environmental History Review* 6.2 (1982): 8–13.

Chapter Three

Cultural Ecology, the Environmental Humanities, and the Transdisciplinary Knowledge of Literature

Hubert Zapf

The environmental humanities have emerged in the twenty-first century as a new interdisciplinary field that promises to restore the epistemic, social, cultural, and political relevance of the humanities as an indispensable part of the knowledge production of contemporary universities. The environmental humanities are being institutionalised around the world as centres of environmental research and teaching that bring together disciplines that were formerly more or less strictly separated both within the humanities themselves and in the dialogue with the natural sciences. While ecocriticism was a development originating of literary and cultural studies and gaining considerable visibility in these disciplines, however, the environmental humanities often tend to be shaped by other disciplines such as environmental history, geography, earth systems sciences, bioethics, philosophy, agriculture, sociology, or science studies. Even though the argument is frequently made that literature as a core area of the humanities has something important to offer to the environmental knowledge, it often remains rather unclear what this special contribution could consist of apart from general moral, culture-critical, and political interventions that can as well be made by sociologists, political scientists, or cultural philosophers—or, in fact, by engaged citizens and environmental activists.

The question remains what literature and the humanities are good for, except to illustrate the knowledge provided by the hard sciences? The prevailing impression is that literature and aesthetics play a relatively minor role in this interdisciplinary dialogue, and I would like to argue here that there are some good reasons why this should be different, and why literature actually has an indispensable part to play in the new ecological episteme that is bridging the former divide between the humanities and the natural sciences. It seems useful at the outset to keep in mind that interdisciplinarity is no self-evidently given but needs some degree of caution and differentiation from an ecological perspective. While interdisciplinarity is a ubiquitous label and trendy marker of innovation in the contemporary sciences, it also has its limits in the fact that the knowledge cultures of different disciplines have a distinct contribution to make—not only in relation to the natural sciences but within the humanities themselves. In the case of the environmental humanities as an interdisciplinary array of disciplines as well, there exist significant differences between its various sub-disciplines such as politics, social sciences, history, geography, media studies, or cultural and literary studies, which cannot always as easily be bridged as the abstract postulate of interdisciplinarity would suggest.

With these caveats in mind, I would like to employ the perspective of cultural ecology here to address the question of how the place and function of literature and literary studies can be newly assessed as a distinct form of contemporary ecological knowledge within the dynamic and increasingly globalised development of the emergent interdisciplinary field of the environmental humanities. I can obviously only give a highly condensed account here of some key aspects of a cultural ecology of literary knowledge and will address the topic in the following steps: (a) briefly discuss the increased attention to literary knowledge in non-literary disciplines; (b) sketch some general premises of a cultural ecology of literary knowledge; (c) indicate a number of transdisciplinary contexts of cultural ecology that illustrate some of the ways in which the cultural knowledge of literature can be relevant to the environmental humanities: (i) metaphor and ecological knowledge, (ii) literary knowledge and the life sciences, and (iii) postcoloniality, ecoglobalism, and literary knowledge.

LITERARY KNOWLEDGE IN THE VIEW
OF OTHER DISCIPLINES

It seems first of all useful to turn around the perspective for a moment and look at the development in other disciplines of the humanities and social sciences, in which there is a notable tendency towards an increased attention to literary texts as models for the experiential concretization and methodological differentiation of their inherited codes of knowledge. Thus, in religious studies, the awareness of the textual and literary dimension of sacred scriptures has led to a shift of focus to questions of language, metaphor, narrative, and genre, which, interestingly enough, is connected with an increased awareness of interreligious and transconfessional issues. The dialogue of religious studies with literature has clearly become more important in recent decades, and it is instructive to see that wherever this is the case, dogmatic versions of religious thought are becoming questionable, because the recognition of the textual mediatedness of even the most sacred scriptures prevents any fundamentalist assertion of absolute truth claims. Thus it would certainly be productive to look not only at the Bible but also at the Quran from a literary perspective to integrate it into a wider non-dogmatic, intertextual, and transcultural discourse. Philosophy, too, especially philosophical ethics, has recently been looking to literature as a site of exploring ethical issues in particularly relevant and illuminating ways. As ethical theorists such as J. Hillis Miller, Paul Ricœur, or Martha Nussbaum have pointed out in their different ways, ethical issues seem to require the fictional mode of narrative, because the ethical is a category that resists abstract systematization and instead needs concrete exemplification of lived experience in the form of stories that allow for the imaginative transcendence of the individual self towards other selves.

In historiography or sociology as well, literary texts such as historical novels, but also other genres, have become sources of knowledge about the complexities of lived experience in specific historical periods and social conditions. Already in 2008, an article in the *Journal of Developmental Studies* pointed in this direction, authored by two social scientists from the London School of Economics and an economist of the World Bank, and bearing the remarkable title 'The Fiction of Development: Literary Representation as a Source of Authoritative Knowledge' (Lewis, Rodgers, and Woolcock 2008). In the article, the authors put forward the argument that works of literary fiction can contribute in unique ways to knowledge about developing cultures, which is not available in the same way to the 'positivist scientific discourse' (3) that is characteristic of social scientist documents both in academic writings and in other fact-and-statistics–oriented accounts such as by the World Bank or also by NGOs. Well intentioned as these may be, the authors argue, they still often miss important aspects of the situation of developing countries and regions, because they neglect such factors as personal experience, emotions, cultural memory, and the impact of the modernization process on the values, identities, and concrete lives of people, and especially of those whose voices are silenced in the official reports and blueprints for developmental programmes. Literature thus helps to provide what Walter Benjamin, as quoted by Lewis, Rodgers, and Woolcock, calls 'a concept of knowledge to which a concept of experience corresponds' (2), and which the authors see as a necessary counterpart to the generalizing and objectifying disciplinary knowledge on which developmental studies has almost exclusively depended. Literature's power to 'effectively convey complex ideas' (4) is considered as an indispensable complementary source of knowledge, which in their view should be taken seriously and be included in the ways in which the current situation of developing countries is to be assessed and their future to be envisioned more adequately. It is this potential of representing the otherwise unrepresented and the statistically ungraspable 'other' of empirical science and rational discourse in their symbolic scenarios that gives literary texts a special authority of insight: 'The creative imagination of the literary artist often has achieved insights into social processes that have remained unexplored in social science' (4).

Such considerations, I would like to argue, are also of relevance to the newly emerging field of the environmental humanities as an interdisciplinary array of approaches and issues that, however, are so far mainly dominated by disciplines such as environmental history, geography, anthropology, and the social and political sciences but in which the place of literature has yet to be assessed.

CULTURAL ECOLOGY AND LITERARY KNOWLEDGE

I would like to suggest that the paradigm of cultural ecology is one such transdisciplinary frame that can help to place literature and literary studies in the larger context of the environmental humanities, without reducing it to a mere illustrative function for other disciplines. A key figure in extending ecology beyond its biological-anthropological origins and in establishing it as a transdisciplinary approach in the humanities has been Gregory Bateson. Bateson's work itself spans a broad range of disciplines ranging from anthropology to logic, from psychology to epistemology, from ethnology to language theory, from cybernetics to philosophy. It does not cohere into a unified scientific system, but rather brings together heterogeneous fields of knowledge in a form of 'consilience' (Wilson 1998) or 'conciliation', as Greg Garrard calls it (see Garrard 2016), in which the deeply entrenched epistemological divide between the natural and the human sciences is bridged and common patterns of mind and life are explored beyond disciplinary boundaries. These patterns are shared across different epistemic and cultural fields, but they also vary according to specific contexts and do not designate fixed properties of given realities but rather emphasises nonlinear, emergent processes characterised by interacting networks and recursive feedback relations.

In Peter Finke's integrative approach of an Evolutionary Cultural Ecology, Bateson's 'ecology of mind' is developed further in ways that even more explicitly relate to crucial issues of the environmental humanities. Finke's *Ökologie des Wissens* (Ecology of Knowledge) fuses ideas from Bateson's ecology of mind with concepts from evolutionary biology on the one hand, and from social systems theory and linguistics on the other. Finke's aim is likewise to reconnect the various cultures of knowledge that have evolved in history, and that have been separated into more and more specialised disciplines and subdisciplines in the development of modern science. Building on the biologist Jakob von Uexküll's distinction between *Umwelten* and *Innenwelten*, i.e., between external and internal environments, which Uexküll ascribes to nonhuman as well as to human life, Finke develops the notion of *cultural ecosystems*, which have emerged in coevolution with natural ecosystems but have generated their own rules of selection and self-renewal, of production, consumption, and reduction of energy, along with their functionally differentiated tasks within society and culture. Language as a cultural ecosystem is especially important here as a shaping factor in the process of cultural evolution. Language represents a 'missing link' between cultural and natural evolution (Finke 2005), because it relates back to concrete biophysical forms of information and communication in the pre-cultural world of nature, but also transforms them into more abstract, symbolic, and generalizing systems of human interpretation and self-interpretation. Language thus decisively contributes to the emergence of internal worlds of consciousness and culture that are characteristic of the cultural evolution. Language and other cultural sign systems, in turn, are the material and the medium of art and literature, whose task is the constant critical examination, imaginative exploration, and creative self-renewal of these cultural sign systems.

In this more specific sense, literature can itself be described as the symbolic medium of a particularly powerful form of cultural ecology (see Zapf 2002, 2016b). This theory integrates insights of general cultural ecology with insights of literary theory and, indeed, of the literary texts themselves, which in this view must be taken seriously as sources of cultural knowledge in their own right. A central assumption of a cultural ecology of literature is that in its aesthetic transformation of experience, literature acts like an ecological force within the larger system of cultural discourse and knowledge. From its beginnings in storytelling and oral narratives, in legends and fairy-tales, in the genres of pastoral and nature poetry, but also in modes of the comic, gothic, and grotesque, literature has symbolically expressed the fundamental interconnectedness between culture and nature in tales of human genesis, of metamorphosis, of symbiotic co-evolution between different life forms. This attention to the life-sustaining significance of the mind/body and culture/ nature interaction became especially prominent in the era of romanticism, but continues to be characteristic of literary stagings of human experience up to the present. As an ecological force within culture, literature has presented human experience as part of a shared world of bodily natures and embodied minds (see Iovino and Oppermann 2014), exemplified in the motif of what Louise Westling calls the 'human-animal dance', a fascinating closeness between human and nonhuman life that has pervaded literary narratives from archaic to modern times, from the Gilgamesh epic to Virginia Woolf (Westling 2006, 11).

The aesthetic mode of textuality involves an overcoming of the mind–body dualism by bringing together conceptual and perceptual dimensions, ideas and sensory experiences, reflective consciousness and the performative staging of complex dynamical life processes (Ette 2004). From the beginnings of modern aesthetic theory in Baumgarten's *Aesthetica*, Kant's *Critique of Judgement*, Hegel's *Aesthetics* and Adorno's *Aesthetic Theory* up to Gernot Böhme's contemporary ecophilosophical 'aesthetics of nature', theory has struggled with the double status of the aesthetic as both an experience and a form of knowledge, a paradoxical, non-systemic form of *sinnliche Erkenntnis*, of 'sensuous knowledge', in which the tension and ambiguous co-agency between mind and body, thought and life was part of the ways in which the productivity of aesthetic and imaginative processes was conceived. Literature is an ecological cultural force not only in a thematic sense as in explicitly environmental forms of writing, but in a more fundamental sense in the forms and functions of aesthetic communication as they have evolved in literary and cultural history and are inscribed into the generative matrix of texts. Characteristic features of aesthetic texts such as recursive complexity, dynamic feedback relations, diversity-within-interconnectedness, or individuality-in-context are also the hallmarks of a contemporary ecological epistemology, which goes beyond inherited binaries and establishes the ineluctable interdependency of mind and body, culture and nature, human and nonhuman world as a fundamental given of all human (self-)knowledge.

There are meanwhile a growing number of voices from both the natural and cultural sciences that support this position. Current forms of complexity theory; biosemiotic and biocultural theories of literature as formulated by Wendy Wheeler and Nancy Easterlin; neuroscientific theories such as Paul Armstrong's concept of literature as creative engagement of the various faculties of the brain (see Armstrong 2013); theories of texts as an alternative form of *Lebenswissen*, of knowledge of living, as Ottmar Ette calls it (Ette 2004); or indeed cultural-ecological views of literature as a 'reintegrative interdiscourse' (Link 236) that brings together in metaphor and narrative what is separated in institutionalised concepts, categories, and discourses—all of these approaches corroborate the claim that literature has indeed something relevant and indispensable to contribute to contemporary and, indeed, to future knowledge. The fusion of heterogeneous semiotic material creates cognitive ambiguities, which provoke the interpretative engagement of the reader with the imaginative world of the text, and open up the space for the interdisciplinary perspectives that are required in the study of literary works, but that are also always incomplete and insufficient as explanatory models, since they are embedded in the explorative relational epistemology that the works themselves employ. This also implies that the various disciplines that are brought into play in this polyphonic dialogue of cognitive frames cannot simply remain unchanged but have to adjust and constantly transcend their own premises in the encounter with the text.

The knowledge of literature that emerges from this interplay of multiple perspectives is perhaps better described as *trans*disciplinary rather than *inter*-disciplinary knowledge, because interdisciplinarity could as well be applied to the relation between given scholarly disciplines to each other without the mediating power of literature and the aesthetic. But it is precisely the latter that accounts for the surplus value of literature as a form of knowledge that both includes and transforms the various frames of disciplinary knowledge that go into it and that make up their cognitive material. In its relational polarities, literature is a form of cultural ecology that does not follow a traditional binary logic but a transdisciplinary thinking in complexity, which according to Basarad Nicolescu is based on the 'nonseparability' and fundamental 'indeterminism' that characterise complex living processes from the natural to the cultural levels (Nicolescu 2008, 17–19). This thinking in complexity extends the binary logic of mutually exclusive contradictions towards a logic of the 'included middle', which associates opposite terms in nonlinear correlations interacting on always new emergent levels. 'The tension between contradictories builds a unity that includes and goes beyond the sum of the two terms' (29–30). Transdisciplinarity in this sense 'concerns that which is at once between the disciplines, across different disciplines, and beyond all disciplines', exploring in-between spaces of knowledge that are however not empty but on the contrary, are 'full of all potentialities' (44).

TRANSDISCIPLINARY CONTEXTS OF A CULTURAL ECOLOGY OF LITERATURE

Metaphor and Ecological Knowledge

One such domain, which opens up transdisciplinary perspectives, is the role of metaphor in ecological knowledge, which has been pointed out by Gregory Bateson and Wendy Wheeler among others. In a biosemiotics context, Wheeler emphasises the crucial role of metaphors both in processes of life and in its poetic transformation. Wheeler brings together evolutionary biology, eco-phenomenology, cultural history, and the semiotics of Charles Sanders Peirce, to apply to literature the approach of biosemiotics that has been developed since the 1960s by Friedrich S. Rothschild, Thure van Uexküll, Thomas Sebeok, and Jesper Hoffmeyer among others (see Hoffmeyer 2008). The sciences and literary studies appear as 'complementary epistemologies' (Westling 2014, 75) in the context of recent developments in the biological life sciences, which are moving from an 'Age of Reduction' to an 'Age of

Emergence' (Wheeler 2006, 12). This has made it possible to find new common ground with the human sciences in terms of a shared knowledge of 'complex structures of life' and of creative evolutionary processes that characterise nature as well as culture (13). Nature in this view is no opposite of cultural concepts of creativity and cooperation but is itself driven by multiple processes of semiosis and co-evolutionary emergence. Rather than solely a principle of monogenetic selection and dominance, this 'symbio-genetic co-operative communication' is fundamental to all life and makes it possible to see in nature a basis of 'human sociality' and of the 'fundamentally social nature of human existence' as well (12).

   Natural and cultural evolution, though qualitatively different through the higher degree of complexity and 'semiotic freedom' that has emerged in human culture (Wheeler 2006, 153), are nevertheless linked by the basic insight of biosemiotics that '*all* life—from the cell all the way up to us—is characterised by communication, or semiosis' (Wheeler 2011, 270). This semiotic dimension of life is evidenced in the functional cycles of semiotic loops 'flowing ceaselessly between the *Umwelten* (semiotic environments) and *Innenwelten* (semiotic inner worlds) of creatures' (272)—concepts that Wheeler borrows from the biologist Jakob von Uexküll, one of the most influential precursors of cultural ecology. Creative processes in nature and culture share an element of agency and improvisational flexibility, with which they respond to changing demands of their environments by rearranging and recombining existing patterns of life, communication, and interpretation. As in the 'reading' of the DNA structure by proteins, signs are constantly read in bodily natures within a survival-oriented process, which transforms itself into the various semiotic communication levels of organisms and ecosystems. What is of special significance in our context is that this transference of similarities across different scales of living systems in their survival-oriented forms of self-organization suggests that, as Wheeler points out, processes of creativity in life can be likened to the operation of metaphors on the level of language, discourse, and art. The 'meta-phorical' reading of one form or pattern and its transference to another is at the core of creative activity both in processes of life and in processes of literature and art, and 'creation via metaphor' (275) constitutes a common ground between them. In this sense, the (auto-)poiesis of life becomes an analogue for the (auto-)poiesis of the aesthetic dimension, since in fact the 'human grasp of the world is essentially aesthetic' (276). Art is thus also always implicitly self-reflexive, constituting a cultural medium that thematises the 'mysteries of human meaning-making itself' (276). This means that 'art, and especially art in language, remains the best place of our hopes of self-understanding' (276). Literature becomes a paradigmatic cultural form representing the play of similarities and differences that make up the ecosemiotic processes of life itself. Indeed, the reflexive interactivity between mind and body, culture and nature, constitutes one of the most characteristic sites and sources of literary creativity. This interactivity combines a cognitive with an affective and ethical dimension.

Wheeler's ideas resemble in significant aspects the ways in which Gregory Bateson views the relation between ecology, metaphor, and poetic language. Bateson likewise suggests a similarity between the processes of life, as they are characterised by feedback relations and infinite structural analogies, and the basic poetic form of speech, the metaphor. His own ecological thinking, he states, follows a metaphorical rather than a classical-logical principle, and in this respect, his mind functions like the mind of a poet, focusing not on the generalizing logic of the subject but on the analogies that can be constructed between different spheres and phenomena of life on the basis of shared predicates. The 'patterns which connect' (Bateson 2002, 7ff.) heterogenous domains of life and mind to each other are basic forms of knowing the world, and they are characteristic of the procedures of metaphor that are performed most explicitly and self-reflexively in poetic language. Relational, metaphorical thinking, rather than syllogistic reasoning, corresponds to the principles on which the living world is built and on which an ecology of the mind can orient itself. An example of a traditional, subject-centred syllogism is: '*All men die / Socrates is a man / Socrates dies*'. Bateson replaces this classical syllogism by what he calls '[a]ffirming the consequent', or 'syllogism in grass': '*Grass dies / Men die / Men are grass*'. According to Bateson, this meta-phorical procedure, which relates domains separated in traditional categories of thought to each other on the basis of common predicates, is closer to the processes of life, which are characterised by structural similarities and shared properties, than the abstract classifications and exclusionary boundary lines of logical-conceptual thought. It is a form of detecting 'connecting patterns' between different spheres of the living world (Bateson 2002, 7 ff.), which also describes his own relational form of ecological thought: 'it seemed to me that indeed this was the way I did much of my thinking, and it also seemed to me to be the way the poets did their thinking. It also seemed to me to have another name, and its name was metaphor. Meta-phor. And it seemed that perhaps, while not always logically sound, it might be a very useful contribution to the principles of life' (240–241).

Bateson's 'syllogism in grass' as an alternative mode of meta-phorical ecological knowledge as distinct from traditional logocentric forms of thought has clear affinities to processes of literary creativity as enacted in literature. A prime example in American literature is Walt Whitman's collection of poems, *Leaves of Grass*, in which the title already establishes the central analogy between humans and grass that is explored in ever new variants in the texts, thereby becoming a main source of their poetic energy and creativity. In 'Song of Myself', for example, grass alternately becomes an expression of the inner state of the poet, a hieroglyph of the creation, a sign of democracy, a symbol of the cycle of death and rebirth, and an analogue to poetic polyphony ('O I perceive after all so many uttering tongues'; 'Song of Myself' 26). It is the basis for always new metamorphoses of the self and the world in which the poet, too, includes himself, and which he passes on as his testimony to his readers: 'I bequeath myself to the dirt to grow from the grass I love/ If you want me again look for me under your bootsoles' (78). 'Men are Grass'— Bateson's ecological syllogism is transformed by Whitman into an ecopoetic process, which at the same time extends and expands the metaphor into a source of constant metamorphosis. Many more examples could be given for this, but Whitman remains one central inspiring precursor who has inscribed this transformative eco-poetic knowledge into American poetry.

Life Sciences Versus Literary Knowledge of Life

The metaphorical mode of ecological thought raises the question of the relationship between mind and life, life writing and the life sciences as another important potential of the transdisciplinary knowledge that literature can provide. In the context of contemporary knowledge landscapes, the life sciences represent an inevitable frame of reference. As part of the experimental natural sciences, the life sciences are not only drawing public attention and money to their disciplines, but are also often credited with discursive authority in the definition of what is currently seen as constituting 'life'. Indeed, the life sciences have recently expanded their research into areas that have been considered genuine domains of the humanities and of literary studies—e.g., in the debates about mind, consciousness, and ethics in the neurosciences. Yet as Ottmar Ette among others argues, it would involve a severe epistemic as well as ethical reductionism to assume that the natural life sciences could cover the whole spectrum of what constitutes 'life' in a sufficiently complex, i.e., also cultural, sense, or that they could claim a superior authority of truth over the phenomena that they are taking as their objects of research within the premises of their quantifying, causal-empirical, and objectifying methodology (Ette 2004).

It is useful to start from the recognition that if we try to define life, we realise that life means different things in various disciplines and branches of knowledge within and beyond the life sciences: in biology, it is the genetic structure and evolutionary process of living systems; in medicine, it is the physical and biochemical life of the human organism in the ever precarious balance between sickness and health; in psychology, it is the emotional, intellectual, and communicational life energies that help maintain or restore the vitality of a person in the face of crisis, alienation, or traumatization; in sociology and political science, it means the right to life as a form of personal and social self-determination as well as the various forms and problems of 'living together' between individuals and cultures (Ette 2004); in philosophical ethics, the doctrine of the 'good life', however it may be defined in detail, becomes a guiding principle, which, again, relates not only to the individual self but includes respect for the life of other people and living beings. In the view of cultural ecology, and in the light of the discussed above, literature can be seen as a multiperspectival form of writing that potentially encompasses and participates in all of these different meanings and manifestations of life.

I would like to elucidate the relation of literature and life with reference to two theoretical models that offer nonreductionist adaptations of the contemporary life sciences, Nancy Easterlin's biocultural theory of evolution and Evan Thompson's phenomenological theory of embodied dynamicism in his substantive study *Mind in Life*. As Easterlin critically remarks in her book, *A Biocultural Approach to Literary Theory*, the aesthetic has not fared well with literary and cultural studies during the past few decades. Yet as she also points out, art and the aesthetic have been a vital factor in cultural evolution since its beginnings. From prehistoric pottery, ritual, or cave painting, to the later emergence and diversification of more and more visual, aural, plastic, kinetic or verbal art forms, art has evolved into an integral part of human societies, in which existential issues of fear, threat, reproduction, and survival were symbolically enacted and communicated. As art was increasingly dissociated from religion, myth, and ritual on the one hand, and from economy, philosophy, and science on the other, it was assigned a special, quasi-autonomous sphere outside everyday cultural practices; however, as a communally shared space of mimetic play and performative representation, it gained vital importance by reflecting and transacting fundamental problems, contradictions, and unresolved tensions that could not be otherwise articulated within the available discourses of the community (see Easterlin 2012).

These products and processes of art, however, do not provide definitive answers to the culturally crucial questions they address but rather create polysemic 'cognitive objects that offer themselves for interpretation' (Easterlin 2012, 26). From her biocultural perspective on literature, in which Easterlin combines literary scholarship with the current state of knowledge in the bio-evolutionary life sciences, this is not an unnecessary luxury and distraction from truly relevant, decision-oriented survival tasks, but 'is of a piece with our distinct species logic' (26). Interpretation, as it is called for by literary texts, is an activity that foregrounds and makes conscious the meaning-making impulse itself as one of the most basic and unique features of our evolved species (34). In their very openness, sensory concreteness, and semantic complexity, art and literature express a deep-rooted human disposition to relate otherwise neglected aspects of our interior worlds in sufficiently complex ways to external environments: 'Artworks . . . have an unusual capacity to bring back into the consciousness aspects of selves, bodies, behaviors, and the like, that may otherwise remain hidden' (26). Reconnection of consciousness to the unconscious, mind to body, external to internal ecosystems, discursive knowledge to prediscursive experience, is thus one significant function of art and literature for a fully developed capacity of human societies for self-representation, self-reflection, and self-renewal. As she put it: 'Considered as a whole, the semantic power of imaginative literature bears witness to the centrality of meaning-making for the human species, for the business of producing and consuming texts is primarily about extending our meaning-making capabilities, not about something else during which meaning-making happens to become some secondary kind of adventure' (24). In the adaptive analogies between imaginative play, meaning-making, interpretation, and aesthetic experience, which a biocultural account of literary evolution brings to light, literature becomes a space of explorative possibilities, which balances the one-sided economic-utilitarian interpretation of cultural evolution. Through its 'defunctionalizing' distancing from the pragmatic imperatives of society and the everyday life-world, imaginative literature is enabled to respond to 'dysfunctional aspects' of the sociocultural system and to transform traumatic experiences into potentially regenerative processes (139–140). Literature combines the invitation to complex interpretation with the capacity of (re-)structuring disconnected experiences in acts of symbolic sense-making, in which the human preference for 'patterned information' (31) and 'our ability to use compositional, recursive language' are brought to expression in full intensity, acknowledging 'our shared human nature' beyond individual, historical, and cultural diversities (33–34).

As Easterlin demonstrates in examples from Wordsworth's romantic poetry to postcolonial novels like Jean Rhys' *Wide Sargasso Sea*, literature links experiences of cultural alienation and traumatization with experiences of our complex embodiedness and embeddedness in the natural world. This activity is shaped by a culturally evolved artistic impulse, since 'the capacity to see nature properly, as one of our interrelated and essential attachments, is a product of mind and imaginative effort' (133). Poems are relational, communicative acts, which articulate unarticulated thoughts, feelings, wishes, fears, conflicts, and desires that make up as much of our shared psychosocial 'reality' as the externally visible and publicly represented social world. In this counter-discursive dynamics, literature combines a diagnostic with a therapeutic function, (re-)enacting personal and collective traumas and crises in ways that involve the potential for 'healing functions' (140). This biocultural description of literary functions implies an affirmative attitude to life but also, ultimately, to the human mind and to cultural evolution. Ecocriticism, according to Easterlin, has an enormous potential for the environmental humanities if it combines its attention to the revaluation and agency of nonhuman nature with an awareness that the mind, the imagination, culture, human agency, and intersubjectivity, which are rather sidelined in some versions of ecocentric theory, are indispensable for all cultural evolution, for ecological engagement, and, indeed, for all ecological studies of the culture–nature relationship (151). Starting from bio-evolutionary premises, this kind of ecocriticism arrives at cognitive, communicational, psychological, and ethical dimensions of ecology in which the aesthetic becomes a special site and source of ecological sensibility and knowledge.

Another enriching perspective for a transdisciplinary positioning of literature within contemporary knowledge cultures is provided by Evan Thompson's *Mind in Life*, even though Thompson himself does not explicitly develop his argument in this direction. Thompson offers a broadly framed, phenomenologically grounded interpretation of the life sciences that insists on the necessity to include an experiential, subject- and consciousness-oriented dimension in the ways in which the 'embodied dynamic systems' of living organisms are to be conceived (Thompson 2007, 10 ff.). Reconsidering guiding paradigms of the contemporary life sciences such as autopoiesis, system, and emergence from a complementary set of phenomenological notions such as consciousness, experience, or embodied vision, Thompson arrives at complex descriptions of autopoetic and, by extension, of 'ecopoetic' life processes (118–122), which in terms of their constitutive culture–nature and mind–body interactivity, are also and specifically relevant for literary texts. As he writes in a strangely reflexive formula borrowed from Hans Jonas, 'life can be known only by life' (164). Thompson goes on to say that what makes this kind of knowledge of life possible in the first place is the capacity for 'empathy' with other living organisms, which is derived from our own 'lived experience of our bodily being' (165). We cannot grasp the phenomenon of 'autopoetic selfhood' (162), which forms the basis of all living organisms in their self-sustaining constructions of inside/ outside, system/ environment, without taking recourse to our own embodied experience of inwardness and purposiveness: 'empathy is a precondition of our comprehension of the vital order, in particular of the organism as a sense-making being inhabiting an environment' (165). If imaginative literature is a cultural mode of communication that is based on 'empathy' in a broad sense, i.e., on the generic potency of stepping outside oneself into an alternative world of fiction while yet remaining oneself as a reader;[1] of taking ever new perspectives of strangers while never fully escaping one's own; of immersing oneself in the embodied minds of other human and nonhuman beings while depending on one's own previous experiences—then literature has indeed a special contribution to offer in terms of that more comprehensive knowledge of life envisioned by Thompson. As empathetic creation of multiperspectival worlds and self-reflexive staging of concretely imagined life processes, literature is a form of cultural knowledge in which the maxim that 'life can be known only by life' is part of its generative and epistemological code.

POSTCOLONIALITY, ECOGLOBALISM, AND LITERARY KNOWLEDGE

Another domain or frame in which I want to indicate the transdisciplinary knowledge of literature as part of the environmental humanities is the domain of postcolonial studies and its ecoglobal implications. Postcoloniality in literature reflects not only colonial traumas and asymmetrical power relations as a long-term consequence of colonial history, but it also 'writes back' in critical and transformative ways from the perspectives of non-western knowledge traditions that, as 'alternative knowledge systems' (Rigby 2015, 5), often provide sources of a critical and more complex assessment and evaluation of western scientific approaches. Indeed, indigenous knowledge of culture–nature interdependence often represents a source of imaginative counterdiscourses in postcolonial texts that help to frame western scientific paradigms in a broader and more holistic form.

Radical postmodernism insisted on the absoluteness of difference, on the ultimate unbridgeability of the rift between signs, texts, and cultural identities. With the transition to postcolonial and ecoglobal paradigms, this doctrine of absolute difference became more and more questionable (see Banerjee 2016). Even though in earlier versions, postcolonialism tended to simply reverse former binaries and claim radical incompatibility not only of cultures but of fundamental verities and values, its main impact on literary and cultural studies has been to call attention to various forms of cultural and textual hybridity, liminality, and ambiguity as productive features of postcolonial literature and art, without of course advocating any levelling of differences, conflicts, and asymmetries of power in favour of superficial harmonizations. This is where postcolonialism and cultural ecology converge in important ways. In ecological thought, there are no absolute but only relative, or *relational*, differences. Binary semiotics is opened up to the ecosemiotic diversity of historically, culturally, and personally distinct manifestations of human life within its irreducible connectivity with all other life on the planet. This is not to claim an ahistorical universal validity of the model of a cultural ecology but to assume a *transcultural* potential of texts that, by the very logic of ecological thought, provides the basis for such a cross-cultural interpretation and dialogue, while at the same time always also offering resistance to easy appropriation and generalization.

I would like to illustrate this briefly in a text that has been widely discussed in postcolonial ecocriticism, Amitav Ghosh's *The Hungry Tide*

(2005), a novel that helps to demonstrate the enormous complexities in the relationship between the local and the global as both a challenge and a source of literary knowledge in an age of eco-globalism. In the novel, the huge mangrove wetlands of the Sundarbans, a cluster of low-lying islands in the Bay of Bengal off the easternmost part of India, form the narrative site of multiple interactions between nature, culture, politics, and personal lives against the background of violent ethnic strife and displacement, but also of conflicting models of culture–nature relations between myth and modernity. The radically unstable boundary between water and land in the Sundarbans is omnipresent in the novel as a both destructive and life-enabling environment of human culture. Piyali Roy, or Piya, an American marine biologist of Indian descent, comes to the Sundarbans to pursue a scientific research project on a rare river dolphin species, the *Orcaella brevirostris*, a project that leads her into a journey of rediscovering her cultural roots in her family ancestors' battles for social and environmental justice. Politics, ecology, kinship, and love are interwoven in a richly textured network of interacting plots and narrative voices. 'Western' ecological science as represented by Piya at first sharply contrasts with the 'indigenous' knowledge of nature represented by Fokir, a native fisherman, whose perspective is associated with the deep-time story-world of legends and songs that alternates with the postmodern time-shifts of the narrative. Significantly, however, the novel's process consists in bringing Piya and Fokir ever closer together. In the course of the novel, their apparently incompatible approaches to nature are presented as mutually enriching and complementary rather than as merely contradictory and mutually exclusionary forms of ecocultural knowledge.

A third major character, who illustrates this interplay between local and global epistemologies and narrative frames is Kanai Dutt, a worldwide connected businessman, who returns from his upper-class urban milieu in Delhi to his native Sundarbans to retrieve the diaries of his dead uncle Nirmal. The diaries record the personal role of Kanai's relatives in the Bengali resistance against their forced resettlement in the historical Morichjhanpi massacre of 1978–1979, when thousands of Bengali refugees were forcibly evicted on the alleged grounds of environmental protection of the Mangrove forests and Bengal tigers. In these conflicts, humanist and environmentalist issues clash in sometimes unsettling and ethically incommensurable ways, while the traumas of the past are still present as deep-time scars in contemporary social and political life. This continued presence of the past is inscribed into the novel's narrative structure in multiple time shifts, mainly between the politico-personal stories of conflict and resistance recorded in Nirmal's diaries, and the narrative present that is revolving around the triangle of interactions between Kanai, Piya, and Fokir.

In their narrative functions, these three characters can be loosely associated with the triadic model of cultural ecology (see Zapf 2016b). Kanai's behaviour and mentality display features of a culture-critical metadiscourse in that he approaches the complex entanglements of history and human–nonhuman relations from a posture of superior intellectual knowledge, relying on the unquestionable authority of social status, learning, and literate culture. From this mindset, he looks down on the illiterate native Fokir as incarnating naïve pre-modern ignorance, whereas for Piya and the implied reader, in contrast, Fokir gains considerable counterdiscursive stature precisely because of his intimate, experiential knowledge of nature's ways that he has acquired in his day-to-day life as a fisher in the mangrove waters. On a textual level, this knowledge is woven into the narrative in the traditional mythic stories, songs, and poems of the Bengals about the tide and the tigers as natural forces shaping humans' lives and options of survival. The novel's title condenses the hunger of humans, tigers, and the tide into one complex signifier for all those forces that both drive and limit human life and culture under the conditions of this vast liminal region between land and water, rivers and sea, plant and animal, solid and fluid forms of existence. And it is the deeper intuitive knowledge of these complex interconnections that Fokir personifies. Piya stands between Kanai and Fokir in this triangle of characters, in which Fokir is associated with a biosemiotic life knowledge linked to water, eros, the body, and the kinship to nonhuman life, while Kanai, in contrast, represents civilisational reason and organised knowledge. Even though she cannot communicate with Fokir through language, Piya is irresistibly drawn to him, while establishing a kind of working relation with Kanai. She thus embodies a reintegrative force in the narration, bringing together modern and premodern, scientific and experiential, global and local forms of life and ecological knowledge. This mutual eco-epistemic enrichment is underlined in the final turn of the novel's plot: the hidden habitats and movements of the dolphin, which Fokir knows from personal experience and to which he has initiated Piya, are saved on the data files of Piya's GPS (Global Positioning System) after Fokir dies in a typhoon during their common exploration of the dolphin's life patterns. They are becoming one symbiotic being in this climactic storm at the end, in which Fokir meets his death in saving Piya's life, who in turn commits her survival to preserving his legacy ('it was as if the storm had given them what life could not: it had fused them together and had made them one', Gosh 390). Fokir's data provide the 'empirical' basis for Piya's future scientific research, in which she will possibly be supported by the cosmopolitan intellectual Kanai, who has himself profoundly changed in the encounter with Fokir and his indigenous ecological knowledge of the Sundarbans (see Heise 2008; Bartosch 2013).

Again, of course, this interdiscursive dimension of the novel implies no superficial harmonization of conflicts or erasing of existing differences. On the contrary, like other postcolonial novels, it acts out a 'logic of complexity' (Nicolescu 2008) that relates positions contradictory to each other in multi-layered ways while at the same time maintaining their irreducible distinctness and difference. In interweaving otherwise separate cognitive and experiential domains, this reintegrative function reveals incompatibilities and internal contradictions that can, however, enrich ecological knowledge in narratives that resist easy solutions and instead, in the words of Roman Bartosch, open up 'clefts and gaps that have to be filled with meaning in the interpretive process' (Bartosch 2013, 179) and that require and enable transdisciplinary perspectives to account for their richly textured epistemic complexities.

These different contextual frames—metaphor, life sciences, postcoloni-ality/ecoglobalism—are only an exemplary selection from a much wider spectrum of possible contextualizations. By taking them together, it becomes evident that literature provides an invaluable source of transdisciplinary knowledge that should be seriously pursued especially by those profession-ally engaged in both the field of literary studies and in the broader domain of the environmental humanities.

NOTE

1. This reminds us of Wolfgang Iser's adoption of the Greek notion of 'ek-stasis', or ecstasy, for the act of writing and reading fictional texts, also in the sense of step-ping outside of oneself while simultaneously remaining oneself on a different plane. See Iser (1993).

WORKS CITED

Armstrong, Paul. *How Literature Plays with the Brain: The Neuroscience of Reading and Art*. Baltimore: Johns Hopkins University Press, 2013.
Banerjee, Mita. 'Postcolonial Ecocriticism'. *Handbook of Ecocriticism and Cultural Ecology*. Ed. Hubert Zapf. Berlin: De Gruyter, 2016. 194–207.
Barad, Karen. *Meeting the Universe Halfway: Quantum Physics and the Entanglement of Matter and Meaning*. Durham: Duke University Press, 2007.
Bartosch, Roman. *EnvironMentality: Ecocriticism and the Event of Postcolonial Fiction*. Amsterdam: Rodopi, 2013.
Bateson, Gregory. *Steps to an Ecology of Mind*. London: Paladin, 1973.
Bateson, Gregory. *Mind and Nature: A Necessary Unity*. Creskill: Hampton Press, 2002.
Böhme, Gernot. *Für eine ökologische Naturästhetik*. Frankfurt: Suhrkamp, 1989.

Clark, Timothy. *Ecocriticism on the Edge: The Anthropocene as a Threshold Concept.* London: Bloomsbury, 2015.

DeLoughrey, Elizabeth and George B. Handley, eds. *Postcolonial Ecologies: Literatures of the Environment.* New York: Oxford University Press, 2011.

Easterlin, Nancy. *A Biocultural Approach to Literary Theory and Interpretation.* Baltimore: Johns Hopkins University Press, 2012.

Ette, Ottmar. *ÜberLebenswissen: Die Aufgabe der Philologie.* Berlin: Kadmos, 2004.

Finke, Peter. *Die Ökologie des Wissens: Exkursionen in eine gefährdete Landschaft.* Freiburg: Alber, 2005.

Garrard, Greg. 'Conciliation and Consilience: Climate Change in Barbara Kingsolver's *Flight Behaviour*'. *Handbook of Ecocriticism and Cultural Ecology.* Ed. Hubert Zapf. Berlin: De Gruyter, 2016. 295–312.

Ghosh, Amitav. *The Hungry Tide.* New York: Harper Collins, 2005.

Goodbody, Axel and Kate Rigby, eds. *Ecocritical Theory: New European Approaches.* Charlottesville: University of Virginia Press, 2011.

Gould, Stephen Jay. *The Hedgehog, the Fox and the Magister's Pox.* New York: Harmony Books, 2003.

Heise, Ursula. *Sense of Place and Sense of Planet: The Environmental Imagination of the Global.* Oxford: Oxford University Press, 2008.

Hoffmeyer, Jesper, ed. *A Legacy for Living Systems: Gregory Bateson as Precursor to Biosemiotics.* Heidelberg: Springer, 2008.

Huggan, Graham and Helen Tiffin, eds. *Postcolonial Eccocriticism: Literature, Animals, Environment.* London: Routledge, 2010.

Iovino, Serenella and Serpil Oppermann, eds. *Material Ecocriticism.* Bloomington: Indiana University Press, 2014.

Iovino, Serenella. *Ecocriticism and Italy: Ecology, Resistance, and Liberation.* London: Bloomsbury, 2016.

Iser, Wolfgang. *The Fictive and the Imaginary: Charting Literary Anthropology.* Baltimore: John Hopkins University Press, 1993.

Lewis, David, Dennis Rodgers, Michael Woolcock. 'The Fiction of Development: Literary Representation as a Source of Authoritative Knowledge'. *Journal of Developmental Studies* 44.2 (2008): 198–216.

Link, Jürgen. 'Interdiskurs'. *Metzler Lexikon Literatur- und Kulturtheorie: Ansätze— Personen—Grundbegriffe.* Ed. Ansgar Nünning. Stuttgart: Metzler, 2001. 236–237.

Luhmann, Niklas. *Ecological Communication.* Cambridge: Polity Press, 1989.

Müller, Timo. 'Between Poststructuralism and the Natural Sciences: Models and Strategies of Recent Cultural Ecology'. *Anglistik: International Journal of English Studies* 21.1 (2010): 175–191.

Müller, Timo. 'From Literary Anthropology to Cultural Ecology: German Ecocritical Theory since Wolfgang Iser'. *Ecocritical Theory: New European Approaches.* Eds. Axel Goodbody and Kate Rigby. Charlottesville: University of Virginia Press, 2011. 71–83.

Nicolescu, Basarab, ed. *Transdisciplinarity: Theory and Practice.* Cresskill: Hampton Press, 2008.

Nussbaum, Martha. *Love's Knowledge: Essays on Philosophy and Literature.* New York: Oxford University Press, 1992.

Oppermann, Serpil. 'Transnationalization of Ecocriticism'. *Anglia* 130.3 (2012): 401–419.

Rigby, Kate. 'Gernot Böhme's Ecological Aesthetics of Atmosphere'. *Ecocritical Theory: New European Approaches.* Eds. Axel Goodbody and Kate Rigby. Charlottesville: University of Virginia Press, 2011. 139–167.

Rigby, Kate. *Dancing with Disaster: Environmental Histories, Narratives, and Ethics for Perilous Times.* Charlottesville: University of Virginia Press, 2015.

Schliephake, Christopher. *Urban Ecologies: City Space, Material Agency, and Environmental Politics in Contemporary Culture.* Lanham: Lexington Books, 2014.

Thompson, Evan. *Mind in Life: Biology, Phenomenology, and the Sciences of Mind.* Cambridge: Harvard University Press, 2007.

Westling, Louise. 'Darwin in Arcadia. Brute Being and the Human Animal Dance from Gilgamesh to Virginia Woolf'. *Anglia* 124 (Winter 2006): 11–43.

Westling, Louise. *The Cambridge Companion to Literature and the Environment.* Cambridge: Cambridge University Press, 2014.

Westling, Louise. 'Merleau-Ponty and the Ecoliterary Imaginary'. *Handbook of Ecocriticism and Cultural Ecology.* Ed. Hubert Zapf. Berlin: De Gruyter, 2016. 65–83.

Wheeler, Wendy. *The Whole Creature: Complexity, Biosemiotics and the Evolution of Culture.* London: Lawrence and Wishart, 2006.

Wheeler, Wendy. 'The Biosemiotic Turn: Abduction, or, the Nature of Creative Reason in Nature and Culture'. *Ecocritical Theory: New European Approaches.* Eds. Axel Goodbody and Kate Rigby. Charlottesville: Virginia University Press, 2011. 270–282.

Wheeler, Wendy and Louise Westling. 'Biosemiotics and Culture: Introduction'. *Green Letters* 19.3 (2015): 215–226.

Whitman, Walt. 'Song of Myself'. *Leaves of Grass and Other Writings: Authoritative Texts, Other Poetry and Prose, Criticism.* Ed. Michael Moon. New York: Norton, 2002. 26–78.

Wilson, Edward O. *Consilience: The Unity of Knowledge.* New York: Random House, 1998.

Zapf, Hubert. *Literatur als kulturelle Ökologie: Zur kulturellen Funktion imaginativer Texte an Beispielen des amerikanischen Romans.* Tübingen: Niemeyer, 2002.

Zapf, Hubert, ed. *Kulturökologie und Literatur: Beiträge zu einem transdisziplinären Paradigma der Literaturwissenschaft.* Heidelberg: Winter, 2008.

Zapf, Hubert, ed. *Literature and Science.* Special issue of *Anglia: Journal of English Philology* 133.1 (2015).

Zapf, Hubert, ed. *Handbook of Ecocriticism and Cultural Ecology.* Berlin: De Gruyter, 2016a.

Zapf, Hubert. *Literature as Cultural Ecology: Sustainable Texts.* London: Bloomsbury, 2016b.

Chapter Four

Where Is Feminism in the Environmental Humanities?

Greta Gaard

Was Rachel Carson primarily an environmental scientist, or a writer of creative nonfiction? Published just two years prior to her death in 1964, Carson's *Silent Spring* (1962) combined careful observations, scientific data, and eloquent prose to expose the toxic links between pesticides, environmental degradation, and inter-species health. Carson's work is often credited with sparking the environmental movement of the 1970s and beyond, but rarely is she seen as the foremother of second-wave feminism. Like Carson, the work of Dian Fossey and Jane Goodall is usually classified as primatology, but academic training for these women came well after their field research was already underway. Like Barbara McClintock's work with corn, both Fossey and Goodall had 'a feeling for the organism' (Keller 1983, 198) that powered their work more completely than their belated scientific training. Could their research more aptly be described as critical plant studies, transspecies communication studies, or posthumanist anthropology? The interdisciplinary perspectives of both Feminist Studies and the Environmental Humanities defy such exclusionary categorizations.

In the year 2016 of the Anthropocene Era, the crises of climate change prompt us to advance the methods of Carson, Goodall, Fossey and McClintock by thinking across the disciplines. The Environmental Humanities have been key in this regard, bridging environmentally inspired interests in literature and literary criticism, journalism, philosophy, history, communications, theatre, the arts, political and social sciences, education, religion and spirituality. In the past decade, scholars in these subfields have drawn on each other's scholarship and methodologies, producing the broader environmental arts and humanities, inspiring the growth of over seventy research centres and programmes around the world, and the launch of new online journals such as *Resilience* (USA) and *Environmental Humanities* (Australia). In this transitional moment, the environmental humanities function both as 'a useful umbrella' facilitating conversations among these environmental subfields, and as a challenge to their disciplinary fields of origin, suggesting a 'more interdisciplinary set of interventions directed toward some of the most pressing issues of our time' (Rose et al. 2012, 5).

Environmental humanities scholars tend to believe that these 'pressing issues' emerge from a confluence of (a) dualistic and divisive ways of seeing and knowing the world, and (b) developments in science, economics, and technology that *enact* these dualistic and divisive epistemologies to the detriment of all life on earth. The failure of the environmental scientists' and economists' strategy of defending ecosystem services by translating them into monetary terms was critiqued long ago in Aldo Leopold's essay on the 'Land Ethic' (1949, 210–214, 224). Professor of environmental history in Sweden, Sverker Sörlin attributes the formation of the environmental humanities to 'the current inadequacy of the established science, policy, and economics approaches' and the understanding that 'in a world where cultural values, political and religious ideas, and deep-seated human behaviors still rule the way people lead their lives, produce, and consume, the idea of *environmentally relevant knowledge* must change' (Sörlin 2012, 788). Agreeing that 'environmental science and policy [have failed] to provide all the answers or to achieve significant environmental behavioral change' (Kaza 2005, 5), University of Vermont environmental studies professor Stephanie Kaza argues that 'the environmental humanities expand our understanding of environmental problems and our capacities to address them' (4). In the premiere issue of the Australian online journal, *Environmental Humanities*, Deborah Bird Rose and her colleagues explain that 'the whole world, at all scales, is a "contact zone"' : "the deepening environmental and social crises of our time are unfolding in this zone where the nature/culture divide collapses and possibilities of life and death for everyone are at stake" (2). In Sweden, Gender Studies scholars Cecilia Åsberg, Redi Koobak, and Ericka Johnson open their essay, 'Beyond the Humanist Imagination', with a litany of eco-political problems with strong material manifestations: hurricanes, floods, water pollution and garbage that does not go 'away' (2011, 218–219).

Acknowledging the shortcomings of the environmental sciences in responding to these crises, environmental science scholars are turning to the environmental humanities for alternative approaches and strategies. What can the environmental humanities contribute? Stephanie Kaza claims that 'we draw on the methods and skills of the humanities disciplines to raise questions often overlooked by scientific and economic approaches to problem-solving' (4). These are 'questions of meaning, value, ethics, justice, and the politics of knowledge production', Rose and her colleagues explain (2). While humanities fields have commonly focused 'on critique and an unsettling of dominant narratives' the environmental humanities is 'an effort to inhabit a difficult space of *simultaneous critique and action*' responding to a 'dire need for all peoples to be constructively involved' in addressing these environmental crises (Rose et al. 2012, 3). Thus, the environmental humanities require a convergent theory and praxis, performing both critique and action—analogous to feminism, a movement that 'emerged through women who recognised their own lived experiences of marginalisation, oppression, and inequality (whether via race, gender, class, sexuality, age, ability—and usually some nexus thereof) not as personal deficits or biological necessities to be accepted and endured, but rather as socially produced political problems to be challenged' (Gaard 2012, 29). Given this compatibility, along with the fact that feminist analyses are at the roots of the environmental humanities, feminism and its multiple articulations—feminist animal studies, material feminisms, indigenous feminisms, queer ecologies, feminist science studies, feminist environmental and climate justice analyses, antiracist and anticolonial activisms—should all be prominently addressed in the programmes, research agendas, and community engagements of the Environmental Humanities. The contributions of feminist epistemologies and methodologies, the climate and culture of academia, and the imperative of political relevance all require it.

FEMINIST EPISTEMOLOGIES AND METHODOLOGIES

Not merely an academic endeavour or a 'way of seeing', feminism emerged from the lived experiences of women who recognised their own experiences of injustice as socially produced political problems. As material circumstances allowed (and often when they did not), these women stepped forward to work with other women, feminist men, and gender outlaws (Bornstein 1994) to challenge social hierarchies and create social change. From the start, feminism has been a movement for justice: at its heart is the centrality of praxis, the necessary linkage of intellectual, political, and activist work. Feminist methodology—articulated through such foundational texts as Stanley and Wise's *Breaking Out: Feminist Consciousness and Feminist Research* (1983), Harding's *Feminism and Methodology* (1987), and Stanley's *Feminist Praxis* (1990)—requires that feminist research puts the lives of the oppressed at the centre of the research question, and undertakes studies, gathers data, and interrogates material contexts with the primary aim of improving the lives and the material conditions of the oppressed. Feminists work to bridge the 'town/gown' division through socially engaged scholarship, designing research that builds upon community knowledge, addresses oppression in its many intersectional forms, and works for liberatory outcomes.

One contemporary example of feminist methodology can be seen in Beth Stephens and Annie Sprinkle's queer ecosexual documentary on coal mining and working class, queer resistance, *Goodbye Gauley Mountain* (2013). A West Virginia native (albeit relocated to California), Stephens opens the film by reconnecting with the places where she grew up, the mountains and streams, forests and towns, friends and family that together form her ecocommunity of origins. She recalls her family's roots in West Virginia's mountains and in coal mining, establishing that she has both a right and a responsibility to stand with this community, to bring her whole self and all her relations to the struggle for environmental justice. 'The places where people are born are genetically imprinted on people, in their psyche and in their hearts', Stephens explains. Her approach utilises feminist relational ontology, which suggests we are born and come into being through relationships, and these relationships are not only human to human but also human to more-than-human, including relations with other animals, plants, waterbodies, rocks, soils, and seasons.

Most obviously, the practice of mountaintop removal (MTR) used in coal mining involves intersections of race, class and rurality. Stephens takes care to review the history of Black miners who died of silicosis in the 1930s, while later the 'Hawks' Nest Tunnel Disaster' became Hawks Nest golf course, with the clubhouse built on the site of shanties that housed hundreds of black workers. Mining companies have long manipulated the poor hillbillies into working for the mine as the only job in town. The film shows corporate mining rallies, where CEO spokesmen preach propaganda to the workers, but later sell the company after an explosion kills 29 workers, and go on to retire with an $86 million bonus—and start a new company. Appalachians have often been looked down on, considered illiterate, uneducated, unimportant, disposable, expendable. 'So who cares if a few "hillbillies" have to be moved out of their homes or end up with cancer', asks Stephens, 'so that [urbanites] can have cheap electricity?' This is the urban/rural schism dividing queer communities and environmental communities alike. 'I don't think people really care about Appalachia', Stephens reflects. 'I believe that coal mining has become a protracted form of genocide'—a form of *slow violence* (Nixon 2011) that is rural environmental classism, wiping out the culture and eco-communities of West Virginia, where a monoeconomy keeps people in thrall to one industry. Bringing queer performance artists to West Virginia's embattled mining communities, Stephens and Sprinkle invite local activists to join them in performing ecosexual polyamorous weddings that bridge the urban/rural, queer/straight schisms by affirming a shared and longstanding love of the mountains, and celebrating love in drag and polyamorous, posthumanist commitment to land, flora, and fauna.

Goodbye Gauley Mountain recuperates a feminist aesthetic of ecocommunity where interconnections emerge through reciprocal flows. Hillbillies and urban queers come together to love, honour, and cherish all vibrant matters of ecocommunity. For what produces ugliness, if not the renaming of ecologically diverse forests and streams as 'overburden', a naming that authorises the scraping away of human and more-than-human lives to expose the coalblack dirt that can be blasted and hauled, creating ill health for all? Such derogation parallels the naming of queers that authorises hate crimes and exclusions in housing, marriage, employment, and justice. As the filmmakers inform us, communities near MTR have a 50% increase of cancer, and are 42% more likely to have children born with birth defects. Joining rural MTR activists with queer ecosexuals, *Goodbye Gauley Mountain* brings the tools of queer feminist eco-activism to the mountains of West Virginia and beyond. 'We shift the metaphor from earth as mother to earth as lover', says Annie Sprinkle, 'to entice people to have more love of the planet'. And they are not alone.

A whole new movement of ecoqueers is emerging from the back-to-theland lesbian communities of the 1970s, and the gays cruising each other in city and national parks, on beaches and river gorges (Mortimer-Sandilands and Erickson 2010). In the new millennium, more queers have insisted on bringing their sexual and ecological passions together, and eco-queer organizations have flourished: the gay and lesbian Sierra Club chapters in California, Colorado, and Washington State; the Washington-based Out4Sustainability, the U.S.-based Queer Farmer Film Project, San Francisco–based Rainbow Chard Alliance (Sbicca 2012), Toronto's Ecoqueers (Gosine 2001), and Minnesota-based Outwoods. At the September 2014 People's Climate March in New York City, activists gathered at the 'Queers for the Climate' workshop to brainstorm ways for bringing a queer social movement repertoire to our work for climate justice.[1] Our answers included many characteristics and skills emerging from queer sensibilities and experiences: love of beauty, appreciation for nonviolence, understanding of intersectional oppressions (exacerbated in times of crisis), marriage equality victories and challenges, AIDS mobilization skills, and the joys of queer performativity, pageantry, drag, and polymorphous erotics.

Queer feminist scholars have documented the ways that erotophobia and hegemonic heterosexuality are not only part of dominant Western ideas of nature, but are interstructured with environmental degradation (Sandilands 1994; Gaard 1997). Colonialism, white heteromale supremacy, heteronormativity, and the linked the devaluations of the erotic and all those associated with/ seen as 'nature'—indigenous people, women, nonhumans, queers—intersect to *naturalise heterosexuality* and *heterosexualise nature*, together influencing Western culture's erotophobia, as argued by Catriona Sandilands in her 2001 article 'Desiring Nature, Queering Ethics'. From a queer feminist perspective, heteronormativity is 'threatened with the revelation of other erotic possibilities as potentially natural' and in fact 'richer and more genuinely affirmative' (Sandilands 2001, 182). An 'environmental erotogenics', Sandilands concluded, 'might inspire fleeting and exciting contacts among a multiplicity of active and desiring others' (184). Perhaps anticipating Stacy Alaimo's concept of trans-corporeality, Sandilands suggested an erotogenic practice that would involve 'a desiring re-mapping of body and self in passionate contingency with an Other', creating 'a relational understanding of self' (186).

Intuitively enacting Sandilands' theory, Annie Sprinkle, former porn star and Beth Stephen's wife, defines ecosexuality as 'a way to create a more connected relationship' with earth. 'We like to have skygasms', says Annie in *Goodbye Gauley Mountain*. 'Beth and I have intercourse with the air that we breathe'. Their *Ecosex Manifesto*[2] elaborates:

> We shamelessly hug trees, massage the earth with our feet, and talk erotically to plants. We are skinny dippers, sun worshippers, and star gazers. We caress rocks, are pleasured by waterfalls, and admire Earth's curves often. We make love with the Earth through our senses. We celebrate our E-spots. We are very dirty . . . We are everywhere. We are polymorphous and pollen-amorous.

The EcoSex pledge reconnects *eros* and *thanatos* in a ecocycle of sensual embrace: 'I promise to love, honor, and cherish the earth until death brings us closer together forever'.

Made visible from a queer ecological feminist perspective, the clear intersections of queer theory, feminism, anticapitalist, and environmental thought in the United States have contributed to an expanded understanding of the Environmental Humanities.

THE CLIMATE AND CULTURE OF ACADEMIA

As reported via international news media, the United States is experiencing an epidemic of campus sexual assault. In January 2014, President Obama responded to this crisis by charging a task force with investigating campus rape. That same year, *Ms. Magazine* reported that one in five women students on college campuses experience sexual assault (Heldman and Dirks 2014). Descriptions of a 'rape culture'—that is, a culture that authorises rape as a normal, acceptable, and protected behaviour for college athletes, students, and professors—have re-emerged from the feminist scholarship of the 1980s and beyond. This antifeminist culture in academe matters to the students, pedagogy, and faculty in the Environmental Humanities.

For students, it means that in our Literature and Environment courses, our Environmental Humanities and Ecocriticism courses, students are learning in an environment where their bodies and minds are under assault. Since good teaching makes connections between the objects of study and the students' own lived experiences, pretending that one-fifth of our students have not experienced sexual assault, or ignoring the fact that all of us are working and studying each day under the stress of a rape culture, will fail to take advantage of an important environmental justice connection to the environmental humanities. Addressing antifeminism in campus climate and culture is thus a matter of critical eco-pedagogy.

Campus climate matters for faculty in the environmental humanities as well. Perhaps scholars tenured at Research 1 institutions may feel they no longer need feminism because they live in a 'postfeminist' climate where—thanks to the persistent work of feminists (because rights do not just 'happen')—the essential workplace adjustments for gender equality among faculty involving recognition and awards for feminist scholarship and course development, spousal hires, paid maternity leave, stop-the-clock policies, on-campus child care, lactation rooms for nursing mothers, and family caregiving leaves have already been instituted. But these policies leave institutionalised racism and classism intact, and even elite institutions may enact a ' "revolving door" concept of diversity . . . in which token junior faculty of color are brought in to diversify the faculty pool, only to be let go at tenure time like so many downsized autoworkers' (Cotera 2010, 330). In 2016, as public universities continue to become yet another branch of corporate power, faculty face increased teaching loads and reduced job security, as more tenure lines are becoming replaced with adjunct, temporary positions. Women make up the majority of contingent faculty in today's academy, and as Tamura A. Lomax observes, women of colour are 'alarmingly overrepresented' in these unstable ranks (K. Hogan 2016–2017, 1). In the United States, the majority of faculty now work as adjuncts in teaching institutions (Edmonds 2015) where many policies around family leave, flextime, and work/life balance have persisted unchanged since the 1950s.

I teach at one such institution, where I am now a full professor. But in 2009 and 2010, I was fired from that institution—first denied retention, then retention and tenure—on the grounds of being uncollegial and unavailable to students, charged with poor teaching, and irrelevant scholarship (at the time I had published four books with University presses, delivered invited presentations at international conferences, and served as a referee for numerous scholarly journals and presses). In Wisconsin of 2010, I had to use every feminist tool for scholarly research and activist organizing to uncover data that confirmed second-wave feminism's slogan, that 'the personal is political'. Institutional research showed my workplace had been mandated to provide a Campus Report on the Status of Women at all levels, 10 years earlier, and had failed to do so. Snowball interviewing led me and my allies—the

Affirmative Action officer, the Chair of the Faculty Grievance Committee, and an untenured feminist professor in Physics—to uncover over 19 cases of women faculty denied retention or tenure, harassed out of their positions, their offices opened and their files taken, their performance reviews slanted against their motherhood status, against their activist scholarship and socially engaged teaching, against their race and ethnicity. In administrative documents, this harassment, maternal profiling, and sex discrimination is concealed with these terms: 'lack of collegiality'. 'Unavailable to her students'. 'Poor scholarship'. 'Poor teaching'.

I contacted other feminist scholars who were harassed and fired, notably Andrea Smith, who held a joint appointment in Ethnic Studies and Women's Studies at the University of Michigan, and whose ground-breaking book on the rape of Native American women, *Conquest: Sexual Violence and American Indian Genocide* (2005), was seen as insufficient scholarship to merit her tenure. I also reconnected with Annette Kolodny, whose work *The Lay of the Land* (1975) effectively founded ecocriticism and feminist ecocriticism, but was deemed as 'insufficient scholarship' for tenure because of its feminist methodology, and Kolodny was denied promotion and tenure at the University of New Hampshire in 1975. She sued on the basis of anti-Semitism and sex discrimination, and after five years of debilitating legal battles, was awarded an out-of-court settlement. Decades later, writing as a Dean of Humanities at the University of Arizona, Kolodny (2008) reflected on the barriers and supports needed to ensure a feminist campus: they are the same policies I mentioned, those enjoyed by some (not all) faculty at Research-1 institutions and progressive small colleges today; they are the same supports I needed in 2010 Wisconsin.

Although I won the battle for my own promotion and tenure, I have not succeeded in transforming a workplace culture of racism and antifeminism, which takes a heavy toll on those who fight back: the Affirmative Action Officer was fired. The Chair of Faculty Grievance died. The Physics professor was tenured but continues to be harassed by her department and is on antidepressants. So I continue to speak about the climate and culture of antifeminism in academe, because it matters. In a context of institutional harassment, feminist scholarship will not flourish, diminishing our field.

Feminism is a transformative perspective that challenges humanist dualisms of gender, culture, and nature, and undergirds any notion of interdisciplinarity since Feminist Studies cuts across all disciplines, transforming our very definitions of knowledge, knowers, and known.

How could the Environmental Humanities help but have an activist and feminist orientation, with these feminist roots, and these wildly varying institutional contexts?

RACE, CLIMATE, AND WOMEN'S LEADERSHIP

Sparked by the shooting-death of African-American teenager Trayvon Martin in a wealthy Florida suburb—and the acquittal of his killer—the #BlackLivesMatter movement began in July 2013 as a response to institutionalised racism in the United States, manifested specifically through police violence, judicial decisions and incarcerations all disproportionately targeting African-Americans. Experienced queer feminist activists Alicia Garza (Executive Director, People Organised to Win Employment Rights, San Francisco), Patrisse Cullors (founder of Dignity and Power Now, a prison reform organization, based in Northern California), and Opal Tometi (Executive Director, Black Alliance for Just Immigration, New York) created #BlackLivesMatter 'out of a profound sense of Black love' as they sought to affirm the self-worth, hope, and community of Black people confronting yet another surge of racial injustices and hatred (King 2015). Through Facebook, the hashtag was picked up and used on posters in rallies and marches, along with the slogan 'Hoodies UP' as activists in this emerging multiracial movement wore hooded sweatshirts as emblems of solidarity for this slain Black youth. Another year later in Ferguson, Missouri, 18-year-old Michael Brown was shot and killed by a police officer, Eric Garner died in a choke-hold under police arrest while repeatedly telling New York City's officers 'I can't breathe!' and the #BlackLivesMatter movement surged into the national media. Antiracist activists picked up the slogans 'hands up, don't shoot!' and 'while you're on your shopping spree, Black people cannot breathe!'—both chanted at the December 2014 Mall of America rally in Minnesota, temporarily shutting down this epicentre of US consumerism—and even the staid American Dialect Society voted the hashtag phrase its 'word of the year' for 2014 (McCulloch 2015).

Ten years after Hurricane Katrina and its aftermath of Federal neglect destroyed the lives and livelihoods of predominantly poor African-Americans living in New Orleans, the connections between environmental justice and climate justice have become even clearer: poor communities, communities of colour, indigenous communities, Third World nations and the two-thirds world communities within the First World are all disproportionately affected by the operations and wastes of industrial capitalism, militarism, and colonialism (Yeampierre 2014). In 2014, both Pesticide Action Network (PAN) and the Sierra Club came out in support of #BlackLivesMatter, as did 350.Org and Greenpeace. As PAN has documented, chemical plants creating pesticides operate in predominantly Black communities, and the air pollution falls predominantly on African-American communities: 'Blacks and whites actually breathe different air', writes Max Ehrenfreund in *The Washington Post* (2014), thus explaining the elevated rates of asthma in poor communities of colour. Taking feminism's intersectional approach to institutional racism, the founders of #BlackLivesMatter describe the problem thus:

> When we say Black Lives Matter, we are talking about the ways in which Black people are deprived of our basic human rights and dignity. It is an acknowledgement Black poverty and genocide is state violence. It is an acknowledgment that 1 million Black people are locked in cages in this country—one half of all people in prisons or jails—is an act of state violence. It is an acknowledgment that Black women continue to bear the burden of a relentless assault on our children and our families and that assault is an act of state violence. Black queer and trans folks bearing a unique burden in a hetero-patriarchal society that disposes of us like garbage and simultaneously fetishises us and profits off of us is state violence; the fact that 500,000 Black people in the US are undocumented immigrants and relegated to the shadows is state violence; the fact that Black girls are used as negotiating chips during times of conflict and war is state violence; Black folks living with disabilities and different abilities bear the burden of state-sponsored Darwinian experiments that attempt to squeeze us into boxes of normality defined by White supremacy is state violence. And the fact is that the lives of Black people—not ALL people—exist within these conditions is consequence of state violence. (Garza 2014)

The environment described here is a socially constructed environment that affects the economic, material, social, physiological and psychological well-being of Black people. Drawing insight from bell hooks' *Feminist Theory: From Margin to Center*, Garza clarifies that while 'all lives matter', the movement is specifically termed 'Black Lives Matter' because starting from the margins is more likely to make social justice movements inclusive: 'when we are able to end hyper-criminalization and sexualization of Black people and end the poverty, control, and surveillance of Black people, every single person in this world has a better shot at getting and staying free. *When Black people get free, everybody gets free*'. Garza's intersectionality—a term coined by Black feminist Kimberlé Crenshaw (1989)—means that issues of race, gender, sexuality, economics, ability, and age are not seen as separable, and thus must be addressed simultaneously.

Companioning the feminism of #BlackLivesMatter founders is the renewed attention directed to the oppression of Black women. Reflecting on her critique of sexism in the Black community in *Black Macho and the Myth of the Superwoman* (1979)—a Black Feminist classic credited as a precursor to Black Lives Matter (Lemieux 2015)—Michelle Wallace observes,

'people don't ask the question, "How many black *women* have been shot?"'
(Harris 2015). The recent #SayHerName campaign launched by the African
American Policy Forum aims to correct this lacuna, as founder Kimberlé
Crenshaw explains its purpose: 'although black women are routinely killed,
raped and beaten by the police, their experiences are rarely foregrounded in
popular understandings of police brutality' (Kucera et al. 2015). According
to #BlackLivesMatter co-founder Alicia Garza (2014), the environment
created by 'hetero-patriarchy and anti-Black racism' is both toxic and
life-threatening

The intersectional perspective of queer Black feminists is companioned
by the environmental justice standpoint of indigenous women. Preceding
the Black Lives Matter movement by less than a year, the Idle No More
movement was organised at a November 2012 teach-in by four indigenous
women—Nina Wilson, Sheelah Mclean, Sylvia McAdam, and Jessica
Gordon—in response to Canadian Prime Minister Stephen Harper's omnibus
budget bill C-45, which diminished the scope and powers of the Navigable
Waters Protection Act of 1882. The 1882 legislation had presented a significant barrier to industrial development, especially to projects such as pipelines that crossed many rivers on First Nations lands. But Harper's bill C-45
challenged the sovereign rights of First Nations people in Canada, making
changes to the control of First Nations' lands (essentially making them easier
to lease), and thus facilitating the Enbridge Northern Gateway Pipelines
Project plan for numerous pipelines transporting bitumen from Alberta's tar
sands to the Pacific Ocean, the Gulf of Mexico, and beyond to China. From
December 2012 and into 2013, Idle No More grew with numerous flash mobs
of round dancers across North America, gaining national and international
attention through Attawapiskat Chief Theresa Spence's hunger strike. By
the end of the year, *Foreign Policy* magazine had named the four women
founders of Idle No More among its list of 100 Leading Global Thinkers of
2013. Two years later—building on the inspiration of Idle No More activists
and allies—First Nations communities had won major legal victories against
environmentally destructive corporations whose operations relied on extracting the resources, livelihoods, and hopes of indigenous people: after numerous legal challenges from the Athabasca Chipewyan First Nation, Royal
Dutch Shell withdrew plans for developing tar sands near Fort McMurray,
Alberta (Serrano 2015); and in June 2014, a Canadian Supreme Court ruling
granted the Tsilhqot'in First Nation title to a 1,700-square-kilometre area of
traditional land outside its reserve, giving indigenous people more power in
negotiating major projects such as the Northern Gateway pipeline, targeted
for carrying tar sands oil from Alberta to British Columbia (Hildebrandt
2014).

Indigenous feminists have long advocated for gender, species, and environmental justice. As Winona LaDuke (1999) observes, Katsi Cook's Mohawk Mother's Milk Project addressed species, gender, and indigenous justice by connecting the PCBs stored in the bodies of Beluga whales and in Mohawk mothers' breastmilk, both contaminated by toxics in the St. Lawrence seaway; in Hawai'ian, sisters Haunani and Mililani Trask have served key roles in the native sovereignty movement, aimed at ridding indigenous lands of military bases, colonial plantations, and a tourist economy sexualizing native women's hula dances and commodifying native culture; Virginia Sanchez spoke out against nuclear testing and its effects on the Western Shoshone, as did Grace Thorpe, who later became Director of the National Environmental Coalition of Native Americans. To resist these environmental justice assaults, writer Linda Hogan, a Chickasaw poet and novelist, has argued that 'we need new stories, new terms and conditions that are relevant to the love of land, a new narrative that would imagine another way, to learn the infinite mystery and movement at work in the world' (1995, 94).

Accordingly, Hogan has provided us with those stories, making a strong contribution to the literature of the environmental humanities. In *Solar Storms*, Hogan links the environmental devastation brought about by the hydroelectric power projects of Manitoba Hydro, tracing this present moment back to the origins of colonialism in North America, and linking its effects to the hunting and near-extinction of fur-bearing animals, the rapes of women and children, the loss of community, language, livelihood, hope. Hogan's novel *Mean Spirit* explores the effects of oil drilling in Oklahoma on the displaced indigenous community of the Osage. *Power* links the endangered Florida Panther with the endangered Taiga tribe. *People of the Whale* offers a fictional approach to the Makah Whaling controversy—variously portrayed as an assault on an endangered species, or as an attempt to revive culture and economy for the Makah, arguably another endangered species, living on the tip of Washington's Olympic peninsula. In each of these texts, indigenous women narrators use an intersectional perspective that is the hallmark of indigenous feminism, Black feminism, and environmental feminism. As Nathan Heintz argues in *Earth Island Journal*, 'women activists and leaders have been at the core of the environmental movement since its inception' (2014).

How do the three queer Black feminist founders of #BlackLivesMatter define 'environment', or the connection between climate justice and institutional racism and sexism? And are these definitions being reflected in the curriculum and scholarship of Environmental Humanities programmes?

ENVIRONMENTAL HUMANITIES
PROGRAMMES, FEMINISM, AND THE
IMPERATIVE OF POLITICAL RELEVANCE

Comparing three introductory definitions of the environmental humanities from scholars in Sweden (Sörlin 2012), Australia (Rose et al. 2012), and the USA (Kaza 2005), we find there is widespread agreement on the inclusion of environmental philosophy, history, politics, literature, and writing—but less agreement on the relevance of environmental spirituality, feminism, critical race studies, indigenous studies, labour studies, or human–animal studies. Environmental justice is not directly listed in these recitations of primary humanities disciplines, nor is any iteration of feminism: at the nexus of these two perspectives, the scholarship and activism of indigenous women and women of colour should be conspicuous. Graduate programmes in the Environmental Humanities are even more specific in their scope, listing core (required) courses as Environmental Foundations, Methods, Writing Seminar, and a Field Course, leaving room for electives, which is where courses such as Environmental Justice, Women and (other?) Natural Resources, Ecofeminism, and Native American Philosophy usually appear, sometimes clustered and competing against one another in the 'environmental activism' section of electives, as if the content, methods, and perspectives offered by these courses could not fit equally well in course clusters of 'environmental imagination' or 'environmental thinking'.[3]

My concern here is that *environmental humanities scholars can too easily perpetuate the limitations of the very knowledge systems we critique* if our definitions and programme offerings replicate the culture/nature, mind/body, white/non-white, man/woman and human/animal binaries that have kept the sciences and humanities apart, and which impede our interdisciplinary collaborations in addressing the eco-social emergencies of climate change.

Placing indigenous women and multicultural, feminist environmental perspectives more prominently in these definitions and programme offerings of the environmental humanities is not only strategically useful, it is also intellectually honest: indigenous women's experiences and activisms, like feminist environmental scholar-activists, have crossed the disciplinary boundaries of the humanities, social sciences, and physical sciences at least four decades (that is for feminist environmentalisms—it is millennia, for indigenous knowledge) before the concept of the 'environmental humanities' emerged. Programmes such as York University's Faculty of Environmental Studies in Toronto, Canada, and Linkoping's Environmental Humanities Collaboratory in Sweden have foregrounded feminist scholarship, made connections with indigenous communities and indigenous scholars, built research projects that bridge academe with larger communities, and utilised the arts as both research sources and communication vehicles. Their precedent-setting approach demonstrates the enormous potentials of feminist methodologies and epistemologies in advancing the environmental humanities.

CONCLUSION

The writing and activism of women scientists, indigenous women leaders, Black Lives Matter activists, and the knowledge produced by the interdisciplinary fields of Indigenous Studies and Feminist Studies defy restrictive disciplinary categorizations—as do the environmental humanities. It is the environmentally attuned methodologies that bring us together. In North America, the signature of many indigenous methodologies includes listening to and honouring the leadership of women elders. In Women's Studies, the signature of a feminist methodology is its inclusiveness, which involves bringing together diverse forms of knowledge, acknowledging situated perspectives and listening to the information provided by each, creating structures for collaboration whereby the research subjects can themselves set the agenda, express needs, and benefit from the scholarly endeavour. Just as Women's Studies has been known for 'asking different questions', the humanities have been lauded for their ability to foster critical thinking, an asset many see as marketable to the 'corporate and financial sectors' of the world that 'have been notoriously challenged in the ethics department, to say the least' (Jay and Graff 2012). Both feminism and the environmental humanities have the aim of taking action, responding to eco-social crises, and motivating humans to make behavioural changes to address these crises. But not all definitions of the environmental humanities include feminism, or place the perspectives of indigenous women with other core disciplinary perspectives at the centre of study, and this exclusion limits the reliability and utility of environmental humanities research and teaching.

To ensure the contributions of feminism will flourish in the environmental humanities, we must look not only at the mere presence of diversity in the embodiment and perspectives of environmental humanities scholars (i.e., a race, class, gender, sexuality, ability, age, nationality representative of the regional or global human population) or at this diversity reflected in Environmental Humanities course offerings, but equally important, we must look at the topics chosen for research and study, at the epistemological assumptions that shape the research questions, and the methodologies used in researching those questions. It is not enough to have a 'liberal feminist' gender balance among elite scholars in the environmental humanities and environmental sciences (the latter have yet to achieve even that, I am afraid). 'It does not matter if academic institutions all of a sudden engage in a mass hiring of one hundred new black bodies, women or otherwise', argues Tamara A. Lomax, 'if those bodies represent and maintain the status quo, or if their radical resistance is met by macro or micro aggressions and other silencing tactics' (Hogan 2016–2017, 6). It is the presence and influence of postcolonial, antiracist and posthumanist feminist perspectives and methodologies that will make the most meaningful interventions in the environmental crises of our time.

On the front lines of movements for environmental justice and climate justice around the world, indigenous women, poor and working class women, women of colour, and women of the Two-Thirds World understand what is at stake (Mohanty 2003). Their vision and voices—their scholarship and fields of knowledge—need to be central to any definition of the environmental humanities.

NOTES

1. See 'Our Fight Too: An LGBTQ Response to Climate Change'. Available at http://peoplesclimate.org/lgbtq/2014/07/22/our-fight-too-an-lgbtq-response-to-climate-change-2/

2. See http://sexecology.org/research-writing/ecosex-manifesto/.

3. My summary here draws on descriptions of the University of Utah's Master's in Environmental Humanities and the Master's in Environmental Arts and Humanities at Oregon State University, Corvalis.

WORKS CITED

Alaimo, Stacy. *Bodily Natures: Science, Environment, and the Material Self.* Bloomington: Indiana University Press, 2010.

Åsberg, Cecilia, Redi Koobak, and Ericka Johnson. 'Beyond the Humanist Imagination'. *NORA: Nordic Journal of Feminist and Gender Research* 194 (December 2011): 218–230.

Bornstein, Kate. *Gender Outlaw: On Men, Women, and the Rest of Us.* New York: Routledge, 1994.

Burroughs, Gaylynn, and Debra S. Katz. 'Won't Back Down: Student Activists and Survivors Are Using the Legal System to Fight Sexual Assault and Harassment on College Campuses'. *Ms. Magazine* 25.3 (Summer 2015): 24–29.

Carson, Rachel. *Silent Spring.* New York: Houghton Mifflin, 1962.

Cotera, Maria E. 'Women of Color, Tenure, and the Neoliberal University'. *Academic Repression: Reflections from the Academic Industrial Complex.* Eds. Anthony J. Nocella, II, Steven Best, Peter McLaren. Oakland: AK Press, 2010. 328–336.

Crenshaw, Kimberlé. 'Demarginalizing the Intersection of Race and Sex: A Black Feminist Critique of Antidiscrimination Doctrine, Feminist Theory and Antiracist Politics'. *University of Chicago Legal Forum* 1989: 139–167.

Edmonds, Dan. 'More Than Half of College Faculty Are Adjuncts: Should You Care?' *Forbes.* 28 May 2015. Web. 12 October 2015.

Ehrenfreund, Max. 'The Racial Divide in America Is This Elemental: Blacks and Whites Actually Breathe Different Air'. *The Washington Post.* 4 December 2014. Web. 19 September 2015.

Environmental Humanities Graduate Program at the University of Utah. Web. 1 June 2014.

Gaard, Greta. 'Toward a Queer Ecofeminism'. *Hypatia* 12.1 (1997): 114–137.

Gaard, Greta. 'Speaking of Animal Bodies'. *Hypatia* 27.3 (2012): 29–35.

Garza, Alicia. 'A Herstory of the #BlackLivesMatter Movement'. *The Feminist Wire.* 7 October 2014. Web. 10 September 2015.

Gosine, Andil. 'Pink Greens'. *Alternatives* 27.3 (July 2001). Web. 3 September 2015.

Harding, Sandra, ed. *Feminism and Methodology.* Bloomington: Indiana University Press, 1987.

Harris, Tamara Winfrey. 'Revisiting Black Macho: Is America Finally Ready to Embrace Black Feminism—and Black Women?' *Ms. Magazine* 25.3 (2015): 30–31.

Heintz, Nathan. 'Amazon Women: On the Frontlines of Grassroots Climate Leadership'. *Earth Island Journal.* 14 January 2014. Web. 12 September 2015.

Heldman, Caroline and Danielle Dirks. 'Blowing the Whistle on Campus Rape'. *Ms. Magazine* 24.1 (2014): 32–37.

Hildebrandt, Amber. 'Supreme Court's Tsilhqot'in First Nation Ruling a Game-changer for All'. CBC News. 27 June 2014. Web. 11 September 2015.

Hogan, Katie. 'Complicit: On Being a WGSS Program Director in the Neoliberal University'. *Works and Days 65/66* 33.1–2 (2016–2017): 1–8.

Hogan, Linda. *Mean Spirit.* New York: Atheneum, 1990.

Hogan, Linda. *Dwellings: A Spiritual History of the Living World.* New York: Touchstone, 1995.

Hogan, Linda. *Solar Storms.* New York: Scribner, 1997.

Hogan, Linda. *Power.* New York: W. W. Norton and Company, 1998.

Hogan, Linda. *People of the Whale.* New York: W. W. Norton and Company, 2009.

hooks, bell. *Feminist Theory: From Margin to Center.* Boston: South End Press, 1984.

Jay, Paul and Gerald Graff. 'Essay on New Approach to Defend the Value of the Humanities'. *Inside Higher Education.* 5 January 2012. Web. 10 October 2015.

Kaza, Stephanie. 'Why Environmental Humanities?' *Bittersweet Vine* (Fall 2005): 4–5.

Keller, Evelyn Fox. *A Feeling for the Organism: The Life and Work of Barbara McClintock.* New York: Freeman, 1983.

King, Jamilah. '#BlackLivesMatter: How Three Friends Turned a Spontaneous Facebook Post into a Global Phenomenon'. *The California Sunday Magazine.* 1 March 2015. Web. 10 September 2015.

Kolodny, Annette. *The Lay of the Land.* Chapel Hill: University of North Carolina Press, 1975.

Kolodny, Annette. 'Women's Studies and the Trajectory in Academe'. *Minds of Our Own: Emerging Feminist Scholarship and Women's Studies in Canada and Quebec, 1966–76*, Eds. Wendy Robbins, Meg Luxton, Margrit Eichler, Francine Descarries. Waterloo, Ontario: Wilfred Laurier Press, 2008. 170–177.

Kucera, Kat, Emma Niles, Julia Robins, Carter Sherman. 'Short Takes'. *Ms. Magazine* (Summer 2015): 13.

LaDuke, Winona. *All Our Relations: Native Struggles for Land and Life*. Boston: South End Press, 1999.

Lemieux, Jamila. 'This Black Feminist Classic Was a Precursor to Black Lives Matter'. *New Republic*. 1 June 2015. Web. 10 September 2015.

Leopold, Aldo. 'The Land Ethic'. *A Sand County Almanac*. London: Oxford University Press, 1949.

McCulloch, Gretchen. 'Is Hashtag a Word? The Case of #BlackLivesMatter'. *Slate*. 29 January 2015. Web. 10 September 2015.

Mohanty, Chandra Talpade. '"Under Western Eyes" Revisited: Feminist Solidarity through Anticapitalist Struggles'. *Signs: Journal of Women in Culture and Society* 28.2 (2003): 499–535.

Mortimer-Sandilands, Catriona and Bruce Erickson, eds. *Queer Ecologies: Sex, Nature, Politics, Desire*. Bloomington: Indiana University Press, 2010.

Nixon, Rob. *Slow Violence and the Environmentalism of the Poor*. Cambridge: Harvard University Press, 2011.

Oregon State University's Environmental Humanities Initiative: What Is Environmental Humanities? 1 June 2014. Web. 15 October 2015.

Rose, Deborah Bird, Thom van Dooren, Matthew Chrulew, Stuart Cooke, Matthew Kearnes, Emily O'Gorman. 'Thinking through the Environment, Unsettling the Humanities'. *Environmental Humanities* 1 (2012): 1–5.

Sandilands, Catriona. 'Lavender's Green? Some Thoughts on Queer(y)ing Environmental Politics'. *UnderCurrents* (May 1994): 20–24.

Sandilands, Catriona. 'Desiring Nature, Queering Ethics: Adventures in Erotogenic Environments'. *Environmental Ethics* 23 (2001): 169–188.

Sbicca, Josh. 'Eco-queer Movement(s): Challenging Heteronormative Space through (Re)imagining Nature and Food'. *European Journal of Ecopsychology* 3 (2012): 33–52.

Serrano, Melissa. 'Athabascan Chipewyan First Nation Victory over Shell Oil Canada'. *Women Donors*. 3 March 2015. Web. 11 September 2015.

Smith, Andrea. *Conquest: Sexual Violence and American Indian Genocide*. Cambridge: South End Press, 2005.

Sörlin, Sverker. 'Environmental Humanities: Why Should Biologists Interested in the Environment Take the Humanities Seriously?' *BioScience* 62.9 (September 2012): 788–789.

Stanley, Liz, ed. *Feminist Praxis*. New York: Routledge, 1990.

Stanley, Liz and Sue Wise. *Breaking Out: Feminist Consciousness and Feminist Research*. Boston: Routledge and Kegan Paul, 1983.

Stephens, Beth and Annie Sprinkle. *Goodbye Gauley Mountain*. Fecund Arts. 2013. Film.

Wallace, Michele. *Black Macho and the Myth of the Superwoman*. New York: Dial Press, 1979.

Yeampierre, Elizabeth C. 'Hurricane Katrina Proved That if Black Lives Matter, So Must Climate Justice'. *The Guardian*. 24 August 2014. Web. 10 September 2015.

Chapter Five

Seasick among the Waves of Ecocriticism

An Inquiry into Alternative Historiographic Metaphors

Scott Slovic

The deep roots of ecocriticism—or, the exploration of human–nature relationships through textual analysis, as one might define the field in brief—run far back in the field of literary studies. After more than three decades of doing this work, I still cannot pinpoint the Urtext of ecocriticism, the absolute source, but I have the sense that ancient commentaries on the Dead Sea scrolls or the Upanishads, if they happen to refer to natural motifs in these works, would count as precursors to twenty-first-century discussions of the stories embodied in the lives of toads and stones and in the traces of industrial waste found in human bodies, textual representations of the flâneur's experience in urban South Africa, and the ecopoetics of language that is, on the surface, neither poetry nor attuned to the nonhuman environment.

Despite the ancient roots of ecocriticism and the more recent history of proto-ecocriticism traced in David Mazel's *A Century of Early Ecocriticism*, which highlights the emergence of the field between 1864 and 1964 (the latter being the date when Leo Marx's landmark study of pastoralism in Western culture, *The Machine in the Garden*, appeared), the discipline is generally thought to be a product of the surge of environmental awareness that rippled across academic disciplines in the 1970s, following the first Earth Day on 22 April 1970. The publication of William Rueckert's 'experiment in ecocriticism' in a 1978 issue of *The Iowa Review* is as good a temporal marker as any for the beginning of the self-conscious ecocritical movement, although most scholars of 'nature writing', 'ecofeminist literary studies', and 'interdisciplinary wilderness issues' did not think of themselves as being 'ecocritics' until the late 1980s when Cheryll (then Burgess) Glotfelty circulated her now-famous, community-building letter to fellow graduate students and literary luminaries such as Wallace Stegner and the mid-1990s when Glotfelty and Harold Fromm began compiling *The Ecocriticism Reader: Landmarks in Literary Ecology*, which appeared from the University of Georgia Press in 1996.

I am quickly rehearsing this history because what interests me in this chapter are not only the details of ecocritical history—the names of scholars, dates of publications, and evolution of ideas—but the language used by ecocritics and fellow scholars of the environmental humanities and the implications of the historiographic metaphors that characterise the development of this field. It may come as a surprise to some that the dominant metaphor employed in ecocritical historiography was predicted at the very inception of ecocriticism as a self-conscious scholarly movement. Although Rueckert coined the term in his 1978 article, the word 'ecocriticism' was not actually adopted to describe an entire discipline until Glotfelty and Fromm published their anthology in 1996. Cheryll Glotfelty's influential introduction to that book compares the potential importance of ecocriticism to feminist and multicultural approaches to literary studies, which had become prominent in North America in the 1970s and 1980s. She went into particular detail concerning the 'developmental stages' of feminist criticism, writing:

> Elaine Showalter's model of the three developmental stages of feminist criticism provides a useful scheme for describing three analogous phases of ecocriticism.
>
> The first stage in feminist criticism, the 'images of women' stage, is concerned with representations . . .
>
> Showalter's second stage in feminist criticism [. . . is] the women's literary tradition stage . . .
>
> The third stage that Showalter identifies in feminist criticism is the theoretical phase. . . .
>
> (Glotfelty 1996, xxii–xxiv)

Although Glotfelty used the term 'stages' to describe Showalter's model for the history of feminist criticism, most scholars have come to associate the word 'waves' with feminist historiography. The first wave of feminism, which occurred during the nineteenth and early twentieth centuries, emphasised the overturning of legal inequalities between men and women, with a strong focus on women's suffrage; the second wave, especially in the 1960s through the 1980s, highlighted issues pertaining to gender norms and the status of women in society; the current third wave of feminism continues to advance many of the aims of second-wave feminism, but is marked in North America by the advancement of women to positions of academic, corporate, and political power and by the emergence of a new 'material feminist' focus that augments the previous discursive approach to feminist ideas. As becomes clear in Stacy Alaimo and Susan Hekman's 2008 collection *Material Feminisms*, the danger of essentializing women by recognizing the material differences between male and female bodies, which discouraged the adoption of material approaches in the 1980s and 1990s, eroded in the new millennium as scholars began to study the real differences in how people live embodied lives in society and in the physical world. Alaimo's work, especially, in this collection and in her subsequent book, *Bodily Natures* (2010), brought home the trans-corporeal realities of how different bodies react to contaminants—both physical and discursive—in the environment, reinforcing the importance of the material approach.

Glotfelty's brief sketch of the historical development of feminism and feminist criticism in *The Ecocriticism Reader* curiously merged the details of feminist thought with the terminology ('stages') more commonly used in describing the development of academic fields, such as psychology. Psychology is notable because of the frequent use of biographical development as a metaphor for disciplinary history. Kurt Danziger, the author of *Naming the Mind: How Psychology Found its Language* (1997), wrote the following in his opening address for the August 2001 meeting of the European Society for the History of the Human Sciences:

> Approaching the history of psychology in terms of the biography of psychological objects has significant implications for the relationship between the discipline and its history. Traditionally, practitioners of the discipline have too often made use of a historical perspective to create two essentially false impressions, namely, that the field of psychology represents some kind of unity, and that, in spite of some ups and downs, history is a story of progress. . . .
> . . . If one treats the history of psychology in terms of the history of psychological objects one need claim no more coherence for the field than is implied by an assembly of such objects.

Describing the progress of the discipline as if the entire discipline were an individual organism, developing from infancy to childhood and eventually maturing with the proliferation of new branches and applications, as Danziger suggests, has two particular results and might serve as a cautionary example for other disciplines. Whether we are talking about feminist politics (or feminist scholarship), psychology, or ecocriticism, the adoption of biographical metaphors (e.g., the hypothetical statement, 'Ecocriticism was born in the late 1970s with Rueckert's coining of the term . . . The field matured and became richly interdisciplinary with the emergence of material approaches near the end of the first decade of the twenty-first century') ascribes a sense of coherence and unanimity unlikely to exist amid a diverse community of scholars and also conflates change with progress, implicitly denigrating the sophistication of earlier thinkers.

Similar concerns arise in commentaries on the wave metaphor in feminist historiography. Some scholars note the oversimplification of complex, diverse bodies of thought into dominant 'waves', erasing the true nuances of the movement or discipline. The less well-known ideas, or merely the ideas that tended not to be favoured by those who wrote the histories of the field, disappear by the wayside, as if they never existed at all. In her 2008 article 'Talking Waves: Structures of Feminist Moments and the Potential of a Wave Economy', Emily Hoeflinger states:

> True, the wave system, as a rhetorical structure, tends to establish binaries, blind spots, and inaccurate definitions in reading the feminist past and present, which risks the loss of histories not prominent enough to be readily factored into the common notion of the 'Second' or 'Third' wave. Also true, however, is the way in which the wave system, not as a rhetorical device as much as an economy, carries a stock of information from one feminist moment to the next, so losing or rejecting this structure seemingly poses a threat to feminism's collective history (or perhaps a better term would be 'arsenal').

If we think of a social movement's ideas as the tools necessary to achieve traction towards positive transformation, and if we understand the importance of including multiple voices and strategies in order to achieve far-reaching effects, then it seems important to retain as many of these tools/ideas as possible and not discount the potential impact of relatively obscure concepts and vocabularies. Hoeflinger's notion of an economy of ideas that aims to preserve an abundance of diverse events and participants prioritises the retention of small and less popular 'moments' in addition to recognizing dominant trends. All of the work adds up to an 'arsenal' that militates towards achievement of the movement's social goals.

Other feminist scholars, such as Astrid Henry, who wrote the 'Waves' chapter in the 2011 volume *Rethinking Women's and Gender Studies*, critique the historical distortion that occurs when contested ideas are held up as undisputed, unanimously accepted perspectives. The actual richness of a discipline disappears in retrospect when the minority opinions are not respectfully retained. There is also a historiographic tendency for writers of history to distort previous eras. In a 2012 interview, Henry commented:

> I think that terms and metaphors, like 'waves', help us to bracket and cordon off complex things, whether a broad span of history with a lot going on in it, competing ideas, disagreements in political strategy, etc. In my Intro class [at Grinnell College], for example, even though we've spent most of our semester discussing a very wide range of feminist theories and theorists (plural) from what could be described, historically speaking, as the 'second wave' period, when we get to third wave writing about the second wave, a flattened-out caricature of the second wave sometimes seems to take hold—even though students

actually know much better having just studied 'second wave' theory and history. ('Interview with Astrid Henry')

Perhaps it makes sense that social movements would be particularly leery of casting aside minority philosophies and previous generations in rampant pursuit of the new. Historiography, at its heart, seeks to capture the reality of ideas and actions, combining the messiness of nuance and the clarity of broad-brush overviews. The necessity of efficiency also prevents the full retention of detail. In other words, all histories are inevitably written in ways that are less intricate and multifaceted than the realities of the communities that lived those histories. However, in critiquing historical models and in writing the histories of our scholarly fields and other communities to which we belong, it is important for us to recognise the limitations of our historiographic language. This kind of self-critique comes through vividly in Sarah Bebhinn's 2006 piece 'Generations in Conflict—Grappling with the Feminist Wave Metaphor':

> Here is where the wave metaphor becomes difficult for me to embrace. Why would I willfully choose to separate myself into a group that excludes other feminists based on age? The answer is simple: I wouldn't. I think it's much more useful to use the wave metaphor to describe a period of time rather than a group of people. In that case, we would all be in the third wave of feminism, working together. . . .
>
> . . . So why do we need to differentiate the waves? Can't we all just work together? My response to this is that yes, we should all be working together and many of us are. Although, generationally speaking, I belong to the third wave, I consider myself inter-wave.

The scholar here acknowledges that she belongs, in truth, to multiple waves of her discipline simultaneously, not merely to the most recent wave. There is a current-wave bias among most scholars—I have witnessed this on numerous occasions when I have summarised the waves of ecocriticism, as I will do below. Colleagues often come up to me afterwards, expressing relief that they 'belong to' the most recent wave or disappointment that their scholarship apparently harkens back to an earlier wave. Perhaps this comes from scholars' fear of becoming passé, especially in cultures that prize new and original thinking as the ultimate goal of academic work. Bebhinn's disarming statement about being 'inter-wave' actually describes the true, layered historical concatenation of most scholars' vocabularies and conceptual apparatus.

Despite the fact that feminist scholars have long had misgivings about the dominant wave metaphor in their own discipline, other fields, including ecocriticism, have followed suit in describing their historical development in

terms of waves. The best known example of this comes in the introduction to
Lawrence Buell's *The Future of Environmental Criticism* (2005):

> No definitive map of environmental criticism in literary studies can . . . be
> drawn. Still, one can identify several trend-lines marking an evolution from a
> 'first wave' of ecocriticism to a 'second' or newer revisionist wave or waves
> increasingly evident today. This first-second wave distinction should not,
> however, be taken as implying a tidy, distinct succession. Most currents set in
> motion by early ecocriticism continue to run strong, and most forms of second-
> wave revisionism involve building on as well as quarreling with precursors. In
> this sense, 'palimpsest' would be a better metaphor than 'wave'. (17)

What is notable in Buell's identification of these broad 'trend-lines' is both
the lack of specificity within the trends he has named 'first wave' and 'second wave' and also his immediate critique of the wave metaphor, suggesting
that 'palimpsest' might describe the historical development of the field more
accurately. Of course, even a palimpsest, a text that has been written upon
repeatedly, does not precisely capture the overlapping and intersecting of different historical phases/modes of a discipline such as ecocriticism, but at least
the term implies the actual simultaneity of the phases without falsely suggesting a discrete process of succession by which each new phase somehow
cancels out and replaces the previous phase(s).

Buell published his book attaching the wave metaphor to ecocriticism in
2005, and shortly thereafter Joni Adamson and I reused the term as we wrote
our introduction to the 2009 issue of *Multiethnic Literatures of the United
States* devoted to the special topic of Ecocriticism and Ethnicity. Here, allow
me to back up and sketch (reductively!) the essential facets of first-wave
through fourth-wave ecocriticism, rehearsing briefly the territory of my 2010
article 'The Third Wave of Ecocriticism: North American Reflections on the
Current Phase of the Discipline'. In describing all waves of the field, I take
pains to avoid attaching an end-date to each wave—in other words, the wave
metaphor immediately breaks down for me in that the waves are never-ending,
describing as they do practices and ideas that remain current and meaningful,
even years after they initially emerged as pronounced features of scholarly
practice. Here, in any case, is my quick rehearsal of the three waves described
in the 2010 article as well as the fourth wave I have noted more recently (in
my Editor's Note for the Fall 2012 issue, 19.4, of *Interdisciplinary Studies in
Literature and Environment*):

• Starting around 1980, there was an initial surge (a 'first wave') of ecocritical work, even before people were generally using the term 'ecocriticism'. This ground-breaking work tended to focus on literary nonfiction

(so-called 'nature writing'); there was a strong emphasis on nonhuman nature (or 'wilderness'), as represented in literature; initially the field was oriented towards American and British literature; and 'discursive' ecofeminism was one of the most politically engaged sub-movements within the field.

- We can date the second wave to approximately the mid-1990s, when the field began to expand to encompass multiple genres (and even popular culture—some would call this 'green cultural studies'); the works and authors being studied became increasingly multicultural; we saw a growing interest in local environmental literatures around the world; environmental justice ecocriticism began to emerge at this time, especially with the publication of *The Environmental Justice Reader: Politics, Poetics, and Pedagogy* in 2002; and the scope of ecocriticism expanded to include urban and suburban contexts in addition to rural and wild locations.

- In our introduction to the Summer 2009 special issue of *Multiethnic Literatures of the United States*, Joni Adamson and I focused on the *comparatist* tendency in recent examples of ecocriticism, dating back to approximately 2000—comparisons across national cultures and across ethnic cultures. But later I began to describe other notable trends: the melding and tension between global concepts of place ('eco-cosmopolitanism' a la Ursula Heise's *Sense of Place and Sense of Planet*) and neo-bioregionalism (as in Tom Lynch's discussion of 'nested' bioregions in *Xerophilia*); a rising emphasis on 'material' ecofeminism and multiple gendered approaches (including eco-masculinism and green queer theory); a strong interest in 'animality' (evolutionary ecocriticism; animal subjectivity/agency, vegetarianism, justice for nonhuman species, and post-humanism); critiques from within the field (such as those by Dana Phillips and Michael P. Cohen) that have contributed to the growing sophistication of ecocriticism; and various new forms of ecocritical activism (such as John Felstiner's use of poetry as a means of environmental engagement).

- In 2008, Stacy Alaimo and Susan Hekman published the book *Material Feminisms*, which included Alaimo's article 'Trans-Corporeal Feminisms and the Ethical Space of Nature', a study that vividly demonstrates how the human body is essentially embedded in the physical world with its host of discursive practices, and how literary texts illuminate both the material and the ethical implications of physical phenomena that pass between our bodies and the body of the Earth. In the Editor's Note for the Autumn 2012 issue of *Interdisciplinary Studies in Literature and Environment*, I referred to the growing tendency among ecocritics to focus on 'the fundamental materiality . . . of environmental things, places, processes, forces, and experiences' as a new 'fourth wave of ecocriticism'. This was soon manifested in the 2014 book *Material Ecocriticism*, edited by Serpil Oppermann and Serenella Iovino.

As someone who is often called upon to explain the field of ecocriticism to new audiences ranging from undergraduates to government officials, I have found the wave metaphor to be useful shorthand as I have tried to mark the changes the field has undergone in the past thirty years. However, it strikes me that there has been a tendency to microhistoricise ecocriticism, to scrutinise its subtle changes and divergences during brief spans of time (1980–1995, 1995–2000, 2000–2008, 2008–2012). I observe these habits in myself, as a commentator on the field, and I see some of this in my colleagues, too, as they seek to chart the scope and development of ecocriticism in such articles as Ursula K. Heise's 'A Hitchhiker's Guide to Ecocriticism' (2006), Loretta Johnson's 'Greening the Library: The Fundamentals and Future of Ecocriticism' (2009), Andrea Campbell's 'Reading beyond a Universal Future: My Hopes for the Future of Ecocriticism' (2010), and Greta Gaard's 'New Directions for Ecofeminism: Toward a More Feminist Ecocriticism' (2010). The alternative to the minute analysis of multiple waves or subsets of ecocritical practice tends to be the approach demonstrated in Ken Hiltner's 2015 collection, *Ecocriticism: The Essential Reader*, which is divided into two broad sections, titled 'First-Wave Ecocriticism' and 'Second-Wave Ecocriticism', with no particular rationale for separating the selected texts except that 'first wave' is everything up to the publication of *The Ecocriticism Reader* in 1996, and 'second wave' is everything that has come since 1996. The closest Hiltner comes to a precise assertion of the specific foci of second-wave ecocriticism occurs in his observation that the more recent wave encompasses such topics as environmental justice and scale and that the second wave approaches 'environmental issues from a decidedly theoretical position' (132). What is conspicuously absent from the 2015 volume is an acknowledgement that scholars had, for several years, been thinking of ecocriticism within the broader, interdisciplinary rubric of 'the environmental humanities'. Although the University of Nevada, Reno, was home to a Center for Environmental Arts and Humanities from 1995 to 2002, the widespread use of the phrase and concept 'environmental humanities' seems to have percolated around 2010 and to have been prominently institutionalised with the emergence in 2012 of the Australian journal *Environmental Humanities*, founded by editors Thom van Dooren and Deborah Bird Rose.

In light of the current environmental humanities imperative to acknowledge and benefit from the 'conjunctions across environmental philosophy, environmental history, ecocriticism, cultural geography, cultural anthropology, and political ecology' (as the field is described in the statement 'What

Is the Environmental Humanities?' on the homepage for The Environmental Humanities at UCLA), it strikes me as particularly appropriate, nearly two decades into the twenty-first century, to reconsider the wave metaphor for ecocritical historiography that the discipline inherited almost accidentally from feminism. The goal of such a reconsideration is not to immediately adopt a similarly restrictive and distortive metaphor, but to provoke some self-conscious reflection on how we characterise the temporal changes within ecocriticism and the field's intersections with sister disciplines.

I began contemplating alternative historiographic metaphors for ecocriticism in the fall of 2013 in preparation for the University of Washington's symposium titled 'The Future of the Environmental Humanities', where there would be opportunities to engage with leading figures such as Lawrence Buell, Greg Garrard, George Handley, Ursula Heise, and up-and-coming colleagues, including Allison Carruth and Jesse Oak Taylor. Prior to the symposium, I conferred with my colleagues at the University of Idaho (including Anna Banks, Erin James, and Jennifer Ladino) and with other participants in our monthly Ecocriticism Reading Group in Moscow, Idaho. I asked reading group members, 'What metaphors might enable us to place ecocriticism within a broader temporal and disciplinary perspective than the wave metaphor encourages?' Aaron Moe, who had recently completed his PhD thesis on zoopoetics at Washington State University, proposed the idea of 'fractals' (self-same patterns), which would highlight the comparability of ideas and vocabularies in fields ranging from textual studies to philosophy. Anna Banks, deeply engaged with yoga philosophy and practice, held up the term 'spanda', which alludes to the primordial vibration of the universe, and which could serve as a reminder that all ecocritical gestures echo the deepest rhythms and yearnings of existence—but perhaps such an idea was some-what too expansive to be practical. Visiting scholar Wendy Harding from the University of Toulouse half-jokingly suggested 'airport terminals' as a metaphor, as ecocritics (perhaps she meant me, in particular) tend to spend so much time traveling to far-flung places, encouraging audiences to be environmentally conscious—but also because this phrase echoes Buell's description of ecocriticism as a 'concourse of discrepant practices' (2005, 11). She also proposed the idea of ecocriticism as 'a house with many rooms', reminiscent of Toni Morrison's ideas in the recent novel *Home*. These strikingly diverse terms succeeded in exploding the notion that only waves might represent patterns within ecocriticism and exploring the field's relationship with other fields, but none quite captures the sense of meta- and trans-disciplinarity, and the idea of development over time, that I was looking for.

I found myself contemplating the basic idea of how thinkers understand the historical era(s) to which they belong and the process of transition to a new era. One of the central studies of this is Thomas Kuhn's 1962 book, *The*

Structure of Scientific Revolutions. In the chapter 'The Response to a Crisis', Kuhn writes:

> Let us then assume that crises are a necessary precondition for the emergence of novel theories and ask next how scientists respond to their existence. [. . . T] he act of judgment that leads scientists to reject a previously accepted theory is always based upon more than a comparison of that theory with the world. The decision to reject one paradigm is always simultaneously the decision to accept another, and the judgment leading to that decision involves the comparison of both paradigms with nature *and* with each other. (77)

While there have been minor flare-ups, such as the so-called 'Estok-Robisch Affair' in 2010, which briefly pitted theoretical and anti-theoretical ecocritics against each other, for the most part ecocritical change has occurred evolutionarily rather than revolutionarily. If we were to stop microhistorizing and describing (as I have done above) every brief shift in the field as a separate epoch, we might be able to think paradigmatically about the field. This is what the 'big picture' historical span of ecocriticism might look like:

1. Proto-ecocriticism (as in David Mazel's *A Century of Ecocriticism*, but encompassing studies of natural themes in literature throughout the world, not only in North America and also acknowledging the history of such work before 1864, which is the beginning point of Mazel's project): nature writing studies;
2. Ecocritical modes during the post-1970 (Earth Day) environmental movement up through the early years of the 2000s: response to environmental crisis;
3. Growing sense of ecocriticism's coexistence and intersections with a host of sister disciplines, from environmental history to conservation biology: the development of interdisciplinary 'environmental humanities' in the 1990s and 2000s (crisis intensifying—the era of climate change acknowledgement)

I began this chapter by suggesting that there may be ancient exegetical studies of sacred texts that refer to natural phenomena, reflecting ideas about environmental ethics and sense of place—and that such studies might be considered the earliest inklings of the ecocritical imagination. However, perhaps it would be more reasonable to consider the dawn of ecocriticism as a process that occurred in conjunction with the emergence of modern literary criticism in the mid-nineteenth century, as Mazel does and as Joe Moran sketches in his book *Interdisciplinarity* (2nd ed. 2010). If so, then one could argue that the entire span of what we think of as ecocriticism has occurred during the era now described as 'the Anthropocene', which was preliminarily articulated in George Perkins Marsh's 1864 book *Man and Nature: or, Physical Geography as Modified by Human Action,* long before Paul Crutzen proposed the term 'Anthropocene' as a new geological epoch.

The macrohistorical sketch of ecocriticism I have written just above suggests to me a steady process of broadening and picking up energy and momentum—from individual scholars closely reading and describing specific texts to locating these texts within cultural and ecological contexts (and crises), to appreciating the conversations between literary texts and ideas emerging in cognate disciplines. Rather than waves or a palimpsest—or a spanda or a house with many rooms—what I find myself imagining is a vast intellectual drainage system or watershed that encompasses various early and recent developments within ecocriticism per se, alongside other river systems demonstrating small creeks of intellectual, artistic, and activist thought that later merged with each other to form broader, swifter currents, eventually converging with other systems of thought and then finally emptying into the vast sea of 'environmental studies', which encompasses all human efforts to understand our place on this planet. Take a look at a diagram of a river system that shows several sources emerging as tributaries, flowing towards points of confluence with the main river channel and ultimately towards the 'mouth' of the river, where it enters the sea. Doesn't this look like the intellectual milieu to which we currently belong as participants in the environmental humanities?

Perhaps, living in Idaho, where all waters collected in the Lochsa, Selway, Clearwater, Salmon, and Snake Rivers, or their various tributaries, flow eventually into the mighty Columbia and out towards the Pacific Ocean, I simply have rivers on the brain. When I presented a version of this chapter as a talk at the 2013 symposium in Seattle, the room burst into conversation when Professor Buell, who chaired the session, asked for questions and comments. Some listeners latched onto the river metaphor, but others were eager to propose alternatives that had not occurred to me. One man envisioned ecocriticism and neighbouring fields as a tapestry of language and ideas, the warp and weft knotting together disparate fields into a beautiful and intrinsically connected carpet of human desire to belong to the world and to understand this belonging. Despite my fascination with the flow of water and the systems that describe such movement of the stuff of life, I also love the tapestry idea—and I can be convinced to appreciate the partial suitability of various other historiographic metaphors.

My purpose here, as I have suggested above, is not to propose the ultimate metaphor for describing where ecocriticism came from and where it is going, but rather to highlight the artificiality and contingency of all historiographic metaphors. As we flow forward with the present wave of environmental humanities scholarship, let us remember that this current, too, will eventually strike a submerged reef (a radical new idea, a potential collaboration, a social or material crisis) that will raise it up, bring it crashing down on some distant shoreline, and distribute its waters among the endless succession of waves to follow. Although I sometimes find myself 'seasick among the waves of ecocriticism', the search for alternative historiographic metaphors often leads me back to the waves, perhaps with slightly more circumspection and self-awareness than before.

WORKS CITED

Adamson, Joni, Mei Mei Evans, Rachel Stein, eds. *The Environmental Justice Reader: Politics, Poetics, and Pedagogy*. Tucson: University of Arizona Press, 2002.

Adamson, Joni and Scott Slovic. 'Guest Editors' Introduction: The Shoulders We Stand On'. *Multiethnic Literatures of the United States* 34.2 (Summer 2009): 5–24.

Alaimo, Stacy. *Bodily Natures: Science, Environment, and the Material Self*. Bloomington: Indiana University Press, 2010.

Alaimo, Stacy and Susan Hekman, eds. *Material Feminisms*. Bloomington: Indiana University Press, 2008.

Bebhinn, Sarah. 'Generations in Conflict—Grappling with the Feminist Wave Metaphor'. *MatriFocus: Cross-Quarterly for the Goddess Woman* (2006). Web. 26 October 2013.

Buell, Lawrence. 'The Emergence of Environmental Criticism'. *The Future of Environmental Criticism*. Malden, MA: Blackwell, 2005.

Campbell, Andrea. 'Reading beyond a Universal Nature: My Hopes for the Future of Ecocriticism'. *Schuylkill Graduate Journal* 8.1 (2010): 7–10.

Cohen, Michael P. 'Blues in the Green: Ecocriticism under Critique'. *Environmental History* 9.1 (January 2004): 9–36.

Danziger, Kurt. *Naming the Mind: How Psychology Found Its Language*. Los Angeles: Sage Press, 1997.

Danziger, Kurt. 'Revised Opening Address'. European Society for the History of Human Sciences Meeting. Amsterdam, Netherlands. August 2001. Web. 26 October 2013.

Gaard, Greta. 'New Directions for Ecofeminism: Toward a More Feminist Ecocriticism'. *Interdisciplinary Studies in Literature and Environment* 17.4 (Autumn 2010): 643–665.

Glotfelty, Cheryll. 'Introduction'. *The Ecocriticism Reader: Landmarks in Literary Ecology*. Eds. Cheryll Glotfelty and Harold Fromm. Athens: University of Georgia Press, 1996.

Heise, Ursula K. 'A Hitchhiker's Guide to Ecocriticism'. *Publications of the Modern Language Association of America* 121.2 (March 2006): 502–516.

Heise, Ursula K. *Sense of Place and Sense of Planet*. New York: Oxford University Press, 2008. Print.

Hiltner, Ken, ed. *Ecocriticism: The Essential Reader*. London: Routledge, 2015.

Hoeflinger, Emily. 'Talking Waves: Structures of Feminist Moments and the Potential of a Wave Economy'. *Thirdspace: A Journal of Feminist Theory & Culture* 8.1 (Summer 2008). Web. 26 October 2013.

'Interview with Astrid Henry, author of "Waves" chapter'. *Rethinking Women's and Gender Studies*. 20 January 2012. Web. 26 October 2013.

Iovino, Serenella and Serpil Oppermann, eds. *Material Ecocriticism*. Bloomington: Indiana University Press, 2014.

Johnson, Loretta. 'Greening the Library: The Fundamentals and Future of Ecocriticism'. *Choice* (December 2009): 7–13.

Kuhn, Thomas. *The Structure of Scientific Revolutions*. Chicago: Universty of Chicago Press, 1962.

Lynch, Tom. *Xerophilia: Ecocritical Explorations of Southwestern Literature*. Lubbock: Texas Tech University Press, 2008.

Marsh, George Perkins. *Man and Nature; or, Physical Geography as Modified by Human Action*. 1864. Seattle: University of Washington Press, 2003.

Mazel, David. *A Century of Early Ecocriticism*. Athens: University of Georgia Press, 2001.

Moran, Joe. *Interdisciplinarity*. 2nd edn. New York: Routledge, 2010.

Orr, Catherine M., Ann Braithwaite, Diane Lichtenstein, eds. *Rethinking Women's and Gender Studies*. London: Routledge, 2011.

Phillips, Dana. *The Truth of Ecology: Nature, Culture, and Literature in America*. New York: Oxford University Press, 2003.

Rueckert, William. "Literature and Ecology: An Experiment in Ecocriticism." *The Iowa Review 9.1* (Winter 1978): 71–86.

Slovic, Scott. Editor's Note. *Interdisciplinary Studies in Literature and Environment* 19.4 (Fall 2012): 619–621.

Slovic, Scott. 'The Third Wave of Ecocriticism: North American Reflections on the Current Phase of the Discipline'. *Ecozon@* 1.1 (April 2010). Web. 26 October 2013.

Part II

VOICING THE ANTHROPOCENE

Chapter Six

The Extraordinary Strata of the Anthropocene

Jan Zalasiewicz

Geologists tend not to think about history, much. Perhaps not even about Earth history. The theme is—one hastens to add—always somewhere there in the background. A planet that bears countless and *detailed* imprints of what has happened to it—to a greater extent, almost certainly, than any other body in the Solar System—is fertile ground for such thought. But the sheer scale and complexity of the narrative is a considerable barrier to speculation, whether idle or embarked upon with serious intent. There is simply too much of it. That extraordinarily insightful geologist and palaeontologist, Richard Fortey, once described geology as *everything* that is present or happening on, within and above the Earth, now and over the past four and a half billion years.

To that substantial compendium of Earthly time, events and matter, one might now add the Earth's future, of something like another five billion years, to the 'to do' list—and, just for good measure, all the other planetary bodies whirling around the Sun, which we now know have their own *quite* individual geologies. Then, there are all of the planets and moons orbiting other stars in this galaxy, and that we are just beginning to glimpse; they are about a billion strong, at a conservative estimate. (We may leave from consideration, for the time being, the planetary bodies that will be present in the one hundred billion or so other galaxies within the known Universe: it will be some time before our telescopes can be effectively trained on those.) All in all, it is enough to make one's head spin, and a head thus revolving is not ideally placed to undertake cool and considered assessment of planetary history, let alone of the place of any particular, strange and novel event within it, such as—for instance—the extraordinary set of processes that we humans have precipitated. So, what is to be done? And where does one start?

The starting point—to revert back just to this small planet—has tradition-ally been fragments: small shards of the greater whole that have attracted the attention of some passing geologist, using that last word extremely loosely. It is rather like approaching one of Seurat's *pointililliste* paintings, in a dark room, with one of those fine-beam pen flashlights that will illuminate just a few of the dots of paint at one time. Examine, then, those one or two splashes of paint—in great detail. Become absorbed by them, to the extent that they become a central pursuit in one's life. Slowly develop a methodology to study them, and a grammar to discuss them (in reality, to consider just a few aspects of the paint specks, that then—by definition—become of critical importance). Suddenly, the flashlight is aimed elsewhere, and a few other paint spots come into view. These are then minutely examined in turn—particularly as regards those chosen aspects, which have now become channels for directed thought. It will be a long time before any sensibly coherent parts of the panorama come into view. It is clear that that the paint specks are part of a greater whole, but also that, gazed at intently enough, they have a fascination of their own, and particular aspects—their shape, colour, sheen, surface roughness— can become a basis of classification.

The Earth, of course, is somewhat larger than a Seurat canvas. Those dots of information are arranged three-dimensionally. They have not stayed in their relative positions since being put into place, but have been torn apart and reassembled through the unspeakably long tunnel of the fourth dimension. Many have just . . . disappeared. Quite a few have changed colour. And, they are still being added to.

Nevertheless, focusing on such particulars can make the whole exercise *manageable*. On the larger canvas of the Earth, therefore, some geologists may focus on the chemistry of the crystals in a basalt; others, on certain long-dead types of plankton; others still, on the patterns that sand grains take up when sped along a sea floor by a current; and yet others, on the patterns of space that develop *between* those sand grains (an exercise that is not just the inverse of looking at the sand grains themselves). And so it goes on; for much of the science, the devil really is in the detail (the angel is somewhere there too, of course, to be even-handed about this).

The synthesis, to try to pick out some more general truth from the mass of detail, typically emerges once sufficient of that detail has been collected to show patterns emerging from what seemed initially to be bewilderingly chaotic. The major steps in this process are now classics of geological history. William Smith,[1] for instance, in the early nineteenth century, demonstrated that rocks and fossils made sense. He showed that the broad patterns of their arrangement—their *superposition*—could be followed from region to region, from country to country. Coal, he said, only occurred in certain layers: if you are a speculator, and sink a mineshaft too high or too low amid the endless strata, you will end up losing your shirt (as many did, before his insights were appreciated).

The most notably coal-rich succession became divided off as the Carboniferous System. This is emphatically a rock unit. Within its several kilometres of thickness, fortunes were made and lost, and miners lived and worked—and all too often died too, as the overstressed rocks exploded in rock-bursts around them. To better make money—and to attempt to avoid tragedy—generations of geologists mapped out the exquisitely complex arrangement of the hundreds of individual coal layers within that mass of rock, in ever greater detail. Even after the coal is exhausted, that knowledge is still needed to predict where the overlying ground may or may not still subside to damage houses, and where sulphurous, iron-rich waters, percolating through old mine-workings, can make their way to the surface to pollute streams and rivers.

This is detailed, practical, absorbing work—a jigsaw puzzle that can take many lifetimes to (only partially) solve. It is work of the here-and-now. In analysing the endless detail, the realization that those Carboniferous rocks are a memory of something else entirely—of a world of primeval swamp forests, with amphibians and giant dragonflies, but without flowers, or birds, or mammals—is generally very much at the back of a working mind. Nevertheless, this distant past, now separated off as a segment of time some 60 million years long, is the basis for the Carboniferous Period, that may be reconstructed in imagination—but never again touched, or seen, or experienced—from the rocks of the Carboniferous System.

And so it has developed, this compartmentalization of Earth history. The Cretaceous, to take another example, is separated out on the basis of a kilometre-thick stratum of almost pure chalk (now known to be virtually worldwide), that marked one of the ultimate greenhouse worlds of substantially drowned continents. The Permian was found almost by accident when that grand man of Victorian geology, Sir Roderick Murchison, travelled to deepest Russia (Collie and Diemer 2004). There, he was actually following the rocks of the Silurian and Devonian systems, which he had been instrumental in carving out of the rocks of Wales and southwest England, to see if they had global significance (they did). But while there, in the rock strata around the city of Perm, he noticed strata with fossils in them that were different from those of the underlying and familiar Carboniferous strata—and also very different to those of the Triassic System, by then well known from Europe. By a quirk of ancient geography, ancient Perm had been covered by a shallow sea, teeming with life, while Britain and Europe were a virtually lifeless desert—and so these Russian rocks revealed an entirely new dynasty of life and of Earth's history: the Permian Period, of long-gone time, the happenings of which may be inferred from the solid rock strata of the Permian System.

The history business has loomed larger within geology in the last few decades, true—not least because enough *pointilliste*-style evidence has accumulated to make sensible inroads into such large questions as the journeys that continents have taken, or the manner in which Earth's climate has changed. Nevertheless, when the Anthropocene was born—in a practical sense, at least—with Paul Crutzen's inspired improvisation at a conference in Mexico just fifteen years ago, the usual procedures were turned upside down.

This new epoch (using the term 'epoch' provisionally, for neither formal status nor hierarchical level have been decided) burst upon the scene as a time unit, quite fully formed. It was explicitly a geological time interval, the logic proposed being that the Holocene had ended. And yet, the evidence foremost in mind was of the most insubstantial kind: a change in the air, indeed. And the particular change with which Paul Crutzen's name is indelibly associated—the thinning of circumpolar stratospheric ozone because of tiny amounts of highly reactive human-made chemicals, chlorofluorocarbons—is almost perversely counter-geological. While other changes of atmospheric chemistry, such as variations in methane and carbon dioxide levels, can leave an imprint in rock strata—if you look hard enough and devise sufficiently ingenious analyses—this particular change leaves no stratigraphic trace that I am aware of. It is a ghost—albeit one that is convincingly driving significant change in a planetary machine.

Small wonder that it took a while for the geological community—and in particular the formal stratigraphic community (i.e., the one that has the responsibility for maintaining the Geological Time Scale)—to catch on. The idea of the epoch was out there, first among the Earth systems science community, monitoring planetary change in real time, and then spreading widely, among the sciences more generally, and among the arts and humanities too.

Only towards the end of the decade was the concept considered as a potential stratigraphic unit, by the Stratigraphy Commission of the Geological Society of London—a national body with no power to change the Geological Time Scale, but nevertheless one that can provide informed comment, and opinion. And, on the strength of that opinion (a cautious one, that the Anthropocene 'may have merit' geologically) there came the invitation to form the Anthropocene Working Group of the Subcommission on Quaternary Research, a component body of the International Commission on Stratigraphy (the decision-making body that oversees the Geological Time Scale, more technically known as the International Chronostratigraphic Chart)—which itself is under the aegis of the International Union of Geological Sciences, which must ratify any decision.

The process of analysing the Anthropocene formally is certainly novel, in many respects. The term emerged from an evidence base that was largely observational, of global conditions of the present and recent past. It was not—as is the case with all of the other units of the Geological Time Scale—a synthesis of stratal patterns that became evident after long years of study of the rocks. So, one of the first tasks is to see whether there is in effect, a stratal unit on Earth that may be systematically recognised and assigned, as a material body, to the Anthropocene Epoch. In the parlance used, this material or 'time-rock' unit, parallel to the 'time' unit, would be termed an Anthropocene Series.

When considering this material record, it becomes necessary to reconsider one's notion of what geology *is*. For instance, a field geologist mapping the geology of a region would certainly consider the ancient strata below ground as geology. Then, above that, there may be much younger glacial deposits such as boulder clay. Those too, are geology and are mapped as geological units (they may be the focus of interest of geographical studies, too). Above that, and present almost everywhere, is the present-day soil—and that by contrast is very rarely seen as the province of geology, or shown on a geological map, even though it is very emphatically part of the Earth system, and these days considered as a key part of the 'critical zone' of this planet (Richter and Billings 2015) (curiously, fossil soils—or 'palaeosols'—are considered as geology).

Then, there are those rock and soil deposits transported and reworked by humans around cities, motorway and railway embankments, in quarries and landfill sites. Here there is an even more curious contrast in geological practice. If the material forms part of waste or rubble layers, then it is typically mapped as strata of 'Artificial Ground' on a geological map—and likewise the empty spaces left by the extraction of raw materials such as brick clay and sand and gravel may be mapped as 'Worked Ground', and have their own symbol on geological maps (indeed these deposits dominate the surface geology of most urban areas). However, when these materials are in use, in the fabric of homes and factories, roads and railways and airport runways, then they are typically seen as outside the realm of geology (though they will re-enter it as the buildings are demolished and the road material is ripped up, and these wastes are spread over the ground or dumped within landfill sites).

These are differences only of working practice—and disciplinary territoriality. In reality, the materials, whether within functional human-made constructions or as discarded rubble, represent a new and substantial new subsystem within the rock cycle, that, as a large part of the physical structure of Peter Haff's technosphere (2014), is reworking rocks and minerals in new patterns. It is now *very* large in scale. The human-made new rock par excellence is concrete, of which some half a trillion tons have now been made, by far the greater part since the 'Great Acceleration' (Steffen et al. 2007, 2015) of the mid-twentieth century, and more than half of this (given the current acceleration of the Great Acceleration) in the last twenty years. Most of this new rock is within buildings, dams, roads, embankments (and so technically outside geology as traditionally understood). Within a century, though, most of these constructions are likely to be abandoned or demolished, and so this rock will then be travelling on, somewhere within the planetary rock cycle. Thinking through the Anthropocene necessitates such rethinking and recategorization. Arguably, it is getting the science of geology closer to seeing things as they really are.

There is a similar tension in interpretation when considering minerals. A mineral is, in standard definition, a solid of more or less fixed chemical composition. According to the International Mineralogical Association, the body that vets and approves new minerals (with about 50 being added each year to the total of some 4,500 that have been recognised), a mineral is by definition also natural and not human-made. This is sensible in one way, in that it keeps a pristine view of perhaps the most fundamental set of building blocks of this planet. From another view, though, it masks the scale of the mineralogical reconstruction of the Earth's surface by humans, who have produced pure metals (something that, with a few exceptions such as gold, does not characterise the natural world) in multimillion-ton amounts, who have produced large amounts of other novelties such as tungsten carbide (that forms the ball of your ball-point pen), boron nitride (that is harder than diamond), and probably thousands more, that emerge from the laboratories of the materials scientists. These new materials are minerals in everything but formal definition, and their sudden release on to our planet's surface marks, almost certainly, the single largest change to the Earth's mineral storehouse since the early Proterozoic era, some two and a half billion years ago when, in what is now known as the 'Great Oxygenation Event', the world changed colour, going from the greys and greens of a chemically reducing world to reds, oranges and browns, as a swathe of oxide and hydroxide minerals appeared (Zalasiewicz et al. 2014; cf. Hazen et al. 2008).

Even more striking are the 'mineraloids', those substances where the chemical composition changes within set limits. The human-made varieties include glass of different kinds, far more pure and transparent than the volcanic glasses obsidian and pitchstone—and, that symbol of the modern world, plastic. Plastic in its various forms is essentially a post–World War II phenomenon, now being produced in hundreds of millions of tons per year and—hard-wearing, decay-resistant, light and easily transportable—is finding its way to the oceans. There, particularly in the almost invisible 'microplastic' form (the thousands of fibres, say, that come from your fleece after it has been through a wash cycle), it is transported by currents and within animal bodies to reach the most distant beaches and the deepest sea floors (Ivar do Sul and Costa 2014). To regard these phenomena as part of the fabric of geology is certainly novel—but is defensible, in that it does appear to reflect a genuine departure within the Earth system. However, once accepted as a stratigraphic marker, new materials such as plastics, glass and ceramics may be straightforward to use—especially the first of these, which is a widely and easily recognizable time marker.

Other aspects of the Anthropocene are more difficult, simply in practical geological terms. The new minerals and rocks of the Anthropocene are components of strata, and one of the prime tasks of a geologist is to fix the location of strata within three-dimensional space, where they intersect with other three-dimensional surfaces (the topographic surface of the landscape, for instance) to produce geological outcrops. Learning this particular skill is often one of the most challenging parts of the life of a student of geology, as it needs several mental images to be manipulated simultaneously inside one's head—and it is often thoroughly counter-intuitive. The simplest of horizontal strata may show up as terribly complicated outcrops, if cut through by a network of streams and rivers, for instance. Conversely, severely structurally deformed strata commonly have very simple outcrops (a stratum pushed by mountain-building forces to a vertical position will appear as a just a pair of straight parallel lines, no matter how rugged is the topography that it transects.

Now, Anthropocene strata can be very simple and predictable (the layers of polluted snow on an ice-cap, for instance—material that even conventionally is regarded as rock these days). But go to the 'urban strata' of a major city and the geometrical complexity can seem limitless, almost fractal.[2] An ancient city such as Rome will have components that are thousands of years old, interlaced with filigrees of material from successive ages and periods of history, now in turn interlaced with new buildings and foundations, roadways, electric pipes and cables and modern sewage systems, fibre-optic cables, and so on. This is the kind of terrain that archaeologists are skilled at analysing and depicting on plans, but for geologists—who typically have to move rather more quickly over larger areas of terrain, simplifying as needs be as they go—it is more challenging to separate out, say, an 'Anthropocene' unit (if defined with a mid-twentieth-century boundary, for instance) from a 'pre-Anthropocene' one. Simplification of such a three- and four-dimensional patchwork is not straightforward.

One can think of a few partial analogues in nonhuman geology—cave deposits, for instance, and some of the complex structures that form as strata fluidise underground to inject into both older and younger layers of rock. But the challenge here is novel in scale and extent.

Curiously, there may be less of an issue in considering the extreme youth of the Anthropocene, and in locating its boundary outside those crazily mixed-up urban areas. Most geological epochs, it is true, are much longer than the Anthropocene, almost no matter how it is defined. The five formal epochs of the 'Tertiary' period average a little over twelve million years in duration each. But the revolutionary change in duration has already been shown by the Holocene, at a little under twelve thousand years long. This is a full three orders of magnitude shorter than that 'Tertiary' average—and the Anthropocene (if defined to start with the 'Great Acceleration') is just—so far—some two orders of magnitude shorter than the Holocene. The big time jump in classification has already happened, much earlier in the history of geological time classification (the Holocene was first proposed at the third International Geological Congress in 1885, though formally adopted in 1967 by the U.S. Geological Survey), and for eminently practical reasons.

Holocene strata may, for the most part be wet and sloppy (and smelly, too, quite often) and most unlike the public understanding of a 'rock'. But, they cover a good deal of both landscape and sea floor of our planet, being the three-dimensional unit that underlies the two-dimensional surfaces of river floodplains, coastal plains, delta tops and so on. Take the English Fenland, for instance—some four thousand square kilometres of flat agricultural land-scape, a segment of which was one of my first mapping assignments when joining the British Geological Survey as a rookie field geologist (a bemused one, for I had mostly studied and trained on the eminently hard and ancient rocks of Wales). The Fenland, beneath its surface, was a wedge of muds and silts more than ten metres in thickness, all deposited after the retreat of the last ice age, and with an intricate and delicate internal structure reflecting changes in the position of land and sea, and reflecting too the life and death (almost literally) of spectacular tidal waterways (Smith et al. 2010, 2012). The Holocene suddenly made the most perfect geological sense—especially as the realization came that the Fenland, huge by English standards, is tiny by comparison with the world-scale examples of Bangladesh, the Louisiana wetlands, Bangladesh, the Yellow River delta and so forth. A mere eleven millennia may be almost nothing at all in the immensity of Earth time, but when it is up-close then it can encompass world-shaping forces—and similar logic may be applied to the Anthropocene.

However, a difference appears when the possible futures of these two epochs—the formal and the still informal one—is contrasted. The Holocene—like the Quaternary Period that it is a part of—is essentially defined on the basis of climate. It is defined to start as the world warmed in emerging from the last glacial phase (just as the Quaternary is defined to start as the world cooled from the last gasp of Tertiary warmth represented by the Pliocene Epoch). The Holocene is just one interglacial of many in the Quaternary (all the others being lumped together in the Pleistocene Epoch, that makes up almost all of the 2.6-million-year span of the period). In a normal state of affairs, the Holocene as a unit might be expected to terminate within some millennia, given considerations of its 'natural length', when the ice would be expected to advance again to cover the currently temperate regions of the Earth, and sea level to fall by a hundred metres or so as the ice-caps grow huge once more (Tzedakis et al. 2012).

But—and this is a large 'but'—the Anthropocene departs from this state and expectation in a number of ways. Firstly, of *all* the characters by which this emerging interval of geological time might be characterised, climate— and sea level too—are currently among the most trivial and insubstantial ones. True, temperature has risen by almost a degree, globally on average, in the last century—and this is almost certainly (*quite* certainly, if one shakes off inbuilt scientific caution) due to the human-driven rise in greenhouse gas levels. And, sea level has risen by about 30 centimetres over the same time, as the oceans have warmed and expanded, and ice has begun to melt and release water into the sea. But both global temperature and sea level remain within more or less normal interglacial levels. Indeed, temperature would have to rise by about another degree and sea level by more than ten metres to exceed levels seen at peak warmth and sea level of the last interglacial, some 125 thousand years ago, when there was no significant human interference to the Earth system whatsoever. It is much more likely than not that these levels of temperature and sea level will be exceeded, later this century and in a few centuries respectively—but this has not happened yet.

It is in a whole variety of other parameters that the Anthropocene is expressed. Some have a long geological pedigree, and there is a sense of planetary déjà vu—such as a marked increase in species extinction and (especially) invasion rates, and changes in sedimentation rates, and changes in greenhouse gas levels and associated changes in the carbon isotope com- position of the global atmosphere. Others, though, include marked planetary novelty, as in the appearance of enormous city-structures that make up the urban strata, and of novel material such as plastics and aluminium and the extraordinary diverse and rapidly evolving technofossils (Zalasiewicz et al. 2014) into which they are shaped. And, while some of these new geological constructions will currently only continue to be produced as long as humans persist—the urban strata and technofossils, for instance—in other ways, particularly in the restructuring of the biosphere, we have, in the most funda- mental way, changed the course of Earth history.

As Antonio Stoppani realised back in the late nineteenth century (1873), humans are changing not just the present, but also the future. The survivors of the current mass extinction event (like the climate event, in its early stages, but already palpable), and the myriad transplanted (and thriving) invasive species are the ancestors of the life of the future—and hence of the fossils that will be entombed within future strata too. Geologically, the Anthropocene is not just a passing phase—it is *already* a fundamental boundary that might (loosely, and involving a good deal of cross-disciplinary averaging) be assigned an epoch status (see the discussion of biosphere transformation in Williams et al. 2015). Once the climate exceeds Quaternary norms to put very many species lethally outside their comfort zones, and the mass extinction event unfolds to become the 'sixth' great such event, as is likely in the next few centuries (Barnosky et al. 2011) *even discounting the effects of climate change*, then the scale of global change becomes much more reflective of something like a period- or even era-scale boundary.

The nature of the boundary is worth considering. As has been widely noted, there are now many Anthropocenes out there, used for different purposes along different lines of logic in different disciplines. So, one has to draw back the Anthropocene perhaps not quite to its original definition (as a geological time unit, broadly proposed by the atmospheric chemist Paul Crutzen—and the lake biologist, Eugene Stoermer, who had independently invented the same term a little earlier—within an overall Earth systems science context) to the one that is now the subject of formal enquiry (as a stratigraphical time term that must function both as a unit of Earth history—i.e., a geochronological unit—and as a parallel time-defined material stratal unit—i.e., a chronostratigraphical unit [3]).

The question of the boundary has aroused a good deal of comment, not least as regards the protracted and progressive nature of significant human influence on the Earth, ranging from the beginnings of the extinctions of the terrestrial megafauna, starting as long as 50,000 years ago as the culturally modern humans sharpened their co-operative hunting skills, through the development and spread of agriculture beginning some ten thousand years ago, to the origin and spread of urbanization a little later. As farms spread and cities slowly grew, a time-transgressive, human-altered surface layer resulted, which has been termed the archaeosphere; it has been suggested that this complex, time-transgressive imprint of human influence might equate with the Anthropocene, as its most easily visible reflection (Edgeworth et al. 2015). This would be a parallel of archaeological time terms such as 'Palaeolithic', 'Bronze Age' and so on, which are of different ages in different regions, reflecting the cultural state of the local human populations (and would also in part parallel the suggestion of the 'Palaeoanthropocene' by Foley et al. 2013).

However, this would run counter to a peculiarity of geological time, which is that, at heart, it is simply time—albeit in very large amounts. A time boundary (whether geochronological or chronostratigraphical) is just an interface in time, of no duration whatsoever—it is less than an instant—between one interval of time (which may be millions of years long) and another. It is inherently synchronous within the domain across which it operates, which is that of the home planet. This 'pure' use of time intervals has been drilled into successive cohorts of geological students as one of what used to be called 'the holy trinity' of rocks, fossils, and time—which are tightly interrelated, but are separate, and *need* to be kept separate in analysis: broadly, one might say, to keep Earth scientists honest. For rocks can be wildly time-transgressive: think of a stratal unit of beach sand, slowly migrating across wide areas of a landscape as sea level rises over thousands or millions of years—the resultant rock unit will be of different ages in different places. Fossils, now, are often used as hugely effective *proxies* for time—they are still the default tool for dating sedimentary rocks. But they are not the *same* as time; it takes perceptible amounts of time for animal or plant species to evolve from some ancestor—and then yet further time to migrate across whatever part of the world they will eventually come to occupy. So keeping these concepts separate in geology is utterly indispensable—especially as new time proxies, such as chemical and magnetic properties of rocks, have appeared to join the 'holy trinity'.

The lengths taken by stratigraphers to preserve this separation in boundary definition can appear ludicrous, especially when time overall in geology is measured in millions of years. The end of the Cretaceous Period (and indeed of the whole Mesozoic Era that contains it), and the beginning of the Palaeogene Period (and of our current Cenozoic Era) has been placed at the very moment of impact of the asteroid that impacted on Mexico (because it was recognised that the iridium-rich meteoritic debris layer at the 'golden spike' global reference locality in Tunisia would have taken some hours, or days, to traverse the intervening distance and fall to the ground (Molina et al. 2006). The boundary between the Silurian and Devonian periods (Martinsson 1977) has been 'placed' in the middle of a 'turbidite' layer—effectively a turbulent submarine 'avalanche' deposit, which in total probably represents a sediment deposition event lasting less than an hour. An exaggerated precision? Perhaps—but there are times when such precision can be employed in geology. Volcanologists can track 'entrachrons' in pyroclastic flow deposits—successive stages in the evolution of these catastrophic and almost (but not quite) geologically 'instantaneous' deposits (Brown and Branney 2013), for instance.

That does not mean that, in normal practice, the carefully tabulated units of the Geological Time Scale can be followed so precisely across the world. The neat coloured units of this chart might suggest an equivalent neatness and order in geologically documented nature—but, usually, alas, it is not so. Take one of the more effective boundaries in the ancient rock record as an example: the boundary between the Ordovician and Silurian periods (or in 'time-rock' chronostratigraphic terms, the Ordovician and Silurian systems (see Melchin et al. 2012). This boundary postdates most of the main, tumultuous events that separated the Ordovician and Silurian worlds—a glaciation, enormous sea level changes, two large pulses of mass extinction, an ocean anoxic event (Zalasiewicz and Williams 2014)—to be placed at the appearance of a particular, distinctive fossil graptolite (a type of extinct marine plankton) species, the 'golden spike' being set where this has been documented in the shales of a steep and rather scrambly stream gully named Dob's Linn, in southern Scotland.

This fossil appearance seems to represent the rapid spread of this species across part of the oceanic realm—though whether 'rapid' means centuries, millennia or tens of millennia cannot yet be ascertained. In some parts of that formed oceanic realm, this species—it is suspected (but not proven) that it may have arrived substantially later—by some fraction of a million years—than in that part of the ocean that is now southern Scotland, and that the boundary (Kore'n and Melchin 2000) there must be 'guesstimated' using other fossil species as guides to time. Once outside the deep sea realm, in provinces that represent the shallow seas of those times, the task becomes yet harder, as the graptolites did not venture much into shallow water, and are rare or absent in these strata—here again, other fossils or other types of evidence need be used to try to constrain the boundary. In strata representing the land surface (lakes, rivers, and such) of those Ordovician-Silurian times, then there are no graptolites at all—and precious few fossils of any kind—and so locating the boundary precisely is currently effectively impossible, and locating it even very imprecisely is difficult. That simply represents current reality in stratigraphy. The kind of error bars involved are rarely quantified, but in these ancient rocks a 'precisely located' boundary in strata may have error bars of quite a few thousands of years, while the more conjecturally placed boundaries may be plus or minus some millions of years. Some stratal successions have age uncertainties exceeding a hundred million years (e.g., Kryza and Zalasiewicz 2008).

Such error bars in locating boundaries become smaller as the strata become younger, but even in fossiliferous strata of the current Quaternary Period, uncertainties can be many thousands of years, and correlation of the Holocene boundary 'golden spike' section for the Holocene (based on chemical changes in an ice core drilled out of Greenland) involves uncertainties—even to five other carefully chosen and closely studied 'associate' global reference sections (Walker et al. 2009) of up to a couple of centuries.

So, how does a potential Anthropocene boundary measure up to this imperfect reality? The 'measurability' or (in stratigraphical terms, 'correlation potential') of the boundary is here the foremost aspect of a geological unit that comes to a geologist's mind: thus, the question 'how well can it be defined and traced?'—may well come before 'how globally important is it?' and 'when was the first sign of influence of some major new factor in the Earth system?' And, in terms of the definition of a 'stratigraphical Anthropocene', we are dealing with change to the Earth system rather than a change in the extent to which we are recognizing human influence. This kind of definition is seen as a planet-centred, rather than human-centred, phenomenon. So, it is important that the planetary system is *recognizably* changing, and it just happens to be the activities of the human species that are currently the main perturbing force. The Anthropocene would remain just as important geologically, because of the scale of the planetary (and hence stratal) effects, if it had some other cause. Indeed, the concept would then probably be rather easier for humans to comprehend and to react to. Given that, it is important that it is optimally recognizable from the physical evidence. So far, the Anthropocene seems to be effectively distinct—especially if it is 'optimally' recognised as the stratal equivalent of the 'Great Acceleration' and all that followed.

The mid-twentieth century seems so far to be the best candidate for the boundary, not so much because of its historical importance, but because events around that time left traces that can be detected pretty well everywhere around the globe (Waters et al. 2016). The radionuclides from bomb blasts (Waters et al. 2015), the fly ash particles (Rose 2015) effectively a thin, worldwide—and supremely fossiliseable—dusting of fossilised smoke around the world, the plastic fragments on land and in the sea (Ivar do Sul and Costa 2014); the changes in carbon chemistry associated with fossil fuel burning, present in the tissues, bones and shells of all living things, and plethora of abundant new technofossils (those ball-point pens, for instance). From polar ice layers to tropical swamps, from beach sands to abyssal oozes there are detectable traces that, with decadal and in places even annual precision, detect such a boundary of pre-Anthropocene below and Anthropocene: as so defined, one must remember. These are human constructs, albeit ones that try to reflect stratal and geohistorical reality. 'The rocks don't lie' says Bryan Lovell, former President of the Geological Society and one who understands the human meaning of 'abstract' palaeoclimate studies. He is right, even if rocks do not always speak the easiest of languages. Such an Anthropocene has geological reality, and durability too; that does not necessarily mean that it will, or even *should* be formalised in the Geological Time Scale (that will depend just as much on the perceived usefulness of formalization, a knottier problem)—but it does mean that it is not just a mirage conjured from human overeagerness to see human influence on an ancient planet. More's the pity, perhaps.

The last few pages have, if nothing else, shown something of the stratigrapher's focus—some might say obsession—with details of definition and recognition; and with strata, of course. The wider Anthropocene, and its possible significance to human society and culture, or to significance as regards, say, the perceived relations between humanity and nature (e.g., Chakrabarty 2014; Latour 2015), or as a rallying call to environmental protection (or conversely as counsel of despair) does not loom large here. Indeed, these larger issues are often quite forgotten, as one wrestles with questions such as whether industrial fly ash particles can be consistently distinguished from smoke particles released by natural forest fires, or how long it takes plutonium particles to travel from the atmosphere after a bomb blast to be eventually incorporated into deep ocean muds (Waters et al. 2015). This approach may be blinkered, but also seems best placed to exploit the truthfulness of rocks.

The wider use of the Anthropocene is hence beyond the narrative of this essay, or the competence of the writer. But one of the wider inferences drawn seems at odds with standard patterns of geological thought. Thus: the suggestion that, if the deleterious changes associated with the Anthropocene—global warming, biosphere degradation and so on—are considered as arising from the collective actions of humans, then this hides the fact that some groups of humans (rich ones, in developed countries) drive the process more acutely than others (impoverished communities in developing countries).

This seems to rather oversimplify the logic—perhaps on the assumption that arguments should be oversimplified in geological analysis generally, because of the huge distances of time and space involved. Such an assumption, it seems to me, does not do justice to a geological appreciation of the relation between the complex reality of what happened in the past, and the generalizations that need to be made in making interpretations from the patchy evidence available on the ground.

For instance, one might say that incoming asteroids cause mass extinctions. Well, there are asteroids and asteroids. As example, the town of Nördlingen in Germany is sited in a ca. 14-million-year-old impact crater. It is a *large* crater—almost 25 kilometres across, and the impact would have been totally devastating to the region. Yet, it did not precipitate a mass extinction episode, and the impact is now placed comfortably inside an epoch (the Miocene) rather than providing a catastrophically generated boundary to it.

The end-Cretaceous asteroid impact does represent such a geological boundary. It was a larger body, that made a larger crater, true—but it also impacted upon different bedrock geology (limestones including sulphate deposits) that would have vapourised to produced environmentally damaging gases. And, it impacted at a time of monstrous, successive volcanic eruptions in the Deccan region of India, that likely were already affecting the fabric of the global biosphere (Qiu 2015). So, an interplay of these (and other) factors likely contributed to the scale of ecological collapse.

Even with these eruptions—and others of their kind that seem to have triggered other mass extinction events (at the 'Great Dying' of the Permian-Triassic boundary, for example)—it is not simply a case of volcanoes as blanket cause. Some volcanic eruptions are (much) bigger than others—and their spacing through time is a major factor in determining how quickly, for instance, greenhouse gas levels might rise, or how much recovery time might have been available between eruptions. The devil is truly in the detail (while any remaining angels are keeping a safe distance).

And so, in trying to understand the processes driving Anthropocene change, it is clear that one must understand the behaviour and effect of the human drivers. But—just as with the asteroids or volcanoes—this should not mean that the driving force should necessarily be ascribed to 'humanity' per se. It seems clear that there will be large differences in geological motive force (if one puts it this way) in scale and kind between different groups of humans categorised in different kinds of ways and with different levels of detail and perspective. With making comparative analyses would be both useful and fascinating, but the approach should be *at least* as subtle and nuanced with as one allows for volcanoes and asteroids. In reality, humans as agents of planetary change are far more complicated and less predictable than are these more ancient forces. Understanding the Anthropocene will not be a small task—particularly when one has the privilege (we should consider it in no other way, because we have no alternative option) of living through the infancy of this new and extraordinary phase of our planet's history.

NOTES

1. William Smith was that rare thing, an early-nineteenth-century pioneer of geology who was not 'of independent means', but who had to work for a living as a surveyor. Nevertheless, he is generally credited with inventing the disciplines of lithostratigraphy and biostratigraphy, and he single-handedly produced the world's first national geological map, that covered most of Great Britain. Done by horse and carriage and on foot, it remains an almost unbelievable feat.

2. Ford et al. (2014) discuss the geological practicalities of dealing with urban strata.

3. For an exploration of how these two parallel time-cataloguing systems are related today, see Zalasiewicz et al. (2013).

WORKS CITED

Barnosky, Anthony D., et al. 'Has the Earth's Sixth Mass Extinction Already Arrived?'. *Nature* 471 (March 2011): 51–57. Web. 10 December 2015.

Brown, Richard J. and Michael J. Branney. 'Internal Flow Variations and Diachronous Sedimentation within Extensive, Sustained, Density-Stratified Pyroclastic Density Currents Flowing Down Gentle Slopes, as Revealed by the Internal Architectures of Ignimbrites on Tenerife'. *Bulletin of Volcanology* 75.7 (2013): 727.

Chakrabarty, Dipesh. 'Conjoined Histories'. *Critical Inquiry* 41 (Autumn 2014): 1–23.

Collie, M. and J. Diemer, eds. *Murchison's Wanderings in Russia*. British Geological Survey Occasional Publication 2, 2004.

Edgeworth, Matt, Dan de B. Richter, Colin Waters, Peter Haff, Cath Neal, Simon James Price. 'Diachronous Beginnings of the Anthropocene: The Lower Bounding Surface of Anthropogenic Deposits'. *The Anthropocene Review*. 2.1 (April 2015): 33–58.

Foley, Stephen F., et al. 'The Palaeoanthropocene: The Beginnings of Anthropogenic Environmental Change'. *Anthropocene* 3 (2013): 83–88.

Ford, Jon R., Simon J. Price, Anthony C. Cooper, Colin N. Waters. 'An Assessment of Lithostratigraphy for Anthropogenic Deposits'. *Geological Society, London, Special Publications* 395 (2014): 55–89.

Fortey, Richard. *Life: A Natural History of the First Four Billion Years of Life on Earth*. 1997. New York: Vintage Books, 1999.

Haff, Peter. 'Technology as a Global Phenomenon: Implications for Human Well-being'. *Geological Society, London, Special Publications* 395 (2014): 301–309.

Hazen, Robert M., Dominic Papineau, Wouter Bleeker, Robert T. Downs, John M. Ferry, Timothy J. McCoy, Dimitri A. Sverjensky, Hexiong Yang. 'Mineral Evolution'. *American Mineralogist* 93 (2008): 1693–1720.

Ivar do Sul, Juliana and Monica F. Costa. 'The Present and Future of Microplastic Pollution in the Marine Environment'. *Environmental Pollution* 185 (2014): 352–364.

Kore'n, Tatjana N. and Michael J. Melchin. 'Lowermost Silurian Graptolites from the Kurama Range, Eastern Uzbekistan'. *Journal of Palaeontology* 74 (2000): 1093–1113.

Kryza, Ryszard and Jan Zalasiewicz. 'Records of Precambrian-Early Palaeozoic Volcanic and Sedimentary Processes in the Central European Variscides: A Review of SHRIMP Zircon Data from the Kaczawa Succession' (Sudetes, SW Poland). *Tectonophysics* 461 (2008): 60–71.

Latour, Bruno. *'Face à Gaïa'*. Les Empécheurs de Penser en Rond/La Découverte, Paris, 2015.

Martinsson, A., ed. *The Silurian-Devonian Boundary: Final Report of the Committee of the Siluro-Devonian Boundary within IUGS Commission on Stratigraphy and a State of the Art Report for Project Ecostratigraphy*. International Union of Geological Sciences, Series A.5 (1997): 347.

Melchin, Michael, Peter M. Sadler, Brad D. Cramer. 'The Silurian Period'. *A Geological Time Scale*. Eds. F. M. Gradstein, J. G. Ogg, M. Schmitz, G. Ogg. 2 Vols. (2012): 526–558.

Molina, Eustochio, et al. 'The Global Boundary Stratotype Section and Point for the Base of the Danian Stage (Paleocene, Paleogene, "Tertiary", Cenozoic) at El Kef, Tunisia: Original Definition and Revision'. *Episodes* 29.4 (2006): 263–273.

Qiu, Jane. 'Dinosaur Climate Probed'. *Science* 348 (2015): 1185.

Richter, D. de B. and S. A. Billings. ' "One Physical System": Tansley's Ecosystem as Earth's Critical Zone'. *New Phytologist*. Web. 15 June 2015.

Rose, Neil L. 'Spheroidal Carbonaceous Fly Ash Particles Provide a Globally Synchronous Stratigraphic Marker for the Anthropocene'. *Environmental Science and Technology* 49.7 (2015): 4155–4162.

Smith, Dinah M., Jan Zalasiewicz, Mark Williams, Ian Wilkinson, Martin Redding, Crane Begg, C. 'Holocene Drainage of the English Fenland: Roddons and Their

Environmental Significance'. *Proceedings of the Geologists' Association* 121 (2010): 256–269.

Smith, Dinah M., Jan Zalasiewicz, Mark Williams, Ian P. Wilkinson, James C. Scarborough, Mark Knight, Carl Sayer, Martin Redding, Steven G. Moreton. 'The Anatomy of a Fenland Roddon: Sedimentation and Environmental Change in a Lowland Holocene Tidal Creek Environment'. *Proceedings of the Yorkshire Geological Society* 59 (2012): 145–159.

Steffen, Will, Paul J. Crutzen, John R. McNeill. 'The Anthropocene: Are Humans Now Overwhelming the Great Forces of Nature?' *AMBIO: A Journal of the Human Environment* 36.8 (2007): 614–621.

Steffen, Will, Wendy Broadgate, Lisa Deutsch, Owen Gaffney, Cornelia Ludwig. 'The Trajectory of the Anthropocene: The Great Acceleration'. *The Anthropocene Review* 2.1 (April 2015): 81–98.

Stoppani, Antonio. *Corso di geologia*. Vol. 2. Eds. G. Bernardoni and G. Brigola. Milan, 1873.

Tzedakis, P. C., E. W. Wolff, L. C. Skinner, V. Brovkin, D. A. Hodell, J. F. McManus, D. Raynaud. 'Can We Predict the Duration of an Interglacial?' *Climate of the Past* 8.5 (September 2012): 1473–1485.

Walker, Mike, et al. 'Formal Definition and Dating of the GSSP (Global Stratotype Section and Point) for the Base of the Holocene Using the Greenland NGRIP Ice Core, and Selected Auxiliary Records'. *Journal of Quaternary Science* 24 (2009): 3–17.

Waters, Colin N., et al. 'Can Nuclear Weapons Fallout Mark the Beginning of the Anthropocene Epoch?' *Bulletin of Atomic Scientists* 71.3 (2015): 46–57.

Waters, C.N. et al. "The Anthropocene is functionally and stratigraphically distinct from the Holocene." *Science* 351. 6269 (January 2016): 137.

Williams, Mark, Jan Zalasiewicz, Peter K. Haff, Christian Schwägerl, Anthony D. Barnosky, A. D. Erle Ellis. 'The Anthropocene Biosphere'. *The Anthropocene Review*. Web. 10 September 2015.

Zalasiewicz, Jan, M. B. Cita, F. Hilgen, B. R. Pratt, A. Strasser, J. Thierry, H. Weissert. 'Chronostratigraphy and Geochronology: A Proposed Realignment'. *GSA Today* 23.3 (2013): 4–8.

Zalasiewicz, Jan, Ryszard Kryza, Mark Williams. 'The Mineral Signature of the Anthropocene in Its Deep-Time Context'. *Geological Society, London, Special Publications* 395 (2014): 109–117.

Zalasiewicz, Jan and Mark Williams. *The Goldilocks Planet: The 4 Billion Year History of Earth's Climate*. Oxford: Oxford University Press, 2013.

Zalasiewicz, Jan and Mark Williams. 'The Anthropocene: A Comparison with the Ordovician-Silurian Boundary'. *Rendiconti Lincei—Scienze Fisiche e Naturali* 25.1 (2014): 5–12.

Zalasiewicz, Jan, Mark Williams, Colin N. Waters. 'Can an Anthropocene Series Be Defined and Recognised?' *Geological Society, London, Special Publications* 395 (2014): 39–53.

Zalasiewicz, Jan, Mark Williams, Colin N. Waters, Anthony D. Barnosky, Peter Haff. 'The Technofossil Record of Humans'. *Anthropocene Review* 1 (2014): 34–43.

Chapter Seven

Worldview Remediation in the First Century of the New Millennium

J. Baird Callicott

MUSINGS ON THE TERM 'ANTHROPOCENE'

That I do not title my chapter for this collection of 'Worldview Remediation in the Anthropocene', but instead, for 'Anthropocene' substitute 'the First Century of the New Millennium' is not because I am oblivious to the subtitle of the volume. And it's not because I loathe the term 'Anthropocene'. I actually quite like the 'Anthropocene' neologism, but I think it should refer to the geological era that is ending rather than to the geological era that is beginning. Up to about now, for ten to twelve thousand years, an unusually stable and optimal (for a bipedal primate) climate regime has prevailed on Earth—and that made being 'on Earth' almost 'as it is in heaven', so to speak (Mackay et al. 2003). That Goldilocks climate fostered the development of settled agriculture. The development of settled agriculture fostered the development of cities. The development of cities fostered the development of civilization—art, music, letters, organised and institutionalised religion and government, law, politics, philosophy, science, sophisticated technologies. And all of this fostered a tremendous increase in the human population. I do not doubt that the penultimate expression of those sophisticated technologies has triggered global climate change nor that, with a new climate regime, the end of the Anthropocene (aka the Holocene) is in the offing. But what we are entering is the post-Anthropocene geological age, not the Anthropocene, which is just coming to an end.

Two visions of the fate of *Homo sapiens sapiens* in the post-Anthropocene are current.

According to the 'transhumanist' techno-optimistic vision, *Homo sapiens sapiens* evolves (in a Lamarckian manner) into *Homo sapiens cyborgiens* (Bostrom 2014). Nanotechnologies will be embedded in our brains and other organs; our genes will be redesigned to eliminate aging and maybe even death by natural causes; synthetic biology will compensate for the diminishment of Darwinian-evolved biodiversity after the sixth mass extinction has run its course. Humans will colonise and terraform Mars and eventually Earth-like planets throughout the galaxy.

According to the eco-apocalyptic vision, in a more energetic biosphere, the ocean will acidify and stagnate, sea levels will rise precipitously, cycles of flood and drought will intensify, crops will fail, diseases will proliferate; resource wars will ensue; nation states will devolve into failed states; the human population will crash; the remnants will be led by sociopathic warlords; and an irreversible Dark Age will descend upon the what's left of humanity (Lovelock 2006, 2009). To see that future first hand, go (if you dare) to Syria, Somalia, Mali, Libya.

The right name for neither of these futures is the 'Anthropocene'. In the former vision, *Homo sapiens sapiens* will have evolved into a new species; in which case, a term derived from ανθρωπος is hardly the fitting name of the era of its origin. And in the latter vision, while ανθρωποι will still be around, their populations will be reduced to scattered remnants and they will no longer be members of the dominant species on the planet. As are most other environmentalists, if I had to choose—not what I would prefer but what is the more likely future to come about—I am more inclined to share the eco-apocalyptic view. But, as for rectifying names, my personal sensibilities are beside the point. Either way—the techno-optimistic way or the eco-apocalyptic way—the right name is not the 'Anthropocene'.

I have no clue what the future will hold, but I doubt that either of these extreme visions of it will unfold. Hopefully human civilization and biodiversity will squeeze through the present bottleneck relatively intact and the favourable climate of the Anthropocene (or Holocene if you insist) will not exceed a threshold of positive feedback loops and ratchet into a post-Anthropocene climate as-it-is-in-Hell instead of as-it-is-in-Heaven (and as it has been since the Pleistocene). To vouchsafe a livable and pleasant future climate, one thing we need is what I have come to call 'worldview remediation'. That's just one thing among many others, but it's a fundamental thing and the only thing, as a philosopher, I am competent to address. So what this chapter is about is worldview remediation cast mainly in terms of the history of philosophy.

C. P. SNOW'S 'TWO-CULTURES' DISCONNECT

According to Aristotle in Book IV (Γ) of the *Metaphysics*, the philosophy of being as such—being *qua* being—is 'first philosophy'. By 'first', Aristotle did not mean that the philosophy of being as such was first in the order of time—although Heidegger seems to ignore the distinction—but rather first in the hierarchical order of thought. In the temporal sequence that Aristotle himself outlines in Book I (A) of the Metaphysics, the first philosophy that the Greeks pursued—beginning with Thales, according to Aristotle—was natural philosophy. Aristotle maps the progress of the natural philosophy of his predecessors onto his own scheme of causes. Thales and his fellow Milesians in the sixth century BCE were concerned with the material cause (positing water, air, and the like as the material 'substrate'). After Parmenides had problematised motion and change, fifth-century philosophers, such as Anaxagoras and Empedocles also concerned themselves with the moving or 'efficient' cause (Mind and Love and Hate, respectively)—the force or forces that move material things. Following the fifth-century Pythagoreans, Plato, in the fourth century, focused attention on the formal cause—the Numbers, according to Aristotle, who was certainly in a better position to know than we. (To understand this equation of Number and Form, we must remember that the ancient Greeks thought of number exclusively in geometrical terms— such 'numbers' as the several species of triangle, the circle, the several species of polyhedron, and the sphere.)

We call the ancient Greek natural philosophers the 'Presocratics'—but not just because they lived and worked before Socrates. Indeed many were contemporaries of Socrates. Rather, Socrates and his fellow moral philosophers—whom Plato, unfortunately as well as unfairly, denigrates as 'sophists'—expanded the scope of philosophy to include epistemology, ethics, and political theory as well as nature. The philosophers coming after Socrates, most notably Plato and Aristotle, were polymaths, taking up and synthesizing—each in his own way—both natural and moral philosophy, the philosophy of nature and the philosophy of things human.

The seamless union of natural and moral philosophy was not a peculiarity of ancient Greek philosophy. The early modern philosophers also united the two. Descartes—'the father of modern philosophy'—was a natural philosopher of the first water. He was better known among his contemporaries for his *Principles* than for his *Meditations*; and even today, outside philosophical circles, he is more celebrated for his analytic geometry, an enduring contribution to mathematics, than for his now-much-maligned contribution to moral philosophy—his rationalistic epistemology. In the eighteenth century, Kant, who is most celebrated today for his contributions to moral philosophy— especially for his epistemology and also for his ethics—was a celebrated cosmologist in his own time. In the nineteenth century, certainly Hegel attempted a synthesis (no pun intended) of natural and moral philosophy. But during the twentieth century almost all the self-styled philosophers who claim to have inherited the grand tradition of philosophy going all the way back to

Thales (if we can trust Aristotle's historical sketch in the *Metaphysics*), have almost totally neglected natural philosophy. To be sure, there is Whitehead and perhaps a few other twentieth-century natural philosophers, but they are the exceptions. In regard to the neglect of natural philosophy—as in regard to so many other of its peculiarities—twentieth-century philosophy is, in my opinion, an anomaly, indeed an aberration. The twentieth century is now over, way over. The signs of the times seem clear: One distinguishing characteristic of twenty-first-century philosophy will be a return to natural philosophy. Or, more precisely put, twenty-first-century philosophers will be more cognizant of the revolutionary natural philosophy latent in twentieth-century science and will use it to inform and reform moral philosophy. The philosophy of the future, I suggest, is NeoPresocratic.

So profound had become the disengagement from science not only of philosophy, but of literature and history, that, in the intellectual depths of the twentieth century, the knighted Cambridge physicist and successful novelist Charles Percy Snow (1962) identified two coexisting but mutually estranged cultures: that of cutting-edge science and that of the humanities. As the twentieth century recedes into the past and twentieth-century philosophy becomes a period in the history of philosophy, just how can we twenty-first-century philosophers reunite those two cultures and fuse them into one? The need to do so is political no less than intellectual. In American politics, at least, the epistemology of science is losing ground to the epistemology of religion. Political parties, especially those on the right—the Republican Party, the Tea Party—have 'beliefs' (ideologies) that are immune to logical criticism, intractable to contrary evidence, and remain firmly held in defiance of disastrous experience forthcoming from pursuing public policies based on those beliefs. I suggest that we philosophers and humanists generally can do our part to reintegrate science and its epistemology into the wider culture by expressing the new nature of Nature, as revealed by the sciences, in the grammar of the humanities. The putatively 'value-free' discourse of science—a mixture of mathematics, statistics, and technical terminology—is not readily or easily accessible. The discourse of the humanities—rich with imagery, metaphor, emotion, and honest moral judgement—resonates with a much wider audience.

THE NEGLECTED OPPORTUNITY FOR A RETURN TO NATURAL PHILOSOPHY IN THE SECOND SCIENTIFIC REVOLUTION

I suspect, however, that many if not most humanists believe that they will find little in science to fire the imagination, to stir the emotions, to stimulate our aesthetic sensibilities, and to touch our deepest moral sentiments. The world revealed by science is as dull as the language scientists use to characterise it—if the attitudes of my incoming philosophy graduate students are any indication of a prevailing humanistic alienation from a scientific worldview. Many appear to be seeking in philosophy a counter-scientific worldview— even an anti-scientific worldview—and seem disappointed when my entic- ingly titled course, 'Philosophy of Ecology', turns out actually to be about ecology, the science.

Science did, indeed, once represent a natural world that was imaginatively, emotionally, aesthetically, and morally unappealing, even repugnant to most non-scientists and especially to most humanists. Well, it was not altogether aesthetically unattractive, but its beauty was of a sterile mathematical kind, that only a logician could love. What did the late Harvard logician Willard Van Orman Quine (1953) once proclaim?—'a taste for desert landscapes'— something like that (4). The erstwhile Newtonian world was populated by inert, externally related bodies, moving along straight lines, subject to various forces that are communicated by impact—a fragmented, material, mechani- cal world, devoid of life, spirit, mind, and meaning. And what of the organic world emergent from the mechanical and ultimately reducible to it? It popped up as a happy accident of chemistry and evolved by the blind (ateological) forces that the ancient Greek philosophers called τυχη and αναγκη—'chance and necessity'. The ever-increasing complexity of the organic world is driven by the competitive interactions among its excessively fecund organisms. It is all a matter of 'survival of the fittest' and 'devil take the hindmost' in a liv- ing nature that is 'red in tooth and claw'. The whole organic world presents a disgusting spectacle—a violent, meaningless, pointless drama, like 'a tale told by an idiot; full of sound and fury; signifying nothing'.

Thus alienated by classical Newtonian and Darwinian science, most twentieth-century philosophers—of both the analytic and continental persuasions—narcissistically occupied their minds with narrowly circum- scribed, arcane, and abstract conceptual 'puzzles' or equally arcane explora- tions of their own states of consciousness. Thus they took little if any notice when a second scientific revolution occurred in the early twentieth century; and, even now, few take much if any interest in exploring and helping to artic- ulate the post-Newtonian worldview. Equally indifferent to the second scien- tific revolution, some other humanists repaired to their hermeneutical studies of the sacred texts, the great secular books, classical music, the old-master painters. Alternatively, yet others provided a playful analysis and celebra- tion of a contemporary literature, art, and music that ignores—or even rebels against—the supposedly sterile world depicted by scientists. That I mean no disrespect for hermeneutic studies is testified to by my personal love of Plato, especially, and the other ancient Greek philosophers, generally—a love that I continue to try to inspire in every new cohort of students that I teach at both the undergraduate and graduate levels. And while I am not personally engaged in the sophisticated study of contemporary high, low, and hybrid culture, I have the greatest respect for my colleagues who are—and I am delighted when I receive an invitation to their hip soirées and salons.

While the two cultures passed one another by in the twentieth century, like the proverbial ships in the night, the scientific worldview was indeed undergoing revolutionary change. At the turn of the twentieth century, space, time, and matter became anything but dull and unexciting. Our universe had become non-Euclidean, with space and time constituting one curved, warped four-dimensional continuum. The solid Democritean/Newtonian corpuscles, which had been located in Euclidean/Cartesian space, had become nanoscaled solar systems, spun out of the very fabric of non-Euclidean space, with only vaguely located, leaping electrons orbiting tightly bound nuclei that might lose mass and emit energy. Not only were energy and matter convertible, mind and energy matter were conversable—as scientific observation of quantum systems actualises one potential reality rather than another. Being is as being is interrogated and observed. At the opposite end of the spatio-temporal spectrum of scale, the unimaginably immense universe of stars and galaxies came to be understood as evolving and expanding, instead of, as formerly, in a static steady state. The universe is now understood to have originated in a dramatic Big Bang and to be riddled with mysterious and awesome Black Holes. A whole new holistic biology—ecology—took shape in the twentieth century. And in contemporary evolutionary biology—thanks in no small measure to Lynn Margulis—symbiosis is as fundamental a driver of organismic novelty as competition. And natural selection operates at multiple levels of biological organization, not just at the genetic level. And just as twentieth-century geneticists mapped the human genome, twenty-first-century microbiologists are mapping the human microbiome. And in the process they are revealing that we are not really individuals; we are, rather, superecosystems, just as ecosystems were characterised by twentieth-century ecologists as 'superorganisms'.

Despite the many popular science magazines, websites, television shows, zoos, aquariums, and other forms of publicity, what is going on in quantum physics, astrophysics, and ecology seems to be popularly underappreciated nor, certainly, does it seem to have rent the fabric of the prevailing metaphysic. Perhaps because the revolutionary worldview latent in contemporary science has gone unexplored and unexplained by humanists, it is not registering in the public zeitgeist. Now and again a scientist with a gift for accessible prose—a Carl Sagan, a Stephen Hawking, a Stephen J. Gould, a Brian Greene, a Jacques Cousteau, a Carl Safina—will popularise one or another domain of new scientific discovery. But articulating the newly enchanted *worldview* latent in science requires the synthesizing genius of philosophers and the capacity of poets to move the human heart. Yet philosophers have pretty much remained indifferent to the opportunity and poets unresponsive to the challenge.

HOW THE HUMANITIES RESPONDED TO THE FIRST SCIENTIFIC REVOLUTION

This is puzzling because the first scientific revolution—which we may regard as a revolution in natural philosophy—did produce a corresponding revolution in moral philosophy and in the fine arts. Why, in the seventeenth century, did Descartes entertain such extravagant doubts about the reliability of his senses, even about the very existence of his own body? Because up until Copernicus, a century before, all humankind had laboured under a colossal and nearly universal deception, fairly attributable to too trusting a reliance on our senses. We believed that the Earth upon which we stand lay immobile at the centre of the universe and that the sun and moon, planets and stars revolved around us. After all, that's how it looks and feels! If we could be so wrong about that, who knows what else we might be wrong about? The old empirical/inductive epistemology inherited ultimately from Aristotle had to be swept away at a stroke and replaced by a new rational/deductive one erected upon fresh and hypercritical foundations—or so Descartes believed. In the visual arts, linear perspective, which is but an application of projective geometry, created the life-like illusion of three-dimensional space, the space of Euclid, Galileo, Descartes, and Newton. New forms of literature, such as the novel, not accidentally or coincidentally emerged. The studied mathematical precision of the music that we now call classical constitutes, in effect, a new modern science of music. Even theology became rational and deistic.

The original scientific revolution, that of the sixteenth and seventeenth centuries, even more insidiously transformed ethics and politics. The free-standing, free-thinking human individual is, in effect, the social analogue of an atom. Formed from the alpha-privative, $\alpha\tau\alpha o\mu o\varsigma$ in Greek means 'indivisible'. We social atoms were conceived by Thomas Hobbes originally to live a life that was 'solitary [as well as] poor, nasty, brutish, and short' as we moved in a pre-social vacuum driven on our inertial courses impelled by two simple forces: desire and aversion. In the absence of a social contract to give law and order to their movements these social atoms were bound to collide in a mutually destructive war of each against all. After the original atomism of Democritus and the correlative ancient social contract theory of the sophists had been forgotten, and prior to the revival of atomism in the seventeenth century, to conceive of human existence in a pre-social condition would have been nearly impossible.

That's right, for better or worse, our vaunted social and political individualism—which seems so natural, a matter of fact not of thought—originated as a conceptual adaptation in the sphere of ethics and political philosophy of atomism in classical physics. That the same sequence of intellectual events occurred two millennia earlier proves my point. Can it be a mere coincidence that—during both the fifth century BCE and the seventeenth century CE—atomism in natural philosophy was soon followed, in moral philosophy, by social and political individualism and the social contract theory of the origin of law, society, and ethics? Just as the ontology of the physical world was reductively conceived to be an aggregation of externally related indivisibles, so the ontology of the social world was also reductively conceived to be but an aggregate of externally related individuals. But whatever the cause, individualistic social ontology took hold of the Western zeitgeist after the seventeenth century and has become the foundation for our human rights, especially our rights to life, limited liberty, and property. The price we pay, however, is a tragic unawareness of the robust ontology of both social and environmental wholes.

This unawareness of the robust ontology of social and environmental wholes is, incidentally, particularly costly today as we face problems, such as global climate change, that are of such unprecedented spatial and temporal scales that they cannot be effectively addressed by individual responses. When I speak to the public about the ethical challenge of climate change, I am invariably asked 'What can I do to address the problem?' The expectation is that I will recite a list of things that each of us, individually and voluntarily, can do to reduce our carbon emissions. I myself do most of those things: replace halogen light bulbs with light-emitting-diode bulbs; reside in a dense urban community and walk or bike practically everywhere I go; etc. But I live in Memphis, Tennessee—not Berkeley, California, Ashland, Oregon, or Boulder, Colorado—in the United States. And Memphis is a more representative microcosm of the United States than those precious centres of progressive sophistication. So I am painfully aware that my individual efforts to lessen the size and weight of my own personal carbon footprint are swamped by the recalcitrance of the overwhelming majority of my fellow citizens. Many of them have never heard of global climate change. Many of those who have prefer to believe that it is the function of a 'natural cycle' or an 'act of God', not that it is anthropogenic. Many others are convinced that global climate change is a hoax cooked up by self-righteous pinko environmentalists who can't stand to see common people enjoy their mechanised fun. And many of those who think that it's for real welcome it as a sign that the End Times are upon us, the horrors of which they will be spared by the

Rapture. It will not suffice, therefore, to simply encourage people individually and voluntarily to build green and drive hybrid. But what's worse is the implication that that's all we can do about it, that the ultimate responsibility for dampening the adverse effects of global climate change devolves to each of us as individuals. On the contrary, the only hope we have to temper global climate change is a collective social response in the form of policy, regulation, treaty, and law. What is required, in the words of Garrett Hardin's classic treatise, 'Tragedy of the Commons', is 'mutual coercion mutually agreed upon' (1968, 1247).

THE FAILURE OF THE HUMANITIES, ESPECIALLY PHILOSOPHY, VIGOROUSLY TO RESPOND TO THE SECOND SCIENTIFIC REVOLUTION

Please forgive this peevish digression. I've just been frustrated by the way discussion of the ethical aspect of anthropogenic global climate change has been limited to individual responsibility. I return now to the two-cultures theme of this essay. So, after the excitement of the Enlightenment, the fine arts and the humanities rebelled against the Newtonian worldview—for better or worse. The romantic counterculture in the humanities was openly antagonistic to the modern scientific worldview in both philosophy and the fine arts—albeit still colonised by the insidious atomic sense of self and aggregative sense of society. And while romanticism per se may have come and gone, indifference—if not antagonism—to the other culture, that of science, became entrenched in philosophy and the humanities generally and in the fine arts.

Perhaps for this reason, the response of the fine arts and humanities to the second scientific revolution, that of the twentieth century, has been anaemic. In the visual arts, Cubism is, arguably, an expression of non-Euclidean geometry, but it hardly conveys the geometry of Einsteinian space-time as perfectly and faithfully as linear perspective conveys the geometry of Euclidean-Galilean-Cartesian-Newtonian space. In music we have the aleatoric music of such composers and performers as John Cage, which beautifully reflects the indeterminacy and stochastic nature of the quantum world—but Cage and his few exponents remain marginalised and unpopular. Twelve-tone compositions, jazz, blues, folk, rock, pop, rap, and hip-hop all may be revolutionary—but in ways disconnected, so far as I can tell, from the second scientific revolution. In literature there have been some interesting experiments with what might be called the relativity genre, in which time is as fractured as Cubist space and characters have incommensurable perceptions of a common reality—James Joyce's *Ulysses*, Virginia Woolf's *Mrs. Dalloway*, and Vladimir Nabokov's *Pale Fire* come to mind—but it remains a genre for the rare genius and has not taken the literary arts by storm. The theory of relativity is best reflected in culture studies, a central dogma of which is that all cultural reference systems are equal and none is privileged. But the scientific worldview, even as it evolves and changes, is regarded in culture studies as illegitimately hegemonic and a prime target for deflation and deconstruction. What about science fiction? With a few exceptions, such as the novels of Isaac Asimov, Arthur C. Clarke, Robert Heinlein, and Kim Stanley Robinson, science fiction is no better informed by state-of-the art science than other genres of pulp fiction.

The reaction of twentieth-century philosophy to twentieth-century science was particularly unfortunate. Phenomenology, the dominant movement in continental philosophy, hubristically aspired to replace science as we know it—disparaged as 'naturalism' by phenomenologists—with something truer to the phenomena immediately given to our intentional consciousnesses. Science had become, in their view, a skein of abstractions, of theoretical entities, such as atoms, which we do not—indeed cannot—directly experience. And the social sciences, especially psychology, are alleged to falsely objectify the pure subjectivity of the transcendental ego, first discovered by Kant and subsequently explored by Husserl. The alternative 'science' that phenomenologists offer up is based on the assumption that we could 'bracket' the abstract concepts that obscure the pure phenomena and accurately and exhaustively describe the phenomena as they present themselves to consciousness in raw form. By the same token, we could reveal to ourselves the very essence of intentional consciousness itself. Such bracketing, of course, is impossible to do; and even if it could be done, the value of doing it is by no means obvious. All along, however, science as we know it—increasingly abstract and theoretical—continued to thrive and attract funding and prestige, while phenomenology remains an arcane and marginalised specialty in academic philosophy, exerting little influence in the larger intellectual community of academe.

By contrast, Anglo-American 'analytic' philosophy held up scientific knowledge as the epitome of positive truth. Anglo-American philosophy of science is largely dedicated to setting forth the methods and means by which such magisterial knowledge is obtained. Surely then the traditional concerns of philosophy—ontology, metaphysics, ethics—could themselves become domains of positive knowledge by imitating the rigorous epistemological methods and means of science. Accordingly, such fields of study were isolated and divided into their microscopic elemental parts and painstakingly argued to putatively certain conclusions—about which, however, little agreement is ever reached. This virtual worship of scientific epistemology—obeisance to the ways and means of positive knowledge—combined with an application of it to the special turf marked out as their own by analytic philosophers, rendered twentieth-century Anglo-American philosophy as isolated from the dynamic *substance* of twentieth-century science as was twentieth-century continental philosophy. Bertrand Russell, for example, a founding figure of twentieth-century analytic philosophy, retrogressively espoused 'logical atomism' and eschewed the notion of internal relations, which characterises the ontology of quantum field theory. Russell typifies, in a particularly spectacular fashion, the way in which twentieth-century Anglo-American analytic philosophy was completely blind and deaf to the holism implicit in the revolutionary theories of relativity and of quantum physics.

THE ONCE AND FUTURE STATUS OF PHILOSOPHY IN REGARD TO ALL INTELLECTUAL ENDEAVOURS

Simply but boldly stated, what I am suggesting is that philosophy reoccupy the place in the panoply of disciplines reserved for theology in the High Middle Ages as 'Queen of the Sciences'. Unfortunately, twentieth-century Anglo-American analytic philosophy exchanged that exalted office for something more like Handmaiden to the Sciences, while Continental philosophy—to continue the royal metaphor here running wild—abdicated the throne of Queen of the Sciences for some little Duchy in the intellectual Balkans. As scientific knowledge grows in volume, scientists themselves must ever more narrowly focus their research, exchanging breadth of knowledge for depth. Unless someone steps forward to synthesise, integrate, interpret, and extract meaning and morality out of all that specialised knowledge, we—scientists and humanists alike—shall remain bewildered and adrift in a world bursting at the seams with information and devoid of sense and direction. That's a heavy burden for us philosophers to shoulder. To ever more narrowly specialise ourselves in the ever more careful and detailed dissection of the relationship of 'sense data' to the 'external world', sentences to propositions, words to objects, supervenient properties to their base properties, Frege to Carnap, the early Wittgenstein to the late is much more comfortable and manageable.

Or is it? Poet and essayist Gary Snyder—who ought to know—thinks it is easier than one might imagine to synthesise, integrate, interpret, and extract meaning and morality from the raw material of the sciences. In a delightful essay titled, 'The Forest in the Library', he compares the academic information community to the biotic community of a forest. In the basements and windowless laboratories scattered across the campus, the data gatherers—the science graduate students and bench scientists—tediously work away at small scales, just like the detritus reducers on the forest floor and photosynthesisers in the understory. At the next trophic level 'the dissertations, technical reports, and papers of the primary workers are . . . gobbled up by senior researchers and condensed into conclusion and theory' (203).

> When asked, 'What is finally over the top of all the information chains?' one might reply that it must be the artists and writers, because they are among the most ruthless and efficient information predators. They are light and mobile, and can swoop across the tops of all the disciplines to make off with what they take to be the best parts, and convert them into novels, mythologies, dense and esoteric essays, visual or other arts, or poems (Snyder 1995, 203).

Settling into a comfortable academic sinecure, in any case, is not what attracted me to philosophy as a young humanist. I was inspired by the audacity of the Presocratics, such as Heraclitus, who tried to paint a picture of the whole universe in a series of enigmatic epigrams, or such as Empedocles, who tried to best Heraclitus in two grand didactic poems, one titled 'On Nature', the other 'Purifications'. For me, the opportunity to do natural and moral philosophy like the Presocratics—to paint in bold strokes with a broad brush—came with the advent of the environmental crisis. Nature was talking back. It was saying that the prevailing, still essentially Newtonian assumptions—about the nature of Nature, human nature, and the proper relationship between people and Nature—that were still informing industrial development, were flawed. The message came across loud and clear in the form of unbreathable air over our big cities, fouled and stinking rivers and seashores, coastal dead zones, disappearing flora and fauna, statistically anomalous outbreaks of cancer, the threat of silent springs. Just as Descartes did half a millennium before me, I felt we needed to rebuild again from the foundations and ask anew the oldest and most fundamental questions of philosophy: What is the nature of Nature? What is human nature? What is the proper relationship between people and Nature?

Other humanists also seized the opportunity afforded by the environmental crisis to try to transform their respective disciplines. The first to respond were a couple of historians. The signal year was 1967. Roderick Nash's *Wilderness and the American Mind* was published that year and so was Lynn White Jr's (in)famous essay, 'The Historical Roots of Our Ecologic Crisis'. Donald Worster, the former dean of environmental history, once remarked that what historians do is to spin good stories based on otherwise mute facts. Nash's classic represents much more than a history of wilderness. The story he tells became the canonical story of the American environmental movement. Nash identifies and delineates its founding figures: George Perkins Marsh, Henry David Thoreau, John Muir, and Aldo Leopold. In addition to these vernacular philosophers, he ranges comfortably over the natural sciences, literature, and the visual arts, discussing the contributions to an evolving environmental awareness of Alexander von Humboldt, Alexis de Tocqueville, James Fenimore Cooper, Thomas Cole, and George Catlin, to mention but a few.

In retrospect, Lynn White Jr's essay provided the mandate and set the agenda for a future environmental philosophy, which got underway in the 1970s. White was a historian of technology and made the obvious point that the then newly discovered environmental crisis was a serious side effect of 'modern' technology. What made modern technology modern was its heretofore unprecedented union with modern classical science. Ever since the Greeks and up until the eighteenth century, natural philosophy and eventually science was pursued only by leisured aristocrats who prided themselves on seeking knowledge of Nature for knowledge's sake and distained any practical application of their theories as beneath their social station. And technology was the concern of only the working classes to whom fell the burden of supporting the privileged intellectuals as well as themselves. Both science and an aggressive technological esprit are Western in provenance, argued White, and could be traced to the late Middle Ages when Europe was steeped in the Judeo-Christian worldview. Created in the image of God, man's mind might recapitulate that of the Creator as He created the world. That was the inspiration for scientific inquiry. And God commanded man to be fruitful, to multiply, to have dominion over the creation and to subdue it. That was the motivation for developing an aggressive technology. In short, White placed ultimate blame for the environmental crisis on Genesis 1:26–28. Of course, White's thesis is both jejune and cavalier. But obscured by his lurid and brassy text was a more general and plausible subtext: that what we do in relationship to Nature depends on what we think about Nature, about ourselves as human beings, and about our proper relationship to Nature; and, corollary to that, effectively to change what we do in relationship to Nature, we first have to change what we think about Nature, about ourselves as human beings, and about our relationship to Nature: worldview remediation.

HOW TO UNDERTAKE WORLDVIEW REMEDIATION

Exposing what we think about things and changing what we think about them is the work of philosophers—or at least it used to be and, hopefully, soon will be again. There are two moments to this process. The first is critical, the second creative. White himself had taken the first, critical initiative. He criticised the ideas about the man–nature relationship that we had inherited from our Judeo-Christian cultural roots. But those are not our only cultural roots. The Greco-Roman cultural roots run at least as deep and bequeathed to modern Western civilisation just as many environmentally noisome notions. Thus a few philosophers and intellectual historians, such as J. Donald Hughes (1975) and Carolyn Merchant (1980), began to reread Plato's otherworldly theory of forms and Aristotle's anthropocentric teleology, Bacon's coercive epistemology and Descartes' divisive dualism through the new lens of environmental crisis. They afford good examples of the way humanists can use their hermeneutical expertise in new, socially relevant, and exciting ways. I, for example, was able to use my knowledge of ancient Greek natural philosophy to call attention to the way physical atomism in natural philosophy was followed by social atomism and social contract theory in ancient Greek moral philosophy. As noted here already, after atomism was revived in the modern scientific worldview, it was followed once more by social atomism and social contract theory in modern moral philosophy. In doing so, my purpose is to provide much more than a nifty historical insight. I aim to reveal the contingency of our prevailing individualistic social ontology and sense of self, opening us up, hopefully, to possibilities for alternative social ontologies and senses of self latent in the ontologies of contemporary science: the ontology of the space-time continuum; the unified quantum fields; the integrated ecosystems (including our ecosystemic selves); and the self-regulating, superorganismic biosphere—which are more commensurate with the political and environmental problems we face as the twenty-first century unfolds.

The second, creative moment in the agenda for an environmental philosophy set by White is more difficult to pull off. How do we generate new ideas about the nature of Nature, human nature, and the proper relationship of people to Nature? We cannot just gin them up from scratch, just make them up out of the blue. Not even Thales, the very first philosopher in the Western tradition, operated in an intellectual vacuum. Two early approaches were (1) to look for an alternative worldview in non-Western intellectual traditions and (2) to scour the theological and philosophical canon of the West for alternative worldviews that had not found their way into the mainstream but had been washed into intellectual side channels. Here again, White showed the way. (1) He suggested, but ultimately rejected, adopting the Zen Buddhist worldview. That got what we now call comparative environmental philosophy started; and essays soon appeared that proposed that we adopt other strains of Buddhism (such as Hwa-yen), or Daoism, Hinduism, and other non-western worldviews. Huston Smith, for example, wrote a piece titled 'Tao Now: An Ecological Testament'. White himself thought that the West was unlikely to convert wholesale to a foreign worldview (2). So he concluded his essay by recommending that we in the West resurrect and mainstream the heretical and radical ideas of St. Francis of Assisi, according to which animals too had immortal souls and man was brother to the Earth and its many creatures. Following White in method, but looking to the secular Western canon, Arne Naess recommended reviving and mainstreaming the monistic philosophy of

Spinoza; Michael Zimmerman suggested we take Heidegger's advice to 'let beings be'; and so on.

(3) The approach that I took—and am here recommending to those of my fellow philosophers looking for a way to escape the twentieth-century analytic and continental culs de sac—is to espress the natural philosophical essence out of contemporary scientific theories. We in the West are no more likely to dust off and collectively adopt an idiosyncratic historical worldview, especially one that never made it into the Western mainstream in the first place, than we are to adopt a foreign worldview. Science is what is happening now in the West. Moreover, while it may have been Western in provenance— as White assumes, albeit that is certainly a questionable assumption—it is no longer Western in practice and pursuit. Science has international cachet and currency. And it is one of the few intellectual endeavours, if not the only one, that is culturally unaccented. While, for example, we can instantly tell the difference between Bollywood and Hollywood cinema, the string theory cogitated in Beijing is no more distinctly Chinese than that cogitated in Berkeley. (That being said, their liminal points of view may enable scientists from marginalised groups to see things missed or distorted by the scientific establishment. Did being a woman have anything to do with Lynn Margulis' endosymbiosic theory of evolution? Perhaps. Did being born into slavery have anything to do with George Washington Carver's scientific interest in peanuts? Most certainly.) Further, as already noted, science serves up some ideas with extremely exciting and congenial philosophical potential. Nor is abstracting a contemporary philosophical worldview from the sciences the exclusive province of philosophers. Theologians, most notably Thomas Berry (1992), have found ideas in contemporary cosmology that bespeak a human harmony with Nature. Scientists themselves who have a philosophical bent have also contributed to the work of worldview reconfiguration. Indeed many of the great architects of the second scientific revolution were well aware that they were the latest contributors to the Western tradition of natural philosophy. Albert Einstein, Werner Heisenberg, Niels Bohr, Erwin Schrödinger all reflected publicly on the new worldview emerging from the new physics. More recently, physicist Fritjof Capra (1975) has explored the general implications of quantum theory for a new more integrative and holistic ontology and physicist Brian Swimme has teamed with Thomas Berry (1992) to tell 'the universe story'.

My own past work dabbled a bit in the philosophical implications of relativity and quantum theory, but has concentrated more on evolutionary biology and ecology than on any of the other sciences. Following the lead of Aldo Leopold (1949), in the former I find three very useful things. First, from an evolutionary point of view, with all other species on our small planet, we are descended from a common ancestor—which would instil in us, if we took the trouble to think about it, Leopold believes, 'a sense of kinship with fellow-creatures; a wish to live and let live' (109). Second, we may derive a kind of neo-pagan spirituality from the theory of evolution, 'a sense', as Leopold put it, 'of wonder over the magnitude and duration of the biotic enterprise' (109). Third, Darwin provided a detailed account of the origin and evolution of ethics in *The Descent of Man*, which represents the best foundation, in my opinion, for contemporary environmental ethics. Darwin himself was no Social Darwinist. If not in *The Origin of Species* then certainly in *The Descent of Man*, Darwin's views are closer to those of Pëtr Kropotkin in *Mutual Aid* than to those of Herbert Spencer in *Progress: Its Law and Cause*. Darwin argued that ethics evolved to facilitate social organization and community. One of the most fundamental concepts in ecology is that of a biotic community. When this ecological concept of a biotic community is overlain on Darwin's analysis of the origin and evolution of ethics, an environmental ethic clearly takes shape. Just as all our memberships in various human communities—in families, municipalities, nation states, the global village—generate peculiar duties and obligations, so our memberships in various biotic communities also generate peculiar duties and obligations. Darwin's analysis of the origin and evolution of ethics involves 'group selection', an idea drummed out of evolutionary orthodoxy in the 1960s. The emergence of multi-level selection in twenty-first-century evolutionary biology serves to underwrite and vindicate Darwin's account.

WORLDVIEW REMEDIATION IN THE
HUMANITIES GENERALLY

Lynn White Jr's (in)famous essay also induced a dialectical response among Christian apologists. They responded less with a revival of Franciscan theology, as White himself had suggested, than with an alternative, theocentric/stewardship reading of the early chapters of Genesis to counter White's anthropocentric/despotism reading of the same texts. The Judeo-Christian stewardship environmental ethic is very potent: His creation belongs to God, not us humans; in declaring it to be 'good', God invested the creation with what environmental philosophers call 'intrinsic value'; and He turned it over to us humans, not to exploit and destroy, but to dress and keep. If Christianity could be greened in this fashion, what about the possibility of greening other religious traditions?

While Westerners are unlikely to convert en masse to a foreign worldview such as Japanese Zen Buddhism, perhaps those for whom such worldviews are not foreign, but are their own living traditions of faith, could also find in them an environmental ethic. We must remember that the environmental crisis, popularly recognised as such in the 1960s, was then understood to be global in scope, and so it remains, now more than ever. If adherents of Buddhism, Islam, Hinduism, etc., could also find a potent ecological ethic in their worldviews, a network of religiously grounded ecological ethics could be formed around the globe. I barely scratched the surface of this possibility in my book, *Earth's Insights* (*Pensées de la Terre* in French translation). But it was fully cultivated and brought to full flower by the great vision and the great work of Mary Evelyn Tucker and John Grim. They gathered leading representatives of the religions of the world in a series of conferences convened at the Harvard Center for the Study of World Religions in the last decade of the twentieth century and then published the fruits of those gatherings in a series of Harvard University Press books.

History, philosophy, theology, religious studies—all humanities disciplines—have taken an environmental turn and in so doing have bridged, to one degree or another, the gulf isolating them from the sciences. It is not accidental that we almost unconsciously link environmental history, environmental philosophy, and so on, with ecology, and thus with the sciences generally, by means of such labels as 'Deep Ecology', 'religion and ecology', 'eco-theology', 'ecological ethics', 'eco-health', and so on. We now even have 'ecological economics' (as distinct from 'environmental economics') that indeed most academic economists would prefer to think of as one among the humanities rather than as one among the social sciences. And we also now have (and have had for nearly three decades) 'ecocriticism' and 'ecofeminism'. As these fields are well represented in this volume I defer to authors more expert than I to characterise them.

CONCLUSION

Let me now bring this essay full circle and return it to the point at which it begins. According to Aristotle, as noted, metaphysics is first philosophy, but by that he meant that it was first in the hierarchical order of knowledge, not the first to be pursued. Aristotle himself is the first systematic historian of philosophy and informs us that the first philosophy, in order of occurrence, is physics, in the Greek sense of the word, περι φυσεως, concerning Nature—that is, natural philosophy. After ancient Greek natural philosophy was recovered during the Late Middle Ages and Renaissance it evolved thereafter into science proper. Natural philosophy got underway in the sixth century BCE and culminated with atomism in the mid-fifth century. While many of the natural philosophers had something to say about ethics and politics—some more than others—moral philosophy did not become a central preoccupation of philosophers until the time of Socrates and his contemporaries (the much maligned

'sophists') in the second half of the fifth century. Plato and Aristotle systematically integrated natural and moral philosophy, each in his own way, during the fourth century. Both were, however, adamantly opposed to ateleological atomic materialism (physical and social) and countered it with their own teleological natural and moral philosophies. This pattern of development—a change in natural philosophy followed by a change in moral philosophy—is repeated after the Renaissance. First comes a revolution in natural philosophy, which was started by Copernicus in the sixteenth century and completed by Newton in the seventeenth, followed by a revolution in moral philosophy, which was started by Hobbes in the seventeenth century and completed by Kant and Bentham in the eighteenth. In both instances we find some overlap, but also a lag-time of about a century between the thoroughgoing changes in natural philosophy and those in moral philosophy.

Why this sequence? In the first instance, the Greek gods were closely associated with the forms and forces of Nature. Zeus, for example, is a weather god. Alternative, naturalistic explanations of weather and other natural phenomena led to scepticism among sophisticated (pun intended) Greeks about the existence of the gods. But Zeus was also the institutor and enforcer of justice. So if there is no Zeus, why should we be just?—the overarching question of Aristophanes's *Clouds* and Plato's *Republic*. The first philosophical explanation of the origin and nature of justice (and ethics more generally) was, as already noted, the social contract theory, a variation on which theme played practically all the so-called sophists—including Thrasymachus in the first book of the *Republic*. And as I have also here repeatedly noted, the moral ontology of the social contract theory—egoistic, externally related individuals colliding in a perpetual state of war, each with all, in a social vacuum—mirrors the physical ontology of the atomists: externally related bits of indivisible matter violently colliding in a physical vacuum.

The sequence is only slightly more complicated in the second instance. The Christian worldview had become entangled with Aristotelian geocentric cosmology and dynamics, due in large part to the efforts of Thomas Aquinas in the thirteenth century. When the Earth was displaced from the centre of the universe by Copernicus; and then, as the sun became a star and the putatively infinite universe lost its centre altogether, not only had Aristotelian dynamics lost its reference point—a centre towards which earth moves and away from which fire moves and around which the ethereal heavenly bodies move—Christianity also lost its locations for heaven and hell. So again, religious scepticism ensued, which in turn led to moral scepticism—because God is the author and enforcer of the Ten Commandments and the lesser moral rules—and the need for a naturalistic theory of the origin and nature of ethics was again felt. And once more the same social contract theory, only slightly modified by Hobbes, filled the void. (Greek social contract theorists —such as Thrasymachus, if we are to believe Plato—thought that some were natu-rally stronger than others. And thus the strong, Plato notes with alarm, would be reluctant signatories of the social contract, because it would deprive them of their natural prey. Therefore, Hobbes insisted—despite clear differences in strength, intelligence, and other natural endowments—that all human social atoms were sufficiently equal that no one could win the war of each against all; and therefore all should be willing signatories of the social contract.)

Given this clear historical pattern, the scientific revolution of the twentieth century should be followed with some overlap, but also after a lag time of about a century, by a revolution in moral philosophy. Evidence that this is occurring has been detectable for somewhere between a quarter and a half-century in the environmental turn in various disciplines of the humanities reviewed here—environmental history, environmental philosophy, religion and ecology, ecotheology, ecological economics. Further, in the two histori-cal precedents, moral ontology mirrors natural ontology. And the ontology of the contemporary sciences appears to me to be more systemic, holistic, and internally related than that in the Newtonian sciences. This of course is highly debatable. While, for example, ecology in biology is all these things, molecular biology appears to be more and more reductive and materialis-tic. However, with the advent of a second moment of environmental-crisis awareness—increasing awareness of the crisis of global climate change—the science thrust to the forefront of attention is biogeochemistry, which reveals a Gaian Earth that is certainly systemic, holistic, internally related, and indeed self-organizing and self-regulating.

Finally, there is an even larger, more profound revolution afoot, the likes of which has occurred only once before in history, so we have a less reli-able basis of anticipating its philosophical ramifications. This is a revolution in communications and information technology. The first such revolution was the shift from orality to literacy. A few humanists—Walter Ong, Eric Havelock, Marshall McLuhan, David Abram—have given it serious study. They generally conclude that the invention of letters was accompanied by a profound shift in human consciousness—from a sense of community identity to personal identity and from mythic thought to abstract philosophical and scientific thought being the most salient. Why after all, did a Thales emerge in Greece, just when he did—neither earlier nor later—to be followed by a steady stream of natural philosophers and then moral philosophers? Because, answers Havelock (1986), the Greeks became literate; and, adds Abram (1996), the Greeks were the first to have a fully phonetic alphabet—in contrast to the Hebrew and Arabic abjads—enabling them perfectly and completely to supplant the oral word with the written word, in contrast to other emerging alphabetical writing techniques. We are presently in the midst of another revolution in communications and information technology, from literacy to Googality—I'm sorry, but I cannot think of a better name. If these scholars are right about the transformation of human consciousness effected by the transition from orality to literacy, then another transformation of human consciousness may be forthcoming as we leave the linear world of letters and the privacy and intimacy of the one-way conversations we have with books, for the simultaneity, interconnectedness, and interactivity of the cyber 'cloud'.

Comprehending, understanding, and making sense of all these things is what twenty-first-century philosophy and the other humanities should be all about—as I see it, as a philosopher; and indeed as I have been doing it, as a philosopher. But not only should philosophers and other humanists witness and testify to these changes, driven by science and communications and information technology, I believe that philosophers and humanists more generally are one of the main channels through which a new worldview and perhaps even a new modality of human consciousness might flow. Not only can we articulate and interpret the wonderful new natural world that the sciences are revealing, we can even steer consciousness change in positive and hopeful ways. In our collective cultural life, as in our individual personal lives, I believe in the power of optimism. A new collective worldview and perhaps even a new modality of human consciousness will come about—if it does come about—partly through an inexorable historical dialectic, which has a life of its own, and partly because we humanists have tried with our historiographies, philosophies, theologies, and other scholarly endeavours to put saddles and reins on current currents of thought and steer them in the best directions that we can make out for them to go. And, as I am sure you can now tell, this essay is also an exercise in such humanistic optimism.

Following reflections on 'first philosophy', in beginning this essay I suggest that the humanities forge a partnership with the sciences to create a new worldview. From all I have written here, one might suppose that the sciences need only go on, pretty much as they have, ignoring the humanities, and that the humanities should take the initiative to open themselves up to the wonders of the sciences. I seem to be suggesting that the humanities are a χωρα, receiving the ειδη of the sciences. But it's not much of a contemporary marriage if the memetic flow is all in one direction. Here I am primarily addressing my fellow humanists. Were I addressing scientists, I would remind them of the origins of science in natural philosophy and that the high-end scientists—'the noble monarchs of the academy forest', in Gary Snyder's idyll, 'who come out with some unified theory or perhaps a new paradigm' (203)—are still essentially natural philosophers, (as the architects of the second scientific revolution were keenly aware), only now they wear lab coats. I would point out the dynamic nature of science, rendering current 'truths' at best provisional. I would argue that facts are theory-laden and theories are value-laden. I would note the insidious ways in which science is embedded in society and not immune from influence by social biases, politics, economics, and funding sources (Latour 1979, 1987). Above all I would insist that claims to objectivity and value-free discourse are a pernicious and dangerous pretense. And finally, I would conclude that—for all these reasons and more—the sciences need to open themselves to the wonders of the humanities. But that is a topic for a whole 'nother essay.

WORKS CITED

Abram, David. *The Spell of the Sensuous: Perception and Language in a More Than Human World*. New York: Pantheon Books, 1996.

Berry, Thomas and Brian Swimme. *The Universe Story from the Primordial Flaring Forth to the Ecozoic Era: A Celebration of the Unfolding of the Cosmos*. San Francisco: HarperSanFrancisco, 1992.

Bostrom, Nick. *Superintelligence: Paths, Dangers, Strategies*. **New York**: Oxford University Press, 2014.

Capra, Fritjof. *The Tao of Physics: An Exploration of the Parallels between Modern Physics and Eastern Mysticism*. Berkeley: Shambala, 1975.

Hardin, Garrett. 'The Tragedy of the Commons'. *Science* 162 (1968): 1243–1248.

Havelock, Eric. *The Muse Learns to Write: Reflections on Orality and Literacy from Antiquity to the Present*. New Haven: Yale University Press, 1986.

Hughes, J. Donald. *Ecology in Ancient Civilizations*. Albuquerque: University of New Mexico Press, 1975.

Latour, Bruno. *Laboratory Life: The Social Construction of Scientific Facts*. Los Angeles: Sage, 1979.

Latour, Bruno. *How to Follow Scientists and Engineers through Society*. Cambridge: Harvard University Press, 1987.

Leopold, Aldo. *A Sand County Almanac and Sketches Here and There*. New York: Oxford University Press, 1949.

Lovelock, James. *The Revenge of Gaia: Earth's Climate in Crisis & the Fate of Humanity*. New York: Basic Books, 2006.

Lovelock, James. *The Vanishing Face of Gaia: A Final Warning*. New York: Basic Books, 2009.

Mackay, A. W., R. W. Battarbee, H. J. B. Birks, and F. Oldfield, eds. *Global Change in the Holocene*. London: Arnold, 2003.

Merchant, Carolyn. *The Death of Nature: Women, Ecology, and the Scientific Revolution*. San Francisco: Harper and Row, 1980.

Nash, Roderick. *Wilderness and the American Mind*. New Haven: Yale University Press, 1967.

Quine, Willard Van Orman. *From a Logical Point of View*. Cambridge: Harvard University Press, 1953.

J. Baird Callicott

Smith, Huston. 'Tao Now: An Ecological Testament'. *Earth Might Be Fair: Reflections of Ethics, Religion, and Ecology.* Ed. Ian Barbour. Englewood Cliffs: Prent-Hall, 1972. 62–81.

Snyder, Gary. 'The Forest in the Library'. *A Place in Space: Ethics, Aesthetics, and Watersheds.* Ed. Gary Snyder. New York: Counterpoint, 1995. 119–204.

Snow, C. P. *The Two Cultures and the Scientific Revolution.* London: Spectator, 1962.

White Jr, Lynn. 'The Historical Roots of Our Ecologic Crisis'. *Science* 155 (1967): 1203–1207.

Chapter Eight

We Have Never Been *Anthropos*

From Environmental Justice to Cosmopolitics

Joni Adamson

Alejandro González Iñárritu's 2006 film, *Babel*, moves its audience, almost dizzyingly, back and forth from set locations in the USA, Mexico, Japan, and Morocco. The film circulates around the story of a wealthy American couple, Richard and Susan Jones, played by Cate Blanchett and Brad Pitt, who are experiencing marital problems. In an attempt to repair their marriage, they travel from their elite neighbourhood in San Diego for a bus tour through Berber villages in Morocco, the North African nation that links the four seemingly separate stories in the film. In a secondary story, the Jones leave their Mexican nanny, Amelia, at home in San Diego to care for their six-year-old twins. When Richard and Susan fail to return home on time, Amalia crosses the US border for her son's wedding in Tiajuana, Mexico, taking the twins with her. A third story involves a wealthy businessman, Yasujiro Wataya, who travels from Tokyo, Japan, to Morocco to hunt big game. The final story involves two young brothers, Yussef and Ahmed, from an isolated indigenous Berber family living in the mountains of Morocco. The boys are given a high-powered rifle by their father, Abdullah, to protect their herd of goats from predatory jackals. Practicing with the rifle, the boys aim at rocks, cans, and a far-away tourist bus on the horizon. Later, the boys are shocked and disbelieving when they learn that one of their bullets hit the bus, critically wounding the American woman, Susan.

Like the citizens of ancient Babylon after the fall of the Tower of Babel, the bullet that hits Susan sends Iñárritu's characters into a 'babble' of confusion, where they must try to make sense of seemingly chaotic global-scale social, political, economic, media and environmental forces that have uneven effects on different groups of people in different nations and regions of the world. *Babel* clearly alludes to the Hebrew story of an enormous tower once built in Babylon, an ancient city in Mesopotamia sited between the Tigris and

155

Euphrates rivers. At the beginning of the story, all humankind speaks a single language and cooperates capably. In their growing hubris, however, they decide to build the tower so high that it will reach the heavens. They build the Tower not for worship and praise of their God, but for their own power and glory. God, seeing what His people are doing, decides to confuse their languages and scatter them across the earth. This story is often told as a thought experiment examining notions of cosmopolitanism in a world where modern nations are failing to communicate, cooperate, and make sense of each other.

Allusion to 'the fall' of the Tower of Babel links Iñárritu film both to the storied 'cradle of civilization' and to modern US-led wars in Iraq said to have fuelled extremism and acts of terrorism around the world. The film's interlinked plots play with contemporary notions of the United States, or any 'superpower', as a cosmopolitan centre of privilege, wealth and consumption. This links the film's themes to debates about power and privilege that have long been central to both American Studies (AS) and ecocriticism. In the last decade, both fields have circulated around keywords such as *anthropos*, nationalism, exceptionalism, cosmopolitanism, ethnic identity, multiculturalism, localism, and environmentalism (Adamson and Ruffin 2013, 1–17). In scenes set inside the tourist bus and in a Berber village, wealthy American Susan is shown to be constantly glancing nervously, through the tourist bus' windows at the 'multicultural' Arab- and Berber-speaking people. She visibly fears the possible risk she faces as an American travelling outside the borders of her nation. 'Why are we here?' she asks Richard. He replies, 'To be alone'. The paradoxical notion that Richard and Susan are escaping to Morocco, the exotic setting of *Casablanca*, an iconic World War II–era film, to be 'alone', gestures to familiar conceptions of exceptionalism in post–World War II American culture.[1] The film thus provides an opportunity to think about the exceptional American, or exceptional humans of any nationality, and offers the opportunity to engage, playfully, with ideas and books that have been influential in the environmental humanities, including Bruno Latour's *We Have Never Been Modern* and Donna Haraway's 'We Have Never Been Human' in *When Species Meet*.

As outlined above, *Babel* provides four imaginative plotlines or 'case studies' for an examination of AS, the interdisciplinary field out of which, many scholars agree, the earliest examples of 'literary environmentalisms', or ecocriticism, emerged in the early 1990s (Nixon 2011, 235). However, my purpose will be to examine a kind of 'babble', or confusion, in which the term 'American Studies' circulates in ecocritical field genealogies. Some of these intellectual histories argue that a 'boundedness' to US literatures in 1990s ecocriticism can be used to explain a 'belatedness' to the insights of the environmental justice movement, or that the 'turn to environmental justice' in the early 2000s led to an early overemphasis on 'environmental racism' (Buell 2005, 116–119; Heise 2008a, 386). Rob Nixon attributes the 'belatedness' to environmental justice in early literary environmentalisms to the fact that Ramachandra Guha's and Joan Martinez-Alier's work on 'environmentalisms of the poor' (1997, 2002) was widely disseminated through the social sciences and philosophy studies but largely absent from AS (Nixon 2011, 253–255).

Notions of 'belatedness' have also been used to propose intellectual histories of ecocriticism based on a 'wave paradigm' in which a predominantly national framework and persistent 'insular and/or exceptional vision' in AS shapes a 'first wave' of ecocriticism, while ecofeminism, postcolonial ecologies, queer ecologies, and environmental justice are categorised as secondary developments (Buell 2005, 17–28; DeLoughrey and Handley 2011, 20). In a 'second wave', the introduction of environmental justice analysis of US literatures set in communities that function 'in the particular social, racial, and ethnic structures of inequality' discourage early practitioners of ecocriticism from engaging 'any of the several approaches to transnationalism' and lead in a direction comparable to politicised 'multiculturalism' in AS (Heise 2008a, 386). In later publications, many of the scholars drawing these conclusions go on to conclude that the 'turn' to environmental justice has been a crucially important one for the development in the environmental humanities (Buell 2011, 96). Others affirm that developing notions of an 'eco-cosmopolitanism' or world citizenship are best understood in the context of environmental justice field work (Heise 2008b, 10, 159). Others, including Elizabeth DeLoughrey and George Handley (2011), Joni Adamson and Kimberly Ruffin (2013), Greta Gaard, Simon Estok, and Serpil Oppermann (2014), and Serpil Oppermann and Serenella Iovino (2014), suggest more satisfyingly complex notions of 'rhizomatic' entanglement among the intellectual genealogies of environmental justice, indigenous, postcolonial, ecofeminist, new material, and queer studies that prove these fields are *not* secondary to a first wave of Anglo-American–centric ecocriticism but have much older roots in philosophies and cultures that account not only for forms of environmentalism that have developed in the USA but among indigenous peoples and in the Caribbean, India, or Africa and in the ancient world (DeLoughrey and Handley 2011, 11, 15, 20).

Building on rhizomatic intellectual genealogies, I will examine the 'babble' of confusion around the term 'American Studies', a field that began forming in the 1920s, long before the emergence of ecocriticism in the 1990s. I will examine what environmental humanists gain through a more precise use of the terms 'American Studies' and 'environmental justice', and how the recuperation of AS legacies of public intellectualism, scholarship, and activism focused on transnational local and global ethnic communities contribute to the reconfiguration of intellectual histories of the environmental humanities.

I will show how 'rhizomatic histories' account much more precisely for cosmopolitical forms of environmentalism that have long been emerging in the
Global South, and that long predate the US environmental justice movement
that emerged in the 1980s. I will also examine how AS legacies point not
towards 'cosmopolitanism' but towards notions of 'a community of rights and
rights of community', understood as a complex allegory for relational ontologies that unravel generally accepted notions of politicized multiculturalism,
identity politics, and even 'human rights'.

THE USA: AMERICAN STUDIES, THE
COMMONS, AND THE COSMOPOLITAN

Babel suggests that Iñárritu, like Rob Nixon, is interested in both the collective story of humanity's impacts on the earth and more divergent and
'fractured' narratives about widening schisms between the rich and the poor
(Nixon 2014). Iñárritu also seems to be challenging American exceptionalism
and questioning idealised notions multiculturalism. Wealthy white Americans
Richard and Susan Jones have the means to travel by choice and the luxury
of hiring a low-wage immigrant as their live-in nanny. While they travel,
Mexican national Amalia remains in San Diego caring for their children.
Amalia's small home in Tijuana, on the Mexico side of the international
border, is very different than the Jones' upscale house appointed with every
modern convenience. In Morocco, this schism between rich and poor is even
more evident as Richard and Susan peer imperially out the windows of their
air-conditioned bus at local Muslim women wearing black robes and travelling on foot or ethnic Berbers wearing colourful loose clothing, some riding
camels. The indigenous Berbers, who play a crucial role in Iñárritu's film
have lived in North Africa since at least the seventh century BCE, putting up
stiff resistance to various invaders, including the Romans and later the Arabs.
Over time, Arabs came to dominate Moroccan cities, forcing the Berbers to
retreat to the mountain areas where they continued to speak their own language and resist assimilation into Arab culture and religion.

Richard's and Susan's imperialist gaze suggests that Iñárritu is critiquing
attitudes and characteristics that have come to be associated with American
nationalist objectives. While post-1945 AS historical and literary scholarship
clearly did exhibit nationalist objectives and questionable assumptions about
European and American 'discoverers' or immigrants becoming 'American'
as 'they moved from cities or urban areas to the unsettled "wilderness"', a
narrow focus on nationalism or exceptionalism in the field misses some of
the important social and environmental justice activist legacies that should
be recuperated in intellectual genealogies of the environmental humanities

(Adamson and Ruffin 2013, 6). Depending on the directions one traces, AS could be shown to exhibit a clear exceptionalist strain that influenced 'mononational' US-centric literary environmentalisms of the 1990s (Nixon 2011, 237–238) or a public intellectualism that helped lay the scholarly foundation for environmental justice studies (Nixon 2011, 251; Adamson and Ruffin 2013, 4–9). Evidence of both can be found in early AS scholarship.

By tracing the roots of environmental justice, what emerges is the work of founding AS scholars, including F. O. Matthiessen who wrote *American Renaissance* (1941), Leo Marx who wrote *The Machine in the Garden* (1964), and Aldo Leopold who wrote *A Sand County Almanac* (1968). Each was considered a public intellectual, literary critic, writer and teacher who worked to situate his practice in ways that, today, would fit into social justice and environmental frameworks. Matthiessen wrote about early American notions of the pastoral, but he also worked as an activist from the 1920s through the 1950s in support of teachers' unions, New Mexican miners, and longshoremen (Adamson and Ruffin 2013, 6). Aldo Leopold, who wrote *A Sand County Almanac*, a nonfiction scholarly and creative book considered foundational to both AS and ecocriticism, was not only a conservationist, but also helped to create the American Wilderness Society, which put into place a Committee on Foreign Relations, chaired by Leopold. The committee charged Leopold with overseeing the creation of a plan for world peace that recognised the slow violence and attritional lethality of nuclear weapons and other weapons of war (Nixon 2011, 251). Matthiessen, Leopold and Marx were well informed about the geopolitics and transnational perspectives of their day, so it is inaccurate to ascribe to all AS scholarship, or all environmental literary analysis focused on American subjects and authors, a narrow Cold War nationalism, white heteropatriarchy, or a single-minded drive to constitute institutional academic authority and power (Deloria 2013, xiv). This work and activism also confirms that the roots of environmental justice are not a secondary concern within early AS.

With its focus on both a privileged first world couple and indigenous peoples who have been driven out of the cities of Morocco to the mountains, *Babel* also suggests that Iñárritu is interested in 'cosmopolitanism', one of the most debated keywords in both AS and ecocriticism. Stopped in a local Berber village high in the mountains of Morocco for an 'authentic' ethnic meal, Richard and Susan sip from cans of Coca-Cola, and are given ice for their drinks. They embody idealised notions about cosmopolitans travelling the world in comfort and luxury. However, Susan worries about the possibility of contamination in her food and fastidiously wipes her hands with antibacterial lotion, indicating that she is not entirely sure that the world is safe for cosmopolitan elites. The cans of Coca-Cola represent the material realities of global capitalism, with their associated environmental consequences, including the movement of consumer goods, waste, toxins, disease, and pollution and thus introduce environmental concerns into the film.

In a special issue of the *Journal of Transnational American Studies* focused on the Anthropocene, Günter Lenz suggests that in AS, accelerating globalization 'in a multipolar world of unequal distribution of power and resources' has called upon scholars to reconsider the possibilities and pitfalls of 'cosmopolitanism' for justice and governance (Lenz 2011, 9). William Boelhower adds that in the face of these inequities, *anthropos* has become an ambivalent figure, possessed of an agency scaled up to embrace and endanger the entire planet as well as 'common humanity, common wealth, and common ground' (2011, 47). Boelhower's use of *anthropos*, the Greek word for 'the human', is linked to the 'Anthropocene', a neologism proposed by Paul Crutzen and Eugene Stoermer in a short essay describing a transition from the Holocene to a new 'Age of the Human' in which humans have become a geomorphic force powerful enough to change planetary processes (Crutzen and Stoermer 2000, 17–18). This transition began with the invention of the steam engine, they argue, an invention that enabled the extraction and exploitation of humans and nature on a grand scale.[2]

The planes and buses that facilitate the Jones' travel in Morocco point to the reasons many humanists find Crutzen and Stoermer's linkage of the invention of the steam engine to the start of the Anthropocene, and the term *anthropos* problematic. When employed unconsciously to mean 'aggregate *Anthropos*', or 'all humans', the word *anthropos* fails to account for unequal human agency or unequal human vulnerabilities (Di Chiro 2015b, 369). As Andreas Malm and Alf Hornborg argue, it is deeply paradoxical that the 'standard Anthropocene narrative' should be couched in terms 'so completely dominated by natural science' and its origins dated to the invention of a technology that benefitted specific nations and races while disadvantaging others (2014, 63). They argue that the causal origins of anthropogenic change were predicated not on the nature of an entire species—*anthropos*—or a kind of 'species-thinking', but on 'highly inequitable processes from the start' (63). As Crutzen and Stoermer propose it, the steam engine is 'referred to as the one artefact that unlocked the potentials of fossil energy' and thereby catapulted *anthropos* to full-spectrum dominance (Malm and Hornborg 2014, 63). However, steam technology, was not adopted by some natural-born deputies of the human species' but by a tiny minority in Britain, and this 'class of people comprised an infinitesimal fraction of the population of Homo sapiens in the early 19th century' (63–64). At no time did the species as a whole vote for a fossil fuel economy or exercise any shared authority over the destiny of Earth systems.

This helps to reveal that the Jones' cosmopolitan travel, facilitated by technology—the tour bus, hinges on a highly appealing and irrepressible point of view, often expressed conceptually through the figure of *anthropos* moving freely in a planetary 'commons'. At the same time, it illustrates the inequities hidden in discussions of cosmopolitanism as a universal or common good (Boelhower 2011, 47). As several AS scholars with deep knowledge of indigenous and ethnic minority groups, and the historical impacts of Western technologies on these groups (including Phillip Deloria, Rob Nixon, and Andrew Ross) have cogently explained, notions of a 'commons' circulate around a much-cited essay by American ecologist Garrett Hardin titled 'The Tragedy of the Commons' (1968). Once understood in pre-colonial Europe as a centrally located tract of land or resource used by a community as a whole, Hardin frames the 'commons' as a metaphoric pasture. Warning of the ecological dangers of human overpopulation, Hardin describes the future as an 'over-grazed pasture' and issues a warning about the damage that increasing numbers of humans (metaphorical herders, read: non-'American' peoples) will inflict on nations that must compete for valuable resources.

Like the story of the Tower of Babel, in Hardin's thought experiment, a 'pastoralist' represents 'aggregate *anthropos*', a universalism that obscures vital social facts about 'the commons'. The story strips 'commonage of its complex cultural histories so that it becomes a blank stage for predictable, biologically driven actions and outcomes' (Nixon 2012, 593). The story justifies racial dominance and the 'privatization through enclosure, dispassion, and resources capture' of 'the commons' deemed necessary for averting 'tragedy' in the nation (Nixon 2012, 593; Deloria 2013, xvi–xvii). One of Hardin's conclusions, writes Phillip Deloria, was that 'mutual coercion, mutually agreed upon' pointed 'to the larger structures of common property resource management' and from there, scaled up quickly 'from the local to the global' (Deloria 2013, xvi). A shift from local tradition to local law suggests a new category of the pastoralist or *anthropos*: the citizen. Concepts of 'citizen' are then employed to structure notions of coercion, consent and governance. Concepts such as 'national citizen' follow and in discussions of cosmopolitanism, the possibility of a 'global' or 'planetary' citizen comes into focus. In turn, discussion of 'planetary citizen' hides the exclusion of global indigenous perspectives antithetical to the 'common good' since indigenous peoples often oppose the enclosure of their lands and capture of their resources (Adamson 2014, 179–181). Also, since it is almost impossible to build a shared identity even on the strength of the concept of 'the nation', notions such as 'planetary citizen' threaten instantly to become metaphoric rather than possible (Deloria 2013, xvi, xvii).

The metaphor of the 'planetary citizen' is exactly the metaphor that Iñárritu exposes as impossible when Susan is critically wounded by a bullet that shatters the implied cosmopolitan safety of her tour bus and disrupts the hegemony of *anthropos*, or the essentialised categories of the 'human' and the 'nation'. As the Tower of Babel story suggests, after the fall, or in a crisis, there is a need not just for talk, or cosmopolitan literacy, but a need for action. Richard acts by reaching out to the American embassy for help, but learns that the USA has recently bombed Iraq, site of ancient Babylon. As a result, the USA has entered into obscure political agreements among Middle Eastern nations that prevent the US Air Force from flying directly over certain international airspaces in Morocco. Because help from the USA will be delayed, Richard is forced to face the reality that when humans and nations fail to communicate, cooperate, and make sense of each other, even seemingly infallible superpowers cannot avert all risk, and individuals, including cosmopolitans like Susan, may die.

This reality forces Richard to place his trust in his indigenous Berber tour guide, Anwar. Richard does not speak the local language and is not familiar with Berber culture. His endeavour to find medical help would fail without the help of Anwar. The other American and European tourists, waiting on the bus, fearing they might be the next targets of terrorist bullets, demand to leave. Susan and Richard remain behind with Anwar, who provides translation and help until a US medical helicopter finally arrives. Here, Iñárritu shows that humans have never been 'aggregate *anthropos*'. However, the alliance between Richard and Anwar seems to be simultaneously critiquing 'planetary citizenship' while gesturing towards what Donna Haraway has called 'a politics of articulation' (Haraway 1992, 304). As many AS scholars and early environmental justice ecocritics have argued, the lasting legacy of the environmental justice movement is its contributions to notions of a 'transformative' coalitional politics that articulate multiple cultural and socioenvironmental perspectives at once (Adamson 2001, 156–159). A politics of articulation asks questions such as, 'How might like and unlike actors partner to successfully transform social and environmental systems and make them more equitable and just?' 'Can 'aggregate *Anthropos*' act collectively as a species for the common good?' 'Can common well-being be imagined outside of global capital?'

For his help, Richard offers Anwar money, but Anwar refuses it. For Anwar, there is more value in thinking and acting outside of global capital and caring for something bigger any one human or human group. This rejection of money suggests the current rhetoric of the environmental justice movement today, which includes hundreds of thousands of activists and groups organised to advocate for 'intergenerational justice' (Di Chiro 2015a, 105). Notions of intergenerational justice have deep rhizomatic roots in AS scholarship and environmental justice activism, but also in a long history of indigenous uprisings and slave revolts that began after European expansionism and colonization began spreading in the fifteenth century (Adamson 2001, 47–62).

For over one hundred and fifty years, indigenous groups in North and South America, Africa and throughout the Pacific Islands, indigenous and ethnic minority groups have been organizing to resist racism by nations and global corporations and discrimination by elite factions of dominant ethnic groups and nations. These groups from around the world have been organizing politically both inside and outside local, regional, state, national and international courts and institutions such as the United Nations ('About UPFII'; Nixon 2011, 105; Adamson 2014, 179). Analysis of this organizational work demonstrates that contrary to the argument that early environmental justice criticism might have been overly focused on racism among US place-bound groups, AS and environmental literary scholars have long been confronting the 'conflation of racism and minority discrimination into a single oppression' (Comfort 2002, 230).

This work has long acknowledged diverse transnational indigenous groups and nations, ethnic minorities and the poor and traced their organization to formally oppose the increasing power and mobility of transnational corporations that—under cover of trade liberalization were gearing up to exploit the 'commons' through uneven economic deregulation (Adamson 2001, 31–50, 128–179; 2014, 178). Joining the discussion about this expanding 'politics of articulation', Bruno Latour has suggested that if there is ever going to be a world in which all beings, indigenous and nonindigenous, human and nonhuman, live peacefully, it will require not just increased (human) literacy or 'cosmopolitanism' but a 'cosmo*politics*' (Latour 2004, 453, 455). In the next section, then, I delve into the connections between environmental justice and the movement coming to be known as 'cosmopolitics'.

MEXICO: THE NATION, THE ETHNIC GROUP, AND INTERGENERATIONAL JUSTICE

At the beginning of *Babel*, Mexican nanny Amalia is depicted as highly capable and working for a better future for both herself and her own children. Although born into poverty in an underdeveloped country, she has been in the USA for 16 years, working illegally for Richard and Susan, in order to acquire a modest income that she sends home to her children who live just across the US-Mexico border on the outskirts of Tijuana. It is no accident that Iñárritu, who is a Mexican national himself, sets one of the plotlines of his film in this place. Amalia, and the money she sends home, gestures towards her care, thoughts, and actions on behalf of 'intergenerational justice' for both her own children and those of Richard and Susan. This concept has become one of the key goals and aims of the milestone documents, summits, and conferences of the environmental justice movement, produced between

1991 and 2012, when the outcome document of the Rio+2012 United Nations Conference on Sustainable Development, 'The Future We Want' confirmed a broad general agreement that global society should strive for a high quality of life and well-being that is 'equitably shared and sustainable' (Costanza et al. 2014, 284). [3]

Over the course of the last quarter-century, in both AS and ecocriticism, the US-Mexico border has often been associated with 'environmental justice', a phrase now used internationally to 'describe a global network of social movements fiercely critical of the disparities and depredations' caused by the unchecked expansion and neocolonial logic of modern nations (Di Chiro 2015a, 100). [4] Amalia is representative of the migrants who began moving north to the USA in a trickle in the 1960s, and then in a fierce flow by the 1990s when neoliberal economic policies and international lending agencies (International Monetary Fund and the World Bank) began disregarding collective rights of indigenous, ethnic and poor minorities who had once earned their livelihoods on communal farms. After passage of 1990s' free trade agreements, such as the North American Free Trade Agreement (NAFTA), Mexico began passing national legislative reforms that enclosed 'the commons', or once communal agricultural lands, for sale to multinational corporations (Adamson 2014, 178). In the decade and a half after the passage of NAFTA, six million farmers and peasants from Central and South America were forced into an 'unequal competition with massively subsidised American agribusiness' (Ross 2011, 186–187). This is the reason both the United Nations Declaration on the Rights of Indigenous Peoples, adopted in 2007, and the Universal Declaration on the Rights of Mother Earth and Climate Change (UDRME), adopted in 2010, include language that supports immigrants moving north because of 'the policies and practices of exclusionary states' (UDRME 2, Preamble).

Babel implies that Amalia is one of these immigrants who come North in search of a livelihood that will support her family. When her employers, Richard and Susan, do not return from their Moroccan vacation on time, and she cannot find alternative care for the Jones' children, she decides to take them across the border to the wedding of her son. After a wonderful time at the wedding, and on the way back to San Diego, US Border Patrol agents become suspicious because Amelia has passports for the two blonde children but no letter of consent for travel from their parents. In a series of dizzyingly confusing events that follow, Amalia is deported from the USA despite her years of service to Richard and Susan. Here, Iñárritu raises questions about who has access to 'the commons' and to common well-being in a fast globalizing world. Amalia represents the ways in which citizens of one nation are often deprived of well-being and economic justice when they travel or work in other nations, even if they have lived in that nation for many years.

Amalia's capture by the US Border Patrol and transformation from capable caretaker to disoriented 'illegal alien' represents the experiences of thousands of immigrants who are displaced by global trade agreements that simultaneously deprive them of civil and human rights and authorise their deportation, despite their contributions to the economy of the nation in which they work.

Amalia's story raises questions about citizenship rights and human rights in the context of destabilizing national frameworks and development schemes that are driving the displacement of ethnic and minority groups on an increasingly large scale. AS scholars taking transnational ethnic studies approaches have been particularly insistent about the importance of interrogating how 'definitions of legal citizenship, within a region or nation, can be wielded in exclusionary regimes to bar whole groups of people from access to the rights and privileges of citizens' (Adamson and Ruffin 2013, 3). As Lauren Berlant points out in a concise definition and history of citizenship, the 'historical conditions of legal and social belonging have been manipulated to serve the economic, racial and sexual power in the society's ruling blocs' (37–38). American Studies scholar Maria Josephina Saldaña-Portillo explains that in Central and South American contexts, since the 1960s, there has been growing recognition that neoliberalism would affect not only indigenous groups and the poor, but the working classes and disadvantaged minoritised groups making all 'citizens' vulnerable to the vagaries of the global market. In response, a number of important indigenous-led meetings, energised by alliance-building with academics, NGOs, and environmental groups, built a case for self-determination, self-representation, and capacity-building among both ethnic minority and indigenous groups in the Global South. The primary goal, writes Saldaña-Portillo, was not violence or a demand for cultural, 'ethnic' or indigenous rights, but for civil and human rights, and also, a place at the table where international social and environmental decisions that affect the poor, indigenous and ethnic minority groups are made (Saldaña-Portillo 2003, 12, 198).

We see why this advocacy for civil and human rights is important in *Babel* when Amalia is first detained and questioned by the US Border Patrol, in a scene that recalls current events linked to the mass migration of Syrian refugees to Europe. Like Amalia, they are escaping bleak economic conditions, displacement or war. This is the reason, writes Saldaña, AS scholars study the work of transnational organization for social, economic and environmental justice. This is also the reason indigenous and ethnic minority activists refuse to have their struggles reduced to ethnicity, race, or set of economic indicators. They are summoning not only indigenous peoples, but all 'citizens' of every nation to the process of ensuring the civil and human rights everywhere (Saldaña-Portillo 2003, 223, 230, 247, 255).

As we will see in the next section, this kind of coalition building represents a dramatic step forward and points to the reasons why delegates to the World

Conference on the Rights of Mother Earth and Climate Change, are insisting on civil rights for every individual within the nation as they also call for a shift in the world's attention from 'living better' to 'living well' by which they mean supporting a society based on social, economic and environmental justice 'which sees life as its purpose' ('Universal' Art. 2).

JAPAN: SHIFTING ATTENTION FROM
CONSUMERISM TO LIFE AND WELL-BEING

Yasujiro Wataya's story, set in both Tokyo, Japan, and the high, rugged mountains of Morocco, raises questions about what 'living well' instead of 'better' in 'society based on social and environmental justice, which sees life as its purpose' might look like ('Universal' Art. 2). While nations such as Japan once constructed their citizens' identity around principles such as shared geographies, languages, and cultures, Wataya's story illustrates the challenges to intergenerational justice and biodiversity being driven by global capital and wealth disparities. Like the Jones' story, rapid air transport transforms the planet into a commons or playground for cosmopolitan hunters to shoot rare animals. *Babel* shows how the purchasing power of the wealthy now takes precedence over shared nationality or the common well-being of human or nonhuman inhabitants of other nations. Iñárritu offers viewers spectacular shots of the Moroccan mountains where the Barbary lion was hunted to extinction by the 1920s and where the Barbary leopard is today on the endangered species list. [5] The film implies that Yasujiro has come to Morocco to obtain a Barbary leopard that he will add to his collection of exotic, trophy animals mounted on the walls in his Tokyo apartment.

Both Yasujiro's carbon footprint and his participation in the deaths of rare animals raise questions about 'who speaks' for the Barbary leopard and who speaks for the commons? These questions, raised by the cosmopolitical movement, encourage humans to advocate for the 'recovery, revalidation, and strengthening of indigenous cosmovisions' that have been 'thousands of years in the making' (UDRME). 'Cosmovisions' are defined as cosmological understandings, scientific literacies, and lived modern experiences of the worlds' indigenous peoples. This movement began taking visible shape after 2010, when thirty thousand delegates from 100 nations convened the World People's Conference on the Rights of Mother Earth and Climate Change, in Cochabamba, Bolivia. The outcome document of this conference, UDRME, proclaims that 'violations against our soils, air, forests, rivers, lakes, biodiversity, and the cosmos are assaults against us'. 'Us' is emphasised to mean all living 'beings' including humans and 'sentient entities' such as significant mountains and animals such as the Barbary lion (UDRME Art. 2).

UDRME is a 'politics of articulation' that parallels the work of many environmental humanists, who, since the turn of the new century, have taken a turn towards interspecies ontologies, and urge their fellow humanists to think in terms of what it might mean to support intergenerational justice for 'multispecies aggregates' or the most vulnerable humans and nonhumans rather than a homogenous '*anthropos* aggregate' (Haraway 2015, 160). Brazilian anthropologist Eduardo Viveiros de Castro has explained that the 'cosmovisions' upon which the UDRME is based gather up philosophies that summon 'natural entities' as allies into the organization of a 'livable' political 'cosmos'. Viveiros de Castro describes this complex philosophy as 'perspectival multinaturalism'. According to this philosophy, humans, animals and spirits participate in the same world, although with different sensory apparati constituting not just multicultural (human) worlds implying a unity of nature and a multiplicity of cultures, but multinatural worlds implying corporeal diversity and its attendant diversity of perspectives (Viveiros de Castro 2004, 467). What is unprecedented about the goals and aims of the cosmopolitical movement, writes anthropologist Marisol De la Cadena, with reference to understandings found throughout the Andean and the Amazonian regions of South America, is that it is calling not just human groups into deliberations but advocating for 'rights' for 'ecosystems, natural communities, species and all other natural entities' to 'continue and maintain their existence' (UDRME Art. 4.1). De la Cadena defines 'natural entities' as culture–nature 'beings' that might include mountains and rivers considered sentient, or dolphins, fungi, or microbes, considered critical to biospheric and ecosystemic functioning (De la Cadena 2010, 334, 341–342). These beings are being marshalled into politics to help create national and international legal frameworks that 'express an epistemic alternative to scientific paradigms (ecological and economic)' that supposedly stand in the way of 'the common good (productive efficiency, economic growth, even sustainable development)' of a supposedly 'homogenous humanity benefiting from an also homogenous nature' (De la Cadena 2010, 349–350).

Yasujiro's story raises many urgent questions about what constitutes 'the common good'. He lives in Japan, the nation in which two nuclear bombs were detonated at the end of World War II, leaving radioactive fallout to move through succeeding generations of the young. The film does not link fallout or toxins to his family, but his daughter, Chieko, is a deaf/mute teenager, and thus his daughter is dealing with a genetic disorder. She is also grieving the death of her mother who recently committed suicide. Although he is a big game hunter, Yasujiro is concerned for Chieko's well-being. This shows him to be, like most humans, complicated. He is not pure monster. He is a man concerned about his own family, and a person who demonstrates common concern for other humans. After his hunt, and in gratitude to his extremely poor Berber guide, for example, he leaves his rifle as a gift. But despite his wealth, his daughter is isolated and in a seemingly literal allusion to the fall of the Tower of Babel, cannot 'speak' or hear the common language of her community. Like her mother did, Chieko lives in a luxury high-rise apartment, filled with dead trophy animals on the walls and pictures of her father, standing over the bodies of exotic animals. There is no discussion in the film about why the mother committed suicide. The film does not answer any questions about whether or not the images of death everywhere in the apartment contributed to the mother's decision to end her life or to Cheiko's isolation. However, as Chieko stands on the balcony of her apartment, looking down at the street below, unsure about her future, the film suggests Iñárritu's interest in whether or not *anthropos* can redefine 'well-being' and 'common good' outside of global consumer culture and see, instead, 'life as its purpose' (UDRME Art. 2).

MOROCCO: CAN *ANTHROPOS* ACT COLLECTIVELY FOR THE COMMON GOOD?

In the film, the Berber relationship to the local and global commons is depicted in scenes in which the Yuseff and Ahmed are charged with protecting the family's goats from jackals, as the milk, skins, and meat of these animals are the family's only means of economic livelihood. This helps to illustrate why indigenous groups are articulating a politics of relationships between themselves and the animals and other nonhumans with which they live. In other words, for them, the 'commons' is not just a place, it is their 'partner in a communal struggle to provide a livelihood' (Adamson 2001, 157). The Berber family lives in extreme poverty and the rifle they purchase from their neighbour, who guided the Japanese businessman on his big game hunt, becomes a symbol of the ways wealthy First World nationals exploit the 'commons' of other groups and nations through activities such as big-game hunting, tourism, mining, logging, and oil extraction while poverty draws the economically disadvantaged into participation in the exploitation of their own environments. Environmental justice activists have long advocated a more inclusive view of human interaction with the biogeophysical world as a 'home' where discussions of 'nature' would go beyond notions of 'wilderness' to address everyday lives lived in places written off as 'sacrifice zones' by local and federal governments, including border regions and communities inhabited by indigenous peoples (Adamson 2001, 42–58, 66–73).

After Yuseff and Ahmed test their aim on a tourist bus, Susan is critically injured, and Richard Jones enters into a protracted attempt to reach the American embassy for help. The global media begins reporting that the bullet that wounded Susan must have come from the weapon of a terrorist. Journalists descend on Marrakesh and represent events in ways that throw the lives of the Berber family into a dizzying vortex that tears them away from their specific histories, cultures, and lands in Morocco. Continuous new reports being broadcasting on televisions around the world reduce events to the word 'terrorists' and thus associate Yuseff and Ahmed and their family with multiple, shadowy extremist groups with which they have never had contact.

When the rifle is traced to Japan, and then to back to Yuseff and Ahmed's father, the family is hunted down like the jackals the gun was purchased to keep away. Cornered and attacked in rugged mountain terrain, Yussef and Ahmed return fire and both are wounded trying to protect their father. They are taken into custody by Moroccan authorities under pressure from the USA to apprehend the terrorists responsible for harming US citizens. Iñárritu's focus on the Berbers draws his audience's attention to concepts of 'rights' and citizenship for the world's poor and displaced, which as discussed above, has long been a focus in AS. Like other indigenous peoples in the world, Berber resistance to colonization has put them at odds with the dominant settler nation. In this case, an Arab elite, has denied them access to education, economic security, and basic rights to citizenship. We see this social inequity depicted in the film by the sharp contrasts in dress, language, and living conditions between the Berber shepherds and the Arab-speaking Moroccan authorities.

On the other hand, scenes with Richard and Anwar working to save Susan's life depict diverse humans—indigenous and non-indigenous—working for 'life' as a common goal. These scenes suggest the ways that diverse groups are forging transnational links with one another and with academics, civil society, NGOs, and international groups to forge new conceptions of 'rights' that go beyond notions that focus on rights only for *anthropos*. As Daniel Fischlin and Martha Nandorfy emphasise in *The Concise Guide to Global Human Rights* and in *The Community of Rights: The Rights of Community*, in a globalizing and corporatizing world, the notions of 'rights', 'citizenship', and 'community' are being pushed beyond problematic notions of identification, symmetry, totality, and unity employed to justify hegemonic and totalitarian actions, by both state and corporations, in the name of community. International cosmopolitical alliances are also pushing the notion of 'rights' and 'citizenship' beyond the confines of 'the human'. Babel suggests the ways that nations, groups and individuals might contribute, or fail to contribute, to dialogue and action that limits or expands opportunities to build a 'community of rights' and 'rights of community' for Susan, Amalia, the Barbary leopard, Chieko, Yuseff and Ahmed, inside and outside the nation, that works for both their livelihoods and well-being.

A FUTURE WE WANT

What do we gain by understanding the deeper, rhizomatic roots of AS, and where they may overlap with early Anglo-American literary environmental-isms or ecocriticism? How do more accurate intellectual genealogies for these entangled but also different fields offer more satisfying and complete understandings of the roots of the environmental humanities? Iñárritu offers imaginative case studies that provide thought experiments for thinking about keywords and relationships between fields. *Babel* illustrates how individuals and groups who are part of nations and who are also planetary citizens may or may not have access to a 'community of rights' or 'rights of community'. The film provides opportunities to discuss how individuals and groups might work to organise and enact policies, laws, and community practices that ensure not 'wealth' but well-being in a multinatural world where 'life' is the goal. The environmental justice movement, now expanding into a 'politics of articulation' based on cosmovisions that are thousands of years in the making, calls upon all of 'Us' to work collectively and in all our cultural and biodiver-sity for a livable 'future we want'.

NOTES

1. *Casablanca*, the iconic film starring Ingrid Bergman and Humphrey Bogart, was shot in Hollywood. However, so many other iconic films have been shot in Morocco, including *Babel* that these films have a Wikipedia page. See online at https://en.wikipedia.org/wiki/Category:Films_shot_in_Morocco

2. 'Anthropocene' has still not gained full approval among the scientific com-munity deliberating it, but it has quickly become a keyword in the environmental humanities when it is used as a metaconcept to think about the social and environ-mental implications or rhetorical possibilities of employing an 'Anthropocene story' or 'Anthropocene discourses' (Zalasiewicz et al. 2015, 14–16; Nixon 2014).

3. 'The Future We Want—Outcome Document' was signed by all UN member states and calls for more social equity–focused definitions of 'sustainable develop-ment'. See online at https://sustainabledevelopment.un.org/futurewewant.html

4. The Environmental Justice movement is often traced to 1991, when over 300 community leaders from the United States, Canada, Central and South America, and the Marshall Islands convened the First National People of Color Environmental Leadership Summit in Washington, DC. For more details, see DiChiro (2015, 101–105).

5. See 'Examining the Extinction of the Barbary Lion and Its Implications for Field Conservation' online at http://www.ncbi.nlm.nih.gov/pmc/articles/PMC3616087/

WORKS CITED

'About UNPFII and Brief History of Indigenous Peoples and the International System'. The United Nations Permanent Forum on Indigenous Issues. http://www. un.org/esa/socdev/unpfii/en/history.html. Accessed August 17. 2009. Web.

Adamson, Joni. *American Indian Literature, Environmental Justice, and Ecocriticism: The Middle Place*. Tucson: Univeristy of Arizona Press, 2001.

Adamson, Joni. 'Cosmovisions: Environmental Justice, Transnational American Studies and Indigenous Literature'. *The Oxford Handbook of Ecocriticism*. Ed. Greg Garrard. Oxford: Oxford University Press, 2014. 172–187.

Adamson, Joni and Kimberly N. Ruffin 'Introduction', *American Studies, Ecocriticism and Citizenship: Thinking and Acting in the Local and Global Commons*. Eds Joni Adamson and Kimberly N. Ruffi n. New York, US and Oxford, UK: Routledge, 2013. 1–17. Print.

Adamson, Joni and Kimberly N. Ruffin. 'Introduction'. *American Studies, Ecocriticism, and Ecology: Thinking and Acting in the Local and Global Commons*. Eds. Joni Adamson and Kimberly N. Ruffin. New York: Routledge, 2013. 1–17.

Babel. Perf. Brad Pitt, Cate Blanchett. *Dir. Alejandro González Iñárritu*. Paramount Vantage, 2006.

Berlant, Lauren. 'Citizenship'. *Keywords for American Cultural Studies*. Eds. Bruce Burgettand and Glenn Hendler. New York: New York University Press, 2007. 37–42.

Boelhower, William. 'Side-by-Side with You: The Common as Foundational Figure'. *Journal of Transnational American Studies* 3.1 (2011): 47–53.

Buell, Lawrence. *The Future of Environmental Criticism: Environmental Crisis and Literary Imagination*. Malden: Blackwell, 2005.

Buell, Lawrence. 'Some Emerging Thoughts on Ecocriticism'. *Qui Parle* 19.2 (Spring/Summer 2011): 87–115.

Comfort, Susan. 'Struggle in Ogoniland: Ken Saro-Wiwa and the Cultural Politics of Environmental Justice'. *The Environmental Justice Reader*. Eds. Joni Adamson, Mei Mei Evans, Rachel Stein. Tucson: Univeristy of Arizona Press, 2002. 229–246.

Costanza, Robert, *et al.* 'Time to Leave GDP Behind'. *Nature* 505 (2014): 283–285.

Crutzen, Paul J. and Eugene F. Stoermer. 'The Anthropocene'. *Global Change Newsletter* 41 (2000): 17–18.

DeLoughrey, Elizabeth and George Handley, eds. *Postcolonial Ecologies: Literatures of the Environment*. Oxford: Oxford University Press, 2011.

De la Cadena, Marisol. 'Indigenous Cosmopolitics in the Andes: Conceptual Reflections beyond "Politics"'. *Cultural Anthropology* 25.2 (2010): 334–370.

Deloria, Phillip. 'Foreword'. *American Studies, Ecocriticism, and Ecology: Thinking and Acting in the Local and Global Commons*. Eds. Joni Adamson and Kimberly N. Ruffin. New York: Routledge, 2013. xiii–xviii.

Di Chiro, Giovanna. 'Environmental Justice'. *Keywords for Environmental Studies*. Ed. Joni Adamson, William A. Gleason, David N. Pellow. New York: New York University Press, 2015a. 100–105.

Di Chiro, Giovanna. 'Environmental Justice and the Anthropocene Meme'. *Oxford Handbook on Environmental Political Theory.* Eds. Teena Gabrielson, Cheryl Hall, John M. Meyer, David Schlosberg. New York: Oxford University Press, 2015b. 362–382.

Fischlin, Daniel and Martha Nandorfy. *The Community of Rights: The Rights of Community.* New Delhi: Oxford University Press/Black Rose Books, 2012.

'The Future We Want—Outcome Document'. 2015. Sustainable Development Knowledge Platform. United Nations Department of Development and Social Affairs. Web. 12 December 2015.

Gaard, Greta, Simon C. Estok, Serpil Oppermann, eds. *International Perspectives in Feminist Ecocriticism,* New York: Routledge, 2014.

Guha, Ramachandra. *Environmentalism: A Global History.* New York: Longman, 2000.

Guha, Ramachandra and Joan Martinez-Alier. 1997. *Varieties of Environmentalism: Essays North and South.* London: Earthscan.

Hardin, Garrett. "The Tragedy of the Commons." *Science* 162.3859 (1968): 1243–1248. Print.

Heise, Ursula K. 'Ecocriticism and the Transnational Turn in American Studies'. *American Literary History* 20.1–2 (Spring/Summer 2008a): 381–404.

Heise, Ursula K. *Sense of Place and Sense of Planet: The Environmental Imagination of the Global.* New York: Oxford University Press. 2008b.

Haraway, Donna J. 'Anthropocene, Capitalocene, Plantationocene, Chthulucene: Making Kin'. *Environmental Humanities* 6 (2015): 159–165.

Haraway, Donna J. 'The Promises of Monsters: A Regenerative Politics for Inappropriate/d Others'. *Cultural Studies.* Eds. Laurence Grossberg, Cory Nelson, Paula Teichler. New York: Routledge, 1992. 295–337.

Iovino, Serenella and Serpil Oppermann, eds. *Material Ecocriticism.* Bloomington: Indiana University Press, 2014.

Latour, Bruno. 'Whose Cosmos, Which Cosmopolitics? Comments on the Peace Terms of Ulrich Beck'. *Common Knowledge* 10.3 (2004): 450–462.

Lenz, Günter H. 'Redefinition of Citizenship and Revisions of Cosmopolitanisms— Challenges of Transnational Perspectives'. *Journal of Transnational American Studies* 3.1 (2011): 4–17.

Leopold, Aldo. *A Sand County Almanac and Sketches Here and There.* Oxford, UK: Oxford University Press, 1968. Print.

Malm, Andreas and Alf Hornborg. 'The Geology of Mankind? A Critique of the Anthropocene Narrative'. *The Anthropocene Review* 1.1 (January 2014): 62–69.

Martinez-Alier, Joan. *The Environmentalism of the Poor: A Study of the Ecological Conflicts and Valuation.* Cheltenham: Edward Elgar Press, 2003.

Martinez-Alier, Joan. 2002. *The Environmentalism of the Poor. A Study of Ecological Conflicts and Valuation.* Cheltenham: Edward Elgar.

Marx, Leo. *The Machine in the Garden: Technology and the Pastoral Ideal in America.* London, and New York: Oxford University Press, 1964. Print.

Matthiessen, F. O. *American Renaissance: Art and Expression in the Age of Emerson and Whitman.* London: Oxford University Press, 1941. Print.

Nixon, Rob. *Slow Violence and the Environmentalism of the Poor*. Cambridge: Harvard University Press, 2011.

Nixon, Rob. 'Neoliberalism, Genre, and "The Tragedy of the Commons"'. *Publications of the Modern Language Association of America* 127.3 (May 2012): 593–599.

Nixon, Rob. 'The Anthropocene: The Promise and Pitfalls of an Epochal Idea'. *Edge Effects*. 6 November 2014. Web. 12 December 2015.

Ross, Andrew. *Bird on Fire: Lessons from the World's Lease Sustainable City*. Oxford: Oxford University Press, 2011.

Saldaña-Portillo, María Josephina. *The Revolutionary Imagination in the Americas and the Age of Development*. Durham: Duke University Press, 2003.

Universal Declaration on the Rights of Mother Earth and Climate Change. *World People's Conference on Climate Change and the Rights of Mother Earth*. 22 April 2010. Web. 17 September 2010.

'United Nations Declaration on the Rights of Indigenous Peoples'. *The United Nations Permanent Forum on Indigenous Issues*. Adopted by the United Nations General Assembly in 2007. Web. 11 August 2009.

Viveiros de Castro, Eduardo Batalha. 'Exchanging Perspectives: The Transformation of Objects into Subjects in Amerindian Ontologies Castro'. *Common Knowledge* 10.3 (2004): 463–484.

Zalasiewicz, Jan, Mark Williams, Colin N. Waters. 'Anthropocene'. *Keywords for Environmental Studies*. Eds. Joni Adamson, William A. Gleason, David N. Pellow. New York: New York University Press, 2015. 14–16.

Chapter Nine

Resources (Un)Ltd

Of Planets, Mining, and Biogeochemical Togetherness

Filippo Bertoni

PROLOGUE

The coarse and dusty, windswept terrain suddenly sinks in a deep and broad crater layered with red ironstone. The outcrops that emerge from the walls of the crater are bustling with activity: a number of wagons, machinery, and men are busy drilling, blasting, hauling and moving the rocks, and extracting pyrites. Perched on a 3-foot-6-inch railway in the bottom of the pit sits a massive Bucyrus 3.5-cubic-yard steam shovel. The steel behemoth has already been steamed up and its drivers are starting to operate the swivel to crowd the bucket with rocks. A team of eight men has been moving ahead of the new machine recently imported from Wisconsin. They are armed with long compressed air drills and dynamite, and blast the boulders, reducing them in smaller fragments. The steam hissing, the smokestack belching, the bucket and the tracks clanking, the husky voices of Spanish miners shouting, the drills rattling and the explosives blasting in the distance, the Bucyrus begins to haul tons of broken slate into massive wagons, as its trackmen are attending to the rails. Removing the overburden, the machine allows the workers to extract the lode's minerals, which will be washed, crushed, leached, cemented, reduced, smelted; its copper extracted to feed the burgeoning electrical industry; its sulfur, sulfuric acid, superphosphates, and other minerals vitalizing a young chemical industry.

This is Corta Atalaya, on its way to become the largest open pit mine in the old continent. Reaching deep in the entrails of the planet and exposing the minerals of the Iberian Pyrite Belt, it lays bare one of the richest copper deposits for the Rio Tinto Company Ltd to extract and sell. The Bucyrus working the newly excavated site is the same model as those that are incessantly moving the soils of Panama to dig Roosevelt's canal. It is early 1908, the dawn of a new century,

175

a modern century. Progress is making its way through mountains and valleys, digging canals, amassing dirt, extracting minerals, laying cables and railways, spreading fertilizers, and blasting the bowels of the Earth open: changing the world. Nature is made into resources that can then circulate, be processed, transformed, accumulated, commodified and sold more easily. The combination of extraction, the streamlined mechanization of production and transformation, the global reach of commodity chains, the workings of capital, with the commensurability offered by a view of nature as resource is at the heart of the Great Acceleration of the late nineteenth and early twentieth centuries. And of its current and future transformations and declinations.

The vast mass of Earth orbits in the darkness of space. It rotates slowly on its axis, and as the sun begins to dawn on the planet's surface we start to recognise its features. 'What will tomorrow look like? Our world is at its limits. And yet, we all want more. And why not? Why shouldn't the future be better than today?' As the voiceover continues, clips of natural and industrial activities on Earth appear on screen. 'But where will it come from? Simple': the camera suddenly zooms past Earth, floating through the solar system and focusing on an asteroid belt, as the voiceover continues: 'our tiny planet sits in a vast sea of resources, including millions of asteroids bathed in the sun's free energy twenty-four hours a day. The same rocks that could fall from our sky also contain everything we could ever need; both out there and down here. It is time someone seize the opportunity'. The asteroids are swept away as the large logo of the company rolls in, noisily carved on the screen: DSI, 'deep space industries'.[1]

In the twenty-first century, technoscientific dreams of spacefaring, colonizing, and terraforming take consistency in a growing commercial and entrepreneurial set of firms, practices, markets, products, and services, to explore outer space as a way out of the limits of Terran resources. A number of companies like Deep Space Industries are investing in developing the infrastructures needed to mine asteroids. This is not science fiction: the possibilities opened by the space race fuelled by Cold War imaginaries have indeed opened space to entrepreneurial offshoots of the contemporary corporate world. *Planetary Resources*, one of the largest firms in this new market, makes the rationale behind this effort very clear: offering the possibility to refuel and restock after exiting our planet's gravity well allows a much cheaper and simpler avenue for space travel. To achieve that, the goal is to mine asteroids for water and precious minerals. Water would provide the hydrogen and oxygen used as fuel for spacecrafts, and the rare metals could be used for in situ, 3D-printed, automatised apparatuses, on top of their potentially exorbitant market values on Earth.

The logic guiding these projects is phrased clearly in DSI's promotional video: resources are limited, but 'we all want more'. It is the same understanding of nature as a pool of limited but commensurable and account-able resources to be extracted, processed, transformed, accumulated, shipped, sold and used that fuelled the machinery of the Rio Tinto Company Ltd. Having exploited and exhausted Earth's nature as resources, this commensu-rability now reaches beyond the atmosphere of our planet. The same logic at work in digging Corta Atalaya a century ago now pushes other firms to reach for the stars (or, better, the asteroids).

Imagining nature as a collection of resources related through arithmeti-cal operations and made commensurable through accounting and balancing is common today. And a similar logic was at work in the making of mod-ernization during the nineteenth and twentieth centuries. This long history, its relatively simple and intuitive character, and its widespread use make commensurability practically ubiquitous and leave it mostly unchallenged. In fact, this way of thinking about the world is so naturalised that it seems ineludible: even those wary of the problems with modern and exploitative politics of nature struggle to find a vernacular that can move past the koine of resources, their limits, and the balancing act of accounting for their inputs and outputs. This becomes clear as soon as we think about the success of notions like 'ecosystem services' or practices like 'carbon trading'. In fact, the whole conceptual apparatus behind the idea of sustainability—designed to patch up the holes made by modernization—depends on the same calcula-bility and commensurability that animates the logic of resources. Considered from this position, the very notion of the *planetary* and its workings—which grounds the Anthropocene in geological strata, atmospheric dynamics, and vital interconnections across the biosphere—relies on the same repertoire of the world as a set of resources in arithmetic balance that motivates mining in Corta Atalaya and outer space. This notion of resources and their accountabil-ity, then, not only affects the way companies work, or the shapes that global neoliberal corporations take. It also informs the way the planet is imagined, and with it many other aspects of current forms of life and life forms on Earth and beyond.

As this commensurability pervades our planet, the possibilities it opens bring other planets, asteroids, moons, comets, and celestial bodies closer to the reach of human extractive industries. The story of escaping the bound of limited resources told by companies like Deep Space Industries suggests that this logic of resources is an incremental one. And this idea of growing precision, knowledge, accuracy, and technical possibilities synchronises well with a vision of scientific progress. But what happens if we revisit episodes in this account of commensurability and resources without the grand narra-tive of progress to guide us? What if, instead, we focus on the details that do not quite fit? Are all resources just the same, can they really be exchanged and accumulated so easily? How do their conversions work in practice? Does the arithmetic of resources just add up everywhere in the same way? Moving between Rio Tinto and the extraplanetary offshoots of resources that grow from there, this text begins to highlight some gaps in this logic of commensurability and to excavate some alternatives to deal with naturecultures that exceed the accounting of resources.

But *how* to tell stories that will not easily fit together in the ways we are accustomed to? Feminist technoscience scholars Donna Haraway and Karen Barad suggested a method of inquiry, a technique for writing and reading, a genre of storytelling, an ethics, and a politics (yes, all those at once!) that is an inspiration for the attempt I make here. They both mobilise the figure of *diffraction* as a move away from the idea that reflexivity can be the solution to the problem of representation. This is a move that does not solve representation in its own impossibility; one that does not renounce its responsibility for saying something, and for what that telling does, for the worlds it conjures. Instead, diffraction embraces the situated, modest interventions that it makes possible, and uses them towards bringing about different worlds, 'to make a difference in the world, to cast our lot for some ways of life and not others' (Haraway 1997, 36) in Haraway's words.

Here, then, diffraction becomes an ethico-political genre for writing, thinking about, and interfering with the world, in a committed, situated, and open-ended way. Diffracting the stories of the Iberian Pyrite Belt and its extraterrestrial reflections, and the histories of earth, planetary, and life sciences that craft and reshape the commensurability of resources, allows for different stories to surface.

PART I—PYRITES AND RESOURCES

The mining in Corta Atalaya joined the ranks of the Great Acceleration since the second half of the nineteenth century in shaping the world in which we live today. Resources and their extraction, accumulation, and circulation are crucial to the historiography focusing on this time and help understanding what followed. As natural and social scientists, historians, humanists and artists turn their attention to this period in search for answers to the challenges and concerns posed by the Anthropocene, the reach of a view of nature as resources takes another dimension. Global nutrient cycles, isotopic signatures, world trade, receding ice caps, wading mineral deposits, all come to matter and are made to account for present and anticipated changes through a similar idea of commensurability. Extractive industries like the one eviscerating the mountains around Corta Atalaya have an immediately evident import in these stories: still today the area is a lunar landscape, scarred by open pits, tracks, causeways, dams, heaps, holes and disseminated with the rusting skeletons and fractures of past operations. Looking closer at this landscape and the histories and practices that sculpted it, though, the idea of resources and their seamless movement and extraction literally hits the rocks.

Hugh Matheson, first chairman of the Rio Tinto Company Ltd, starts gaining experience in trade and in the pragmatics of the global financial market as this begins to take on a more homogeneous structure through modernity and imperialism. He makes his fortune with trades in China—especially opium—and becomes attracted to the concern in Riotinto by the fortune of Tharsis, another mining venture in the same region that had been taken over some years before by a British company and had encountered enormous success since then. As the occasion presents itself to purchase the mining rights for a bargain from the just declared and already troubled First Spanish Republic, Matheson brings together the capital needed, forms the company, and carries the first instalment of the payment to Madrid, riding with it on a train to protect it from the many warring factions opposing the government.

Still, the area needs large infrastructural transformations if it is to reward the company and its shareholders with the anticipated profit. Aside from building a costly and challenging infrastructure, from railways, to mining shafts and open pits, from dams, to roads, and even to entire villages, the company has to find the best ways to extract the precious minerals the founders are after, to treat them at large, efficient, and cost-effective scales, and then to sell them at advantageous prices. In the kind of financial trade Matheson is versed in, resources are commensurable, and their value and importance can be counted, in British pounds. And if infrastructure costs can also be entered in the logs and books of the company and reported to the shareholders, the actual extraction of the minerals is proving to be more refractory than the accounting of the newly established company expected.

To obtain copper and sulfur, lots of work is required: the overburden has to be removed by blasting and drilling, and carried away, while the ores are to be excavated and transported to a number of processing facilities—most of them still to be constructed—where they can be classified and separated according to their grade, grinded down in determinate sizes, and then sent on to different sites where they go through further extraction processes. At its inception, the Rio Tinto Company Ltd focuses on the extraction and sale of crude pyrites, which are crucial raw materials for chemical industries and require minimum processing. These minerals are sold mostly in lumps known as *tal cual* that each customer crushes in his own plant, mostly in the United Kingdom. It is the sulfur in the pyrite—together with the copper—that makes the ore valuable as a source of iron sulfate, sulfuric acid and sulfur dioxide used in the production of textile dye fixatives, inks, antioxidants, reducing agents, and a number of other new commercial chemical products.

But pyrite does not come out of the mine in easy lumps: the elements are often in various combinations and form different ores. To extract these diverse minerals, a number of techniques are used. The major pathway for extraction since the beginning of operations is called artificial cementation. In this process, lower grade ores are amassed in heaps called *teleras* and 'roasted' in the open-air, letting the sulfur escape as sulfur dioxide smokes. The calcines this operation leaves behind are then 'washed' in various baths of acidic water that, over time, release the copper in solution. The liquors are then transferred in 'cementation' tanks where copper is made to precipitate on iron bars.

This process releases enormous quantities of sulfur dioxide in the environment, with devastating consequences. While roasting had been employed for a long time even before the company started, the larger scale of the operation now aggravates local pollution. The smoke is so thick that, especially during winter, it creates an obstacle to movements and transportation: the reduced visibility even causes accidents on the mine's railway. But the worst damage is to local agriculture: the winds carry the smoke all the way to the best land in the area, around the village of Zalamea la Real. To keep the farmers quiet, the company offers compensations and buys off the land. But these measures are not enough. An anti-smoke league is formed, and labour issues merge with the indifference of the company to the problems caused by the roasting, agitating the workers and citizens of the area. The events escalate quickly: on 4 February 1888, during a meeting in the Town Hall in Riotinto, the gathering crowd intimidates the military who open fire, leaving many casualties among the protesting civilians.

Following the events, the Spanish government bans open-air roasting, but the company manages to continue this process until 1907—though at a smaller and decreasing scale. The roasting of pyrites, meanwhile, is drastically changing the landscape of the region: aside from the growing open pits, the mounds of waste slate, and the many new infrastructures, the forests and the surrounding cultivations are obliterated by the acidic smoke. As the land changes ownership and the company attempts to contain the complaints and the loss in reputation, its managers experiment with tree planting in the area. First an Australian, W. G. Nash, head of the land department, introduces *Eucalyptus globulus*. Soon after the company employs Kai Hasse, a Danish forester who implements the planting of *Pinus pinea*. This pine species, a pioneering one, quickly takes over the hillsides. However, it is not the environmental cost of the process that pushes the company to change their extractive techniques.

For the company, the main problem with roasting is that the sulfur is wasted and it becomes impossible to recover it. Besides, the process is labour-intensive: lots of workers are employed in building up the *teleras*, and even more complicated is their breaking down, since the calcines resulting from the process are hot and corrosive. In fact, the railways are frequently in needs of repairs and maintenance, since the acidic minerals weather them fast. Furthermore, the increasing social and political opposition is clearly becoming an obstacle to rising production. Hence, early on the company also encourages the development of new processes of extraction. This leads to the development of two patented processes by Heinrich Doetsch, a trader in Huelva and one of the original partners of the company that facilitated the acquisition of the operation with Matheson. These processes involve washing the ores with liquors mixed with salt and manganese. Faced with limited success, engineers immediately complain about the inefficiency of these processes, but remain unable to introduce better treatments until the death of Doetsch, who manages to obtain royalties for his processes and selling salt and manganese to the company.

It will be the death of Doetsch, and other transformations in the company, the global market of metals, technologies, techniques, and knowledges, that in turn will help in modifying extraction. Engineers and miners will proceed to simplify the 'natural cementation' process Doetsch had taken advantage of: it will be sufficient to leave the ore in large heaps, with enough ventilation, and wash them with the acidic waters of the mines to dissolute the copper in the liquors. These changes will not solve once and for all the problems at Rio Tinto. The heavy demands heap leaching, as the process came to be known, will put on local water supplies are just one of the many gaps extraction will keep encountering in its making of resources. But also the problem will pave the way to tinkering and transformation: the implementation of a complicated system of collection and redistribution of water undergoing constant improvements, with the use of wooden launders and piping systems to resist the corrosive effects of the acidic cuprous waters. It is these gaps and the tinkering they call for that transform the mineral extracted, as they do with the landscape of the Tinto valley, and the history of extractive industries and global capital.

The way pyrite and the other minerals of the Iberian Pyrite Belt react with other substances and to different processes, what they are to the diverse sets of people that handle, tinker and deal with them, how they comply with or resist certain techniques and treatments, all make of pyrite more than a resource, shaking the commensurability of this currency. The conversions that should happen seamlessly between resources—like the process of extraction—actually require lot of work, interfere in environments, change people and social relations, influence politics and practices, bring about different forms of life. These details cannot be simply written off: they all decidedly took part in the histories that unfolded in Rio Tinto and beyond; they all shaped socio-economic and political environments as much as geological and biotic landscapes. In the ores excavated by the Rio Tinto Company Ltd, pyrite was a resource. But it was also much more. These other stories, which exceed the logic of resources and stubbornly refuse to fit its narrative, suggest that how resources work is not merely by following their arithmetic accounting: and this becomes particularly clear if we consider the acidic mine waters more closely.

INTERMEZZO—BIOGEOCHEMICAL RESOURCES

By the beginning of the 1900s, in the Tinto river valley, heap leaching had become the main way to extract pyrites. But the process was working in ways that still escaped the calculations of engineers and chemists. Ferric sulfate would form faster than the standard reaction could account for. As it often happened in mining, this was attributed to idiosyncratic characteristics of the site and its ores and climate. It was common for mining concerns in distant geographical locations to perform very differently, so that processes needed to be locally adjusted. The particular concentration of some trace metals, or the temperatures the heaps were naturally exposed to, or the local sources of water were left to account for differences in the performances of various processes. In this way the coherence of the logic of resources was maintained intact, and specificities were brushed away as particularly local idiosyncratic deviations from the rule. For this reason, even if the precise mechanism of heap leaching was not completely elucidated, the common idea was that its particular success at the site was due to some unspecified physico-chemical conditions at the site.

It is only in the 1960s that another version of what is going on begins to emerge. This new version comes with a reiteration of commensurability: in a world composed of various elements, particles, and compounds that fuel and materialise different natural processes, these materials can also be resources. And not exclusively for humans, but for all kinds of processes and organisms. At the beginning of the twentieth century, microbial life is becoming a tool and a model that takes part in shaping a view of life as entangled in a capillary network of biochemical and biophysical relations. A 'new biology' emerges, and microorganisms are key to the understanding of its molecular and biochemical mechanisms. With it, several compounds take on new meanings as resources for various biogeochemical cycles.

It is in this context that Paul Trussell, a microbiologist directing the British Columbia Research Council, visits Riotinto in 1961. There, he collects samples of mine waters in which pyrite leached. With those samples, as with those he and his colleagues gathered from other commercial copper-leaching plants in Canada and Arizona, he inoculates a special culturing medium called '9K' and obtains cultures of a bacterium that recently caught the attention of other microbiologists: *Thiobacillus ferrooxidans*. In an article Trussell published in 1963 with a colleague, he writes 'Without doubt, this organism has been associated closely with the leaching of copper from chalcopyrite piles at the Rio Tinto mine, Spain'. And he continues: 'It is interesting to observe that the temperature, pH, and oxygen levels found optimal for leaching in the present studies correspond to those conditions arrived at by decades of experience at this mine' (Razzell and Trussell 1963, 602). This is the first report of microbial activity in Rio Tinto acid mine waters.

However, this is not the first description of the organism. The role of micro-organisms in chemical processes characteristic of Acid Mine Drainage like iron oxidation was discovered already in 1947, when Colmer and Hinkle studied leaching in bituminous coal mines in the US Appalachian. In the following years, microbiologists began characterizing the diversity of acidophilic organisms, leading to the first description of the iron-oxidizing bacteria found in 1947, which Temple and Colmer named *Thiobacillus ferrooxidans* in 1951 (and which was later renamed *Acidithiobacillus* in 2000). This opened the way to a number of studies that focus on the physiology of this and other acidophilic, autotrophic and iron-oxidizing bacteria. Elements like sulfur and iron, in the process, are becoming potential resources for extremophile organisms.

Simultaneously, this version of pyrite as a molecular resource for microbial metabolisms, is helping to turn bacteria themselves in a resource for human use. In this molecular world, everything is part of the same physico-chemical cycles and the energy stored in the bonds of $FeSO_4$ can be used as a resource by microbial life. The bacterial work of extracting energy, then, necessarily can also be scaled up to serve human processes. In fact, it did not take long to realise the commercial potential of studies on microbial metabolisms: already in 1955 Kennecott Copper Corporation, who owned the mines where some of the original research was conducted, designed and patented the first heap-leaching process based on bacterial activity. But to effectively use the bacterial metabolism, specific techniques and technologies need to be experimented with to tinker with the resistance of bacteria and deal with the many other obstacles, glitches, and gaps that emerge. Luckily for corporations like Kennecott, a number of other transformations have already brought about techniques and practices that can help in this effort of making microorganisms into resources.

After World War II the success of microbially produced antibiotics like penicillin offered the hope of defeating infectious diseases once and for all. The war emergency created the necessary networks between the British and American governments, academia, research laboratories and institutions, and pharmaceutical companies, bringing together different disciplines and skills.

These efforts led to the development of advanced technologies for the mass culturing of microorganisms. As Robert Bud describes these apparatuses in his history of biotechnology, they are 'enormous continuously stirred fermenters, typically holding 50,000 liters'. And he goes on: 'The skills developed in building and operating these fermenters proved useful for the industrial-scale production of many other microbiological products—including a host of new antibiotics as well as the steroids needed in the new contraceptive pill' (Bud 2003, 534). But also biofuels, like the 'gasohols' made with surplus maize during the Cold War, and foodstuffs, like the 'single-cell protein' that is to eliminate hunger by feeding the poor protein-rich yeasts similar to those developed as cattle feed (*soylent green*, anyone?). And—from the 1950s—metals, through the implementation of bioleaching technologies and 'rational' biohydrometallurgy.

It is a biogeochemical declination of the logic of resources like the one articulated above that drives the new biotechnological industries. And this logic is bolstered and made possible by tools and techniques for the multiplication of bacterial life like fermentation tanks, transnational and transdisciplinary networks and institutions, changing epistemic regimes, and microbial activities that thrive with these techno-social realities.

PROLOGUE TO PART II

Plains of scarlet-grey dust, spotted by flame and gamboge rocks and craters of rust formations surround a small device moving under a vermilion sky beaten by the wind. It is Sol 2864, the 2,864th Martian day of Mars Exploration Rover B Opportunity's operations. The rover is spending its fifth Martian winter on a north-facing outcrop, on the western rim of the Endeavour crater, informally named Greeley Haven. 'The site is of interest not only for its geologic features but because it has favourable northerly slopes to optimise Opportunity's solar energy as winter approaches in the southern hemisphere of Mars'.[2] Here the rover protrudes its robotic arm to analyse rock and soil targets. In the long time spent on the red planet, Opportunity traversed more than 35 km, scouting the vast expanse of Meridiani Planum and exploring a number of craters on its way. The mission, which started on 25 January 2004, lasted way longer than the original 90 Sol envisioned by NASA and still returns a plethora of information on Mars, and especially the equatorial plain where the rover landed, its geochemical composition, and its possible geological history. The site was chosen for the MER-B landing mainly because the region was characterised, according to orbiter based remote sensing, by the presence of sulfites, sulfates, and other minerals, in particular hematite. This mineral generally forms in the presence of water, and for this reason the region promised good insight into the geological past of the planet and its possible habitability.

In the rust, arid landscape, where rocks hide the horizon, and the wind sweeps the dust, a drill is perforating the soil. It is Sol 2864, or 13 Feburary 2012, here, on Earth. The red, arid landscape is that of the Iberian Pyrite Belt, along the basin of the Tinto and Odiel Rivers, not far from where Corta Atalaya was dug to extract metallic sulfides. The drill is an exploration diamond drill, operated by CGS, a Spanish engineering company specialised in geological surveys and prospecting. The company is drilling for the Iberian Pyrite Belt Subsurface Life (IPBSL), a project of the Centro de Astrobiología (CAB) of the Spanish National Research Council and the National Institute of Aerospace Technology and lead by Ricardo Amils.

The similarity between the landscape of Meridiani Planum, in which MER-B Opportunity is operating and the one in which the IPBSL project's astrobiologists are conducting their research is not just a coincidence, and it goes much deeper than the superficial characteristics of the landscape. The rock cores the drill extracts showed the presence of pyrite, together with gossans, iron bearing minerals, sulfites and sulfates, like jarosite and goethite. In fact, the Mössbauer spectra of Río Tinto and those obtained from explorations of Meridiani Planum are strikingly similar. This similarity suggested that the biogeochemistry of the Tinto River could offer insights on Martian geochemistry and the possibility it holds or held for life. This gives a clue for understanding why CGS is drilling a core from the outcrops near Peña de Hierro. The boreholes are instrumental in characterizing the microscopic niches where various microbial communities take part, through their diverse metabolisms, in the geochemistry of the area. Organisms like *Acidithiobacillus ferrooxidans* use pyrite as a resource for their metabolism. To study these microbial metabolisms the most interesting core samples are transported to the field station, where the ores are processed, prepared, sampled, and analysed to extract traces of life, called biosignatures. The IPBSL geologists that follow the drilling examine the formations in the cores, looking for pyrites and other ores rich in iron and sulfur, the same minerals the Rio Tinto Company Ltd was after, and that are now fuelling microbial metabolisms.

The molecular logic of resources that emerges together with the metabolic pathways of *A. ferrooxidans* offers a way out of some of the gaps resources like pyrite seemed to get stuck into. The details of pyrite and its materialities lurching in the Rio Tinto Company Ltd operation could stall the reach of the accountability of resources. But the molecularization of this logic made the challenges of these details into a quest for *more* knowledge and *more detailed* accounting of the physico-chemical elements of the same arithmetic. Even if the actual accounting is still difficult, it is possible to imagine resources as reaching deep into the molecular fabric of reality.

It is this biogeochemical currency that now allows fields as different as life, Earth, and planetary sciences to work together. Providing a coherent framework, the logic of commensurable resources works like Euclidian space in allowing conceptual coordinates to organise research and other practices. The molecular logic of resources sits beyond the controls of Opportunity, reads Mössbauer spectra, and feeds the ecosystems in the subsurface of Rio Tinto. The very analogy between Mars and the Iberian Pyrite Belt relies on the operations of this logic. But, again, how does this biogeochemical and stoichiometric balancing work in the research practices of IPBSL astrobiologists? Does commensurability flow unhindered across organisms and planets, or does it meet with gaps, obstacles and deviations like it did in the mining of Corta Atalaya?

PART II—ASTROBIOLOGICAL METABOLISMS

As the NASA Astrobiology Roadmap authors put it, 'Astrobiology addresses three basic questions that have been asked in various ways for generations: how does life begin and evolve, does life exist elsewhere in the universe, and what is the future of life on Earth and beyond?' (Des Marais et al. 2003, 1). To answer these questions, astrobiologists concentrate on the origin, the evolution, the distribution and the future of life in the universe. Vital to the notion of life they work with is the molecular commensurability of resources, since without it analogies between Earth cases and other planets would be difficult. But, in order to imagine how life could *differ* from how we understand it now, astrobiologists use this biogeochemical commensurability to attend to specific cases and exceptions, and their details. To understand how this commensurability works for these analogs, it is useful to consider the analogies that bring Mars and the Iberian Pyrite Belt closer for IPBSL scientists.

The first thing to attract astrobiologists to Rio Tinto is the same resource that attracted the mining companies: pyrite. The early work on *A. ferrooxidans* shed light on metabolic pathways that were considered unusual and rare. But microbiology increasingly pointed at the ubiquity of these processes and their ecological importance. The world is not only made of photosynthetic autotrophs—primary producers like plants—and heterotrophic organotrophs—consumers like herbivores and carnivores: chemolithotrophy, saprotrophy, mixotrophy, photoorganotrophy and many other metabolic pathways exist. In this context, the main components of pyrite, sulfur, and iron, are essential resources that feed two important nutrient cycles.

This is particularly true in the Iberian Pyrite Belt. After the characterization of organisms in the acidic mine waters, scientists turned their attention to the waters of the 100 km river that crosses the formation. Getting its name from the dark red colour of its waters, the Tinto river is characterised by low pH and high metallic ions content. These conditions had been long understood as the product of the extractive history of the region. But, together with *A. ferrooxidans*, a surprising diversity of organisms—including eukaryotes—was found to live in the river. The acidity and high content of metals were no longer just traces of human activities, but also essential conditions for a particularly lively assemblage of microbial communities, providing them with vital resources. And while the conditions of the river clearly differ from those on Mars, they also pushed astrobiologists to look deeper. To make sense of the high ferric iron concentration in the river, CAB scientists suggested that the surface conditions can be the product of a complex subsurface ecosystem that they call a 'bioreactor'. This is why they are drilling the deep subsurface of Peña de Hierro.

On Mars surface the present conditions are unsuitable for life: extremely low temperatures, no atmosphere and no global magnetic field to shield from cosmic and solar radiation. Still, the geology of the planet, its valleys and formations suggest that there once was an atmosphere strong enough to allow for liquid water on the surface. As Michalski and colleagues put it, 'By the time eukaryotic life or photosynthesis evolved on Earth, the martian surface had become extremely inhospitable, but the subsurface of Mars could potentially have contained a vast microbial biosphere' (Michalski et al. 2013, 133). The subsurface, then, could still host signs of an extinct biosphere, or even protect the remnants of an extant one. Then, as Fernández-Remolar and other members of the IPBSL team wrote in one of their articles, 'given that Mars has lost its atmosphere, which would have provided greenhouse warming and an ultraviolet shield . . . , the most obvious region to search for potential habitats on Mars is the subsurface . . . Aquifers of acidic brines would have provided the ingredients needed to support a feasible metabolic pathway for organisms in martian aquifers in the past or, plausibly, in the current epoch; putative acidic cryptobiospheres can be sustained by iron and sulfur chemolithotrophy' (Fernández-Remolar et al. 2008, 1023). Iron and sulfur are present in large quantities in the Iberian Pyrite Belt, like on Meridiani Planum. These resources, fuelling the cycles of acidophilic life in Río Tinto, could also be the ones potential Martian life depends on.

In fact, pyrite has been at the centre of an important theory on the origin of life, the so called 'iron-sulfur world' theory, proposed in the 1990s by Günter Wächtershäuser. A chemist by formation, Wächtershäuser worked as a patent lawyer, but dedicated his time to thinking about the origin of life. His main idea was that metabolism would predate heredity, and this original metabolism would have been based on the iron and sulfur cycles.

Nevertheless, the IPBSL astrobiologists are not content with the possibility of theoretically accounting for the biogeochemical processes of this scenario, as Wächtershäuser did: they are looking for ways to find more concrete traces of life. In the field, these are called biosignatures: these traces need to be as clearly biogenic as possible but can be chemical, isotopic, morphological, or sedimentary. As traces, biosignatures are rarely definitive, and the more signatures can be found the stronger is the evidence for past or present life. But if biogeochemistry offers a currency to seamlessly move from geological to planetary and to biotic processes, how to recognise traces of life? This is an even more pressing question for IPBSL astrobiologists, since the biosignatures they might be looking for on Mars could be, potentially, of 'life as we *don't* know it'. If life also started somewhere else, it might exhibit a different chirality, or it might be based on different molecular structures from the DNA and RNA we are familiar with.

The biosignatures IPBSL is looking for, then, need to be attuned to the specificities of particular biotic processes, which often escape a simplistic accountability and the reductionist logic of resources. The presence of chemolithotrophic ecosystems in Río Tinto, joined with the possibility of comparing and analysing closely their mineralogical products, offers the rare opportunity to analogically characterise a set of possible traces that have unique features as markers of their biological origin. As Ricardo Amils, the principal investigator of the project, puts it in an article, 'acidophiles actually create the extreme conditions in which they thrive as a consequence of their peculiar metabolism, which, in addition, generates mineral biosignatures such as goethite, jarosite and hematite, that might facilitate their detection in remote locations' (Amils et al. 2007, 370). Characterizing them better on Earth can help to understand similar formations on Mars and recognise biotic mineralogical products when they are encountered by future missions.

As I follow the research of his team, Ricardo explains to me that the life forms they look for

> are chemolithotrophs because they play with inorganic substances, thus they produce products, mineralogical products. So, from the analysis of these types of minerals you also can guess the kind of activities you are facing. So, for instance, sulfur reducers produce sulfhydric acids, sulfhydric acids combine with metals and precipitates sulfites. So, if you can find sulfites or iron oxides or sulfates . . . depending on the kind of elements you find along the drilling site in the sample, they can give the microbiologists ideas of the kind of microorganisms that we can find.[3]

Life leaves traces of the specific activities that characterise it. Different types of metabolism produce different signatures. The most evident ones are offered by cell materials, and for this reason a group of scientists in the project is working with antibodies that are able to recognise different cell products (membrane components, sugars, proteins) present in the samples. These ones would be the best biosignature, since they are constituted by something that cannot be made abiotically. But to find on the fossil record this kind of molecules is not easy, especially because of the recycling activity that goes on, particularly in extreme environments. 'Life recycles everything', Ricardo tells me, showing how deep this logic of limited resources permeates eco-system theory. Furthermore, these traces can undergo intense geochemical pressures and transformation due to morphological and geological processes.

Another type of biosignature is constituted by things that are produced and discarded by microorganisms. These are more easily incorporated in the fossil record, since they are not reused. In this sense, as Ricardo pointed out to me, 'sulfites are interesting because they are not made at the temperature and pressures of geology. So you can distinguish them from the crystal structure. The sulfites made by sulfur reducers, we call these botryoids because they look like cauliflowers, not like perfect crystals as the ones that are the product of geological processes'. The crystal structure of minerals produced by biotic metabolisms can be different from that of abiotically generated ones. The details of how certain minerals are formed goes beyond the calculations afforded by a biogeochemical commensurability. If sulfites can still be accounted for, the details of their crystal structure and their composition can exceed the simplified arithmetic of resources.

There is a long list of possible biosignatures, and the more is known about specific contexts and their histories, the more biosignatures can acquire different meanings. The search for traces of life is simultaneously also reshaping the notion of life and of the kind of traces it could leave. Then, in astrobiology, no signature can, on its own, be considered a very reliable evidence of life: the habitat, the context, and the dynamics and transformation exceed the definition of a single biosignature, and push to constantly research more. Biosignatures depend on the characterisation and schematization of biogeochemical processes at the molecular and planetary scale. In order to know what to look for, it is important to understand the geology and mineralogy of the rocks, but also the metabolisms of microorganisms, their forms of life, and the conditions, present and past, on Mars. And to do so, the shared language of biogeochemistry, and its reliance on the notion of resources, is essential. This language has been shaped by the same post-war histories that gave birth to earth sciences in efforts to know our planet and extract resources and to planetary sciences in reflections on our solar system's workings. Such understandings of metabolic processes and of planetary ones show the traces of shared ancestry: the notion of closed systems, of resources and of processes that can be characterised in accountable ways, always commensurable and amounting to an arithmetical equation, is like the molecular traces of the Last Universal Common Ancestor in 16S rRNA, or like the craters throughout the solar system telling stories of the shared planetary experience of a Late Heavy Bombardment. It is a trace—fleeting and unclear as traces are—of a shared genealogy.

Like these histories, though, this common ancestry is good only as far as one tries to squint her eyes to see the 'whole' story from a distance. Once the details become more visible, it becomes clear that such shared histories come together with specific ways of *telling* stories about them, but also of *knowing* these stories, and the ways in which *we shape* these stories and the worlds they come with. As the astrobiologists use the currency of biogeochemistry, they simultaneously and constantly hit against gaps and details that do not fit so easily. But these gaps are not limits for them: it is this resistance and recalcitrance of the materials and organisms they work with that allows them to push and transform their notion of life. The crystal structure of biogenic sulfites is a case in point: while counting just like any other sulfites, these are importantly different from the ones that originate in geological processes. Many things fall out of the accounting of resources, and just like the details of pyrite ores in the mining of Corta Atalaya, these are not easily dismissed. Instead they are often crucial in shaping histories, landscapes, forms of life, and life forms.

EPILOGUE

The story that can be told following the logic of commensurability and resources is a powerful one. In digging Corta Atalaya, extracting, treating, shipping and selling copper and pyrite; in searching for life on Mars and in the acidic waters of the Tinto river; in building spacecrafts to mine asteroids, nature as a set of resources is a driving force. For astrobiologists, for example, the biogeochemical currency is crucial in understanding and characterizing the contexts they study. 'However, astrobiologists now realise that discriminating possible traces of life from unambiguous traces of life is extremely difficult in the early Earth rock record, and possibly or probably impossible in an extraterrestrial context. Detecting life requires a set of multidisciplinary approaches and criteria and a large (and always improving but never completed) understanding of natural processes' as Javaux notices (Javaux 2011, 182). Even in the work of astrobiologists, then, the accountability and coherence of this logic needs to be pushed, challenged, transformed and never to be written in stone once and for all.

So, while the power of commensurability does not mean we need to dismiss this notion and the accounting that shapes it, it also reminds us to resist the temptation to think that this is *the only* story. Details and gaps always exceed this account. Nature *is* not a resource: instead, naturecultures take place in ongoing and messier practices. The materials that shaped and emerged from the episodes I chose to put forward are not linear and keep escaping the bounds of accountability even if they can be made to fit, partially at least, with it. Simultaneously, they can have important consequences, as they engender specific worlds. To attend to these materials, these naturecultures and their diffractions, the logic of resources is not a good tool. It is not the certainty of calculations and accounts that matter; instead it is the exceptions, the approximations, the not-quites, not-yets, and almosts that matter here. These details animate a different approach, a different logic: instead of starting from the coherence of commensurabilities with the need to be reminded of their limits, they suggest we tell stories that start from the asperity and certainty of idiosyncrasies, exceptions, interruptions, and differences found in details, keeping the grand narratives as one of many possible coherences that can just appear in the background, as we do not look too closely.

If the Anthropocene calls us to try to find alternatives, it does so by articulating a planetary story. But maybe the stories we need to tell fall short of the coherence of the kind of accounting the planetary relies on. The challenge is to find narrative and political genres of theory and practice that can allow us to stay with these excesses, with these troubles. Diffraction and juxtaposition, as I tried to craft them here, are two experimental narrative devices that can allow for this. Maybe these can begin to help us tell stories that are not only about accounting and balancing, and that can envision and evoke other ways of being together, beyond commensurability.

NOTES

1. This is the promotional video of Deep Space Industries. See online at https://deepspaceindustries.com/

2. http://www.nasa.gov/mission_pages/mer/multimedia/pia15119.html

3. This and the following quotes from Ricardo Amils are from interviews and personal conversations collected during fieldwork.

WORKS CITED

Amils, Ricardo, et al. 'Extreme Environments as Mars Terrestrial Analogs: The Rio Tinto Case'. *Planetary and Space Science* 55.3 (2007): 370–381.

Bud, Robert. 'The History of Biotechnology'. *The Oxford Companion to the History of Modern Science*. Ed. John L. Heilbron. New York: Oxford University Press, 2003.

Des Marais, David J. et al. 'The NASA Astrobiology Roadmap'. *Astrobiology* 3.2 (2003): 219–235.

Fernández-Remolar, David C., et al. 'Underground Habitats in the Río Tinto Basin: A Model for Subsurface Life Habitats on Mars'. *Astrobiology* 8.5 (2008): 1023–1047.

Haraway, Donna J. *Modest_Witness@Second_Millennium.FemaleMan©_Meets_ OncoMouse™: Feminism and Technoscience.* New York: Routledge, 1997.

Javaux, Emmanuelle J. 'Biomarkers'. *Encyclopedia of Astrobiology.* Springer, 2011. 182–183. Web. 6 March 2016.

Michalski, Joseph R., et al. 'Groundwater Activity on Mars and Implications for a Deep Biosphere'. *Nature Geoscience* 6.2 (2013): 133–138.

Razzell, W. E. and P. C. Trussell. 'Isolation and Properties of an Iron-Oxidizing Thiobacillus'. *Journal of Bacteriology* 85.3 (1963): 595–603.

Temple, K. L. and A. R. Colmer. 'The autotrophic oxidation of iron by a new bacterium: Thiobacillus ferrooxidans'. *Journal of Bacteriology* 62.5 (1951): 605–611.

Chapter Ten

Lacuna

Minding the Gaps of Place and Class

Lowell Duckert

In that fleeting and powerful disturbance of his being the earth enfolded in
the starlight peace became a shadowy country of inhuman strife, a battle-
field of phantoms terrible and charming, august or ignoble, struggling
ardently for the possession of our helpless hearts. An unquiet and mysterious country of inextinguishable desires and fears.

Joseph Conrad (1997)

A unique gathering. What is happening here?

Nnedi Okorafor (2014)

MINDING GAPS

At the Association for the Study of Literature and Environment's Tenth
Biennial Conference in Lawrence, Kansas, 2013, Rob Nixon closed his
plenary entitled 'This Brief Multitude: The Anthropocene and Our Age of
Disparity' by encouraging the audience to 'mind the gap' between those who
suffer the most at the hands of neoliberalism—the citizens of the Global
South—and those who profit from it. This sort of socio-economic 'gap' manifests what he has called 'slow violence' in a book by the same name: a violence that 'occurs gradually and out of sight, a vilence of delayed destruction
that is dispersed across time and space, an attritional violence that is typically
not viewed as violence at all' (Nixon 2011, 2). The construction of megadams
in places like India's Narmada River Valley, for example, not only physically
displaces indigenous peoples, but it also helps to develop 'spatial amnesia',
a selective form of national memory that leads to 'unimagined communities'

Figure 10.1. *Parego's Lake (Lagoon), Ebey's Landing National Historic Reserve, Whidbey Island, Washington.* **Courtesy of Lowell Duckert.**

(151). The Sardar Sarovar, the largest and most controversial of thirty proposed dams in the valley, has undergone a series of height increases since 1999 that has led to over a million developmental refugees. As inhabitants rendered un-inhabitants, these 'oustees' continue to exist in harm's way while remaining culturally out of mind (163). Yet Nixon has faith in the power of writer-activists to remind others of unjust gaps in environmental policy and place; he cites writer Arundhati Roy's highly publicised protests against megadamming and her call for 'an art that makes the impalpable palpable, makes the intangible tangible, and the invisible visible. An art which can draw out the incorporeal adversary and make it real. Bring it to book' (170). And to film: the documentary *Drowned Out* (2002) focuses on Adivasi families (India's indigenous people) in the village of Jalsindhi in Madhya Pradesh who refused to relocate and whose homes were consequently submerged: 'We'll be drowned but we won't move', one steadfast man swears. 'There is just water all around'; with its distressing images of aqua outspread—envision moats of state-sponsored effluvia surrounding farms, transforming them, foot by foot, into archipelagos of flooded plains—the film aims to prevent the flood from being forgotten: viewers must 'mind the gap' rather than 'wish it away', out, or silent. More than mere metaphors for financial misallocation, these gaps are spaces physically filled: with concrete and thatch; flotsam, jetsam, dereliction; the drowned and the surfaced.

An environmentalism of the poor, then, does not ask what is *not there* but what is *not minded* in order to produce said gaps. The fate of dammed communities like Jalsindhi importantly draws attention to the material, and often 'slow', conditions of environmental health and justice, even if this degradation happens in a flash of flooding, even if their destruction is brought by the burst of a dam. Nancy Tuana's phrase 'materializing ignorance' encapsulates this double injustice of first targeting specific bodies to carry material burdens— like the weight of a water-wall—and second, ensuring their disappearance *perforce* through physical force, the threat of real as well as imagined violence. By paying attention to how the known is rendered unknown, by asking why certain human and nonhuman beings historically are more or less susceptible to the vagrancies of unknowing, we may identity and possibly critique the 'various institutions and motives that have a stake in the production and maintenance of ignorance' (Tuana 2008, 203). The interrogation is simultaneously ontological as it is epistemological; although writing in the wake of Hurricane Katrina in 2005, the 'viscous porosity' she posits—an 'interactionist ontology' that '*rematerialises the social and takes seriously the agency of the natural*' (188)—extends from the Gulf of Mexico to the mouths of Gujarati rivers, for it magnifies matter's capacities for resistance and opposition; presses a need for more distributive (shared) modes of justice and responsibility due to natural-cultural hurricanes abetted by human industry; bears witness to membranous barriers and their stubborn particularities of openness and closure, from skin to systematic racism (and sometimes both: as the still-desolate and predominantly African-American Lower Ninth Ward of New Orleans details ten years after)[1]; and checks the ubiquity, receptivity, and buoyancy of simplistic faith in 'fluidity'. Porosity elaborates on the viscosity of the visceral (and vice versa), incorporates the gaps that stick with you: lacunose leftovers that mark ruptures' making, here, pores filled and sunken, there, civic and 'trans-corporeal' bodies seeking serious articulations of their translations undergoing, everywhere.[2] Minding gaps: not merely a reminder to never forget, not only a reissue of the ecological awareness mantra, but also a pointed assessment of how remembering takes place, with whom and where, if at all.

MINDING (YOUR) GAPS

I must admit: when Nixon spoke of socio-economic gaps that day, I thought of lagoons. I was still minding his argument, however; ecologically speaking, 'lagoons' are fresh- or salt-water lakes separated from the sea or a nearby larger lake or river. 'Lagoon' derives from the Latin word for 'pool', *lacūna*, which comes from *lacus* ('lake'). 'Lacuna'—meaning an unfilled space or interval, a gap—comes from *lacūna* as well, but in the additional sense of 'a hole, pit'.[3] Just as their waters mark an ambiguous hydrographical space that is neither lake nor sea (but both), 'lagoon' is a word that simultaneously acknowledges a gap and its filling, container and contained: an empty space on land and page (via *lacūna*) and the water therein (via *lacus*). Lagoons bring gaps in endangered submergence zones globally to mind. *And so does my body*, I add, its gappy pores serving as tiny demonstrations of precarious porosity. This essay began as a presentation delivered in a wet suit, 'On the Beach', at the Third Biennial Meeting of the BABEL Working Group in Santa Barbara, California. I delved (as deeply as I could) that morning in October 2014 into the conference's shallow waters: the nearby 94-acre Campus Lagoon. Having risen four hundred feet through the geological process of tectonic compression over millions of years (and still rising), the lagoon's non-tidal waters are regularly refreshed by an intricate technological system of weirs that drain from outfalls to beach, a seawater pump that adds seven hundred gallons per minute, and multiple on-campus storm drains.[4] Mindful of salt in the light of approaching dawn, I thought about the gaps I call 'skin', the recreational pleasure I was afforded, as well as the eventual pain of filling up (too much salt and the skin literally slips off). I waded; the coal-black water belied a soft underbottom. While at first it felt far from Iceland's famous geothermal spa, the Blue Lagoon, it took only a few lingering minutes to prove that this Californian cousin promoted the same skinny co-extensiveness between human and nonhuman as an azure 'oasis of relaxation'.[5] Expensive lava exfoliates aside, I was sloughing, moving in and out of gaps. Not mine alone, either; lacunae cannot just be for the exegete of manuscripts, I concluded, for exegesis leaves much to be explained: poverty, injustice, pollution, swelling like the slow but steady influx–outflux of this offshore lagoon; the rise and fall of wealth distribution; empires, even. I had less than an hour to float some thoughts in the brightening inkwell of brine.

Shelter

A lagunal ecology stresses desires for protection in an unpredictable and permanently unstable world. As physical and imaginary waterscapes they provide safe harbours and ports, refuge for the displaced, respite for lagoon/ie/s lost. Sustainability promises an equilibrium to come and that will stand over time, an impervious barrier erected to shut out the world's turbulence. This logic requires something like a sandbar; lagoons' superficial stillness sometime speaks to sustainability's wished-for stillness, the beauty of shallowness, clarity over opacity: 'relaxation' *now* and *later*. But in reality, lagoons emphasise the contrary; they flow. Split into two types—coastal (those sheltered by sand and barrier islands) and atoll (those sheltered by coral reefs)—their shielding does not guarantee impermeability. Rising ocean, temperature, and acidification levels threaten beliefs in and of protection. The planet's largest living (and lagunal) organism, the Great Barrier Reef, is shrinking. Nations primarily at sea level who are dependent upon their lagoons for eco-touristic revenue, such as the Maldives and other Small Island Developing States, are thrown into political unrest and may drown entirely. Venice sinks 2 mm a year into the sea. Pumping groundwater from the aquifer beneath the lagoon worsens the situation. Although relatively stabilised, the city still goes underwater at particularly high tides (110 cm)—four times a year on average—especially when the *acqua alta* strikes (a high tide strengthened by storms and sirocco winds). Higher and higher: global warming questions the effectiveness of Venice's (incomplete) flood barrier project of movable dykes, the Modulo Sperimentale Elettromecaccanico (MOSE), as well as humanity's technological prowess and powers of prevention more broadly. Moses may part the waters but he also knows what exodus entails.[6] Instead of offering an unreachable blue/r harmony impossible to sustain, lagoons should resile us from the ways of harmony altogether so that we may become more resilient. The former fantasy belongs to *The Blue Lagoon* (1980), a film in which Richard and Emmeline Lestrange (played by Christopher Atkins and Brooke Shields) are marooned cousins in the Victorian-era South Pacific. Sheltered from Western civilization, they sexual mature and eventually procreate, ultimately choosing to stay behind on their island paradise of impassioned coexistence when a European ship draws near. (They are finally rescued, but only by accident; adrift at sea after eating some poisonous berries, and just barely alive, they will awaken to a life they clearly do not want.) Let lagoons bespeak a romance with the world, but one that reflects its deepening complications—climatic and otherwise—rather than banishes them; a shelter—even if temporary—that provides a sanctuary of cares surpassing still-life illusions.

Stagnant

The stilling of the world, in fact, can be horrifying. Being on the shelf: stuck in stillness; the fear that nothing changes, can, or will; feeling that things are still the same, *still*. Consider Joseph Conrad's (1897) Malaysian lagoon of motionlessness, 'immobility perfect and final', surveyed by the nameless 'white man' whose canoe cannot break the landscape's languor, but 'only seemed to enter the portals of a land from which the very memory of motion had forever departed' (27). A 'stagnant' lagoon reflects a hopelessly abysmal night that oozes impenetrability (28). Conradian lagoons are ecological hearts of darkness. The unnamed man visits the house of his friend, Arsat, with whom he had fought against the local 'Ruler' (33), one of the region's several 'Rajahs' (37). Arsat had eloped to the lagoon with his lover Diamelen, who is dying of malaria within the hut (presumably from the locale's water-born mosquitos). She 'burns' at the short story's margins (31), unable to hear and speak as the two men talk outside. As Arsat narrates the escape from the 'Ruler' throughout the night—including how he abandoned his brother who had helped them to safety—the lagoon only seems to lend expression to human feelings of guilt and vile self-loathing, revealing the inter-saturation of psychology and the waterscape. '[D]esires and fears' are simply part of the 'shadowy country of inhuman strife' (32). Significantly, it is via these 'unquiet' and 'mysterious' qualities of the lagoon that Conrad contradicts his earlier statement that 'the land and the water slept invisible, unstirring and mute' (32), and, in addition, distances its very visible waters from too-human moralizations (evil) and telos (death). Thus 'in the breath-less silence of the world' (27) there are those wishing, yet unable, to speak. As the two men muse over deaths near (Diamelen) and far (Arsat's brother), their discussion necessarily includes the lagoon; a three-part conversation ensues: 'sounds hesitating and vague floated in the air round him, shaped themselves slowly into words' (32). 'Sounds' of intimacy that word expi-ration as well as aspiration, deaths and 'dreaming': 'A breath of warm air touched the two men's faces and passed on with a mournful sound—a breath loud and short like an uneasy sigh of the dreaming earth' (36–37). Conrad himself seems to struggle with his lagunal interlocutor and its melancholic message; we are told that Diamelen's illness was contracted after 'she heard voices calling her from the water and struggled against [Arsat] who held her' (30). Water, it is revealed, is not quiet; it is worded and word-shaping. What drew her to the water was an 'unquiet' voice that stirs those willing to listen. But the interpretation of lagoon-language is decidedly clear despite its invincible mysteriousness: Diamelen dies before dawn, daylight breaks, the white man pulls away, and '[i]n the merciless sunshine the whisper of unconscious life grew louder, speaking in an incomprehensible voice round the dumb darkness of that human sorrow' (40). The desire for those who have been lost proves 'inextinguishable', the 'inhuman' anti-human (not in the sense of within), the 'country' one in which humans pity their 'helpless hearts' and upon which they project their 'shadowy . . . fears'. For Arsat, the lagoon (and his story about his arrival there) is a passionate 'battle-field' that spur/t/s revenge against the 'Ruler'; he swears he 'see[s] my road' and is 'going back now' (40). More 'uneasy sigh[s] ', battles, 'touched' and go; there is no hope in and of clarity. At its end, the story eerily repeats its beginning: the 'white man', again, 'leaning with both arms over the . . . roof of the little house [cabin]', watching the boat's wake, 'still looking through the great light of a cloudless day into the hopeless darkness of the world' (40). Peace cannot be realised in 'The Lagoon' when lagoons arouse passions that pronounce loss and separation—revenge, the making of further 'phantoms'—and should subsequently be vacated, lest the haunting cycle of lagunal 'strife' disturb you *still*.

The 'road' is also ours to take, importantly; the reaction to this ontological 'disturbance of . . . being' inspired by the waters' 'warm air' unclear. What 'road[s]' are left down the tug and pull of passionate stirrings never stilled? Our homes are held aloft 'by that undulating and voiceless [*sic*] phantom of a flood' (38). Lagoons' disquiet narrativity sponsors stories and searches for peace amidst human and 'inhuman strife' that are never at rest: 'unquiet' Conradian 'countr[ies]', imperial and imperialised 'phantoms' who want only 'starlit peace to enter their hearts'. Violence that moves slowly across time and trauma that we, like Arsat, will not be rid of. Black of bodies and of Malaysian-European entanglement, a lagoon's turbidity that extends into jungle. Stillness is deadly; so seems departure. But as Arsat's retelling of events at the centre of 'The Lagoon' shifts the narration from third to first person perspective, Conrad brings to (his) book the role of storytelling, extending its co-compositional and more-than-human capacities to the reader. Lagunal words come to us in and as water, as Diamelen discovered—they may sicken us, we may die—yet they also prove more than malarial or melancholic, mobile even if 'still'. Notably silent and suffering, Diamelen's garrulous silence expresses the story's true horror: the gaps of *erasure*, the result of human and nonhuman voices rendered voiceless, those shapeless words that companion the unsaid. The quieted should disturb; the enforced stillness in lagoons known to be loquacious should encourage better earth-dreaming. We must attend to these feelings, read the keyword 'stagnant' as indicating affective pools (never dull) with differing depths of help and hope (-lessness included). 'Stagnant' comes from the Latin *stagnum*, 'pool', and, as such, lagoons pool the silenced, pondering how to revitalise the matter-flows of *stagnum* in turn. It is a different 'road' than revenge, one that Arsat travelled earlier in the story, albeit less often, filling a gap in his dialogue by the fire like so: 'A man must speak of war and of love . . . Therefore I shall speak to you of love' (32). Gaps are places for other and others' stories to fill. They are full of lost loves; they propel new ones. Choices like these 'see' the tumultuousness within the seemingly still, and, by interrupting narratives of irreversible stagnancy (read: poverty), try to help the 'helpless hearts' in the 'darkness' that is ecological enmeshment. If the tale's conclusion repeats its opening, it does so, then, in an effort to enact repetition with a difference—indeed, Conrad would later alter the final line[7]—asking us how we will insert ourselves into lagoons, our world, of 'war and of love'.

Lagune

In its etymology, a 'lagoon' indicates colonialist histories and an origination from fraught ecomaterial contacts. The first recorded encounter in English with a lagoon outside Venice—'laguna' had entered the language from Spanish-Italian *laguna* in 1612 to describe the Adriatic archipelago—was at gunpoint in the New World. The Englishman William Dampier's *A New Voyage Round the World* (1697), an account of his first (of three) circum-navigations from 1679 to 1691, is replete with approximately seventy-five 'Lagune[s], or Lake[s] of Saltwater'. He outlines one on the western Mexican coast near Acapulco in particular: 'the mouth of this Lagune is not Pistol-shot wide, and on both sides are pretty high Rocks, so conveniently placed by nature, that many men may abscond behind' (241). The Spanish who were also fishing and watering there ambush the English in October 1685. Pistols are fired; five are wounded. The men row their canoe farther into the lagoon for safety, fearing that a retreat will only send them back through the lagunal gauntlet. Stranded in the middle of the lake for three nights, Captain Townly finally rids the rocks of their oppressors. Lagoons emerged in the English imagination, at least, with early modern conquest and the conflicts of aqua-territorialization: salt and fresh water striated, solid land from slough separated, non/indigenous in- and ex-habitants taxonomised, entrapped. This colonial context has regrettably extended; the International Union for Conservation of Nature's (IUCN) 'Red List' of endangered ecosystems, for example, names specific lagoons at risk: the Coorong in southern Australia, the reefs of New Caledonia in the French Pacific whose 'anthropogenic pressures' manifest the threats that many face.[8] As highlighted sites of encroachment, a lagoon's delicate nature—its fragile beings suspended in blue—easily marks the human's damaging impress: fertiliser run-off and ensuing nitrogen enrichment; various hydraulic engineering feats such as the draining of headwater supply systems and the opening of sandbars to alleviate flooding of farmland; the tracks of off-road vehicles and the scratches of surface mining; the expanding shorelines of livestock manure, factory-farmed lakes. As perilous sites of natural-cultural mixture, even (and especially) when ecotourism riches and biodiversity richness meet, lagoons are places bodies both want into and out of, and, once in, might require rescue: whether by nationality (Townly's Englishness) or by civilization (the Anthropocene's aid). Within this eco/neo/colonial industrial impulse, intervals are not allowed; gaps must be filled, flux obliterated. Since the word began, 'lagoons' and lagoons have been contact zones with the violence of human and nonhuman hyper-separation built-in.

Creature

Antithetical to the terrestrial by their aqueous nature—like their hydrological kin, swamps—lagoons harbour lurking creatures whose unclassifiable natures demand *un*knowing, posing an epistemological quandary thus: a desire to inhabit the unknown, but without settling into configurations of 'fact'-finding (truth). Still, science may police which creatures from multi-colored and -cultured lagoons are assessed, enlighten us as to how opacity is to be made clear, determine the destines of deep dark things. A case study: the *Creature from the Black Lagoon* (1954), the so-called 'Gill-man', who represents the amphibious link—no longer missing—between water and land, fish and human, Devonian and Holo/Anthropo/cene. We watch as 'Gill' unsuccessfully defends his Amazonian home from invasive scientists hunting for fossils. Once discovered, he must be captured; as Dr Mark Williams (Richard Denning) obsessively quips, 'we must have proof'. Stalked and speared by human divers, the creature murders a crewmember. The scientists retaliate with a poison—the piscicide rotenone (still used)—that paralyzes the entire lagoon's population of fish, causing them to surface, asphyxiate, and slowly die. As the rotenone sinks to the bottom, the ichthyologist Dr David Reed (Richard Carlson) presents a philosophy of knowledge at odds with his colleague—who 'deal[s] with known quantities'—and the boat's captain, Lucas, who equates 'everything' in the jungle with 'killers'. The upper Amazonian rainforest represents the utter unknown as well as the impossibility of knowing:

> We've just begun to learn about the water and its secrets. Just as we've only touched on outer space. We don't entirely rule out the possibility that there might some form of life on another planet. Then why not some entirely different form of life in a world we already know is inhabited by millions of living creatures?

Less accumulation, more ambiguous of the amphibious: in Reed's estimation, lagoons are places of limitless onto-epistemological exploration. But how his more open-ended investigation should be put into practice (with rotenone and what else) is endlessly up for debate. 'Gill', shunning the light above-water (and the analysis of the Enlightenment) is eventually captured but easily escapes, taking the heroine Kay (Julie Adams) back to his lair. As the rescue team riddles the creature with bullets in the film's final minutes, Reed allows 'Gill' to slink back into the blackwater. The last shot is of a dark body darkening, its hues deepening monochromatically, the audience uncertain of its death (indeed, two sequels were made shortly thereafter in 1955 and 1956). Capture remains 'evidence' of fact rather than the 'touched' of intimacy, even if the Creature's hand is the body part most visualised throughout, starting with a webbed fossil protruding from a hillside while the Creature's pulsing hand (in prehistoric fast-forward) reaches out of the water nearby. The brackish, in short, too quickly turns to blackish; the blackness of possibility engenders fears of uncertainty, avoids doubt-full dives into lacunae. Science literally spearheads knowability at the expense of darker ecological others, stifles proliferative and pluralised knowledge*s*. Just as the language of extinction has come under pressure, lagoons helps us to scrutinise what counts as the *bio-* of biodiversity: not just a mammalian 'life', but even an inorganic kind. A lagoon is creaturely; 'living creatures' and *the* Creature are the lagoon.

Weird

Dawn had broken but the water was still a warming black. My feet touch something. Weird: I recall the scene from the film in which the Creature mimics (not attacks) the human swimmer in a graceful underwater dance; she dove deeper to examine her partner. Maybe mine is Aristotle's octopus. Armand Marie Leroi's *The Lagoon* (2014) posits the Grecian lagoon of Lesbos as the birth of biology because it served as Aristotle's marine laboratory in the *History of Animals* (ca. 350 BCE): '[T]his is what Lesbos and the lagoon at Pyrrha gave to Aristotle: a *place*, calm and lovely, where he could be among natural things' (7). Leroi's lagoon extols Aristotelian causes; by plumbing the depths of things for their identifiable sources, the philosopher *caused* modern science itself.[9] Knowledge, like the animal, ably slithers up onto the beach and receives its definition. Or perhaps not: Aristotle infamously decried the octopus as 'stupid . . . (for it even comes towards a man's hand if he puts it under water)' (321). Weird: when did a desire for intimacy become *dumb*, or is it that octopoid ink's darkness confounds the philosopher's touch of intelligible translation meant to ink truth into texts? Knowledge eludes; never stagnant, it exudes creation upon creation, actions without causality, touches tied to the specificities of place, modes of experiential knowing—lagunal nodes—left for things to inhabit. A loose cephalopod loosens the human faith in the cephalic. Rinse and repeat: to strive, to seek, to . . . *or just to seek*; this is where, after all, the sensorial French philosopher Michel Serres reminds us, 'Ulysses loses his linear head. Did he ever have it?' (2008, 265).[10] *Did I*, mingled that morning salty-fresh within lagunal middles of not-quite-empty, not-quite-full, minding the political-economic lacunae (gaps) of class and the hydrological lacunae (lakes) of place? I then realised that I had taken a detour. I waded to the lagoon's 'weir', a low dam built to regulate water flow, from Old English *werian* 'dam up', but also that which designates a set of stakes used to trap fish. Too many dams; too few interchanges. Lagoons teach you

Figure 10.2. *Little Blue Run (Lake), Pennsylvania.* Courtesy of Lowell Duckert.

how to feel trapped in a flow. There is a word for it, I think: *weir-d*, the filiation of filtration.

FINDING GAPS

Sometimes the problem is not minding the gaps: it is finding them. Since the early twentieth century, a 'lagoon' has described an artificial shallow pool used in the treatment and concentration of sewage and slurry. In preparation for my talk that October, I entered (probably trespassed) into the largest coal ash impoundment in the country: Little Blue Run in Pennsylvania, about 30 miles northwest of Pittsburgh and immediately adjacent to the Ohio River (Figures 10.2 and 10.3). Built in 1975, this 1,700-acre unlined brilliantly aquamarine lagoon contains 20 billion gallons of coal combustion residuals (also known as coal ash) from FirstEnergy's Bruce Mansfield power plant—poisonous leftovers like arsenic, chromium, lead and mercury—that have been proven to contaminate ground- and surface-water nearby.[11] Large-scale bodies of water nearby need not be necessary; wind-fuelled coal ash storms devastate desert populations: the Reid Gardner Power Plant along the Muddy River in Nevada enshrouds the Moapa River Indian Reservation in 'fugitive' dust. Moapa is but one of many: out of the approximately 1,400 coal ash sites in 37 states that generate 140 million tons of industrial waste each year, 331 dams are deemed either 'high hazard' (loss of life likely) or 'significant hazard' (causing economic and/or environmental damage); 70% are located in low income areas; and, since February 2014, there have been 208 *known* spills into groundwater, wetlands, and rivers. Coal by-product pools like these, also known as sludge impoundments, are common in Appalachia where I live. West Virginia boasts 41 'lagoons' at eleven different power plants. The twelve whose ages are known are over thirty years old. Almost half are unlined. Five are designated 'high hazard'. Their breaches have been devastating: the Buffalo Creek Flood in Logan County on 26 February 1972 drowned 125 people and left more than 4,000 homeless as a 25-foot tidal wave of 130 million gallons of black water slammed into neighbouring towns at seven feet per second. The burst wiped out sixteen towns in the river hollow in its 17-mile course. Here un-inhabitants surfaced only to immediately disappear below: while not in the geographic Global South, the deluge disoriented the compass of degradation by extending to Appalachian poor the status of Third-World citizenship (and it still does; read: 'white trash'). It is no accident that these events happen with greater frequency in unremembered places and to unimagined communities. Although survivors won a then-unprecedented lawsuit against the coal company, Pittston, for thirteen and a half million dollars, and the tragedy helped pass the National Dam Inspection Act of 1972, the company, who had inspected the faulty impoundment dam just days before its failure and rated it satisfactory, infamously called the disaster 'an act of God' (Stern 10). This logic of coincidental causes and corporate exculpation unfortunately continues. Wished-for forgetfulness: when a strip-minded creek, a 'sacrifice zone' for the glory of national industry (Scott 31), additionally becomes one of submergence.

Denise Giardina—born in Bluefield, West Virginia, and raised in a coal camp in neighbouring McDowell County—'[b]ring[s] to book' transgressions like these in her novel *The Unquiet Earth* (1992). Dillon Freeman narrates the feeling of Trace Mountain, another name for the Buffalo Creek sludge slide, rushing down upon him: 'water reaches my thighs, pulls at my legs, I turn to face the wall and stretch my arms wide' (335). The mountain, located in Justice County (a pseudonym for Mingo County in the coalfields of southern West Virginia) had been strip-mined and its waste haphazardly dammed up by the company into smouldering lagoons; at its foot, recalls Dillon, 'I stop and listen, kneel and place the palm of my hand flat on the bone [slate]. It is warm as flesh' (274). The American Coal Company, believing their work of reclamation done, and assuring themselves that the hot 'bone[s]' will hold, ignore his concerns. When heavy rains fall, Dillon grows disquiet about the unquiet earth-water; he returns to the mountain's

Figure 10.3. *Minding the Blues.* Courtesy of Lowell Duckert.

pernicious perch: 'At the top I stop to listen. A low moan swells from the water—it is the tormented spirit of Trace Mountain torn apart. I hear voices in the moan and I step toward them on the dam' (328). Dillon, like Diamelen, is drawn to the water; he likes listening to lagunal 'voices' that are sirens' calls. 'The water sighs' (328). Then it breaks. His body is never found. His daughter Jackie, working at a Pittsburgh newspaper, has a dream that invokes Ariel's song from William Shakespeare's *The Tempest* (1611), fitting for the book's final section called 'The New World': 'I dreamed of his skeleton stripped and blackened and mired in the sludge, becoming one with the bones of the mountains' (338).[12] Giardina's book tries to counter-act Trace's spatial amnesia; to trace the material traces left behind with all their trauma; to enflesh human and nonhuman 'bones' through storytelling; to bear better witness to the gaps of place and class than a highway's 'his-torical marker' that too-easily relegates the 1972 catastrophe to the past; to dole out response-ability to the drowned (out) and intentionally quieted. Newer worlds, still mired; the three worst coal ash spills in US history have occurred in the twenty-first century, Appalachian all: Wolf Creek, Kentucky in 2000; Dan River, North Carolina in 2014; and Kingston, Tennessee, the largest, in December 2008 that comprised over a billion gallons across 300 acres. In 2010 the Tennessee Valley Authority transported four million cubic yards of ash to Arrowhead Landfill in Perry County, Alabama (68% African-American and one of the poorest counties in the state; the closest community, Uniontown, is 88%). *Black lagoons for black bodies.* Increased awareness of ash-lagoons' presence and pollution amassed enough public outrage to force the US Environmental Protection Agency's coal ash rule on 19 December 2014: one of the most significant stipulations being a requirement to post facilities' records of disposal freely.[13] Still sighs, swells moan. On a much smaller scale, I am reminded of chemical lagoons whenever it rains heavily at home in Morgantown, West Virginia; to prevent water contamination from the sewage treatment plant on the Monongahela River, chlorine dioxide, a widely used water purifier, gives my tapwater a plastic taste and smell. I go lagunal with a sip, speak in slurry-ed words. Decker's Creek, a tributary of the river died orange from acid mine drainage, has been diverted by its Friends into a series of lagunal 'remediation' ponds that produce metal-free and pH-neutral water.[14] Over, or out of, time: by treading the toxic wasteland of Little Blue lagoon north of my home in the fall of 2014, I had lost my linear body. Lagunal 'death by water'.[15] My sense of taste, aesthetics, became adulterated. I desired to run into the tainted-turquoise lagoon and dip into the beautiful water we are not supposed to see.

Metamorphosis: lagoons may sponsor another 'dream'—even better: they *are* dream spaces—that sponsor the founding of new communities even as they relate their failures, that speed imaginations and hopes of short-term (but widening) relief even as they strip skeletons and mines in the long term. Finding gaps is a way of making publics, like the West African lake village of Ganvié, Benin, located in the middle of Lake Nokoué. Separated by a channel (known as the Cotonou Lagoon) that runs through the city of Cotonou (built by the French in 1885) into the Gulf of Guinea, the lake, being but a few miles from shoreline, is actually a coastal lagoon. Known as the 'Venice of Africa', and containing about 20,000 inhabitants spread out across vast networks of stilted houses, Ganvié grew in the sixteenth and seventeenth centuries when the Tofinu people evaded Portuguese enslavement; the ruling warrior ethnic group, the Fon, had been capturing and selling various peoples from smaller tribes such as the Tofinu. Because the Fons' religion prohibited them from attacking any person who dwelled on water, the lake-town emerged. While Ganvié began as a slave trade–free lagoon, a haven for the racially oppressed, its security now is threatened by the ocean. Underwater corals provide Ganvians with their livelihood of fish, but rising sea levels have increased the amount of pesticide residuals in the lake, flooded eroded banks, and intensified saltwater intrusion. Houses high: is this the promise of *founding* communities after *finding* injustice? Rather than repeating Euro-American appreciation or curiosity, as it is often described touristically (which has a long history in colonialist depictions[16]), Ganvié's tenuous situation starts to look more like a future: it communicates the global task of resilience. The city's name means, appropriately, the 'collectivity of those who found peace at last'. Another translation is simply, 'we survived'. A peace always in the making, a place that holds our 'starlit' attempts at survival; a lagoon is a locus of energetic emplacement—I confess: I wanted to stay in mine—that affords an active model of dwelling as defined by anthropologist Tim Ingold: 'that immersion of beings in the currents of the lifeworld without which such activities as designing, building and occupation could not take place at all' (2011, 10). Thinking constructively with lagoons requires an ontological reworking of and *with* materials. If, essentially, dwelling 'is . . . literally to be embarked upon a movement along a way of life' (12), lagoons are dream pools; we are within them, at work, occupying the dreaming wet and *Unquiet Earth* of 'The Lagoon' and the metamorphoses of matter-floods; grieving dreams lost in the 'wide' of reality, ashes to ashes, 'fac[ing]' nightmares; building upon ways to find peace, and to peacefully co-collect.

To lagoons, then: the finding of not-too-distant futures. Nigerian author Nnedi Okorafor's science fiction novel *Lagoon* (2014) is set in present-day Lagos, a name, she points out, that was given to the city by the Portuguese when they landed on Nigeria's lagunal island in 1472. *Lagoon* tells the story of three people with unexplained yet extraordinary powers of energy—a marine biologist, Adaora (force field); a rapper, Anthony de Craze ('the rhythm'); and a soldier, Agu (strength)—brought together by a decimating sonic '*BOOM!*' on Bar Beach that transports them to an alien vessel underocean (10). When Adaora awakes on land, she meets the friendly shape-shifting 'marine witch' (155) Ayodele who can contort the molecular structure of matter (attended with the sound of metal on glass). The city erupts in panic: Ayodele's powers are captured on film and her kindred are exposed; their presence has 'enhanced' creatures already hostile to humans because of Lagos's worsening water pollution—'sea beast[s]' such as oil pipe–spiking swordfish and enormous octopuses (241)—turning the lagoon into untouchable poison: 'Lagos's lagoon is filling up, and people's homes, roads, and the beaches have flooded. Neither the military nor scientists have any answers' (42). Rather than providing an omniscient narrator, Okorafor's story cuts back and forth across multiple perspectives, languages (Pidgin English), and even species (like bats), intensifying the *wahala*, or, 'African Chaos', as many experience it (212). The plot centres around Ayodele's attempted captures by various parties: the hypocritical Father Oke and his Christian congregation who intend to convert her; to the closeted transvestite Jacobs and his friends who imagine a sizable ransom; his prostitute sister, Fisayo, turned murderously xenophobic once her desires for a better life on-board the alien ship are denied; to the hooligan Area Boys engaged in endless looting; the LGBTQ organization, the 'Black Nexus', who applaud Ayodele's trans-formative abilities and recognise a potential ally; the machinations of a scared military. Addressing Nigeria's economic dependence upon oil, Ayodele broadcasts a message that appears on all electronic devices nation-wide: '*We have come to bring you together and refuel your future . . . Your land is full of a fuel that is tearing you apart . . . We are here to nurture your world*' (113). A second '*BOOM!*' sends more aliens like her in human forms up from the beach. With the help of the three superhuman As, Ayodele heals the ailing Nigerian president and takes him to meet her three 'Leaders' back on the submerged ship. At this point, Adaora discovers her own transspe-cies hybridity, her body switching between air- and water-breathing at will. Born with webbed digits and conjoined legs, 'I was . . . [already] like a fish', she says (257). *Lagoon* breeds mutability; its lagoons—and the lagoon of Lagos—bespeak the repeated maxim of '*Change begets change*' (193). The aliens become increasingly associated with transmission (as trans-corporeal translation) as the novel progresses: 'We are communicative people', Ayodele admits early on, and, later to the president: 'I am change . . . We *are* technol-ogy . . . We do not want to rule, colonise, conquer, or take. We just want a home' (218). In the end, however, the peaceful message of matter energy she represents is met with violence: soldiers savagely beat her to death as Adaora helplessly looks on. Yet the communication continues; Ayodele, vowing that "You'll all be a bit . . . alien', vaporizes and moves over the city: '[Adaora] knew that this fog was rolling like a great wave over all of Lagos. She could almost see it in her mind. And everyone was inhaling it' (269). In the final pages, the enlivened president takes a deep breath, extolls the aliens now living within and amongst them as 'neighbor . . . brother . . . family', and declares oil-abetted '[c]orruption . . . dead in Nigeria' (276, 278). 'Lagos' redeemed, refreshed, at last.

The president's plan for his country's return to 'pure' land would be a difficult—if not unattainable—task for any community, especially in a place like Lagos, currently the sixth most populated city in the world (at over 15 million people) and one of the fastest growing in Africa, where socio-economic '*change*' accelerates for some but stagnates for alienated others in the city's notorious slums-on-stilts. Okorafor claims that the misrepresenta-tions of Nigerians in the film *District 9* (2009) 'started [her] daydreaming about what aliens would do' if they ever splashed down at home (299). The future-figure of *Lagoon* is its infrequent narrator, Udide (the Igbo word for 'spider'), who feels the '*vibrations*' of the city '*that travel through my webs*', who pushes (puzzlingly) on the protagonists at times, and who, ultimately, serves as a symbol for the authorial dream- and story-weaver herself, Okorafor: '*I see sound. I feel taste. I hear touch . . . But I feel the press of other stories*' (290–291). '*[S]piders play dirty*' (292) Okorafor-Udide promises, and thus the novel seems to end with yet another pledge: this time to ensure that the fictional president's commitment to '*change*'—beginning with the impression of previously unheard stories—will be enacted in the real world. This hopefulness is attenuated just slightly by a postscript in which three pre-med students in Chicago, Illinois—Shaquille, Jordan, and Nature—watch the 'African Chaos' unfold on YouTube, only to causally dismiss it before returning to their Chemistry 101 study session: 'I'm just glad it's all happening over there. It's freaking me out', remarks Nature. And *Lagoon*'s last line concurs: 'In the meantime, the world would take care of itself' (303–304). Acting like its hydrographical namesake, the novel adds to confusion rather than tries to solve it; spins webs of messy human and nonhuman mediation through extended networks of media; sifts, but never settles. I still sense in the book's probing question—'*How would you have felt?*'—an optimism over the 'infinite possibilities' that Okorafor, I would argue, tries to convey (271). Rephrased: once the gaps of lacunae are witnessed, '*what will you do?*' (113). The '*BOOM!*' may be a sound wave that paralyses (it fells aerial animals, for instance), and a misogynistic voice (like Chris's, Adaora's husband) that accuses women of witchcraft—who 'nee[d] to be vanquished . . . nee[d] to be beaten down' (77)—but it is also an alien malfeasance that assembles human and nonhuman beings, bodies *black* and otherwise, into a noisy *nexus* of potentialities, a condition for lagunal 'daydreaming'. The '*BOOM!*' is that of unquiet lagoons, a register of multiple contacts, the vibrations of '*change*' and what they '*bege[t]*', come collapse and connection: *how* to change socially and to change the social; *what*, on a material level, to change into; *whether* to embrace the alien's greeting or to drown it out. *Lagoon* queries as much as it queers the lacunal, finds gaps' oddly optimistic openness: here be havens, freedom in and as lagoons.

MINDING THE BLUES

A final, dark blue thought comes to mind. Perhaps aestheticizing pollution can be an effective strategy for minding trans-corporeal enmeshment, its aim to redress the slow violence involved: the bodily shock of blue; the rush of the wave; here comes that *weir-d* feeling again. Eileen A. Joy poses just such an experiment in her essay 'Blue': 'to think about depression as a shared creative endeavour, as a trans-corporeal blue (and blues) ecology' (213). Far from the paradisiacal blue lagoon (and *Blue Lagoon*) of uninhibited wish fulfilment, the lacunae I have revealed thus far belong in a post-sustainable world of Blue Runs both little and large. Saving energy cannot be the only motivation. Proposed tidal lagoon technology in England's Swansea Bay would be the first of its clean 'green' kind, for example, and it would probably help assuage

socio-economic ills.[17] Timothy Morton's 'ironic gap'—another lacuna—
might be more useful, as he declaims, 'Don't just do something—sit there'
(125). Minding gaps is, after all, a way of thinking 'the ecological thought'.
To appropriate a popular form of protest, however, what kind of *sit-in* is this?
It is hard to sit in a lagoon, as I discovered, for they instil questions impossible to answer (at least in one sitting) but also, and more importantly, impossible to ignore. Yet this is not a reason *not to* do so. Lacunae, if anything, are
about intimacy rather than absence, about negotiating middle spaces between
desire and disaster with beings that stick to the skin like a salty film, layers
upon layers of humans and nonhumans, who, despite their material imbrica-
tions, are vulnerable to cultural 'forgetting', *un*knowing, wished-away by the
spatial amnesiac. Lacunae are, in short, about challenging anthropocentricity
and the political, social, and economical damnation that attend to it. I want to
suggest—no, remind—in closing that art has a role in this process of minding
the gaps of place and class, of minding material agency's ability to reactivate
activism, or even to activate alternative modes of it. 'To strive, to seek, to
mind, and not to yield': Ulyssean ecopoetics, something like "reactivism".
We need lagunal stories that infiltrate genres, temporalities, theories, and ped-
agogies. We will always have more to gain than to lose by avoiding gaps in
periodization, discipline, field, and sub-specialty. Hear the waters in Tuana's
adhesive reprise: 'It is easier to posit an ontology than to practice it' (2008,
209). Water writer-activists, broadly defined, can help bring fraught nonhuman and human submergence zones to the surface to be minded, changed,
charged with the promotion of more more-than-human modes of social justice. They can widen the gap so as to transform it into a call for embrace—
'I . . . stretch . . . wide'—rather than distantiation: whether it pertains to the
geographically or financially dammed, the co-implicated bodies of creatures
that pool together, or the possibilities of love and strife in the lakes. And they
can never protest too much.

ACKNOWLEDGEMENT

Special thanks to Serpil Oppermann and Serenella Iovino for their invitation to contribute to this collection; the audience at BABEL and my
'Precariousness + Risk + Storm + Wreck' co-plenarist, Steve Mentz, who
helped me surreptitiously dip into Campus Lagoon; and to Parego's Lake, a
beautiful place (Figure 10.1) that I have visited since childhood, and a site of
intercultural lacunary conflict (as, I argue, most are) between Euro-American
settlers and northern coastal Indians in the nineteenth century: see http://
www.nps.gov/ebla/learn/historyculture/index.htm.

NOTES

1. Greg Allen. 'Ghosts of Katrina Still Haunt New Orleans' Shattered Lower Ninth Ward'. *NPR*. 3 August 2015. See online at http://www.npr.org/2015/08/03/427844717/ghosts-of-katrina-still-haunt-new-orleans-shattered-lower-ninth-ward.

2. Stacy Alaimo's notion of 'trans-corporeality' convincingly proves that these concerns are just as inseparable as humans are from their environments, since they are 'always intermeshed with the more-than-human world' (2).

3. See s.v. 'lagoon' (n.[1]) and s.v. 'lacuna' (n.) in *The Oxford English Dictionary*.

4. Information retrieved from the Cheadle Center for Biodiversity and Ecological Restoration: http://ccber.ucsb.edu/ecosystem/management-areas/campus-lagoon.

5. Also known as 'One of the 25 Wonders of the World'. See online at http://www.bluelagoon.com/.

6. 'What It's (Really) Like: Venice's Acqua Alta'. *Fodor's Travel*. 16 November 2012, see online at http://www.fodors.com/news/venices-acqua-alta-6194. Also see Serenella Iovino's work on 'cognitive justice': Venetian citizens' right to know what is actually happening to them and their ecology. (And on MOSES as an ecopolitical issue, see Iovino 2016, 55–56.) My emphasis throughout on lagoons' narrativity echoes what Serpil Oppermann and Serenella Iovino have deemed 'storied matter': 'a *material* ecocriticism examines matter both *in* texts and *as* a text, trying to shed light on the way bodily natures and discursive forces *express* their interaction whether in representations or in their concrete reality' (Iovino and Oppermann 2014, 2).

7. 'The Lagoon' was originally published in the London magazine *Cornhill* in January 1897. When reprinted in *Tales of Unrest* (1898), the line read: 'He stood lonely in the searching sunshine; and he looked beyond the great light of a cloudless day into the darkness of a world of illusions' (xxv).

8. For the IUCN's 'Red List', see https://www.iucn.org/about/union/commissions/cem/cem_work/tg_red_list/. New Caledonia's situation is discussed in scientific detail by C. Grenz, R. Le Borgne, J. P. Torréton, and R. Fichez.

9. '[S]ome philosophers and physicians had dabbled in biology before him, but Aristotle gave much of his life to it. He was he first to do so. He mapped the territory. He invented the science. You could argue that invented science itself' (376).

10. Here and later on I intentionally reference Alfred Lord Tennyson's last line in 'Ulysses' (1842): 'To strive, to seek, to find, and not to yield' (50).

11. The US Environmental Protection Agency provides ample information on the hazards of coal ash: http://www2.epa.gov/coalash. Earth Justice's website includes an interactive map and downloadable 'fact sheets' for all states affected by ash: http://earthjustice.org/advocacy-campaigns/coal-ash. West Virginia, for example, is http://earthjustice.org/sites/default/files/files/West-Virginia-Ash-Fact-Sheet-2014-12-15.pdf. The information that follows stems mainly from these two sources.

12.

> Full fathom five thy father lies.
> Of his bones are coral made;
> Those are pearls that were his eyes;

Nothing of him that doth fade
But doth suffer a sea-change
Into something rich and strange. (1.2.400-1.2.405)

13. Read the entire ruling here: http://www2.epa.gov/coalash/coal-ash-rule.

14. These are Friends of Decker's Creek: http://www.deckerscreek.org/about/projects/acid-mine-drainage.

15. Also one of Giardina's chapters, 'Death by Water: 1969–1971', and which references, of course, the fourth section of T. S. Eliot's (1922) *The Waste Land* (16).

16. Consider Walter Ralegh's (1596) description of the Tivitivas tribe: 'In the summer they haue houses on the ground as in other places: In the winter they dwell vpon the trees, where they build very artificiall townes and villages . . . for between *May* and *September* the riuer of *Orenoke* riseth thirtie foote vpright, and then are those Ilands ouerflowen twentie foote high aboue the leuell of the ground . . . and for this cause they are enforced to liue in this manner' (50–51).

17. For more on the project's vision, 'an opportunity to harness indigenous, low carbon electricity that is both affordable and sustainable long-term', see online at http://www.tidallagoonswanseabay.com/

WORKS CITED

Alaimo, Stacy. *Bodily Natures: Science, Environment, and the Material Self*. Bloomington: Indiana University Press, 2010.

Aristotle, *History of Animals*. Trans. D. M. Balme. Vol. 3. Cambridge: Harvard University Press, 1991.

Conrad, Joseph. 'The Lagoon'. *The Lagoon and Other Stories*. Ed. William Atkinson Oxford: Oxford University Press, 1997. 27–40.

Creature from the Black Lagoon. Dir. Jack Arnold. Universal Studios, 1954. Film.

Dampier, William. *A New Voyage Round the World*. London, 1697.

Drowned Out. Dir. Franny Armstrong. Spanner Films, 2002. Film.

Eliot, T. S. *The Waste Land*. Ed. Michael North. New York: W.W. Norton, 1992.

Giardina, Denise. *The Unquiet Earth*. New York: Ballantine Books, 1992.

Grenz, C., R. Le Borgne, J.-P. Torréton, R. Fichez. 'New Caledonia Lagoon: A Threatened Paradise under Anthropogenic Pressure?' *Lagoons: Habitat and Species, Human Impacts and Ecological Effects*. Ed. Mwinylikione Mwinyihija. Hauppauge: Nova Science Publishers, 2013. 31–56.

Ingold, Tim. *Being Alive: Essays on Movement, Knowledge, and Description*. New York: Routledge, 2011.

Iovino, Serenella. *Ecocriticism and Italy: Ecology, Resistance, and Liberation*. London: Bloomsbury, 2016.

Iovino, Serenella and Serpil Oppermann, eds. *Material Ecocriticism*. Bloomington: Indiana University Press, 2014.

Joy, Eileen A. 'Blue'. *Prismatic Ecology: Ecotheory beyond Green*. Ed. Jeffrey Jerome Cohen. Minneapolis: University of Minnesota Press, 2013. 213–232.

Leroi, Armand Marie. *The Lagoon: How Aristotle Invented Science*. New York: Viking Press, 2014.

Morton, Timothy. *The Ecological Thought*. Cambridge: Harvard University Press, 2010.

Nixon, Rob. *Slow Violence and the Environmentalism of the Poor*. Cambridge: Harvard University Press, 2011.

Okorafor, Nnedi. *Lagoon*. New York: Saga Press, 2014.

Ralegh, Walter. *The Discovery of the Large, Rich, and Beautiful Empire of Guiana*. Ed. Robert H. Schomburgk. London: Hakluyt Society, 1848.

Scott, Rebecca R. *Removing Mountains: Extracting Nature and Identity in the Appalachian Coalfields*. Minneapolis: University of Minnesota Press, 2010.

Serres, Michel. *The Five Senses: A Philosophy of Mingled Bodies*. Trans. Margaret Sankey and Peter Cowley. London: Continuum, 2008.

Shakespeare, William. *The Tempest*. *The Norton Shakespeare*. Eds. Stephen Greenblatt, Walter Cohen, Jean E. Howard, Katharine Eisaman Maus. 2nd edn. New York: W. W. Norton, 2008.

Stern, Gerald M. *The Buffalo Creek Disaster: How the Survivors of One of the Worst Disasters in Coal-mining History Brought Suit Against the Coal Company—and Won*. 2nd edn. New York: Vintage Books, 2008.

Tennyson, Alfred Lord. 'Ulysses'. *Selected Poems*. Ed. Christopher Ricks. London: Penguin, 2007. 49–50.

Tuana, Nancy. 'Viscous Porosity: Witnessing Katrina'. *Material Feminisms*. Eds. Stacy Alaimo and Susan Hekman. Bloomington: Indiana University Press, 2008. 188–213.

Part III

NATURE'S CULTURES AND CREATURES

Chapter Eleven

Nature/Culture/Seawater

Theory Machines, Anthropology, Oceanization

Stefan Helmreich

On 17 October 2009, fourteen officials of the Maldives government convened a meeting on the seafloor, 20 feet below the water's surface, to sign a document exhorting nations around the planet to cut carbon dioxide emissions. At an average of 5 feet above sea level, many of the 1,192 coral islands of the Maldives are in danger of vanishing beneath the Indian Ocean if climate change proceeds as many scientists predict. The Maldivian meeting, staged as an elaborate if serious photo opportunity, saw cabinet ministers outfitted in full scuba gear, and it mobilised seawater—in its apparition as what Lévi-Strauss would have called *maleficent water* (against beneficent water, rain water)—as a symbol of drowning.[1] The meeting was a call to recognise a local 'culture' under threat from a global 'nature' transformed by distant 'cultures' of consumption and pollution. Water materialised as a cycling, hybrid substance, at once natural and cultural.

The anthropologically minded analysis I have offered just now presses the nature/culture binary to do a good deal of critical work—conceptual work conditioned by anthropology's wider epistemological inheritance. As Marilyn Strathern might observe: 'Western nature-culture constructs . . . revolve around the notion that the one domain is open to control or colonization by the other' (1980, 181). Water oscillates between natural and cultural substance, its putative materiality masking the fact that its fluidity is a rhetorical effect of how many of us speak and think about 'nature' and 'culture' in the first place. Water as *nature* appears as both potentiality of form and uncontainable flux; it moves faster than culture, with culture often imagined in a land-based idiom grounded in the culture concept's origins in European practices and theories of agriculture and cultivation. Water as nature appears as that flowing substance that culture may be mobilised to channel—think of canal locks, dams, and irrigation networks. Water as *culture*, meanwhile, can materialise as a medium of pleasure, sustenance, travel, poison, and disaster.

I here consider water as substance and symbol in anthropological theory, asking how the nature/culture pair imposes particular qualities on water, which water is then sometimes imagined to overflow. In asking after water this way, I retool historian of science Peter Galison's (2003) notion of a 'theory machine', an object in the world that stimulates a theoretical formulation. For Galison, networks of electro-coordinated clocks in European railway stations at the turn of the twentieth century aided Einstein's thinking about simultaneity. Animal husbandry provided a theory machine for Darwin. For French physicist Sadi Carnot, *water* was a theory machine; his second law of thermodynamics in the 1820s hypothesised that heat was a fluid that behaved like flowing water (Knight 2009). How has water operated as a theory machine in anthropology? How has water been framed by nature/culture? How has it in turn reframed nature/culture?

Water is not one thing. For natural science, water's effects depend on its state (solid, liquid, gas), on its scale (from molecular to oceanic), and on whether it is fresh or salty, still or turbulent, deep or shallow. For interpretative social sciences, water can be sacred substance, life, refreshment, contaminant, grave. I fix in this essay on seawater—mindful that rivers, lakes, rain, irrigation systems, glaciers, bogs , and other aqueous elementalities demand their own accounts.

In 'Common Senses: Water, Sensory Experience and the Generation of Meaning', Veronica Strang compares her ethnographies of water in Aboriginal north Australia and Dorset, England, to suggest that the variety of meanings attached to water issues from its form: 'Water's diversity is . . . a key to its meanings. Here is an object that is endlessly transmutable, moving readily from one shape to another: from ice to stream, from vapour to rain, from fluid to steam. It has an equally broad range of scales of existence: from droplet to ocean, trickle to flood, cup to lake' (98). Strang suggests that water's qualities of mutability 'are crucial in that they provide a common basis for the construction of meaning' (97). I agree with Strang on the mutability and multiple meanings of water but would emphasise that such mutability has no meaning apart from human conceptions of it. Strang's argument offers one kind of theory machine, positing that a formal flexibility in a substance's 'nature' underwrites its flexibility in culture. Strang's claim is emblematic of larger turn to 'the form of water' (15) in recent anthropological and social theory.

In what follows, I track that turn and its history to motivate a discussion of seawater imagery and metaphors in early ethnography, in maritime anthropology, and in recent social theory. I trace a three-part story. First, I suggest that in early anthropology the qualities of seawater were portrayed impressionistically, even Romantically. Using Franz Boas' famous suggestion that the colour of seawater is a matter of cultural construal, rather than of sheer empiricity, I argue that such figures as Bronislaw Malinowski, Raymond Firth, Claude Lévi-Strauss, and Margaret Mead treated water, paradoxically, as atheoretical, a substance upon which to meditate when they were not building social theory. Second, I discuss how, in maritime anthropology, water became a more explicit substance to think with, its materiality a crucial factor in accounts of fisher people. Third, I show how in today's social theory—in the work of Paul Gilroy, Zygmunt Bauman, and Peter Sloterdijk, for example—scientific descriptions of water's form, molecular and molar, have become prevalent in figuring social, political, and economic forces and dynamics.

I argue that seawater has moved from an implicit to an explicit figure for anthropological and social theorizing, especially in the age of globalization, which is so often described in terms of currents, flows, and circulations. Indeed, I suggest that, in light of such tropes, 'globalization' might also be called 'oceanization'. But although directing salutary attention to watery materiality, such turns to 'the form of water' can conjure new reifications, which should prompt anthropologists to puzzle further about how best to think across nature, culture, water, and theory. Rather than treat water as a 'theory machine', then, I conclude—drawing on an image often used in nautical talk—that anthropologists might work *athwart theory*: that is, they might think of theory neither as set above the empirical nor as simply deriving from it but, rather, as crossing the empirical transversely (Helmreich 2009, 23–25). Theory (and, for that matter, seawater) is at once an abstraction as well as a thing in the world; theories constantly cut across and complicate our descriptive paths as we navigate forward in the 'real' world.

ANTHROPOLOGY'S OCEANIC ORIGIN STORIES

One origin story for anthropology goes back to Franz Boas' reflections on the colour of seawater as a matter decided divergently within distinct cultural epistemologies. Looking back on his 1881 University of Kiel physics-geography dissertation, 'Contribution to the Understanding of the Color of Water', Boas wrote:

> In preparing my doctor's thesis I had to use photometric methods to compare intensities of light. This led me to consider the quantitative values of sensations. In the course of my investigation I learned to recognise that there are domains of our experience in which the concepts of quantity, of measures that can be added or subtracted like those with which I was accustomed to operate, are not applicable. (qtd. in Stocking 1974, 42)

Seawater prompted Boas to consider qualitative aspects of seeing. Seawater, seen, became a theory machine for the qualitative, relativist cultural episte-mology for which Boas became known—which perhaps is fitting because the word *theory* derives from ancient Greek for 'to look on' and 'to contem-plate'. Alexandra Lorini takes this argument further, suggesting not only that, 'Water in its different forms, and the human activities related to it, was at the centre of Boas' geoanthropological descriptions of the Northwest Coast' ('The Cultural Wilderness') but also that the mutability of water—in rivers, rain, snow—served as a model for Boas' belief in the mutability of cultural practice.[2]

Seawater figured more practically in early anthropology as the medium supporting passages towards fieldwork. Gisli Pálsson writes that,

> As a result of voyages by sea, different and isolated worlds were connected into a global but polarised network of power-relations. Prior to these voyages, the idea of anthropology did not exist. In a very real sense, then, anthropology, the study of humanity, is as much the child of seafaring as of colonialism. (1991, xvii)

Such European seafaring saw the sea as a blank space between nation-states, as Philip Steinberg (2001) has argued.[3] Malinowski's stay in the Trobriands during World War I resulted from his status as an Austro-Hungarian citizen permitted to substitute internment as an enemy alien in Britain with a stay in the Western Pacific. For Malinowski, the Trobriands became anthropological islands out of history because of a view of the sea as a dissociating space (Kuper 1983).

European anthropologists rhapsodised about waters over which they passed. Malinowski, in his 1922 *Argonauts of the Western Pacific*, wrote of 'intensely blue, clear seas' (49) and reflected on how 'the sea will change its colour once more, become pure blue, and beneath its transparent waters, a marvel-lous world of multicoloured coral, fish and seaweed will unfold itself' (220). Raymond Firth, in *We the Tikopia*, recalls that, 'In the evening the shades of the sea vary from a steely grey where the light is reflected on it through a pale green of the reef waters inshore to a darker green near the reef edge, and an indigo beyond' (29). Lévi-Strauss's *Tristes Tropiques* tells of the 'blue crucible of the sea' and of 'a gleaming, satin-smooth tropical sea' (78, 88).

We can use Boas to help make sense of such imagery. Accounts of the colour of seawater often bespeak qualitative intuitions about the meaning of the ocean. For Malinowski, Firth, and Lévi-Strauss, seawater is a symbol of changeable nature. Water functions not so much as theory machine but as an other to theory: as description. These anthropologists hold 'theory' in abey-ance while at sea, only to set it in motion once the ethnographer hits land. Malinowski's opening tableau in *Argonauts* is canonical: 'Imagine yourself suddenly set down surrounded by all your gear, alone on a tropical beach close to a native village, while the launch or dinghy which has brought you sails away out of sight' (1922, 4). Michael Taussig in *What Color Is the Sacred?* suggests that Malinowski's fixation on colour uses detail to conjure the ineffable. Taussig offers this titbit from Malinowski: 'During that walk I rested intellectually, perceiving colours and forms like music, without formulating them or transforming them' (qtd. in Taussig 2009, 84). Without, that is—in the terms of my analysis—using colour and form as elements for thinking, for theorizing.

Such aesthetic visions of seawater are European, Romantic. They are signs of nostalgia and fantasy. Elizabeth DeLoughrey has argued that 'colonial mystifications of an idyllic South Seas . . . interpellated the Pacific Basin as a vast, empty (feminised) ocean to be filled by masculine European voyagers' (2007, 103), and insofar as this tradition continued in the anthropology of such figures as Malinowski, whose writings are lush with what Malinowski, in *The Sexual Life of Savages*, called a 'half-idyllic South Sea pastoral' (106), one might, following Catherine Lutz in 'The Gender of Theory', detect a masculine cast to these makings of 'theory' as a land-based activity—although Margaret Mead's 1928 rhapsody on the 'gleaming sea' (14) in *Coming of Age in Samoa* also aestheticises the sea. So, too, in an Atlantic context, does Zora Neale Hurston's ethnography of Haiti and Jamaica, *Tell My Horse*—although Hurston *also* writes of ocean floods and drowning, pointing to the Atlantic as a distinct theory machine in African American anthropology.

It is worth noting another chromatic of the sea: the sea at night. This can be another aesthetic reading, but has also been deployed more directly as a theory machine. Consider Henk Driessen's 'A Janus-Faced Sea', in which Driessen uses ethnography among clandestine trans-Mediterranean migrants to 'offer a counterpoint to the romantic image of a benevolent Méditerraée— smooth as glass, bathed in sunshine, blue, green, and turquoise colours and consumed by mass tourists' (42). Writing that, 'Over the past ten years the clandestine, mostly nocturnal, crossing of the Mediterranean has become a dangerous passage into Europe for an increasing number of migrants from Africa and Asia' (45). Driessen employs a distinction between daytime and night-time seas, seas of tourism versus seas of perilous migration, to offer the maleficent waters of the nocturnal sea as a theory machine for understanding dispossession.

MARITIME ANTHROPOLOGIES

Maritime anthropologists centre much of their work on examining how people think about and negotiate property in ocean resources.[4] One objective of such work, often carried out in applied anthropology, has been to demonstrate (to governmental organizations that regulate fishing) the rationality of local knowledges in managing fish stocks. Maritime anthropologists have also studied how technocratic experts are possessed of culturally particular practices around the sea.[5] Maritime anthropology is a fruitful place to look for distinct deployments of seawater as theory machine.[6]

In early articulations, maritime anthropology projected land-based notions onto seafaring life (Hewes 1948). Tim Ingold (2000) observes that foraging wild food resources, on land or sea, has been represented as akin to activities of nonhuman animals, whereas agricultural cultivation has been associated with *production*—and thus, by extension, culture. Early literature on fishing communities focused on the hybrid represented by peasant fishermen, like those studied by Firth (1936). Only with one foot planted on *terra firma*, could these fishermen appear as legitimate subjects of study.

Treating the sea as a zone to be brought under containment has led to what Pálsson, riffing on Foucault, calls 'the birth of the aquarium', the rise of management regimes that treat the sea as a mammoth aquarium that must be enclosed (Pálsson 1998). Such enclosure is predicated on a separation of nature and culture, with the sea scripted as a hypernature until now outside culture. In *Rough Waters*, an ethnography of a Marine Park in Tanzania, Christine Walley (2004) reports that people of Tanzania's Mafia Island did not share the distinction between nature and culture to which transnational marine scientist park consultants were committed; far from seeing the sea as a wild Other to human culture, their seascape was a space of fishing, fish, and biographically meaningful stories of seafaring.

Treating the sea as naturally distinct from the land has other pitfalls. One is to assume that the ocean is ontologically unpredictable, and can therefore explain, say, the apparition of magic in fishing practice. Such a model, owed, canonically, to Malinoswki, operates as a functionalist theory machine: oceanic vagaries produce urgency, which in turn produces a certain kind of ritual engagement. Another hazard is a treatment of the sea as fluid and unbounded prior to its enclosure in 'culture'. When Ingold writes that, 'As terrestrial mammals, we humans stake out our differences on the land; the sea, however, is a great dissolver—of time, of history, of cultural distinction', this must be heard as a summary of an historically particular view (qtd. in Pálsson 1991, x). Such a culturally specific vision animates the fluid ontology that geographer Sarah Whatmore assigns to the sea: 'The spatial codification of "real" property as a grid-like surface finitely divisible into mutually exclusive estates is both unimaginable and impracticable if we substitute the socio-materialities of land for those of air or water' (2001, 60). But seeing the sea as the most unbounded nature there is has a lineage—one connected to colonial projects of keeping the high seas 'free', outside sovereign territorializations.

Western constructions of the 'nature' of the sea—contrasted to the grounded 'culture' of land, as 'fluid' and 'protean' (Raban 1993) or, as early anthropologists who travelled to 'the field' by ship might have had it, as 'another world . . . without human culture' (Davis 1997, 100)—are not universal.[7] But they remain powerful, perhaps nowhere so much as in views of ocean resources as 'by nature' common (Trawick 2001).

Maritime anthropology has demonstrated that how people understand property in ocean resources has to do with local systems of management and meaning rather than with the nature of the sea as such. Liberal economists hold that the seas are a common resource that invites overexploitation owing to a natural selfishness that drives human action. Maritime anthropologists, however, have documented a variety of norms around marine resource use. Pálsson, quoting Arthur McEvoy, notes that,

> Hardin's thesis of the tragedy of the commons represents a 'mythology' of resource use, a model 'in narrative form for the genesis and essence of environmental problems'. The claim that access to the ocean is open for everyone in most fishing societies, and that this is the root of all environmental problems, needs to be qualified . . . The theory of the tragedy of the commons, then, is an important means for making history, an authoritative claim with a social force of its own, and not simply an attempt to understand the world. (1991, 154)

Scholars thus detail the diversity of kinds of sea tenure, 'collectively managed informal territorial use rights in a range of fisheries previously regarded as unownable . . . ways in which inshore fishermen perceive, name, partition, own and defend local sea space and resources' (Cordell and McKean 1992, 183). How that 'space' is imagined is relational. Ajantha Subramanian, in her study of South Indian artisan fishers competing with mechanised trawlers for fish, describes 'fishermen in pursuit of mobile species' (158) who operate at different speeds with respect to the fish they seek. Mobility is not 'in the nature' of fish, so much as a relational category that depends on technologies and speeds of access. The way water operates as a theory machine depends on how quickly one frames it moving, flowing, with respect to 'culture'.[8]

How else might seawater be imagined and engaged? I consider some possibilities by turning now to how seawater is figured in recent social theory.

OCEANIZATION

The black Atlantic is an analytic unit that Paul Gilroy (1993) proposed in the early 1990s in order to link histories kept apart by such landed terms as

African and African American. The Black Atlantic is a term that includes the horrors of the Middle Passage but that also can point to the way that the sea has been a positive presence in the Afrodiaspora. In spaces such as the Sea Islands, off the coasts of Georgia and North Carolina, where people escaping from plantation slavery in the United States sometimes found refuge, water can be a buffer from mainland politics as well as a symbolically baptismal substance associated with swimming escapes from captivity. And, where some writers might suggest that people in such locales as the Sea Islands have a 'local' relation to the sea, it is also the case that such people possess a 'global' imagination of the ocean, one connected to what Gilroy writes of as the 'rhizomorphic, fractal structure of the transcultural, international formation I call the black Atlantic' (4).[9] Gilroy's move—one of the first in a trend in historical studies to pose oceans as units of cultural analysis—operates as a theory machine for renarrating sociality.

Work on the black Atlantic, along with anthropologies of the Indian Ocean (Walley 2004) and cultural studies of the Pacific, mark a moment of rethinking the 'natures' that subtend 'cultures' (often providing a resource for metaphors, too; for example, in Enseng Ho's ethnography of trans–Indian Ocean kinship, he explains, 'Hadramis, especially the sayyids, were a strong current in this restless ocean' 102). I suggest that these works might be read not only as responses to 'globalization', but also as offering a new framework: *oceanization*, a reorientation towards the seas as a translocally connecting substance.[10] John Kurien (2001) has pitched such an approach in a multinaturalist direction, suggesting thinking about 'seacosystems'; he asks social scientists to attend to tropical and temperate seacosystems as enmeshed in distinct ecological and sociopolitical dynamics.

The use of maritime analogies by anthropologists seeking to reconceptualise analysis owes much to the 1972 writings of Fernand Braudel on the Mediterranean and to the introduction into anthropology of a world-systems approach by those, like Sidney Mintz (1985), interested in an Atlantic space crisscrossed by ships, slaves, and sugar. Scholars have become interested in rethinking the world in fluid terms, and also in looking at those entities— refugees, nomads, weapons and drugs, fish—that challenge borders because they flow across them. As Pamela Ballinger writes,

> authors of both popular and scholarly accounts of globalization often employ watery metaphors—of flows, fluidity, circulations—in an effort to capture the increasing unboundedness of movements of capital, communications, and persons. The sea and its qualities thus come to symbolise the growing permeability of borders in a globalizing world, even as the oceans themselves literally represent both medium and site of globalization (2006, 154–155).

Thinking with watery metaphors has become a prescriptivist enterprise. We *should* be thinking with water—even oceans—say many theorists (Chambers 2010).

What kind of theory machine is seawater in new social theory? For some, the ocean is a boundary-blurring body, a space of liberation. Epeli Hau'ofa, of the University of the South Pacific, has argued that Europeans have belittled Oceania by construing it as a scattering of islands, rather than as a 'sea of islands'. This 'sea of islands', holds Hau'ofa (1993), is actually connected, not divided, by water. For others, the rise of the ocean in social thought represents the unwelcome return of 'capital's myth element', the site of unimpeded circulation (Connery 1995, 289).

For still others, the liquidity of water summons up the spectre of maleficent water. Sociologist Zygmunt Bauman, for example, worries that 'liquid modernity' unmoors people from grounds of politics; in liquids, he writes, quoting the *Encyclopedia Britannica*, 'molecules are preserved in an orderly array over only a few molecular diameters' (1), with the result that large-scale structures deliquesce. Philosopher Peter Sloterdijk sees in globalisation a shrinking and multiplication of spheres of human action, fusing and fissioning, and employs the image of 'foam' to describe this state, which he sees as negative. In 'Towards an Amphibious Anthropology', René ten Bos summarises Sloterdijk's position: 'Politically, foam is uncontrollable and unruly: we live our lives in what can best be described as a morphological anarchy' (85). What I have called, drawing on Strang, the turn to the 'form of water' takes shape at a variety of scales, but usually with some appeal to the *formal* properties of water: its hydrography as a connecting element for community and commerce, its molecular structure, and so forth.

If the sea is a potent material for the formation of theory, it may be because, as Taussig has it, 'the sea has disappeared into our heads' (2006)—by which he means that the ocean is not, for many European, American, and other social theorists a quotidian presence but, rather, a space of imagination (a view easily complicated by contrast with the experience of contemporary maritime labourers, such as Filipino workers who can be found in large numbers on cargo and cruise ships the world over; Fajardo 2011). Scholars across disciplines should think critically about this turn to water, recognising, for example, that it often appeals to abstract, scientific descriptions of water as though these have meaning in themselves. But the 'materiality' of water does not tell a self-evident, on-beyond-human story. Attention to materiality is, in part, consequent upon an environmentalist common sense that increasingly takes water to be a self-evidently 'global' substance, one that connects vastly different cultural, political, and economic worlds. Jamie Linton, in *What Is Water? The History of a Modern Abstraction*, suggests that water has come into view as an abstraction—in accounts of the hydrological cycle, in debates about bottled water, in discussions of contaminated ground water—at the very moment when it is at risk. Similar arguments may apply to the specific case of seawater, overfished, acidifying, irradiated, polluted, deoxygenated. We should keep in sight the epistemological conditions and contentions of the recent turn to water and to seawater.

Discussions in feminist theory point one way forward. Writers have examined the use of water metaphors—flux, flow, sea—to speak of women's worlds and have pointed to the essentialism such rhetoric can summon (Game 1995, 192). Scholars worry about the 'wave' metaphor (first, second, third) in histories of feminism. Edna Keah Garrison argued in 2005 that the *feminist oceanography* (a term coined by Deborah Siegel) of the wave narrative homogenises women, linearises movement, and posits times of lulls, which mismeasures histories of activism. Alison Wylie is more sanguine about water waves, suggesting that

> waves do not so much overtake and succeed/supercede one another as rise and fall again and again in the same place, transmitting energy in complicated ways. . . . waves propagate and interact even in the simplest of circumstances . . . waves are generated in many different ways: by river or tidal currents, by snags and obstructions under water, by wind and traffic on the surface, and, on rare and catastrophic occasion, by grinding shifts in tectonic plates (2006, 173).

Wylie's is a call to think with the form of water, yes, but it is also tuned to empirical variation as well as the inescapable rhetoricity of such thinking.

Thinking with water might best be done with such fusing of the theoretical and empirical. In anthropology, Celia Lowe's *Wild Profusion*, an analysis of biodiversity in Indonesia, asks readers to take the view of Sama fishers in the Togean archipelago off the coast of Sulawesi:

> For those without intimate experience with the sea, land and water can seem binary entities. The land is start and finish; the sea is a way to get there. The land represents the rich world of human history and domestication; the sea is a temporary pathway. But in many places with watery histories—the Mediterranean, the Pacific Islands, the Netherlands—land and water join together in configuring senses of place (2006, 92).

Where the Indonesian state has seen Sama as 'extraterrestrial others', outside institutional frameworks because of maritime nomadism, Lowe details how sites like lowland swamps are considered anthropogenic spaces by Sama people. Lowe does and does not use water as theory machine; Sama views structure her own, but she does not generalise them.

WORKING ATHWART THEORY,
THINKING THROUGH WATER

In a review essay on water and sustainability, Benjamin Orlove and Steve Caton (2010) urge anthropologists to treat water as 'a total social fact' Crucial to such treatment, they insist, is an understanding of 'the materiality of water' (402) anchored in water's molecular properties, which shape the quantities in which water can manifest (from drop to deluge) and the qualities that water can support (from purified to polluted). Although Orlove and Caton allow that, 'quantity and quality are always experienced as social constructions' (403), they suggest that limits to such constructions inhere in water's materiality (and insofar as Orlove and Caton appeal to molecularity, that materiality is itself a kind of form).

My petition to think critically about the turn to the form of water in social theory asks not for the further reach of 'social construction', although attending to historical controversies about water's materiality form (when did people come to believe that it was an element? a compound?) can generate useful hesitations about ontological claims.[11] Rather, I am interested in how simultaneously to employ water as a theory machine, when useful, and to treat both water and theories as things in the world. I think of this approach as operating 'athwart theory': that is, as tacking back and forth between seeing theories as explanatory tools and taking them as phenomena to be examined. Such an account does not separate meaning and materiality because such sequestering only reinstalls a preanalytic nature–culture.

I return, in conclusion, to an oceanic phenomenon of recent contemporary 'global' concern, a bookend to the Maldives vignette with which I began this chapter. The 2010 Deepwater Horizon Gulf of Mexico oil spill—like the crisis faced by the Maldives, bound up with fossil fuel use—also churned up nature and culture and may best be understood by refusing that binary. The spill became available to comprehension because of an intermingling of the empirical and the theoretical. Awareness of the spill and its extent emerged at a variety of levels, from shoreline experiences of a slick arriving on beaches to fishers' and shrimpers' experience of their poisoned supply chain. But the phenomenon was also made apprehensible through models—simulations that use data from satellites and submarine sensors and that plug these into algorithms that model flow and currents. As David Bond (2013) has noted in his ethnography of the spill, what counted as 'the environment' was an outcome, not a stable category already in place before such representations. The very 'empiricity' of the spill—including as a 'national' and 'global' event—became manifest through machines instantiating theories of seawater behaviour.[12] Such simulations are both theoretical models of the world and things in the world that are mobilised in the service of social priorities and agendas.

Rather than use water as a theory machine itself, then, I would suggest that any social scientific or historical account of events such as this spill—or of hurricanes, of storm surges, of tsunamis—track how oceanographers, politicians, corporations, citizens, NGOs, and other actors themselves used water as a theory machine to motivate their analyses. Such a reading does not treat the form or substance of water as the privileged province of scientific description, which is then simply drafted into cultural accounts that give that form different 'meanings' (following Ivan Illich in *H₂O and the Waters of Forgetfulness*, the reading I suggest would 'refuse to assume that all waters may be reduced to H_2O' [4]). Rather, such an analytic practice takes scientific accountings—including social scientific ones—as events in the world in need of examination. Put another way, I suggest that scholars import the anti-essentialist insights developed to rethink biogenetic, bioengineered, and ecological 'nature' in the age of biotech into their understandings of the 'nature' of seawater.[13] Seawater is both good to think with and here to live with, in multifarious actuality.[14]

NOTES

1. 'Lévi-Strauss commented . . . on the ubiquity of two kinds of water in South American myths, creative water of celestial origin and destructive water of terrestrial origin' (Shanklin 1989, 234). For a classic anthropology of water symbolism, see Patricia Hidiroglou (1994).

2. Boas' reflections on water as encultured substance contrast with Durkheim, who naturalises water as preanalytic stuff: 'Sensual representations are in a perpetual flux; they come after each other like the waves of a river, and even during the time that they last, they do not remain the same thing' (1915, 433).

3. This view, supported by the legal making of the High Seas (in Dutch jurist Hugo Grotius's 1609 *Mare Liberum* [*Freedom of the Seas*]), has in European philosophy been leveraged into a claim about ocean ontology. Barthes 'claimed that the sea "bears no message", not merely because of its power to reflect rather than contain a gamut of different meanings but because of its seeming absence of evidence' (qtd. in Nandita Batra and Vartan P. Messier 2008, 4).

4. Maritime anthropology offers ethnographies of fishing communities. See, for classic texts, Frederik Barth's *Models of Social Organization* (1966), James M. Acheson's *The Lobster Gangs of Maine* (1988), Bonnie J. McCay's *Oyster Wars and the Public Trust: Property, Law, and Ecology in New Jersey History* (1988), Gísli Pálsson's *Coastal Economies, Cultural Accounts: Human Ecology and Icelandic Discourse* (1991). Also important have been anthropological histories of seafaring.

See Thomas Gladwin's *East Is a Big Bird: Navigation and Logic on Puluwat Atoll* (1970), Ben Finney's *Voyage of Rediscovery: A Cultural Odyssey through Polynesia* (1994). On coastal tourism, see Jane Desmond's *Staging Tourism: Bodies on Display from Waikiki to Sea World* (1999). Scholars have examined beliefs about fishing symbolism, e.g., John Cordell and Judith Fitzpatrick's 'Cultural Identity and the Sea in Torres Strait' (1987). Such work has documented how fishing is structured around gender, race, class, and indigeneity. See Barbara Garrity-Blake's *The Fish Factory: Work and Meaning for Black and White Fishermen of the American Menhaden Industry* (1994); Irene M. Kaplan's 'Women Who Go to Sea: Working in the Commercial Fishing Industry' (1984), Olga Nieuwenhuys's 'Invisible Nets: Women and Children in Kerala's Fishing' (1989), S. Søreng's 'Fishing Rights Discourses in Norway: Indigenous Versus Non-indigenous Voices' (2007). Maritime anthropologists have tracked fishing alongside migration, trade, development, and environmentalist politics. See Serge Dedina's *Saving the Grey Whale: People. Politics, and Conservation in Baja California* (2002), Theodore C. Bestor's 'Supply-side Sushi: Commodity, Market, and the Global City' (2001), Jane Nadel-Klein's *Fishing for Heritage: Modernity and Loss along the Scottish Coast* (2003).

5. For an account of how new kinds of marine biotechnology might be imagined—both by social theorists and practitioners—as continuous with older practices of fishing, see Stefan Helmreich's 'A Tale of Three Seas: From Fishing through Aquaculture to Marine Biotechnology in the Life History Narrative of a Marine Biologist' (2003).

6. An early angle through which seawater was viewed anthropologically was as host to natural resources for human cultural enterprise. Lewis Henry Morgan named fishing as a skill marking humanity's transition to the Middle Stage of Savagery, his logic being that fish required cooking to eat. See page 10 in Lewis Henry Morgan's *Ancient Society, or Researches in the Lines of Human Progress from Savagery through Barbarism to Civilization* (1877). In 1906, Marcel Mauss documented coastal lifeways of the Inuit, reporting that Eskimo sociality was organised around summer and winter regimes and noting that 'if a child is born during the summer, his first meal consists of soup made from some land animal, or from a river fish cooked in fresh water; the "winter" child's first meal is soup from some sea animal cooked in salt water' (Mauss 1979, 60). See also Alfred L. Kroeber's 'Fishing among the Indians of Northwestern California' (1960).

7. Nor are they monolithic, even within the so-called West, as historians of the modern seaside have demonstrated. See Alain Corbin's *The Lure of the Sea: The Discovery of the Seaside 1750–1840* (1995). Looking at 'culture and nature underwater' (53), to borrow Susan Davis's phrase, can demonstrate that there are many ways to parse watery realms.

8. Maritime anthropology also contests the idea that the ocean is naturally dangerous: '[H]istorian Marcus Rediker has argued in *Between the Devil and the Deep Blue Sea* (1989) that we distort 'the reality of life at sea by concentrating on the struggle of man and nature', which effectively obscures the role of exploitation and economic pressures in seafarers' lives' (Howard 2010, 9).

9. For one argument about what this sort of theory machine might leave out—perhaps Indian Ocean and Pacific Ocean Afrodiasporas and other Black Oceans—see Stefan Helmreich's 'Kinship, Nation, and Paul Gilroy's Concept of Diaspora' (1992).

10. 'Oceanisation' has a natural science meaning: 'The conversion of continental crust into the much thinner and petrologically distinct oceanic crust' (OED 2008). I would not suggest that social scientists develop their own unitary definition of 'oceanization'. Indeed, even in oceanography, the properties assigned to seawater are not fully generalisable but, rather, are particular to oceans on Earth: currents are motored by wind, modulated by the planet's rotation, and organised into loops called gyres; circulations refer to the three-dimensional conveyance of water across hemispheres based on temperature and saltiness; tides depend on the moon.

11. Hasok Chang, *Is Water H₂O? Evidence, Realism and Pluralism* (2012). See also Ivan Illich, *H₂O and the Waters of Forgetfulness: Reflections on the Historicity of 'Stuff'* (1985).

12. On models of climate and associated oceanic events, see Paul Edwards's *A Vast Machine: Computer Models, Climate Data, and the Politics of Global Warming* (2010). Another example that could be elaborated here would be the disastrous civic planning and politics that permitted the waters consequent to 2005's Hurricane Katrina to drown or otherwise cause the deaths of at least 1,833 people in Louisiana. Shaped by racialised and racist city planning, the infrastructural failure of the levees in New Orleans hit African American neighbourhoods hardest, an outcome that requires an analysis that looks at how the formalisms of city and hydraulic planning can encode and/or be calibrated to ruling assumptions about which places and people are worth protecting. See J. Anthony Paredes's 'Introduction to "The Impact of the Hurricanes of 2005 on New Orleans and the Gulf Coast of the United States"' (2006).

13. See Arturo Escobar's 'After Nature: Steps to an Antiessentialist Political Ecology' (1999). It is not clear to me that treating water as an 'actor' in the sense encouraged by some posthumanism is the way to go here. Jessica S. Lehman, in 'Relating to the Sea: Enlivening the Ocean as an Actor in Eastern Sri Lanka' (2013), offers an intriguing narrative in which seawater is an actor—though one of the difficulties of this approach, ironically, turns out to be that 'the ocean' is treated as a category before the analysis gets underway.

14. This phrasing plays with Lévi-Straussian ideas but also invokes words of Donna Haraway's. In *The Companion Species Manifesto*, Haraway writes: 'Dogs are not surrogates for theory; they are not here just to think with. They are here to live with' (2003, 5).

WORKS CITED

Acheson, James M. *The Lobster Gangs of Maine.* Hanover: University Press of New England, 1988.
Ballinger, Pamela. 'Watery Spaces, Globalizing Places: Ownership and Access in Postsocialist Croatia'. *Contemporary Studies in Economic and Financial Analysis. Vol. 88: European Responses to Globalization: Resistance, Adaptation and Alternatives.* Eds. Janet Laible and Henri J. Barkey. Bingley: Emerald Group Publishing, 2006. 153–157.

Barth, Frederik. *Models of Social Organization.* London: Royal Anthropological Institute, 1966.

Batra, Nandita and Vartan P. Messier. 'The Multitudinous Seas: Matter and Metaphor'. *This Watery World: Humans and the Sea.* Eds. Vartan P. Messier and Nandita Batra. Newcastle upon Tyne: Cambridge Scholars Publishing, 2008. 1–19.

Bauman, Zygmunt. *Liquid Modernity.* Cambridge: Polity Press, 2000.

Bestor, Theodore C. 'Supply-side Sushi: Commodity, Market, and the Global City'. *American Anthropologist* 103.1 (2001): 76–95.

Boas, Franz. *The Mind of Primitive Man.* New York: Free Press, 1938.

Bond, David. 'Governing Disaster: The Political Life of the Environment during the BP Oil Spill'. *Cultural Anthropology* 28.4 (2013): 694–715.

Bos, René ten. 'Towards an Amphibious Anthropology: Water and Peter Sloterdijk'. *Environment and Planning D: Society and Space* 27.1 (2009): 73–86.

Braudel, Ferdnand. *The Mediterranean and the Mediterranean World in the Age of Philip II.* Vol I. Trans. Siân Reynolds. 1949. New York: Harper and Row, 1972.

Chambers, Iain. 'Maritime Criticism and Lessons from the Sea'. *Insights* 3.9 (2010). Web. 10 September 2015.

Chang, Hasok. *Is Water H₂O? Evidence, Realism and Pluralism.* Dordrecht: Springer, 2012.

Connery, Chris. 'The Oceanic Feeling and the Regional Imaginary'. *Global/Local: Cultural Production and the Transnational Imaginary.* Eds. Rob Wilson and Wimal Dissanayake. Durham: Duke University Press, 1995. 284–311.

Corbin, Alain. *The Lure of the Sea: The Discovery of the Seaside 1750–1840.* Trans. Jocelyn Phelps. Harmondsworth: Penguin, 1995.

Cordell, John and Judith Fitzpatrick. 'Cultural Identity and the Sea in Torres Strait'. *Cultural Survival Quarterly* 11.2 (1987): 15–17.

Cordell, John and Margaret A. McKean. 'Sea Tenure in Bahia, Brazil'. *Making the Commons Work: Theory, Practice, and Policy.* Ed. David Feeny. San Francisco: Institute for Contemporary Studies Press, 1992. 183–206.

Creighton, Margaret and Lisa Norling, eds. *Iron Men, Wooden Women: Gender and Seafaring in the Atlantic World, 1700–1920.* Baltimore: Johns Hopkins University Press, 1996.

Davis, Susan. *Spectacular Nature: Corporate Culture and the Sea World Experience.* Berkeley: University of California Press, 1997.

Dedina, Serge. *Saving the Grey Whale: People. Politics, and Conservation in Baja California.* Tucson: University of Arizona Press, 2002.

DeLoughrey, Elizabeth. *Routes and Roots: Navigating Caribbean and Pacific Island Literatures.* Honolulu: University of Hawaiian Press, 2007.

Desmond, Jane. *Staging Tourism: Bodies on Display from Waikiki to Sea World.* Chicago: University of Chicago Press, 1999.

Driessen, Henk. 'A Janus-Faced Sea: Contrasting Perceptions and Experiences of the Mediterranean'. *Maritime Studies* 3.1 (2004): 41–50.

Durkheim, Émile. *The Elementary Forms of the Religious Life: A Study in Religious Sociology.* Trans. Joseph Ward Swain. London: George Allen and Unwin, 1915.

Edwards, Paul. *A Vast Machine: Computer Models, Climate Data, and the Politics of Global Warming*. Cambridge: MIT Press, 2010.

Escobar, Arturo. 'After Nature: Steps to an Antiessentialist Political Ecology'. *Current Anthropology* 40.1 (1999): 1–16.

Fajardo, Kale Bantigue. *Filipino Crosscurrents: Oceanographies of Seafaring, Masculinities and Globalization*. Minneapolis: University of Minnesota Press, 2011.

Finney, Ben. *Voyage of Rediscovery: A Cultural Odyssey through Polynesia*. Berkeley: University of California Press, 1994.

Firth, Raymond. *We, the Tikopia: A Sociological Study of Kinship in Primitive Polynesia*. London: George Allen and Unwin, 1936.

Firth, Raymond. *Malay Fishermen: Their Peasant Economy*. London: Routledge and Kegan Paul, 1946.

Galison, Peter. *Einstein's Clocks, Poincaré's Maps: Empires of Time*. New York: Norton, 2003.

Game, Ann. 'Time, Space, Memory, with Reference to Bachelard'. *Global Modernities*. Eds. Mike Featherstone, Scott Lash, Roland Robertson. London: Sage, 1995. 192–208.

Garrison, Edna Keah. 'Are We on a Wavelength Yet? On Feminist Oceanography, Radios, and Third Wave Feminism'. *Different Wavelengths: Studies of the Contemporary Women's Movement*. Ed. Jo Reger. New York: Routledge, 2005. 237–256.

Garrity-Blake, Barbara. *The Fish Factory: Work and Meaning for Black and White Fishermen of the American Menhaden Industry*. Knoxville: University of Tennessee Press, 1994.

Gilroy, Paul. *The Black Atlantic: Modernity and Double Consciousness*. Cambridge: Harvard University Press, 1993.

Gladwin, Thomas. *East Is a Big Bird: Navigation and Logic on Puluwat Atoll*. Cambridge: Harvard University Press, 1970.

Haraway, Donna. *A Companion Species Manifesto: Dogs, People, and Significant Otherness*. Chicago: Prickly Paradigm, 2003.

Hau'ofa, Epeli. 'Our Sea of Islands'. *A New Oceania: Rediscovering Our Sea of Islands*. Eds. Vijay Naidu, Eric Waddell, Epeli Hau'ofa. Suva: School of Social and Economic Development, USP, 1993.

Helmreich, Stefan. 'Kinship, Nation, and Paul Gilroy's Concept of Diaspora'. *Diaspora: A Journal of Transnational Studies* 2.2 (1992): 243–249.

Helmreich, Stefan. 'A Tale of Three Seas: From Fishing through Aquaculture to Marine Biotechnology in the Life History Narrative of a Marine Biologist'. *Maritime Studies* 2.2 (2003): 73–94.

Helmreich, Stefan. *Alien Ocean: Anthropological Voyages in Microbial Seas*. Berkeley: University of California Press, 2009.

Helmreich, Stefan. 'Virtual Water'. *Cultural Anthropology*. Virtual issue on Water. September 2010. Web. 10 November 2013.

Hewes, Gordon W. 'The Rubric "Fishing and Fisheries"'. *American Anthropologist* 50 (1948): 238–246.

Hidiroglou, Patricia. *L'eau Divine Et Sa Symbolique*. Paris: Albin Michel, 1994.

Howard, P. McCall. 'Working the Ground: Life and Death at Sea'. *Anthropology News* 51.2 (2010): 9–11.

Hurston, Zora Neale. *Tell My Horse: Voodoo and Life in Haiti and Jamaica.* Philadelphia: J. B. Lippincott, 1938.

Illich, Ivan. *H2O and the Waters of Forgetfulness: Reflections on the Historicity of 'Stuff'*. Dallas: Dallas Institute of Humanities and Culture, 1985.

Ingold, Tim. *The Perception of the Environment: Essays on Livelihood, Dwelling and Skill*. London: Routledge, 2000.

Kaplan, Irene M. 'Women Who Go to Sea: Working in the Commercial Fishing Industry'. *Journal of Contemporary Ethnography* 16 (1984): 491–514.

Knight, David. *The Making of Modern Science: Science, Technology, Medicine and Modernity, 1789–1914*. Cambridge: Polity Press, 2009.

Kroeber, Alfred L. 'Fishing among the Indians of Northwestern California'. *Anthropological Records* 21 (1960): 1–210.

Kuper, Adam. *Anthropology and Anthropologists: The Modern British School*. London: Routledge, 1983.

Kurien, John. 'People and the Sea: A 'Tropical-majority' World Perspective'. *Maritime Studies* 1.1 (2001): 9–26.

Lehman, Jessica S. 'Relating to the Sea: Enlivening the Ocean as an Actor in Eastern Sri Lanka'. *Environment and Planning D: Society and Space* 31(2013): 485–550.

Lévi-Strauss, Claude. *Triste Tropiques*. 1955. Trans. John and Doreen Weightman. New York: Penguin, 1995.

Linton, Jamie. *What Is Water? The History of a Modern Abstraction*. Vancouver: University of British Columbia Press, 2010.

Lorini, Alexandra. 'The Cultural Wilderness of Canadian Water in the Ethnography of Franz Boas'. *Cromohs* 3 (1998). Web. 17 September 2010.

Lowe, Celia. *Wild Profusion: Biodiversity Conservation in an Indonesian Archipelago*. Princeton: Princeton University Press, 2006.

Lutz, Catherine. 'The Gender of Theory'. *Women Writing Culture*. Eds. Ruth Behar and Deborah Gordon. Berkeley: University of California Press, 1995. 249–265.

Malinowski, Bronislaw. *Argonauts of the Western Pacific: An Account of Native Enterprise and Adventure in the Archipelagoes of Melanesian New Guinea*. London: Routledge and Kegan Paul, 1922.

Malinowski, Bronislaw. *The Sexual Life of Savages in North-Western Melanesia*. London: Routledge, 1929.

Mathur, Anuradha and Dilip da Cunha. *Soak: Mumbai in an Estuary*. New Delhi: Rupa and Co., 2009.

Mauss, Marcel with H. Beuchat. *Seasonal Variations of the Eskimo: A Study in Social Morphology*. Trans. and Foreword by James J. Fox. London: Routledge, 1979.

McCay, Bonnie J. *Oyster Wars and the Public Trust: Property, Law, and Ecology in New Jersey History*. Tucson: University of Arizona Press, 1988.

Mead, Margaret. *Coming of Age in Samoa: A Psychological Study of Primitive Youth for Western Civilization*. New York: William Morrow and Company, 1928.

Mintz, Sidney. *Sweetness and Power: The Place of Sugar in Modern History*. New York: Penguin, 1985.

Morgan, Lewis Henry. *Ancient Society, or Researches in the Lines of Human Progress from Savagery through Barbarism to Civilization*. Ed. Leslie White. New York: Henry Holt and Company, 1877.

Nadel-Klein, Jane. *Fishing for Heritage: Modernity and Loss along the Scottish Coast*. Oxford: Berg, 2003.

Nieuwenhuys, Olga. 'Invisible Nets: Women and Children in Kerala's Fishing'. *Maritime Anthropological Studies* 2.2 (1989): 174–193.

OED, 2008. http://public.oed.com/the-oed-today/recent-updates-to-the-oed/previous-updates/december-2008-update/

Orlove, Benjamin, and Steve Caton. 'Water Sustainability: Anthropological Approaches and Prospects'. *Annual Review of Anthropology*. Volume 39(2010): 401–415.

Pálsson, Gísli. *Coastal Economies, Cultural Accounts: Human Ecology and Icelandic Discourse*. Manchester: Manchester University Press, 1991.

Pálsson, Gísli. 'The Birth of the Aquarium: The Political Ecology of Icelandic Fishing'. *The Politics of Fishing*. Ed. Tim Gray. London: Macmillan, 1998. 209–227.

Paredes, J. Anthony. 'Introduction to "The Impact of the Hurricanes of 2005 on New Orleans and the Gulf Coast of the United States"'. *American Anthropologist* 108.4 (2006): 637–642.

Raban, Jonathan, ed. *The Oxford Book of the Sea*. Oxford: Oxford University Press, 1993.

Raffles, Hugh. '"Local Theory": Nature and the Making of an Amazonian Place'. *Cultural Anthropology* 14.3 (1999): 323–360.

Shanklin, Eugenia. 'Exploding Lakes and Maleficent Water in Grassfields Legends and Myth'. *Journal of Volcanology and Geothermal Research* 39 (1989): 233–246.

Søreng, Siri U. 'Fishing Rights Discourses in Norway: Indigenous versus Non-indigenous Voices'. *Maritime Studies* 6.2 (2007): 77–99.

Steinberg, Philip E. *The Social Construction of the Ocean*. Cambridge: Cambridge University Press, 2001.

Stocking, George W. Jr. *The Shaping of American Anthropology, 1883–1911: A Franz Boas Reader*. New York: Basic Books, 1974.

Strang, Veronica. 'Common Senses: Water, Sensory Experience and the Generation of Meaning'. *Journal of Material Culture* 10.1 (2005): 92–120.

Strathern, Marilyn. 'No Nature, No Culture: The Hagen Case'. *Nature, Culture and Gender*. Eds. Carol MacCormack and Marilyn Strathern. Cambridge: Cambridge University Press, 1980. 174–222.

Subramanian, Ajantha. *Shorelines: Space and Rights in South India*. Stanford: Stanford University Press, 2009.

Taussig, Michael. *Walter Benjamin's Grave*. Chicago: University of Chicago Press, 2006.

Taussig, Michael. *What Color Is the Sacred?* Chicago: University of Chicago Press, 2009.

Thomas, Nicholas. *In Oceania: Visions, Artifacts, Histories*. Durham: Duke University Press, 2007.

Trawick, Paul. 'The Moral Economy of Water: Equity and Antiquity in the Andean Commons'. *American Anthropologist* 103.2 (2001): 361–379.

Vestergaard, Torben A. 'The Fishermen and the Nation'. *Maritime Anthropological Studies* 3 (1990): 14–34.

Walley, Christine. *Rough Waters: Nature and Development in an East African Marine Park*. Princeton: Princeton University Press, 2004.

Whatmore, Sarah. *Hybrid Geographies: Natures Cultures Spaces*. London: Sage, 2001.

Williams, Raymond. *Keywords: A Vocabulary of Culture and Society*. New York: Oxford University Press, 1976.

Wylie, Alison. 'Afterword: On Waves'. *Feminist Anthropology: Past, Present, and Future*. Eds. Pamela Geller and Miranda Stockett. Philadelphia: University of Pennsylvania Press, 2006. 167–176.

Chapter Twelve

Revisiting the Anthropological Difference

Matthew Calarco

A number of discourses associated with the 'animal turn' in theory take as their point of departure the contemporary challenge to traditional ways of drawing the human/animal distinction. Most theorists who write from within this turn agree that classical binary and hierarchical notions of an anthropological difference—which is to say, a difference that would definitively demarcate human beings from other animals—are ontologically and normatively untenable.[1] In opposition to this approach, there are currently efforts by many theorists throughout the humanities and social sciences to develop alternative conceptions of an anthropological difference that take into account many of the standard criticisms of traditional human/animal distinctions but that reassert strong divisions between human beings and animals. How might pro-animal theorists respond to such discourses? In this chapter, I undertake an analysis of a recent text by Hans-Johann Glock that offers a paradigmatic instance of this countertrend. Glock is an analytic philosopher who argues that an anthropological difference—that is, a generic distinction between human beings and animals—should be established along new lines in order to continue work in philosophical anthropology and the human sciences. My reading of Glock's text aims to demonstrate that his version of the anthropological difference, while successfully responding to certain scientific challenges raised against essentialist conceptions of human nature, contains a number of problematic conceptual and scientific limitations. I further argue that Glock's approach is open to serious ethical and political challenges, which, when taken into consideration with the other problems concomitant with his approach, suggest we might consider leaving behind altogether the project of determining an anthropological difference. I close the chapter with a brief sketch of how a thought that holds the search for an anthropological difference in abeyance might proceed.

ESSENTIALIST HUMAN NATURE AND
THE BIOLOGICAL CHALLENGE

The title of Glock's article takes the form of a question: 'The Anthropological Difference: What Can Philosophers Do to Identify the Differences between Human and Non-human Animals?'. As an initial response to this question, one might wonder: why it is the task of philosophers to determine the anthropological difference? After all, if the assumption that there is or must be an anthropological difference has long been the reigning *doxa*, ought not the task of philosophy be to challenge that *doxa*? That there is a felt need to pose and answer this question concerning the anthropological difference suggests that the human/animal distinction is currently in trouble. If that is indeed the case, why might it not be the task of philosophy to accelerate or intensify this trouble? Against this critical possibility, Glock would seem to want to reaffirm the reigning image of thought. To be fair, Glock acknowledges that his project is a somewhat contentious one. He hopes to defend a traditional (albeit modified) vision of philosophy as philosophical anthropology, despite the well-established problems with such an approach; and he seeks to maintain an anthropological difference, even as he acknowledges that previous attempts to identify a sharp distinction between human beings and animals are unpersuasive. With regard to the first point, Glock aligns himself with the Enlightenment and neo-Kantian versions of philosophy as philosophical anthropology, an approach that proposes that many of the central questions in philosophy revolve around the more basic question of human nature. This long-standing approach to philosophy, which represents a significant portion of the work still done in the discipline today, would fall by the wayside if the anthropological difference were fatally compromised. And, as Glock notes, the fate of the human social sciences is also tied up with the fate of philosophical anthropology, inasmuch as a significant amount of the research done in the social sciences is founded on a conception of 'the human' that allows human beings to be clearly distinguished from animals. It is in view of salvaging and reworking this joint intellectual heritage that Glock's argument is developed.

In view of the second point, Glock is entirely forthcoming about the troubles that plague the identification of an anthropological difference, although even his stark admission of the seriousness of the problems might still underestimate just how much trouble the anthropological difference is actually in at present. Before exploring the full depth of the trouble, let us first follow Glock as he lays out what he takes to be the chief problems with traditional versions of the anthropological difference and how he charts a path beyond those limitations. Glock suggests that developments in evolutionary biology and cognitive ethology have led to a 'general crisis in our self-image as human beings' (2012, 108). Nearly all of the traditional proposed candidates for the anthropological difference have been shown to be conceptually problematic or empirically false, either appearing in some form among some animal species (or at least among certain individuals within a given animal species) or lacking in certain groups of human beings (or in individual human beings).[2] Glock lists some twenty 'features' of claims to human uniqueness— from tool use to moral sense—that have all been found questionable in one way or another as essential markers (110–111). That none of the traditional candidates for the anthropological difference have held up to scrutiny should not be surprising if we view the issue from within a naturalistic, evolutionary framework. Ideally, the anthropological difference should delimit a capacity, characteristic, or behaviour (or a set of such things) that is found in *all* members of the species *Homo sapiens* and *only* in members of that species. Such would be the kind of essential difference that marks human beings off from animals and that provides the necessary and sufficient conditions for group membership. But there is no reason to believe evolutionary processes should produce such clean demarcations between species. The variations found in and among species often make it difficult to identify any specific trait or set of traits that holds for all and only members of a given species. And even if such a break were to be identified, it would not indicate some timeless or essential difference between species but rather the temporary and contingent result of an ongoing process of evolution (Hull 1989, 11).

As Glock concedes, it is of little help to move the search for the anthropological difference to the level of the genotype because the historical and current variation within the human species and the overlap with the genotypes of related species rule out any clean division. Phenotypical differences (where markers of propriety have traditionally been sought) are no more promising as candidates, inasmuch as the variation among human beings at this level is enormous. No matter what specific trait, function, or behaviour is proposed for human uniqueness, there will always be individual human beings without it; and if the characteristic or behaviour chosen is so general as to be truly universal among *Homo sapiens*, it will almost certainly be found among one or more related species. Likewise, appeals to 'potentiality' or 'normality' will do nothing to resolve these problems within a naturalistic framework because variation within a species is neither accidental nor aberrational. Glock suggests that, at best, we might try to delimit a range of reaction norms that specify the range of possible developmental pathways for a given genotype in relation to different environments. However, given how wide this range is among human beings, such an approach would do little to help distinguish human beings from animals as such.

HUMAN PROPRIETY AND THE SOCIAL TURN

Readers who have been immersed in debates regarding philosophy of biology and animal ethics in recent years will be familiar with these and related problems concerning the establishment of an anthropological difference. Viewed collectively, they constitute a devastating attack on the very notion of human nature and rule out the possibility of establishing (at least on biological grounds) any traditional, essentialist version of the anthropological difference. Despite the widespread acceptance of the critical ontological implications of these views among biologists and naturalistic philosophers, there is still no shortage of attempts to re-establish essentialist theories of human nature. Much to Glock's credit, he acknowledges the intractable problems with essentialism and jettisons this approach. He refuses, however, to accept the conclusion that the concept of human nature should be eliminated; he believes that the anthropological difference can still be maintained, albeit in a less ambitious form (he labels his approach *anthropological difference 'light'*). What we need to face squarely, Glock argues, is that there is no version of an anthropological difference starting from basic biological and naturalistic premises that can delimit a range of relevant capacities or traits found among all and only members of *Homo sapiens*. If we still wish to speak of human nature and the anthropological difference in light of these limitations, we must shift our attention away from individual human beings and towards *social life*—towards *species-typical behaviour* in cultural settings.

Glock has much to say about these specific, post-essentialist constraints for defining an anthropological difference. Before examining his remarks on the matter, we should note just how problematic this 'social turn' is. Glock's move away from individuals and towards species-typical behaviour effectively means that when we speak of an anthropological difference—of a break between human beings and animals—there will be a significant number of individual members of the human species who do not fully match the definition of what is human. Thus, we should underscore that such an approach to the anthropological difference is not actually interested in attending to the remarkable variation characteristic of the human species. It is instead focused on 'the human', a partial and carefully delimited segment of human beings that is believed to be cleanly and definitively separated from animals. As one might suspect, there are problems and dangers with such an approach; indeed, the constraints at work in Glock's approach move uncannily in lockstep with the logic of the anthropological machine as described by Giorgio Agamben, determining and fracturing the human along social lines and creating those caesuras in view of a specific difference in relation to animals (Agamben 2004, 29). Glock maintains, though, that 'there is nothing problematic about the idea that in contemporary circumstances humans typically develop in certain ways and hence have typical features and capacities' (2012, 128). Although one could imagine certain contexts in which such a statement might be true, it is most certainly *not* true in the context of debates about human nature and the anthropological difference. Few contexts, it could be reasonably argued, carry higher stakes.

Even with the adoption of this less ambitious notion of an anthropological difference based on the social turn and species-typical behaviour, Glock acknowledges that it remains difficult to locate a definitive human/animal difference. In order to do so, we have to be able to answer the following two questions: 'What features and capacities, if any, are present in all human societies and absent in animal societies? Which capacities are prerequisite for the functioning of human societies?' (129). To explain what is at issue in the second question, Glock offers the following troubling illustration: 'no human society comprised exclusively of severe autists would be viable' (129). Such variations among human beings, then, will need to be set aside if we are to determine an anthropological difference based on the social turn. (That there are currently calls among autistic self-advocates of many sorts to have their communities recognised as cultures is not considered by Glock here.[3]) In regard to the first question, Glock has to tread an even finer line of inclusion and exclusion. As a first step, he argues it is necessary to take a synchronic approach to the study of human cultures and examine only *extant* societies among modern-day *Homo sapiens*. A diachronic and genealogical approach would lead us into the rather problematic issue of how to separate *Homo sapiens* from certain extinct hominids, some of which likely shared with *Homo sapiens* nearly all of the social features and capacities that Glock has in mind. In addition, Glock acknowledges that even 'viable' human cultures sometimes do not display certain features that are often claimed to be universal among human cultures. Here, Glock has to appeal to a modified notion of potentiality and suggest that these societies should still be seen as belonging on the side of the human inasmuch as they are *capable* of exhibiting all such typical features (his example is 'cultural development') 'given a suitable social context' (129). Conversely, behaviour from animals who have been 'enculturated' (that is, trained to acquire specialised behaviours in scientific settings) can be safely ruled out of the discussion, Glock maintains, inasmuch as the behaviours exhibited in those settings do not form part of the normal developmental pathways of animals. Whatever one's opinion of such research practices, the fact that animals *can be* and *are* raised in enculturated environments entails that, by definition, such environments are not strictly outside their normal developmental pathways (except in a limited, statistical sense). As is the case with human beings, many species of animals are capable of living within an enormous variety of environments. Thus, to rule enculturated

behaviours out of the discussion strikes me as a questionable gesture, inasmuch as the varied environments that structure development in animals are
essential to understanding phenotypic plasticity in a given species.[4]

If, however, we were to allow all of these constraints to govern the discussion, what kind of anthropological difference might emerge? For Glock, there
is not one human/animal difference that comes to the fore but rather a cluster
of properties. He isolates the following behaviours and capacities as the best
candidates for anthropological differences: a 'special and highly complex'
language; a 'special and highly complex' form of sociality, which includes
institutions and norms; and a 'special' rational-technological plasticity that is
built on uniquely human cognitive abilities (130). With this cluster of properties in mind, Glock hopes to avoid the traditional requirement to determine
a single anthropological difference (although if forced to do so, he notes that
his 'money would be on language' [130]) and move the discussion instead
to the cluster of differences that can be found on the other side of the social
turn. Of course, in adopting this kind of cluster approach, his position will be
open to objections of various sorts. This section of Glock's paper is especially
problematic because he cites no biological, sociological, or anthropological
literature to support the notion that any of these behaviours or capacities are,
in fact, entirely absent among all animals. A fuller discussion of that literature
would no doubt force Glock to acknowledge that, *even within the narrow set
of constraints he advocates*, the differences between 'the human' and all other
animals are primarily quantitative rather than qualitative. Given his obvious
familiarity with the ethological and comparative psychological literature,
Glock is certainly aware that claims about some kind of special plasticity and
sociality being absent in *all* animals are highly contentious.[5] Even the more
'promising' claims concerning recursive language being absent in animals are
by no means assured at present. Prior to laying out his three candidates for
anthropological differences, Glock himself provides a caveat on the issue of
animal language (carefully couched in terms of 'natural communication') in
a footnote: 'We may not know enough about the various channels of natural
communication between cetaceans, in particular bottlenose dolphins, in order
to decide how far they approximate linguistic communication' (129, n. 45).
The same could be said, of course, about other animal species.

Even if Glock were to concede these objections, one gets the sense that
they would fail to have any critical force for his project because the idea of
actually trying to attend to the complexity and variation of both human and
animal life has long been left behind in this and most other discussions about
the anthropological difference. On this issue we are enduringly committed—
and a priori, as well, it would seem—to a distinction between the human and
all other animals and to certain practices and forms of life that are built on
that distinction.[6] If the distinction is troubled by some empirical finding or

conceptual problem, one can always move the goalposts, change the constraints, redraw the lines, and get back to the task at hand, as Glock has done in view of previous scientific challenges. It might make more sense, then, to examine what is actually driving this project of separating human beings from animals than rebut Glock point by point on his proposed candidates for anthropological differences. Why does it matter whether we carry out this project? Clearly, his is not a neutral exercise in classification, so where do the ultimate stakes lie?

For Glock, the stakes are to be found primarily in maintaining the practice of philosophical anthropology mentioned at the outset of our analysis. In defending the notion of anthropological differences, Glock hopes to preserve philosophical anthropology as a specific philosophical approach in its own right as well as in relation to the grounding work it does for the human social sciences, anthropology in particular. Thus, the concern here is that, without some conception of human uniqueness, a great deal of philosophical, scientific, and social scientific research will be undercut. This is a common worry among analytic philosophers who work on the topic of human nature and human/animal differences. In a survey of recent research in this area, Maria Kronfeldner, Neil Roughley, and Georg Toepfer argue, like Glock, that the concept of human nature should be maintained. They suggest that human nature should be understood in a pluralistic manner, doing different work in different theoretical contexts depending on 'our epistemic needs' (Kronfeldner et al. 2014, 650). Inasmuch as 'different scientific fields draw on different epistemic roles (definitional, descriptive, and explanatory)' (650), they argue we will need to make use of different notions of the human, of several human natures.

Such pragmatic concerns about maintaining the anthropocentric and exceptionalist underpinnings of scientific and social scientific inquiry are, from a certain perspective, entirely reasonable. After all, how can we expect to maintain the disciplinary orientations of these fields without *some* notion of human nature that is relevant to 'our epistemic needs'? If we lose hold of human uniqueness and have no way cleanly to differentiate human beings from animals (as well as other 'others' of the human), what would become of the humanities and social sciences in particular? They would, of course, undergo a radical and thoroughgoing revision. *Perhaps, though, that is precisely what is needed.* The current destabilization of the anthropological difference could lead to a complete rethinking of how 'the human' has been configured within these disciplines and how the disciplines might themselves be reconfigured in the face of these challenges. These are different epistemic needs, to be sure, but such needs are precisely what is at issue. We are engaged here in a struggle over the future of thought, and it is not entirely obvious that traditional work in philosophical anthropology or the epistemic requirements of current research in the sciences and social sciences should be our sole guide in thinking through the anthropological difference.

Rosi Braidotti makes the important point that this kind of unmooring of the humanities and social sciences from their epistemological and anthropocentric foundations serves as a unique opportunity to create alternative lines of inquiry in the form of posthumanities. This would not be a sceptical project content simply to undo the anthropological difference but would instead be aimed at pursuing a thought and practice of the human as being irreducibly caught up in a series of relations, networks, and contexts. According to Braidotti, the critique of anthropocentrism and human exceptionalism reconfigures the human so as to stress its 'radical relationality, that is to say nonunitary identities and multiple allegiances' (2013, 144). She offers animal studies and ecocriticism as examples of the kinds of research programs and practices that have emerged from this postanthropocentric approach. Following Braidotti, I would suggest that this line of nonanthropocentric thought could be accelerated in order to reconfigure existing disciplines and also allow additional fields of thought to emerge through what she calls 'humble experimentation' (150) with the theoretical and practical implications of nonanthropocentrism. Important examples of such work are already unfolding in fields as diverse as anthropology, sociology, geography, and political theory.[7]

THE ETHICS AND POLITICS OF THE HUMAN

Let us pause for a moment to restate the line of thought we have pursued up to this point. We have seen that the conceptual and general biological issues with determining an anthropological difference pose intractable problems for trying to draw essentialist lines between human beings and animals. The only viable option available to broadly naturalistic philosophers like Glock who wish to maintain an anthropological difference of some sort is to redraw the distinction in a rather constrained way, setting aside diachronic, genotypic, and phenotypic variation in view of a highly circumscribed subset of members of *Homo sapiens*. This approach, as we have suggested, is still open to serious scientific objections even on its own terms; likewise, the presupposition that some version of the anthropological difference is necessary for work in philosophical anthropology and the human and social sciences is less than persuasive. But there are a host of other problems—primarily ethical and political in nature—with the search for an anthropological difference with which Glock seems largely unconcerned.[8] These ethical and political criticisms of the anthropological difference, however, carry even more force and provide us with an additional set of compelling reasons for trying to develop different ways of thinking and living beyond the human/animal distinction. Here I examine briefly just a handful of the more important criticisms germane to the argument being developed in this chapter.

The first critical point to consider is that the determination of an anthropological difference must be seen as being to a large extent performative in nature, in the sense that this term is given in Jacques Derrida's reading of J. L. Austin and in Judith Butler's influential account of gender performativity.[9] As a performative practice, this project is participating in and reiterating networks of power relations that structure the intersection of human and animal. Again, the stakes could hardly be higher here. The definition of human propriety in dominant cultural and intellectual practices and discourses informs how we perceive the widespread variation among human individuals and cultures and delimits what we take to constitute genuine humanity. Further, given the hegemonic tendency within the dominant culture towards a hierarchical value system based on an anthropocentric measure, all beings who are seen to lack full humanity—whether human, animal, plant, machine, or some other kind of entity—tend to be devalued to the degree that they divert from the anthropocentric norm. This kind of hierarchical value system does not, of course, necessarily follow in a strict logical sense from the attempt to determine an anthropological difference. One could argue that the distinction between human and animal is simply neutral and denotative and carries no necessary value implications. Such an argument, however, would be profoundly ahistorical and apolitical. As Judith Butler notes in her recent work, *Undoing Gender*, the category of the human 'has been crafted and consolidated over time' and carries within it 'existing differentials of power' (2004, 13–14). To fail to address this sedimented history when dealing with the anthropological difference risks reinforcing and extending deeply problematic power relations.[10]

One of the more subtle ways in which the anthropological difference has been used to institute and reproduce problematic forms of power is through the employment of logics of sub- and dehumanisation. In line with the point just made concerning the performative and ideological nature of the anthropological difference, David Livingstone Smith argues that defining what is properly human is far from 'a morally innocent exercise in descriptive taxonomy' (2013, 42). The human, he argues, is perhaps best understood as an indexical term that refers back to what one considers to be genuine members or representatives of one's natural kind—a grouping that does not typically include all members of the species. As Smith suggests, this understanding of how human propriety is indexically established sheds important light on the mistreatment of animals as well as discrimination against marginalised human beings. Violence against animals occurs, in Smith's account (and contra standard accounts of speciesism), *not* because animals are understood as belonging to a different species. Rather, they are often treated violently or occupy precarious situations inside and outside the *socius* because 'they are believed to be sub-human (less than human)' (52). In other words, animals are often characterised as not being genuine members of 'our' natural kind and, as such, are marked as being outside the scope of full concern and standing.

As Smith goes on to note, understanding the mistreatment and marginalisation of animals in terms of subhumanisation has important implications for how we think about the marginalisation and dehumanisation of certain groups of human beings. He explains that 'there is a striking resemblance between the way that we habitually conceive of other animals and the way that we conceive of those members of our own species whom we dehumanise' (52). This resemblance leads Smith to propose that 'research into dehumanisation might benefit from drawing on research into the moral marginalisation of other animal species and, conversely, that investigations into the ramifications of human exceptionalism might be enriched by the study of our propensity to dehumanise our fellow *Homo sapiens*' (52) Although Smith does not cite any work done along these specific lines, there is in fact an emerging body of social scientific literature that investigates the particular connections between beliefs about anthropological differences and the dehumanisation of various marginalised peoples. Nick Haslam, a leading researcher in dehumanisation studies, notes that the human/animal distinction is one of the chief axes along which dehumanisation is reproduced (Haslam 2006). In addition, a number of recent studies have sought to tease out how the alignment of certain groups of human beings with animals provides the 'logic' whereby violence and marginalisation are justified and naturalised.[11] What this literature suggests is that the anthropological difference often functions to differentiate sharply human beings from animals and to establish caesuras in and among human beings themselves. Thus, if we wish to reconsider what it means to be human, we must do so with a critical awareness of this long and sedimented history of division, power, and violence. We cannot proceed as if subdividing humanity into species-typical behaviours, and then further dividing that subset of humanity sharply from animals, does not run the risk of creating the conditions for the development of pernicious attitudes and practices.

Another critical limitation in Glock's analysis concerns the rather ethnocentric nature of his approach to defining human nature and human/animal differences. As Judith Butler suggests, our dominant ideas about what constitutes the human tend to be 'distinctively western . . . and, therefore, partial and parochial' (2004). Recent work associated with such anthropologists as Eduardo Kohn (2013), Eduardo Viveiros de Castro (2014), and Philippe Descola (2013) suggests that the dominant manner of determining human propriety over and against all animals is, in fact, deeply ethnocentric.[12] Descola in particular argues that, beyond the kind of approach we have examined in

Glock (which Descola labels 'naturalism', a framework that allows for biological continuity between humans and animals at the physical level but posits a sharp break at the level of the mental registers of interiority, subjectivity, and cognition), there are other, important frameworks for thinking about human–animal relations and culture–nature interactions. He explores three other general ontologies under the rubrics of *totemism, animism*, and *analogism*, all of which generate very different orientations towards human beings, animals, personhood, subjectivity, and so on (Descola 2013, 129–231).

Such alternative ontologies and epistemologies of human, animal, and more-than-human relations ought to be taken into account within discussions of the anthropological difference as more than ethnographic novelties. To treat them as such would simply reinforce the ethnocentrism of the dominant approach by other means. What is needed instead is a full respect for these and other alternative frameworks as viable and valuable on their own terms, as engendering alternative and ongoing forms of life and thought with which we must enter into deeper dialogue. The dominant culture is structured by human/animal and human/non- and subhuman dualisms that serve to institute, reproduce, and justify nearly unthinkable and ever-increasing forms of violence against any being or collective that falls outside the orbit of the human. This form of life is already complicit with mass death on an unprecedented historical scale, is currently initiating another mass extinction event, and is poised to undercut in fundamental ways many of the biophysical systems on which all life-forms—human and more-than-human—depend. In Michel Serres' words, 'We are dying, in effect, of separating ourselves from the world' (2008, 129). It would thus seem pressing to engage with and learn from other ways of seeing, knowing, and being in the world that seek to heal this split instead of retreating to familiar terrain and trying to re-establish traditional frameworks that emphasise human exceptionalism and sharp breaks from animals and all other nonhuman beings.

HUMAN–ANIMAL INDISTINCTION

In this final section, allow me to sketch in some of the basic elements of what such a shift in orientation might include. I make no pretence of offering a complete or final account here, for not only are the fields of relation and difference we are considering inexhaustible, but also because the task at hand (namely, considering how me might live and relate differently) is inherently collective and experimental. Now, the most general point to be gained from our analysis thus far is that there is a profound need, if not entirely to eliminate the human/animal distinction, then at least to set it aside provisionally so that other modes of thought might come to the fore. To hold the anthropological difference in abeyance is to begin from the premise that the traditional distinctions drawn between human beings and animals fail to designate anything of ontological significance, which is to say, such differences do not denote any kind of meaningful 'joints' carved in nature.[13] As we have seen, the opposition that is being set aside is an extremely clunky one that tries to differentiate countless numbers of species, individuals, and relations into two general sets. Although such an ontological approach has been dominant throughout the Western metaphysical tradition and permeates multiple spheres of contemporary thought and practice, we are in no way obligated to maintain it and refine it. Not all inherited frameworks and concepts are worth maintaining, no matter how venerable their origins might be. Given the centrality and dominance of the anthropological difference, I am not suggesting, of course, it can be easily overcome or forgotten. There will long be a need to engage in critical analysis of and resistance to this heritage, and hence it will remain necessary to risk reproducing its terms in order to displace it. But there is a marked difference between critique of the established order and creating the space to imagine other configurations of relation and other forms of life. The attempt to place the anthropological difference in abeyance is driven by a desire to open that alternative space and to experiment with other modes of thought and relation.

The most common concern voiced against placing the anthropological difference in abeyance is that such a strategy would seem to entail flattening the differences between human beings and animals and reducing this rich field of beings to a single, undifferentiated set. Such flattening would be particularly problematic if it were to proceed by way of demonstrating that 'animals are like us', which is to say, by showing that animals are relevantly similar to or identical to human beings in various ways and viewing animals solely along those lines. Such a strategy, which is commonly employed in analytic animal ethics and animal minds discourses, leaves the human at the centre of the analysis and measures animal being, value, and standing in terms of quintessentially human properties. The path of thought that I am sketching out here does not deny that many of the traits considered to be exclusively 'proper' to human beings are, in fact, present among many animal individuals and species, but the assimilation of animals to various anthropocentric measures is not what is at stake. Instead, the point is to situate what we call human beings within a history and a set of relations that precedes and exceeds them in innumerable spatial and temporal directions.

Thus, to set aside the anthropological difference means thinking from zones in which human beings and animals become indistinct. Becoming indistinct refers neither to a simple, common sense identity nor to the erasure of difference. What this concept points to is (1) the surprising and profound ways in which human beings find themselves situated within and alongside animals, and (2) the manner in which differences among human beings and animals come to be redistributed along other axes. In regard to the first point, the concept of indistinction is meant to situate human beings within a series of relations that fundamentally challenge claims to human propriety and exceptionalism. Such undercutting of human propriety suggests that those whom we call human beings are in a fundamental sense latecomers to a series of regional and planetary relationships and modes of existence, both in evolutionary-ecological and in ontological terms. We find a particularly powerful example of this way of characterizing human existence in artist Francis Bacon, whose paintings align human bodies with animal flesh to create a zone of indistinction between them.[14] Following Bacon, if we think of human bodies not as securely organised and atomised organisms but rather as a kind of meat or flesh that is exposed to relations and becomings, we come to situate human beings within a broader set of relations that are proper neither to them nor to animals. To live as a fleshy body is to discover that one shares in a mode of life-death that undoes any and all attempts to establish human propriety. Here, human flesh is seen to be like animal flesh, and animal flesh is seen in turn to participate in a series of other iterations of vulnerable, finite, and living materialities. Human–animal indistinction thus encourages us to rethink the *socius* far beyond the confines drawn by philosophers like Glock, who seek to limit sociality to intrahuman relations.

In regard to the second point, by rendering the traditional human/animal distinction indistinct, there is indeed a risk of eliminating a generic difference; but this risk is taken in in order to point up how other differences are generated and distributed along other axes. Jacques Derrida recurrently makes the important point that the generic human/animal distinction functions to block important differences among animals.[15] This point is true as far as it goes, but if we limit ourselves (as deconstruction does) to remaining on the terrain of this distinction in order to refine and multiply it, we tend to underestimate just how unruly and differential the field of beings and relations is. Thus, rather than relaunching a more complex version of the question of the proper of the human in relation to the animal, we might consider foregoing ontologies of propriety altogether. For what we are trying to do here is catch sight of a variety of differential relations—which is to say, alternative identities, differences, and assemblages—that undercut any and all forms of propriety. Relations between human beings and animals are so differentially complex that attending to them requires a very different kind of logic and ontology. In *What Animals Teach Us about Politics* (2014), Brian Massumi offers such an approach under the rubric of a logic of *mutual inclusion*, a logic that aims to displace the generic human/animal difference in order to highlight the singularities that emerge in and around the edges of the traditional distinction. A logic of mutual inclusion calls for us to experiment with the singularities and alternative modes of relation that become possible beyond generic differences. Indistinction and mutual inclusion are, then, the wellsprings from which alternative modes of thought and new forms of life emerge. To view human–animal relations and differences in terms of indistinction is to begin from the premise that the field under consideration is irreducibly aporetic for thought, that it is inexhaustible, that singularities continually emerge from and then fall back into the field of differences, and that this field of differences always threatens to undo any kinds of generic differences we might seek to draw.

These ontological points about indistinction might seem to indicate an implicit commitment to a process ontological approach; and there is, in fact, certain aspects of that framework that are of immense importance in trying to carve out a space for thinking beyond the anthropological difference. Similarly, it might seem that the preceding analysis is pointing in the direction of a companion species ontologies and multispecies ethnographies; here, too, there are undoubtedly multiple gestures and insights worth preserving. There are additional consonances that could be underscored between this analysis and certain nonwestern, indigenous, and radical environmental frameworks as well. What is to be said about such seemingly eclectic ontological implications? Is there not an overarching framework that could properly sort and order these varied ontological tendencies? In the context of the contemporary race for theory, we are encouraged to engage in just such a project, to adopt a monistic perspective, to choose and defend one of these ontological approaches over the others, to pit one framework against the others, and to be on the lookout for the next major ontology and the major thinker who proposes it. Against these monistic and exclusivist tendencies, I want to stress the fundamentally aporetic nature of the field we are considering and, hence, the aporetic nature of the ontological task. What is at stake in thinking beyond the anthropological difference is not the establishment of a single, comprehensive, denotative ontology, but rather the practical and experimental task of developing forms of life that seek to think through and practice more respectful relations. As such, ontological profligacy (which is rather different than a single pluralist or profligate ontology) is to be expected. Given the invariably complex and experimental nature of such forms of life, and the difficulties of attending to various levels and registers of salient relations across a wide range of domains, there will be a need for ontologies of various sorts.

What, then, of the ethical and political implications of setting aside the anthropological difference? The vast majority of thinkers in the fields of animal ethics and animal studies have framed the ethical issue of violence and discrimination against animals as one of *speciesism*. Yet, our analysis of Glock and the alternative ontological approach we have been sketching out in this section point towards a slightly different conception of the ethical issue at hand. Speciesism is typically defined as an irrational prejudice on behalf of the human species that leads many individuals to discriminate against members of other species solely on the basis of their lack of human species membership. The guiding assumption in analyses of speciesism is that most of us extend ethics to all members of the human species but not beyond that species line, and that withholding such an extension without good reasons constitutes an illogical, unjustifiable gesture.

But as we saw with our critique of Glock, the delimitation of the human does not typically track along lines that would include all members of the biological species. The anthropological difference seeks to establish a difference between the human and other animals, to be sure, but also between the human and other human beings (as well as a host of others entities who are deemed subhuman and nonhuman). Thus, in tracking and contesting reactive efforts to establish an anthropological difference, what we are analysing is not so much a speciesist prejudice held by individuals but rather a socio-political apparatus aimed at instituting and reproducing the specific subject position associated with *the human*—a position that has always only been available to a limited number of human beings. Anthropocentrism goes well beyond individual prejudices and irrational ethical judgments to include a wide variety of practices, discourses, and institutions that revolve around the maintenance of the privilege of the human over and against the subhuman and the nonhuman.

To mount a genuine critique of the apparatus of anthropocentrism thus entails a contestation and rethinking of a variety of caesuras and oppositions, both those internal to the human as well as those considered to be nonhuman and external to the human. Thinking beyond the anthropological difference is, from this perspective, to refuse these rifts and to introduce another economy of relations that redraws the field of differences and identities. What needs to be underscored here is that a thought that proceeds beyond the anthropological difference is not limited to displacing the human/animal binary; rather, the critique of this variety of anthropocentrism must be linked with other discourses and practices aimed at calling into question a whole host of other oppositions and rifts between the human and its others. If the human has been constituted in and through a series of such problematic oppositions, a thought that seeks to go beyond such an approach must be prepared to rethink a number of oppositions, each in terms of its specific history and in its relation to the others. It entails in short, a complete rethinking of *all* relations and the constitution of forms of life that seek to do justice to these myriad relations.

NOTES

1. Among critical animal studies theorists, there can be found numerous ways of negotiating and rethinking the human/animal distinction. But what is widely shared

in this context is the sense that attempts to draw binary distinctions between human beings and animals have been thoroughly challenged by developments in evolutionary theory, multispecies ontologies, and biopolitical critique. Similarly, in the normative and ethical domains, the traditional notion that purported differences between human beings and animals should engender value hierarchies has received sharp criticism from normative ethical and political theorists, including analytic philosophers, feminist theorists, neo-Levinasian Continental philosophers, and non-Western thinkers from various traditions, among others.

2. I should emphasise here my discomfort with this binary metaphysics of presence and lack, which orbits around a supposed human norm. It will be called further into question as my argument unfolds.

3. See Straus (2013) for more on this point.

4. This point is made in the context of primate studies by Bard and Leavens (2014). The importance of attending to the environmental aspects of development when making cross-species comparisons applies, of course, to claims made about other species as well.

5. For a helpful introduction to these ongoing debates, see Laland and Galef (2009).

6. Tom Tyler makes a similar point about an 'uncritical prior belief in human uniqueness' (24) that pervades theory and prefigures the human/animal distinction along certain anthropocentric channels.

7. See Gillespie and Collard (2015), Haraway (2008), Parikka (2010), Taylor and Twine (2014), Wadiwel (2015), and Wolfe (2010).

8. Unlike Glock, Kronfeldner and her colleagues (2014) do make note of some of these concerns, but they also fail to give them any significant weight in their analysis. The chief and nearly exclusive concern in much of the analytic philosophical work on the anthropological difference tends to be limited to (1) the evolutionary biological challenge to the human/animal distinction, and (2) the implications of this challenge for intellectual work grounded on this distinction.

9. See Jacques Derrida (1988) and Judith Butler (1990).

10. The converse holds true as well when we argue for the *destabilization* of the anthropological difference. Although the desedimentation of the human/animal distinction might help uncover and challenge certain power differentials concomitant with the human, this does not mean that such a gesture is itself liberatory, neutral, or outside of power. As we proceed along this path of thought, it will be essential to attend to this point with great care.

11. An example of such research carried out in the context of perceptions of immigrants can be found in Costello and Hodson (2009). Along similar lines, Bilewicz, Imhoff, and Drogosz (2011) explore how rhetorics of dehumanization and human–animal continuity/discontinuity figure in the eating of animals. For an overview of recent research on these issues, see Haslam and Loughnan (2014).

12. There are, of course, important differences between these thinkers. I list them together only to indicate a certain trend among certain anthropologists towards non-anthropocentric approaches.

13. See Plato (1997, 265e).

14. Such a reading of Bacon is pursued by Deleuze (2003).
15. See, among various places, Derrida (2008, 47–48).

WORKS CITED

Agamben, Giorgio. *The Open: Man and Animal*. Trans. Kevin Attell. Stanford: Stanford University Press, 2004.

Bard, Kim A. and David A. Leavens. 'The Importance of Development for Comparative Primatology'. *Annual Review of Anthropology* 43.1 (October 2014): 183–200.

Bilewicz, Michal, Roland Imhoff, Marek Drogosz. 'The Humanity of What We Eat: Conceptions of Human Uniqueness among Vegetarians and Omnivores'. *European Journal of Social Psychology* 41.2 (March 2011): 201–209.

Braidotti, Rosi. *The Posthuman*. Cambridge: Polity, 2013.

Butler, Judith. *Gender Trouble: Feminism and the Subversion of Identity*. New York: Routledge, 1990.

Butler, Judith. *Undoing Gender*. New York: Routledge, 2004.

Costello, Kimberly and Gordon Hodson. 'Exploring the Roots of Dehumanization: The Role of Animal-Human Similarity in Promoting Immigrant Humanization'. *Group Processes and Intergroup Relations* 13.1 (January 2009): 3–22.

de Castro, Eduardo Viveiros. *Cannibal Metaphysics: For a Post-structural Anthropology*. Trans. Peter Skafish. Minneapolis: Univocal, 2014.

Deleuze, Gilles. *Francis Bacon: The Logic of Sensation*. Trans. Daniel W. Smith. Minneapolis: University of Minnesota Press, 2003.

Derrida, Jacques. *Limited Inc.* Trans. Samuel Weber. Evanston, IL: Northwestern University Press, 1988.

Derrida, Jacques. *The Animal That Therefore I Am*. Ed. Marie-Louise Mallet. Trans. David Wills. New York: Fordham University Press, 2008.

Descola, Philippe. *Beyond Nature and Culture*. Trans. Janet Lloyd. Chicago: University of Chicago Press, 2013.

Gillespie, Kathryn and Rosemary-Claire Collard, eds. *Critical Animal Geographies: Politics, Intersections, and Hierarchies in a Multispecies World*. London: Routledge, 2015.

Glock, Hans-Johann. 'The Anthropological Difference: What Can Philosophers Do to Identify the Differences between Human and Non-human Animals?' *Royal Institute of Philosophy Supplement* 70.1 (July 2012): 105–131.

Haraway, Donna J. *When Species Meet*. Minneapolis: University of Minnesota Press, 2008.

Haslam, Nick. 'Dehumanization: An Integrative Review'. *Personality and Social Psychology Review* 10.3 (August 2006): 252–264.

Haslam, Nick and Steve Loughnan. 'Dehumanization and Infrahumanization'. *Annual Review of Psychology* 65.1 (January 2014): 399–423.

Hull, David L. *The Metaphysics of Evolution*. Albany: State University of New York Press, 1989.

Kohn, Eduardo. *How Forests Think: Toward an Anthropology beyond the Human.* Berkeley: University of California Press, 2013.

Kronfeldner, Maria, Neil Roughley, Georg Toepfer. 'Recent Work on Human Nature: Beyond Traditional Essences'. *Philosophy Compass* 9.9 (September 2014): 642–652.

Laland, Kevin N. and Bennett G. Galef, eds. *The Question of Animal Culture.* Cambridge: Harvard University Press, 2009.

Massumi, Brian. *What Animals Teach Us about Politics.* Durham: Duke University Press, 2014.

Parikka, Jussi. *Insect Media: An Archaeology of Animals and Technology.* Minneapolis: University of Minnesota Press, 2010.

Plato. 'Phaedrus'. Trans. Alexander Nehamas, Paul Woodruff. *Plato: The Complete Works.* Ed. John M. Cooper. Indianapolis: Hackett, 1997.

Serres, Michel. 'Feux et Signaux de Brume: Virginia Woolf's Lighthouse'. Trans. Judith Adler. *SubStance* 37.2 (2008): 110–131.

Smith, David Livingstone. 'Indexically Yours: Why Being Human Is More Like Being Here Than Like Being Water'. *The Politics of Species: Reshaping Our Relationships with Other Animals.* Eds. Raymond Corbey and Annette Lanjouw. Cambridge: Cambridge University Press, 2013. 40–52.

Straus, Joseph N. 'Autism as Culture'. *Disability Studies Reader.* Ed. Lennard J. Davis. New York: Routledge, 2013. 460–484.

Taylor, Nik and Richard Twine, eds. *The Rise of Critical Animal Studies: From the Margins to the Centre.* London: Routledge, 2014.

Tyler, Tom. 'If Horses Had Hands . . .' *Animal Encounters.* Eds. Tom Tyler and Manuela Rossini. Boston: Brill, 2009. 13–26.

Wadiwel, Dinesh. *The War against Animals.* Leiden: Brill, 2015.

Wolfe, Cary. *What Is Posthumanism?* Minneapolis: University of Minnesota Press, 2010.

Chapter Thirteen

Lively Ethography

Storying Animist Worlds

Thom van Dooren and Deborah Bird Rose[*]

SEALS

Unlike the many other seals at home in cold waters, the Hawaiian monk seal (*Monachus schauinslandi*) has taken to life in the tropics. Members of the *Monachus* lineage, their ancestors evolved in the coastal waters off what is now Turkey and Greece. From here they spread into the Atlantic and the Caribbean and eventually the Pacific, via a waterway that is now closed. Different species of monk seal could once be found thriving in all of these places. Today, all are in severe decline or extinct. There are roughly 1,100 Hawaiian monk seals left, making the species one of the rarest marine mammals on Earth ('Hawaiian Monk Seal').

From 15 million years ago up until the early centuries AD, Hawaiian monk seals likely knew nothing of humans. Members of our species were late arrivals in the Hawaiian Islands. The great seafaring Polynesians settled in the main Hawaiian Islands only about 1,500 years ago. Having evolved in a world without people, monk seals show almost no flight response in our presence. As long as they are not threatened, they stay put. This lack of fear is part of what made them vulnerable to incredible commercial slaughter in the past. It is also part of why they remain so vulnerable on land, even today.

Alongside generalised threats like starvation, entanglement in marine debris and the loss of haul out and pupping sites (due to development and beach erosion), today's monk seals are, not infrequently, subject to deliberate and violent attack by people, beaten to death on the beach. 'Hauling out' of the

*This chapter was previously published in 'Multispecies Studies', a special issue of *Environmental Humanities* (2016, 8.1), edited by Thom van Dooren, Ursula Münster, Eben Kirksey, Deborah Bird Rose, Matthew Chrulew, and Anna Tsing.

water is a vital part of monk seal life: it is required for mating and birth-ing, it provides opportunities to rest, avoid predators and feed young pups. Nevertheless, for some people seals are 'out of place' amongst the main Hawaiian Islands where they compete with fishermen for fish. Attempts at conservation have become bound up with deeply unpopular restrictions on fishing and other marine activities (Rose, 'Monk Seals'). But, into this envi-ronment of violence and loss, some local people are injecting narratives and practices of care. When a seal hauls out on a beach in an inhabited part of the islands, volunteers are called. They go to the reported site and set up a perimeter with stakes and plastic tape, they put up signs, they make sure the event is reported, and they stay. They are not so much policemen as educa-tors, so while they make sure that people respect the sleeping seal's need to be left alone, they also answer questions about monk seal biology, history, future, and behaviour. Although the official literature does not put it this way, volunteers are ambassadors for monk seals. Their response, their commitment to being there, is in itself an ethical statement.

In the abstract, the idea of hanging out on the beach all day keeping an eye on a sleeping seal sounds great. In actual fact it is both great and not so great. Sometimes it is wet and cold, sometimes sticky and boring. The volunteers need to be knowledgeable, and they need the patience to have the same conversations over and over, day after day. They need to be able to discuss conflicting views about monk seals in a manner that does not exac-erbate conflict. It helps to be a good story-teller as well as a good listener (Rose 2017).

Through these grounded acts of care, of witnessing and careful storytelling, these volunteers help to daily enact the dream of a flourishing multispecies community on the beaches of Hawai'i. Unexpectedly, interestingly, com-pellingly, a seal arrives. The arrival feels like a message from the deep, a statement of vulnerability brought onto land by those who live in the ocean but also need to haul out. In these times of extinction and extermination, this moment is a fissure, a happening that becomes a recursive attractor that announces that maybe, just maybe, other kinds of communities might still be possible.

ETHOS

The beautiful word 'ethos' (plural: *ēthea* or *ēthē*) is not widely used these days, although it holds a place in anthropological discussions of aesthetics, poetics and performance (Herzfeld 2001, 283–284).[1] In ethnographic usage, Clifford Geertz's definition is a good baseline: 'A people's ethos is the tone, character, and quality of their life, its moral and aesthetic style and mood; it is the underlying attitude toward themselves and their world that life reflects' (Geertz 1996, 126–141). Our point of departure from standard ethnography is the recognition that it is not only humans who are known by their ethos.

'Ethos', though, is more shifty and elusive than this already open-ended definition suggests. It comes from old Greek, where it meant things like character or way of life, but also custom, and customary practices and places.[2] Homer wrote of the ethos of horses—their habits and habitats. Today it can also mean spirit, as in the spirit or character of a time—a zeitgeist, or an overarching set of values and practices—a style. Definitions start to become reflexive—ethos is part of what makes a group, or 'kind' distinct; we know (or think we know) that given individuals are *a kind* because they are distinct. Dominique Lestel et al. express this point well in their discussion of animals' individual and shared 'cultures'. They conclude that 'there will always be a cognitive or behavioral *style* that will characterise chimpanzees as chimpanzees and distinguish them as much from gorillas as from elephants and humans' (Lestel et al. 2006, 171).[3] And so it is clear that ethos arises through the interplay of sameness and difference. If there were no differences, there would be no background and foreground, no pattern to distinguish, no figure to become meaningful. Ethos involves knowledge, sense of self and other, discernment between kinds.

In short, we are using the term 'ethos' to designate broad styles or ways of life. Our interest is in life in all of its diversity. While Lestel and colleagues focus on the 'cognitive or behavioural style' of particular *animal* species, our approach aims to draw in worlds of life beyond the animal kingdom with all of the diverse modes of engagement, entanglement and co-becoming that this implies. In many of these contexts it does not make sense to focus on 'cognition and behaviour'—at least not in their 'standard' ('animal', of perhaps 'human') forms. There are myriad other kinds of difference and distinctiveness to be found: how does a mistletoe plant make its way in the world, attracting and sharing nectar with some and boring into the branches of others? What kinds of relationships do fungi strike up with wind, soil, tree roots and countless others to shape a world of 'intricate but [perhaps] unintended designs?' (Tsing 2014, 233).

Here we are reminded that the wider distinctiveness of ēthea is crafted through relational and participatory intra-action.[4] Ways of being are not formed and sustained in isolation. Each ethos is also a style or way of being and becoming *with others*. Ēthea are not essences, but emergent and performative happenings; never isolated or fixed, bleeding into and co-shaping one another, and yet somehow maintaining their distinctive uniqueness.[5] This co-shaping takes place at multiple 'levels' and across diverse time frames. In addition, as *embodied* ways of life ēthea are not a cultural element somehow added onto a pre-existing biology. Rather, they are the 'product' of the differential biosocial becomings—the evolutionary and developmental intra-actions—of organisms and their species in co-constitutive relationship with others.[6]

Ultimately, our focus on diverse ēthea leads us into an *ecological animism*. To be attentive to ēthea is to inevitably encounter an animated world, woven through with co-forming patterns of responsiveness, attention, desire and communication. Our approach to animism shares much with indigenous understandings (but we will not explore these similarities here).[7] However, we come to animism via our own worldly encounters, read through the refractive lenses of western science and philosophy.[8] Our focus is on what Emma Restall Orr has called the 'relational awakeness' (2012, 194) of the world, an awakeness that resides in the multiple and diverse forms of intentionality—of perception, striving, desiring, sensing, adapting and responding—that we see evidenced all around us.[9]

Moving well beyond the obvious examples of intentional behaviour in our close relatives in the animal kingdom, biochemist Daniel Koshland notes: ' "Choice", "discrimination", "memory", "learning", "instinct", "judgment", and "adaptation" are words we normally identify with higher neural processes. Yet, in a sense, a bacterium can be said to have each of these properties' (qtd. in Margulis and Sagan 1995, 219). In a similar vein, recent work on plant intelligence has increasingly indicated the widespread existence of sentience and agency of diverse kinds. Plants emerge from this work as beings that sensitively detect and respond to their environments in highly adaptive and communicative ways, drawing in resources as well as warding off herbivores, perhaps by synthesizing chemical deterrents or even by releasing other chemicals that provide cues to potential predators of problematic grazing insects (Trewavas 2002; 2003; Hall 2011; Hustak and Myers 2012; Marder 2013).

Ecological animism responds to a world in which all life—from the smallest cell to the largest redwood—is involved in diverse forms of adaptive, generative, responsiveness. This responsiveness may happen in the immediacy of the moment (as two albatrosses sing and dance to form a pair bond), it may happen through drawn out developmental processes (as a plant slowly grows towards the sun), or perhaps even over evolutionary time frames that remake entwined morphological and behavioural forms to better inhabit their worlds. However it happens though, life is saturated in diverse forms of purposeful attentiveness and responsiveness.[10] In paying attention to these processes, ecological animism is grounded in *recognition* as a mode of encounter that 'aims for the greatest range of sensitivities to earth others' (Plumwood 2002, 177). But more fundamental than any specific set of ideas about what plants, bacteria and others are and do, is the cultivation of a kind of *openness* towards the world. As Cheney and Weston note: 'the kind of practice asked of us is to venture something, to offer an invitation . . . and see what comes of it. We are called, in fact, to a kind of etiquette . . . in an experimental key: the task is to create the space within which a response can emerge or an exchange coevolve' (1999, 126). In short, this is a commitment not to assume that we know, that we could know, all of the ways in which our world is lively and responsive. Ecological animism is not a doctrine or orthodoxy, but rather an opening into a mode of encounter.

LAVA

The Hawaiian island chain is a place of immense biological diversity. Spending time in the forest or the surrounding seas it is often easy to be overwhelmed by the sheer abundance, the energy and vitality of life. But out on the lava fields, surrounded by black as far as the eye can see, other kinds of life, other patterns of coming into and out of the world are also taking place. They may be harder to see at first glance, but the lava fields of Hawaiian are equally places to celebrate living processes. The vibrancy of these places starts with the island-forming potential of the lava itself. For many Hawaiian people this is the work of Pele, who both creates and destroys. Pouring out of fissures deep beneath the ocean's surface, lava cools and accumulates over millions of years to build islands that eventually rise above the surface of the water. The youngest member of this island chain, the Island of Hawaiian, is now roughly two million years old. Moving northwest along the chain we pass through progressively older islands. Geological processes over immense periods of time birthed these islands from deep within the fertile Earth. This is a different kind of fertility, a geologic fertility; sterile in biological terms but lively and generative in the worlds of rocks.

Processes of decay operate in this world too. Travelling out beyond the islands in the main Hawaiian chain we encounter islands that are just clinging to life and some that are gone altogether with only faint traces to mark their once-presence. As these islands move away from the hot spot that birthed them—as a result of shifting tectonic plates—processes of erosion by wind and wave gradually return them to the sea. Far out in the chain, Midway Atoll is now nothing more than an accumulation of sand around coral reefs that once encircled a volcanic island long since disappeared. Here, the biotic holds the geologic, its form and its memory. Different processes of living and dying, of coming together and dissipating are working themselves out at temporal and spatial scales that vary across diverse geological, evolutionary and organismal processes: the lifecycles of island chains and that of fleeting coral polyps in intimate entanglement. But coral and the many creatures—like monk seals—that form *marine* communities around it are just some of the biota made possible by these lively rocks. As lava cools it becomes a clean slate in which new possibilities might take root. The lichens are usually the first to take up this offer. Circulating in immense quantities in the Earth's atmosphere, most of their spores will never germinate. The numbers are against them. But every now and again, 'a spore settles onto a patch of bare rock of the right age and texture and with enough moisture and sunlight that it germinates and, if it is lucky enough to find its symbiotic partner, grows' (Flaspohler 2012). This symbiotic partner is an algae or cyanobacterium that provides the photosynthetic capabilities to a fungus. All lichens are cross-kingdom collaborations of this kind.

Over time, lichen growth and death produces the biological material that, in combination with the elemental weathering of rock, produces soil. Plants like 'okina (*Metrosideros polymorpha*) expertly adapted to these environments find cracks in the lava where moisture and nutrients can accumulate and a seed can germinate. As they grow, they contribute to the slow production of soil as their roots further help to break up the rock while their vegetation adds new organic material. Eventually, bare rock becomes a flourishing and diverse forest full of the incredible variety of lichens, plants, birds and others that is now found in this island chain. But this is only one life story, or set of stories. From another perspective this is a story about the vibrancy of rock, as successive forests come and go beneath fresh waves of hot lava. But also it is perhaps a story about water, a story that moves from ocean to ocean as islands come and go. Above all, therefore, this is a story of entanglements, of the lively biotic, geologic, atmospheric and oceanic processes that are our changing planet.

LIVELINESS

Working from the foundation that our world is constituted out of countless, interwoven ēthea, the question becomes: how might we practice and embody this mode of responsive encounter in our own work? Ethnographers try to capture humans' distinct ways of being and becoming, writing them up as ethnographies. Might our encounters in the larger-than-human world be brought into written form as 'etho-graphies' in a way that would give others vitality, presence, perhaps 'thickness' on the page and in the minds and lives of readers? This is an approach that might start with Clifford Geertz's understanding of man as 'an animal suspended in webs of significance he himself has spun' (1973, 5), but that would quickly insist that humans are not the only beings suspended in such a way, and that no one—no group or species—ever spins alone.[11]

The intention here is not to slip into the hubris of claiming to tell another's stories, but rather to develop and tell our own stories in ways that are open to other ways of constituting, of responding to and in a living world. In this context, stories are powerful tools for 'connectivity thinking' (Weir 2009, 47–50). Unlike many other modes of giving an account, a story can allow multiple meanings to travel alongside one another, it can hold open possibilities and interpretations, and it can refuse the kind of closure that prevents others from speaking or becoming (Smith 2005).[12] Of course, not all stories do this in practice. Good ethographic accounts refuse to become the kinds of stories that shut out, or normalise, all others—rendering invisible the conditions of their own telling.[13] They are active sites for the ongoing weaving or braiding of stories; efforts to inhabit multiply-storied worlds in a spirit of openness and accountability to otherness.

Telling these kinds of stories is an inherently multidisciplinary task, one that draws us into conversation with a host of different ways of making sense of others' worlds. In Anna Tsing's terms, it is about 'passionate immersion in the lives of nonhumans' (2011, 29).[14] Our particular approach draws heavily on a subsection of the natural sciences within the fields of biology, ecology and ethology (animal behaviour), but also geology, chemistry, and more. In telling stories informed by these literatures, ethographies invite readers into a sense of curiosity about the intimate particularities of others' ways of life: how they hunt or reproduce, how they relate to and make sense of (or 'story'; van Dooren and Rose 2012) their particular place, how they entice pollinators or throw their spores to the wind. Beyond the natural sciences, ethographies also make use of the detailed observations and understandings of other peoples whom, for a diverse range of reasons, make it their business to understand other forms of life: from the knowledge of hunters and farmers, to artists, indigenous peoples, animal trainers, wildlife carers, 'cat yoga' practitioners[15] and many others. In each of these cases, as with the insights of the natural sciences, knowledges must be evaluated for what they teach us, as well as with a critical eye to the particular political and technical architectures of framing within which they are produced. In short, it matters which stories we use to tell and think other stories with.[16]

While an ethography tends to start with, to be provoked by, other-than-human ways of life, the openness of these accounts inevitably draws humans into the frame. To this end, more conventional *ethnographic* methods are an indispensable component of an ethography. What does the disappearance of flying foxes mean to *this* community of Aboriginal people in Australia for whom the species is kin? How is the absence of vultures in India experienced by the Parsee community who has traditionally relied on these birds to consume their dead?[17] In this way, ethographic work is attentive to other people's ways of life and understanding (including other animisms); to the biocultural complexity of the worlds that we craft with others. In exploring these and other sites of entanglement, ethographies offer important insights into the many *different*, and consequential, ways in which, as Tsing succinctly puts it, '[h]uman nature is an interspecies relationship' (2012, 144).

With relationality and openness in mind, ethographies are always about more than a singular ethos in isolation: these are *multispecies* stories in which entangled becoming across all of the kingdoms of life is an unavoidable reality. In addition, many entities usually considered to be 'non-living' are key parts of an ethographic account. The volcanic rock that forms the Hawaiian island chain offers a sense of what is at stake here. This lively rock prompts us to ask questions differently. It draws our attention towards what Kathryn Yusoff has called the 'minerality' of the biologic, it undoes any sense of a firm border between the living and the non-living, and it throws into question certainty about what this distinction might even mean. And so it is clear that the non-biotic will always be *part* of an ethographic account, but we remain deliberately open—prepared to be invited and to respond—to the possibility that the liveliness of such beings might itself become the *central* (in so far as there is one) focus of an ethographic account. For us, the key issue for ethography is that of taking the other seriously in their otherness—whether cultural, biological, geological, chemical or something else entirely—and consequently learning to ask and to see how we might be called to respond.[18]

CROWS

Tucked away in aviaries on the south side of Kilauea, on the island of Hawaiian, are some of the rarest birds on earth. Amongst a range of smaller honeycreepers are some of the only remaining 'alalā, or Hawaiian crows (*Corvus hawaiiensis*), a species that has been extinct in the wild for over a decade now. Big, beautiful, birds, their absence has not gone unnoticed. With so many of Hawaii's forest birds having already been lost in the last few centuries, it seems that the 'alalā may have been the last remaining seed disperser for at least three plant species: 'okina, halapepe, and the loulu palms. Beyond simply moving seeds—itself important for plant survival—it seems that some of these seeds germinate better, or in the case of 'okina, will only germinate if the outer fruit has been removed (something that 'alalā once routinely did; Culliney et al. 2012). And so it is not surprising that these three plants are in decline: halapepe and the loulu palms are themselves rare or endangered and most of the 'okina trees encountered in the forest today are older with a 'general lack of seedlings or saplings in the wild' (Culliney 2011, 21). A long and intimate history of co-evolution that binds together avian and botanical lives is unravelling here, a shared past creating specific and shared vulnerabilities in which co-evolution can potentially switch over into co-extinction.

In addition to these plants, many local people have also been drawn into the absence of 'alalā. For some (native) Hawaiians, 'alalā is part of the cultural landscape: these birds hold stories and associations in the world; they are an 'aumakua or ancestral deity for some; and the plants and forests that might disappear or change significantly without their seed dispersal are themselves also culturally significant in various ways. Many other locals are also drawn into this experience of loss, trying in their own ways to reckon with the affective burden of living in a place where crows are no longer present, a place in which (paraphrasing one biologist), we have lost the most intelligent and charismatic component of our forests.[19] But 'alalā have themselves also been altered by more than a decade of captivity. There are now suggestions that their once remarkable vocal repertoire—their raucous calls and mournful songs—is being diminished. Perhaps this is because they have less to talk about, or perhaps juvenile birds simply have not been exposed to enough chatter from their elders.[20] Similarly, know-how about predators and how to avoid them many not be being passed between generations in captivity, potentially impacting on their future survival when they are eventually able to be released. And yet, release itself is also a complex prospect. Getting the birds ready is one part of the story, but the forest and the surrounding communities into which they might return are also vitally important. Plans by conservationists to fence a section of a local forest reserve to allow the vegetation to recover as a future release site have been greeted with hostility by some. Fencing itself raises concerns around limited access (concerns that for many Hawaiians are explicitly tied to a long history of occupation and dispossession), as does the proposed removal of pigs and other ungulates that some people hunt (van Dooren 2017).

There are no simple answers here. Crows, plants, pigs, and diverse local people are all bound together in an unfolding story of co-evolution, colonization, conservation, and more. Each of these living beings has an ethos, each has a way of life that has emerged and endured in entangled company with others. In a time of ongoing colonization and extinction, these stories call us into response, but never in a singular or final way.

RESPONSE: BECOMING-WITNESS

It is clear then that ethographies do not aim to impartially produce 'objective' accounts of the world (whatever these might be). Instead, this approach is grounded in the conviction that making others fleshy and thick on the page, exposing readers to their lives and deaths, may give rise to proximity and ethical entanglement, care and concern. At the core of this notion of storytelling as an ethical practice is the understanding that the stories that we tell are powerful contributors to the becoming of our shared world. Explicitly reject-ing a simple division between the 'real' and the 'narrated' (van Dooren 2014, 12), we see storytelling as a dynamic act of 'storying'. As Haraway notes, '"[w]orld" is a verb, and so stories are *of* the world, not *in* the world. Worlds are not containers, they're patternings, risky co-makings, speculative fabula-tions' (2014). Telling stories has consequences: one of which is that we will inevitably be drawn into new connections, and with them new accountabili-ties and obligations. In short, these are *lively* ethographies in both message and form: in their commitment to the openness and continuity of diverse ways of life, and in their attempt to enact stories as world-making, life shaping, technologies. Ethographic storytelling is about the arts of becoming-witness, which include both attention to others and expression of that experience: to stand *as* witness and actively to *bear* witness. As we are seized, so we bear witness in order that others may be seized: telling stories that draw their audi-ences into others' lives in new and consequential ways, stories that cultivate the capacity for *response*.

This focus on response enables a more interesting approach to questions of ethics in multispecies worlds (Haraway 2012). In exploring 'response-ability'—the capacity to respond—we move beyond simplistic framings of 'responsibility' as a question of human agency in a passive and inert world. All living creatures, and others too, respond to the world around them. What it means for each being, in each case, to respond is quite different. *It is, how-ever, through these responses that worlds are constituted.* We are all account-able for—implicated and at stake in—the worlds that our actions bring into being. Here, the line between response and reaction is not an abyssal divide (Derrida 2003), but a site for the ongoing questioning of the various modes of being with others that are open to different forms of life at different times. Similarly, 'the human' does not mark the sole site of 'responsibility' in any straightforward way that again separates 'us' from 'them'. To begin with, we must recognise that our own responses to others are grounded in long processes of evolution and the development of emotional and cognitive com-petencies, many of which are shared with a range of other species. Beyond simple 'biology', all people, and other creatures too, respond in their own ways to given worlds as a result of their own life histories, personal develop-mental dynamics and the diverse forms of knowledge and truth that they have inherited and been disciplined into. In short, response is always an achieve-ment, the outcome of a complex process that combines a range of elements that are often glossed as 'biology', 'learning', 'culture', and more.

As such, there is no singular 'responsible' course of action; there is only the constantly shifting capacity to respond to another. What counts as 'good', perhaps 'ethical', response is always context-specific and relational. It is always being rearticulated, reimagined, and made possible in new ways, *inside* ongoing processes of call and response and the worlds that they pro-duce. Here, responsibility is about developing the openness and the sensi-tivities necessary to be curious, to understand and respond in ways that are never perfect, never innocent, never final, and yet always required. Stories are opportunities to test and explore different modes of responsiveness; to 'learn to be affected' (Despret 2004, 131) in new ways, to cultivate the intellectual, emotional and critical capacities necessary to recognise our own implication in the world, the consequences of our actions, and possibilities for other kinds of futures.[21] More than this though, ethographic storytelling is about respond-ing to others as we encounter them *in the richness of their own stories*. While this response is often grounded in immediacy, more demanding forms of responsibility require a curious attentiveness to another that exceeds the given moment so that we might better understand the other in order to make an *appropriate* response. As Haraway notes, 'caring means becoming subject to the unsettling obligation of curiosity, which requires knowing more at the end of the day than at the beginning' (2008, 36). This form of response takes an interest in what matters to another rather than reading one's own positioning on to them (Rose 1999; 2007). This line of questioning is inseparable from a consideration of *ēthea*: it demands an attentiveness to the ways in which others make and live their worlds, it demands ethography.

But, as we have seen, to witness is also to participate in the world in its *rela-tional* becoming. In this context, our curiosity about and for others must be definitively expansive, perhaps even explosive. Can our awakening response draw us into this particular story, and on into encounters with the many others who are bound up in relationships of nourishment, care, meaning-making and more within a broader 'ecology of selves'? (Kohn 2013, 16).

Responsibility and ethography are delicately and recursively entangled here. Responsibility requires attention to ethographic context, to others' forms of worldly responsiveness; while ethography draws us into new rela-tions and forms of response-ability. In other words, good storytelling is generative—we do not know quite where it will take us.

Much of our own work has brought us into situations where some fateful combination of ignorance, negligence, selfishness, and deeply conflicting values are spelling disaster for individuals and species. Our arts of witness involve turning-toward rather than away. The turning-toward is a material and semiotic kinesis that seeks engagement with the world of life. Confronting atrocity, we are acutely aware of the prevalent slippage between explanation and justification; our approach refuses to reduce deathwork to a rational cal-culation. We are in the most difficult place of witness, where to say nothing is abhorrent, and where to say anything is already to risk reductions. And yet we 'stay with the trouble' (Haraway 2012, 311) because the trouble has seized us, and we cannot turn our backs. An ethics of refusal grounds this work: it is the refusal, following Levinas (1989), to abandon others (83). Put in the positive, it embraces the ethical call others make upon us in the *meaningfulness* of their lives and deaths.

Storytelling is one of the great arts of witness, and in these difficult times, telling lively stories is a deeply committed project; one of engaging with the multitudes of others in their noisy, fleshy, living and dying. It is the aim of lively ethographies to seize our relational imagination. It is an engagement with the joys, passions, desires, and commitments of earth others, celebrating their ēthea in all their extravagant diversity.

ACKNOWLEDGEMENTS

We would like to thank the following people for thoughtful comments on earlier drafts of this chapter: Jennifer Hamilton, Kate Wright, Jeffrey Bussolini, Laura McLauchlan, Etienne Benson and Ursula Münster. Earlier drafts of this chapter were presented at a range of fora including the Mellon Sawyer Seminar series 'The Environmental Humanities: Emergence and Impact', University of California, Los Angeles, and the 2015 Meeting of the American Anthropological Association, Denver. This chapter draws on years of collaborative research, much of it generously funded by the Australian Research Council (DP110102886).

NOTES

1. It also is alive and well in studies of communication and rhetoric and in the scholarly journal *Ethos* (*Journal of the Society for Psychological Anthropology*).

2. Thus ethos (ἦθος, ἔθος, *plurals: ēthē* [ἤθη], *ēthea* [ἤθεα]) is a Greek word originally meaning 'accustomed place' (as in ἤθεα ἵππων 'the habitat of horses'; *Iliad* 6.511), 'custom, habit', equivalent to Latin *mores*.

3. Although it is general differences at a species (or perhaps population/cultural) level that are the focus here, our approach—like that of Lestel and colleagues—also makes room for individual variability among both humans and nonhumans. See also Lestel et al. (2014).

4. On 'intra-action', see Barad (1996).

5. Of course uniqueness in this context can be and is gauged in different ways. In some cases, it is possible to be curious about how others, human and nonhuman, recognise kinds (their own and others): Vinciane Despret urges us to consider how it is that lions understand lion-ness, how they decide who is and is not a lion (2008). Eben Kirksey pays attention to some of the ways that wasps, fig trees, and frogs distinguish between those who are and are not the right 'kinds', developing their own taxonomic praxiographies (Kirksey in preparation). In other cases, we simply do not

know enough about what matters to others to ask this question seriously. On species as 'performative' co-becomings, see van Dooren (2016).

6. See Oyama et al. (2001); Oyama (2000); Haraway (2014). The modes of sociality of any given ethos are rooted in specific biological capacities. While many animals' social lives are immediately recognisable to us (although their existence has nonetheless often been denied), plants, microorganisms, and various others are also deeply social beings in their own ways: exchanging signs and meanings, communicating in ways that we often underestimate (discussed further below). In this sense, sociality is a common feature of all life and should not be restricted to those organisms that possess similar enough modes of interaction to the human to be immediately recognisable as such. Our being social creatures, as well as the specific forms that this sociality takes, is in an important way a feature of our biological makeup. At the same time, however, that biology has itself evolved within the context of very material processes of intergenerational life in company with others. There is no sociality outside of its specific biological possibilities; nor is there any biological form that has not been shaped by its own particular social milieu. It is in this complex space that ēthea emerge.

7. Long histories of Indigenous thought have been concerned with the animated character of the perceptible world, and it is at that scale that people say that other beings have culture. Living beings are 'culture-creatures', and knowledge of this fact is, on the face of it, not at all arcane (Rose 2013). One sees some birds dance; one hears others sing; one watches them finding their food, making their nests, raising their young. The way of participatory ethos is not hidden. Indeed, given the relational and participatory qualities of life, it could not be hidden—but nor is it always addressed to, or perceptible by, humans. And, of course, it may involve hiding, deception, and many other modes of communication and resistance. These indigenous animisms are grounded in the recognition, as Graham Harvey has put it, 'that the world is full of persons, only some of whom are human, and that life is always lived in relationship with others' (2006, xi).

8. On 'refraction', see Haraway and Goodeve (2000) and Metcalf (2008).

9. Others have called this 'mindfulness'. In this context, the point is to move away from a dualistic, Cartesian construction of mindfulness that separates it sharply from the body and sees its fullest expression in abstract forms of rationality. We should not assume that we know what mindfulness is and certainly not that there is only one proper form of it (that is associated with the rationality of the [unmarked] 'human').

10. Val Plumwood explores similarly expansive, more-than-human forms of intelligence and sentience in 'Nature in the Active Voice' (2009).

11. We understand these ethographies as part of a broader field of multispecies studies that is populated by a range of related but distinct approaches, including 'multispecies ethnography' (Kirksey and Helmreich 2010), 'etho-ethnology' (Lestel et al. 2006), 'anthropology of life' (Kohn 2013), 'anthropology beyond humanity' (Ingold 2013), 'extinction studies' (Rose and van Dooren 2011), 'philosophical ethology' (Buchanan et al. 2014), and 'more-than-human geographies' (Lorimer and Driessen 2014; Whatmore 2003). For a discussion of penguin and flying fox modes of storying their worlds, see van Dooren and Rose (2012).

12. For a discussion of the way in which nonhumans might write their own stories in/on the landscape, as well as in humans and our stories, see Benson (2011).

13. On stories that normalise all others, see Haraway (2014).

14. Our particular approach takes inspiration from James Hatley's work on narrative and testimony in the face of the *Shoah*. Hatley forcefully reminds us of the ethical demands of the act of writing, of telling stories. In place of an approach that would reduce others to mere names or numbers, in place of an approach that aims for an impartial or objective recitation of the 'facts', Hatley argues for a mode of witnessing that is from the outset already seized, already claimed, by an obligation to those whose story we are attempting to tell. In the context of ecocide and many other forms of mass death, this mode of storytelling is particularly important. Along with the work of remaining true to the facts of the situation, witnessing insists on truths that are not reducible to populations and data, a fleshier more lively truth, that in its telling might draw others into a sense of accountability and care.

15. For discussions of cat yoga and other fascinating etho-ethnographic encounters with felines, see the work of Jeffrey Bussolini and Ananya Mukherjea at the Feline Studies/Avenue B Multi-Studies Center.

16. Haraway has made this point in conversation with Marilyn Strathern's work on the ideas we think other ideas with (Haraway 2014; Strathern 1992).

17. We have explored these issues in Rose (2011); van Dooren (2011).

18. There is a growing body of work on lively materiality beyond the biotic, some of which is likely compatible with this ethographic approach.

19. Interview with Jeff Burgett (USFWS), conducted by van Dooren on 19 December 2011 in Hilo, Hawaiian.

20. For further information, see http://www.animal-acoustics.com/current-research-phd/hawaiian-crow. Web. 21 August 2013.

21. This project is very much in line with Anna Tsing's call for the cultivation of 'arts of noticing'.

WORKS CITED

Barad, Karen. 'Meeting the Universe Halfway: Realism and Social Constructivism without Contradiction'. *Feminism, Science, and the Philosophy of Science.* Eds. Lynn Hankinson Nelson and Jack Nelson. Dordrecht: Kluwer Academic Publishers, 1996. 161–194.

Benson, E. 'Animal Writes: Historiography, Disciplinarity, and the Animal Trace'. *Making Animal Meaning.* Eds. Linda Kalof and Georgina M. Montgomery. East Lansing: Michigan State University Press, 2011. 3–16.

Buchanan, Brett, Jeffrey Bussolini, Matthew Chrulew. 'General Introduction: Philosophical Ethology'. *Angelaki* 19.3 (2014): 1–3.

Cheney, Jim and Anthony Weston. 'Environmental Ethics as Environmental Etiquette'. *Environmental Ethics* 21.2 (1999): 115–134.

Culliney, Susan Moana. 'Seed Dispersal by the Critically Endangered Alala (*Corvus Hawaiiensis*) and Integrating Community Values into Alala (*Corvus Hawaiiensis*) Recovery'. MS Thesis, Colorado State University, 2011.

Culliney, Susan, *et al*. 'Seed Dispersal by a Captive Corvid: The Role of the 'Alala (*Corvus Hawaiiensis*) in Shaping Hawaiians Plant Communities'. *Ecological Applications* 22.6 (2012): 1718–1732.

Derrida, Jacques. 'And Say the Animal Responded?' *Zoontologies: The Question of the Animal*. Ed. Cary Wolfe. Minneapolis: University of Minnesota Press, 2003.

Despret, Vinciane. 'The Body We Care For: Figures of Anthropo-Zoo-Genesis'. *Body and Society* 10.2/3 (2004): 111–134.

Despret, Vinciane. 'The Becomings of Subjectivity in Animal Worlds'. *Subjectivity* 23.1 (2008): 123–139.

Flaspohler, David J. 'A Delicate Web of Life That Started with Lava'. *New York Times*. June 12, 2012. Web. 10 February 2016.

Geertz, Clifford. 'Thick Description: Toward an Interpretive Theory of Culture'. *The Interpretation of Cultures*. New York: Basic Books, 1973. 3–30.

Geertz, Clifford. 'Ethos, World View, and the Analysis of Sacred Symbols'. *The Interpretation of Cultures*. New York: Basic Books, 1996.

Hall, Mattew. *Plants as Persons: A Philosophical Botany*. Albany, NY: SUNY Press, 2011.

Haraway, Donna J., and Thyrza Nicholas Goodeve. *How Like a Leaf*. New York: Routledge, 2000.

Haraway, Donna J. *When Species Meet*. Minneapolis: University of Minnesota Press, 2008.

Haraway, Donna J. 'Awash in Urine: Des and Premarin® in Multispecies Response-Ability'. *Women's Studies Quarterly* 40.1 (2012): 301–316.

Haraway, Donna J. 'Playing String Figures with Companion Species: Staying with the Trouble'. Published in translation as 'Jeux de ficelles avec les espèces compagnes: rester avec le trouble'. *Les Animaux: Deux Ou Trois Choses Que Nous Savons D'eux*. Eds. Vinciane Despret and Raphael Larrère. Paris: Hermann Publishers, 2014.

Haraway, Donna J. 'Sf: String Figures, Multispecies Muddles, Staying with the Trouble'. Paper presented at the University of Alberta, 24 March 2014.

Harvey, Graham. *Animism: Respecting the Living World*. New York: Columbia University Press, 2006.

Hatley, James. *Suffering Witness: The Quandary of Responsibility after the Irreparable*. Albany: State University of New York Press, 2000.

'Hawaiian Monk Seal' (*Monachus Schauinslandi*). 2013. Web. 10 December 2015.

Herzfeld, Michael. *Anthropology: Theoretical Practice in Culture and Society*. Oxford: Blackwell, 2001.

Hustak, Carla and Natasha Myers. 'Involutionary Momentum: Affective Ecologies and the Sciences of Plant/Insect Encounters'. *differences* 23.3 (2012): 74–118.

Ingold, Tim 'Anthropology beyond Humanity'. *Suomen Anthropologi* 38.3 (2013): 5–23.

Kirksey, Eben. 'Species: A Paxiography in Three Parts'. (In preparation).

Kirksey, S. Eben and Stefan Helmreich. 'The Emergence of Multispecies Ethnography'. *Cultural Anthropology* 25.4 (2010): 545–576.

Kohn, Eduardo. *How Forests Think: Toward an Anthropology beyond the Human.* Berkeley: University of California Press, 2013.

Lestel, Dominique, Florence Brunois, Florence Gaunet. 'Etho-Ethnology and Ethno-Ethology'. *Social Science Information* 45 (2006): 155–177.

Lestel, Dominique, Jeffrey Bussolini, Matt Chrulew. 'The Phenomenology of Animal Life'. *Environmental Humanities* 5 (2014): 125–148.

Levinas, Emmanuel. 'Ethics as First Philosophy'. *The Levinas Reader.* Ed. Séan Hand. Malden: Blackwell, 1989.

Lorimer, Jamie and Clemens Driessen. 'Wild Experiments at the Oostvaardersplassen: Rethinking Environmentalism in the Anthropocene'. *Transactions of the Institute of British Geographers* 39.2 (2014): 169–181.

Marder, Michael. *Plant-Thinking: A Philosophy of Vegetal Life.* New York: Columbia University Press, 2013.

Margulis, Lynn and Dorian Sagan. *What Is Life?* Berkeley: University of California Press, 1995.

Metcalf, Jacob. 'Intimacy without Proximity: Encountering Grizzlies as a Companion Species'. *Environmental Philosophy* 5.2 (2008): 99–128.

Oyama, Susan. *Evolution's Eye: A Systems View of the Biology-Culture Divide.* Durham: Duke University Press, 2000.

Oyama, Susan, Paul E. Griffiths, Russell D. Gray, eds. *Cycles of Contingency: Developmental Systems and Evolution.* Cambridge: MIT Press, 2001.

Plumwood, Val. *Environmental Culture: The Ecological Crisis of Reason.* London: Routledge, 2002.

Plumwood, Val. 'Nature in the Active Voice'. *Australian Humanities Review* 46 (2009): 113–129.

Restall Orr, Emma. *The Wakeful World: Animism, Mind and the Self in Nature.* Uitgeverij: John Hunt Publishing, 2012.

Rose, Deborah Bird. 'Taking Notice'. *Worldviews; Environment, Culture, Religion* 3 (1999): 97–103.

Rose, Deborah Bird. 'Recursive Epistemologies and an Ethics of Attention'. *Extraordinary Anthropology: Transformations in the Field.* Eds. J. G. Goulet and B. Miller. Lincoln: University of Nebraska Press, 2007. 88–102.

Rose, Deborah Bird. 'Flying Fox: Kin, Keystone, Kontaminant'. *Australian Humanities Review* 50 (2011): 119–136.

Rose, Deborah Bird. 'Cosmopolitics: The Kiss of Life'. *New Formations* 76 (2012): 101–113.

Rose, Deborah Bird. 'Death and Grief in a World of Kin'. *The Handbook of Contemporary Animism.* Ed. Graham Harvey. Durham: Acumen, 2013. 137–147.

Rose, Deborah Bird. 'Monk Seals at the Edge: Blessings in a Time of Peril'. *Extinction Studies: Stories of Time, Death and Generations.* Eds. Deborah Bird Rose, Thom van Dooren, Matthew Chrulew. New York: Columbia University Press, forthcoming.

Rose, Deborah Bird and Thom van Dooren, eds. *Unloved Others: Death of the Disregarded in the Time of Extinctions.* Special issue of *Australian Humanities Review* 50 (2011).

Smith, Mick. 'Hermenuetics and the Culture of Birds: The Environmental Allegory of Easter Island'. *Ethics Place and Environment* 8.1 (2005): 21–38.

Strathern, Marilyn. *Reproducing the Future: Essays on Anthropology, Kinship and the New Reproductive Technologies*. New York: Routledge, 1992.

Trewavas, Anthony. 'Plant Intelligence: Mindless Mastery'. *Nature* 415.6874 (2002): 841.

Trewavas, Anthony. 'Aspects of Plant Intelligence'. *Annals of Botany* 92.1 (2003): 1–20.

Tsing, Anna. 'Arts of Inclusion, or, How to Love a Mushroom'. *Australian Humanities Review* 50 (2011): 5–22.

Tsing, Anna Lowenhaupt. 'Unruly Edges: Mushrooms as Companion Species'. *Environmental Humanities* 1 (2012): 141–154.

Tsing, Anna Lowenhaupt. 'Strathern beyond the Human: Testimony of a Spore'. *Theory Culture Society* 31.2/3 (2014): 221–241.

van Dooren, Thom. *Flight Ways: Life and Loss at the Edge of Extinction*. New York: Columbia University Press, 2014.

van Dooren, Thom. 'Authentic Crows: Identity, Captivity and Emergent Forms of Life'. *Theory, Culture and Society* 33.2 (2016): 29–52.

van Dooren, Thom. 'Spectral Crows in Hawaiian: Conservation and the Work of Inheritance'. *Extinction Studies: Stories of Time, Death and Generations*. Eds. Deborah Bird Rose, Thom van Dooren, Matthew Chrulew. New York: Columbia University Press, forthcoming.

van Dooren, Thom. *Vulture*. London: Reaktion Books, 2011.

van Dooren, Thom and Deborah Bird Rose. 'Storied-Places in a Multispecies City'. *Humanimalia* 3.2 (2012): 1–27.

Weir, Jessica K. *Murray River Country: An Ecological Dialogue with Traditional Owners*. Canverra: Aboriginal Studies, 2009.

Whatmore, Sarah. 'Introduction: More Than Human Geographies'. *Handbook of Cultural Geography*. Ed. Kay Anderson, et al. London: Sage, 2003.

Yusoff, Kathryn. 'Geologic Life: Prehistory, Climate, Futures in the Anthropocene'. *Environment and Planning D: Society and Space* 31.5 (2013): 779–795.

Chapter Fourteen

Religion and Ecology

Towards a Communion of Creatures

Kate Rigby

WHY RELIGION?

For better or ill, religion informs the environmental views, values, relations, and behaviour of an overwhelming majority of people around the world, often in profound ways. For this reason alone, studies in religion and ecology should comprise a crucial component of the wider work of the environmental humanities. It is the first task of this essay to show how this has indeed been the case. Among the world's many diverse religions, Christianity has become a dominant force globally. Christianity remains the most populous world religion, with some 3.2 billion followers, constituting over 31.5% of the global population ('Global Religious' 2014). While the global predominance of practicing Christians is being challenged by the growth of Islam, estimated at 23.2% of the total population and growing rapidly, Christian traditions remain culturally influential, informing many of the secular attitudes, assumptions and institutions of modern western societies. Moreover, in light of the continuing geopolitical power of the United States, it is not insignificant that 78% of the US population identify as Christian of one kind or another ('Global Religious'). If, as Larry Rasmussen has argued, it would be foolish for those with an interest in the prospects for a more sustainable world 'to overlook the religious loyalties of some ten thousand religions and 85 percent of the planets' peoples' (2013, 6), so too it behoves religious studies researchers in the environmental humanities to inquire into the potential for the 'greening' of Christianity. In my own case, I should acknowledge upfront that Christianity forms part of my own cultural formation, something that I accept as a problematic inheritance with which I continue to grapple, personally, politically and academically. Accordingly, the latter part of this chapter homes in on

Christianity and ecology, with a view to tracing the lineaments of an emergent 'communion of all creatures' (Rigby 2014).

RELIGION, ECOLOGY, AND THE HISTORICAL
ROOTS OF THE ENVIRONMENTAL HUMANITIES

As the editors of a 2011 *Field Guide to the Study of Religion and Ecology* observe, 'religion' and 'ecology' are both 'complicated and controversial' terms (Baumann et al. 2011, 4). The latter is often used rather loosely as a synonym for the environment, environmentalism, or, ever more problematically, 'nature'. But even in its more narrow usage, to denote a branch of the natural sciences, ecology refers not to a fixed set of facts, a secure ground on which to found or evaluate ostensible green forms of faith, but to an open and evolving field of enquiry. Religious studies scholars, along with other Environmental Humanities researchers, are thereby challenged to grapple with new understandings and current debates, giving consideration, for example, to how the theorization and practice of religious environmentalism might need to be reframed 'for a post-natural world' (Lodge and Hamlin 279–307). 'Religion' is an even trickier term. Emerging from Western history and carrying 'Western baggage' (Baumann 2011, 13), it has been variously understood and researched.

In Clifford Geerz's analysis, religion comprises a system of symbols that 'establish powerful, pervasive and long-lasting moods and motivations . . . by formulating conceptions of a general order of existence' (Baumann 2011, 18). As such, it can function as a major source of social cohesion, as previously discerned by Emile Durkheim. Where its symbols and their interpretation have been captured by the interests of the powerful, religion is liable to contribute to the conservation of the socio-ecological *status quo*, as Karl Marx observed of mainstream Christianity in the mid-nineteenth century, which offered imaginary compensation for 'oppressive social relations' (Baumann 2011, 19). Like all human institutions, religious organizations can also generate their own systems of oppression, harbouring corrupt practices that contradict their own teachings. Yet there is also ample historical evidence to show how the moods and motivations engendered by religious symbolism can become a powerful source of opposition to oppression, as exemplified in Marx's own lifetime by the movements for the abolition of slavery and the prevention of cruelty to animals, both of which were framed through the Christian discourse of justice and compassion that inspired their most effective advocate, William Wilberforce (Metaxis 2007).

Depending on how literally its texts and teachings are taken, religious constructions of reality can come into conflict with other sources of knowledge, as well as engendering exclusionary group identities with the potential to engender social conflicts that sometimes turn violent. From another perspective, though, this kind of literalism constitutes a fundamental misunderstanding of what religion is about. For the great German Protestant theologian, founder of the modern historical-critical method of biblical studies, Friedrich Schleiermacher, religion arises from a universally available human experience of profound connectedness to the becoming of the cosmos. The appropriate ethical response to this experience, in his view (and mine), was recognition of interdependence, combined with respect for the individuated others who co-become as part of this ungraspable, unfolding universe. As Schleiermacher argued in his 1799 talks on religion 'to its cultured despisers' (principally his close friends among the Early German Romantics), the stories and rituals that arose historically as a means of framing and sharing such experiences became mixed up with the metaphysics and morals of the surrounding culture. In literate societies, moreover, these historically limited and culturally contingent ideas about the nature of reality, and how people should behave, got inscribed into sacred texts, which should therefore be treated with caution, understood contextually, and discerningly reinterpreted. From this enlightened perspective (which informs this essay), religion occupies a different place, and serves a different purpose, from science: while the latter is freed to become a preferred source of growing knowledge about the workings of the physical world, the former answers to the desire for the kinds of mystical experience, overarching meanings, and shared ethical orientations that cannot be supplied by empirical science alone. Enhanced understanding of the historicity of any given set of religious symbols and narratives facilitates inter-religious dialogue by counteracting bigotry and fostering the reinterpretation of inherited beliefs in response to new knowledge and changing socio-ecological circumstances.

The branch of the environmental humanities that studies these two 'complicated and controversial' phenomena in their complex and varied interrelations can be traced back to at least the early 1970s. Attending to both intellectual frameworks and lived practice, '[s]cholars of religion and ecology help people to think critically about how religion has been shaped by the natural environment and can be shaped by environmental degradation' (Baumann et al. 2011, 8). They also consider how specific religious perspectives and practices might work to either impede or advance the mitigation of socio-ecological ills, hampering or hastening the creation of more just, peaceful, and sustainable ways of living. While it is always risky to try to fix beginnings, the early stirrings of the study of religion and ecology have justly been traced to Lynn White Jr's oft-cited (if all too frequently misread) article in *Science* from 1967, 'The Historical Roots of our Ecologic Crisis'. That White's article first appeared in a scientific journal reflects the extent to which environmental destruction was at that stage still seen as a largely scientific and technical issue. Yet the burden of White's article was precisely that while science was crucial to diagnosing ecological ills, it provided an inadequate basis for understanding, let alone resolving, a problem which was largely cultural and social in origin. In White's analysis, '[w]hat people do about their ecology depends on what they think about themselves in relation to things around them. Human ecology is deeply conditioned by beliefs about our nature and destiny—that is, by religion' (1967, 1205). For this reason, White maintained that it was necessary to look to the dominant religious traditions of the West, whence originated that mode of industrial development now ravaging the Earth, in seeking to identify the primary source of those attitudes towards the natural world, which in his view had led to the current crisis.

White's view of the primacy of religion as *the* underlying driver of environmental damage might be overstated. But the significance of this slim article, in my analysis, pertains to far more than his critique of Christianity (which, as discussed below, was actually far more nuanced than is generally assumed). For in his method of analysis and argumentation, White, who studied theology before becoming a pioneering scholar in the cultural history of science and technology (Riley 2014a), effectively lays out the entire project of the environmental humanities as an inter- or trans-disciplinary undertaking, as well as initiating the study of religion and ecology in particular. To begin with, White's explanation of the aetiology of industrial modernity's 'ecologic crisis' incorporates an environmental historical dimension, entailing the recognition of nonhuman entities as historical actants: namely, the thick, sticky, clayey soils of northern Europe, which resisted being worked by the light scratch-plow, drawn by a single beast of burden, which originated in the Fertile Crescent and had been adopted throughout the Mediterranean region as agriculture spread north and westwards; and the heavy iron plough, which was invented towards the end of the seventh century, in order to work such resistant soils more effectively. This innovative technology reshaped northwestern European farmers' relations with one another, their domesticated animals, and the land. White sees the impact of these changes in the altered depiction of the seasons in early medieval illustrated calendars, the imagery of which implied that 'Man and nature are two things, and man is master' (1967, 1205). This assumption also began to inform Western Christian interpretations of the biblical injunction to humans to 'have dominion' over other creatures and 'subdue the earth' (Gen. 1.26–1.28). In this respect, White's method also incorporates a proto-ecocritical dimension, as the editors of the first ecocriticism reader, Glotfelty and Fromm, rightly discerned in choosing to include it in their anthology. In addition, his article raises questions about the underlying onto-epistemological and normative assumptions informing the peculiarly Western alliance of science and technology, which would subsequently be pursued by environmental philosophers. In particular, White's identification of the profoundly dualistic and 'anthropocentric' (1205) dimension of the mentality that came to predominate in modern Western society prefigures the influential line of 'deep ecological' analysis initiated by Arne Naess and the Routleys (later Richard Sylvan and Val Plumwood) in the mid-1970s. At the same time, however, White pre-empts more recent critiques of the "wilderness area mentality', which 'advocates deep-freezing an ecology, whether San Gimignano or the High Sierra, as it was before the first Kleenex was dropped' (1204).

It is, however, above all as a first foray into the field of ecologically oriented religious studies that White's slim article has borne most fruit. In view of the formative role of Western Christian attitudes and assumptions in the genesis and application of modern science and technology, White argued that, '[s]ince the roots of our trouble are so largely religious, the remedy must also be essentially religious, whether we call it that or not. We must rethink and refeel our nature and destiny' (1967, 1206). For this reason, he concludes with the recommendation that St. Francis, who 'tried to substitute the idea of the equality of all creatures, including man, for the idea of man's limitless rule of creation', be made the 'patron saint of ecologists' (1206). This call was answered by Pope John Paul II in 1979 when he declared Francis the Patron Saint of Animals and the Environment. Meanwhile, the urgent ecospiritual and eco-justice advocacy of the Pope who bears St. Francis' name promises to advance efforts already underway to effect the radical transformation envisaged and embodied by the 'spiritual revolutionary' (1206) from Assisi. Later in this essay I will return to White's own proposal for the deep greening of Christianity. Firstly, though, I want to delineate the subsequent development of studies in religion and ecology, as part of the wider field of the environmental humanities.

White's 1967 article triggered an efflorescence of this area of study, with '[h]undreds of books and articles . . . written as a direct response to it' (Riley 2014b, 241). While White stressed that 'Christianity is a complex faith and its consequences differ in different contexts' (1967, 1206), his assertion that 'Christianity bears a huge burden of guilt' (1206) for the industrial despoliation of the earth contributed significantly to the combination of self-critique and apologetics that characterised much early ecotheology; but it also gave impetus to the quest among many environmentally concerned Westerners for ecospiritual alternatives to Christianity. White himself referred to the affinity of the 'beatniks' for Zen Buddhism as manifesting a 'sound instinct', while worrying that since Buddhism was 'as deeply conditioned by Asian history as Christianity is by the experience of the West' (1206) it might not offer a viable alternative for Euro-Americans. Be that as it may, much Western environmental philosophy would subsequently be informed by an engagement with

Eastern thought and spirituality, from Arne Naess' borrowings from Gandhi's reformed Hinduism to Freya Mathew's creative extension of Daoism, with different traditions of Buddhism, variously interpreted, a pervasive presence (Macy 1991; Fox 1995; Morton 2010). In the meantime, Buddhist thinkers from East Asia, such as Thich Nhat Hanh, have helped to globalise the ecospiritual conversation.

This eastward turn was manifest outside the academy in the ecologically inclined counterculture that followed that of the beatniks. Here, though, ecospiritual inspiration was also being found elsewhere: namely in the indigenous traditions of colonised peoples. While many popular (and often lucratively marketed) manifestations of this enthusiasm for eco-indigeneity are unquestionably superficial, sentimental, and disturbingly appropriative, Native American voices, such as those of Linda Hogan, and scholars of Native American history and culture, such as Joni Adamson, have made a vital contribution to the development of the environmental humanities. In Australia, too, the emergence of the environmental humanities was informed by the teaching of traditional Aboriginal Elders, as well as by Indigenous philosophers, such as Mary Graham (Mathews 2003, 179–183; Plumwood 2008; Rose 2011; 2013). Such endeavours to recover an indigenous understanding of the material world as communicative, agentic and ethically considerable respond to a yet deeper-lying dimension of the impact of the Christianization of Europe: namely, the extirpation of pagan animism, which, as White lamented, proclaimed 'Man's monopoly on spirit in this world' and 'made it possible to exploit nature in a mood of indifference to the feelings of natural objects' (1967, 1205).

This lament has a long pre-history in Western thought, dating back at least to the Romantic counter-movement to the 'death of nature' (Merchant 1980), beginning in the late eighteenth century (Rigby 2004, 45–52). More recently, the German Critical Theorists, Theodor Adorno and Max Horkheimer, wrote ruefully of the 'disenchantment' of the world in the baleful 'dialectic of enlightenment', whereby progress in the techno-scientific 'domination of nature' was bought at the price of human self-alienation, fuelling a desire for new forms of pseudo-belonging. Fascistic nationalism with its murderous exclusions was the one of most immediate concern to these Jewish Marxist intellectuals in exile, but they also targeted the mollification of the masses effected by the capitalist culture industry. Adorno and Horkheimer took the term 'disenchantment' (actually 'demagicification', *Entzauberung*) from the German sociologist Max Weber, who stressed that this process, while initiated by Roman Christianity, was advanced by the Reformation, and completed only with the rise modern science (1920/1991). As Weber (1958) had previously argued in his *magnum opus* of 1905–1906, moreover, it was no coincidence that the wedding of science and technology with capitalist economics took off in Europe's reformed North West, with its Protestant ethic of hard work, self-restraint, and the accumulation of financial wealth.

This brings me to a notable omission in White's *Science* article (if not in his wider work, as Riley demonstrates in *Deeper Roots* [2015]): namely, the socio-economic drivers and ramifications of environmental degradation. While he was of course quite right to point to this as characteristic of the Communist East no less than the capitalist West, it was under the economically favourable conditions of nineteenth-century industrial capitalism that Francis Bacon's ethos of techno-scientific mastery, conjoined with Cartesian dualism and Newtonian atomism, acquired widespread cultural traction, becoming a core constituent of modern thought: one that the political movements that subsequently sought unsuccessfully to realise the Communist project in Eastern Europe (as in China) failed adequately to critique. As Adorno and Horkheimer emphasise, moreover, the industrial capitalist mastery of nature has always also entailed the exploitation of human labour, as well as the domination of those other others, and dimensions of the self, that are ideologically aligned with that nature requiring mastering: namely women, animals, and the body. This critique has subsequently been taken further by ecofeminist historians (Merchant 1980; 1995) and philosophers (Plumwood 1993; Salleh 1997), who also point to the incorporation of indigenous peoples into the subordinate domain of nature within what Plumwood terms the 'logic of colonization' (see also DeLoughrey and Handley 2011). In addition to being variously exploited and marginalised in the process of the domination of nature, many groups of socially subordinate humans (especially people of lower socio-economic status, African Americans, children, subsistence farmers, and Indigenous peoples) generally bear the brunt of its 'slow violence' (Nixon 2011).

GREENING RELIGION: CHALLENGES AND ACHIEVEMENTS

The interconnection between social injustice and environmental degradation has become a central matter of concern within the study of religion and ecology in recent years. However, it was broached considerably earlier by those who brought a feminist lens to this field of research and praxis. This was the terrain of my own first major venture into this arena with an essay on 'Eecofeminist Reconfigurations of Gender, Nature, and the Sacred' (Rigby 2001) that focused on post-Christian feminist ecospiritualities drawing their inspiration from Europe's pre-Christian past (Gimbutas 1982). The 'return of the Goddess' forms part of a wider revival (probably better described as reinvention) of the West's own indigenous traditions of Earth-honouring. The first international academic conference devoted to contemporary paganism was hosted by the University of Newcastle-upon-Tyne in 1994, and was followed two years later by another (appropriately enough, given the Romantic precursors of this project) at Ambleside in the Lake District. Organised by the Religious Studies Department of the University of Lancaster, this conference on 'Nature Religion Today' gave rise to a landmark book of that name (Pearson et al. 1998). Since 2004, Pagan Studies has boasted an academic journal, *The Pomegranate*, and a book series, beginning with *Researching Paganisms* (Blain et al. 2004). Not all neo-pagans profess an ecological orientation. But Graham Harvey (2013) puts his finger on what is at stake for those who do: namely 'the attempt to live respectfully as members of the diverse community of living persons (only some of whom are human) which we call the world or cosmos'.

Within the broad spectrum of contemporary paganism, feminist ecospiritualities are distinguished by their attention to the interlinkage of the patriarchal domination of women and the 'anthroparchal' (Cudworth 2005, 8) domination of nature. Ecofeminist paganism draws on a variety of traditions and comes in diverse guises, from Melissa Raphael's 'the*a*logy', through Carol Christ's Goddess pantheism, to Starhawk's queered Wicca. Rather than seeking to restore past cultural forms and social structures, though, feminist neo-paganism typically involves the creation of new narratives, rituals, and modes of co-becoming, in response to the insights and interests of contemporary collectives concerned with social injustice and environmental degradation. Whereas some forms of neo-paganism unquestionably construct their male and female deities along conventionally gendered and heteronormative lines, spiritual ecofeminists such as Starhawk (formerly Miriam Simos and of Jewish descent), deny that women are intrinsically 'closer to nature' than men, and critique gender stereotypes that erase salient differences among women and men pertaining to class, race, gender identity, and sexual orientation (1989, 214–218).

While any kind of religious practice might become a substitute for social action, ecospirituality can also provide vital nourishment for ecopolitical engagement (Spretnak 1986). Many challenges nonetheless confront the new 'dark green' (Taylor 2010) spiritualties, no less than the established religions, tasked as they are with rethinking not only particular religious symbols, stories and rituals, but also the role of religion per se in an ever more technologised, urbanised, globalised, anthropogenic, and ecologically imperilled world. Also cutting across the religious divide are two further risk factors. Firstly, there is the idealist assumption that wider socio-ecological changes can be effected by altering the way people think: that what we need is simply a 'new story'. As White argued with the respect to the changes attendant on the invention of the iron plough, and Weber demonstrated in the case of the

Protestant ethic, new stories become powerful only when they resonate with everyday practices and social relations. Moreover, within modern Western societies, characterised as they are to a high degree by the separation of distinct spheres of life, what goes on in the domain of religion, generally considered a cultural dimension of private life, is not necessarily correlated with what goes on in, say, the political or economic arenas (Cudworth 2005). While I do not subscribe to the view that these sub-systems are hermetically sealed from one another, the historical record suggests that the greening of religion will only take off, and strike longer lasting roots, if it is interlinked with other societal changes, relating in particular to the political and economic drivers of continued environmental degradation, and the invention and deployment of technologies more consistent with environmentally sustainable and socially just forms of development.

The other overarching hazard is the all-too-familiar one of claiming that one's own story is the truest and the best. For eco-religionists to get into a fight with one another about who is the 'greenest' would be highly counterproductive when what is most badly needed is a collaborative effort, ideally undertaken in consort with non-religious environmentalists as well. While the assumption of supremacy tends to be most common among proselytizing religions, notably Christianity and Islam, all belief systems, including apparently secular and indeed explicitly atheist ones, are liable to be mistaken by their adherents for the one and only truth. As Heather Eaton observes, 'religions are like languages, and it is folly to ask which language is true or superior' (2014, 215). My own view, supported by a growing body of research in ecology and religion, is that virtually all faith traditions contain elements that can be drawn upon to shape a sturdy environmental ethic. However, given the unprecedented nature of our current geo-historical moment, in the midst of the 'Great Acceleration' of human impacts upon all Earth's natural systems, no pre-existing tradition has ready-made answers to today's problems: all require some degree of re-interpreting and re-imagining, preferably, as feminist ecotheologian Rosemary Radford-Ruether puts it, by those who 'claim community in them' (1992, 11).

Since the early 1990s, that work of re-visioning has been proceeding apace around the world, as can readily be seen from the website of the international, multi-faith Forum on Religion and Ecology. Now based at Yale University, FORE was founded in 1995 at Harvard University's Center for the Study of World Religions. Under the directorship of Mary Evelyn Tucker and John Grim, it has to date hosted 25 conferences and published numerous books and articles. In addition to a series of monographs on individual religions arising from the initial series of conferences held at Harvard (on Buddhism, Christianity, Confucianism, Daoism, Hinduism, Indigenous Traditions, Islam, Jainism, Judaism, and Shinto), several of which have been translated into other languages, the website provides introductory essays, bibliographies, sacred texts, official statements, and grass-roots projects for each of these traditions, plus Baha'i. Some 8,000 people around the world subscribe to FORE's monthly newsletter, and similar organizations have also been created elsewhere, including the Canadian Forum on Religion and Ecology, the European Forum for the Study of Religion and Environment, the Australia-Pacific Forum on Religion and Ecology, and the (US-based) International Society for the Study of Religion, Nature, and Culture. These associations have a strong commitment to interdisciplinarity, fostering dialogue between religion and science.

This burgeoning of eco-religious scholarship finds a counterpart in the growth of both grassroots religious environmentalism and religious leadership on ecological issues (Kearns 2011; Gottlieb 2006a; 2006b). While the extent of the greening of religious practice across different faith traditions around the world remains unclear, there has been a rapid rise in the number of faith-based environmental social movement organizations in the United States from the early 1970s (Haluza-DeLay 2015). Meanwhile, secular organizations dedicated to animal welfare and conservation, such as the American Humane Society and Worldwild Fund for Nature, have recognised the motivational role of religion by creating faith outreach programs. Among the activities indicating a growing ecological orientation among diverse faith communities are the 'greening' of worship centres through practical sustainability measures; local environmental initiatives, such as community food gardens; the inclusion of environmentally oriented prayers and songs into worship services; the creation of ecospiritual retreat centres, publications, and educational initiatives; and various forms of eco-political engagement, including participation in protest movements, for instance in favour of divestment from fossil fuels, or against mountain top removal mining (see Elvey et al. forthcoming). Many religious leaders have begun to take a stronger stand on socio-ecological concerns in recent decades. Among the first to do so was the Ecumenical Patriarch Demetrios, then head of the Orthodox churches, who in 1989 released an encyclical on the environment, initiating the prophetic response to 'Earth's cry' that has been extended under his successor, Bartholomew, the so-called 'Green Patriarch' (Chryssavgis 2015). Similarly, John Paul II focused on the environment in his 1990 World Day of Peace message, and advocated an 'ecological conversion' to promote better custodianship of the earth. The FORE website includes official statements from across the world's religions, many of them directed towards major international bodies, such as the Hopi Message delivered to The United Nations General Assembly meeting in New York in 1992, and the World Council of Churches statement to the Third Session of the Conference of the Parties to the UN Framework Convention on Climate Change in 1997. The most significant of such statements thus far are Pope Francis' May 2015 encyclical *Laudato si'* ('Praise be to you') and the Islamic Declaration on Global Climate Change of August 2015, not least because of their timing: namely, with a view to putting moral pressure on the delegates to the UN Climate Change summit in Paris later that year.[1]

Significantly, the papal encyclical is addressed not only to Catholics, nor even to all Christians, but to 'every person living on this planet' (4). Similarly, the Islamic Declaration calls on people of all faiths worldwide to take urgent action to curb climate change and transition swiftly to a fossil-free economy. This reveals how socio-ecological concerns have opened up common ground for inter-religious dialogue, as can be seen also in the release of many interfaith statements, especially concerning climate change (Rauterbach et al. 2014), and in the formation of inter-religious environmental initiatives, such as the global Alliance of Religions and Conservation, Interfaith Power and Light (USA), and the Australian Religious Response to Climate Change (now allied with Greenfaith Australia). Counteracting sectarian fundamentalism, this trend was manifest also in the 2009 Parliament of the World's Religions in Melbourne, addressed to the challenge of 'Making a World of Difference: Hearing Each Other, Healing the Earth'. Bringing together some 8,000 people from around 200 countries and dozens of faith traditions, this congress coincided with the UN's climate summit in Denmark and many delegates chose to sign a petition urging those meeting in Copenhagen to take concerted action to limit global warming. This was followed in 2014 by an Interfaith Summit on Religion and Climate change in New York, organised by the World Council of Churches and Religions for Peace. Immediately preceding the UN climate change summit there on September 24–25, it enabled delegates from around the world to join the People's Climate March and participate in an interfaith service at the Episcopal Cathedral of St John the Divine, where Terry Tempest Williams, Vandana Shiva and Al Gore were among the speakers.

EARTHING CHRISTIANITY: TOWARDS
A COMMUNION OF CREATURES

Considerations of Christianity and ecology can be traced back (at least) to the mid-1950s when Lutheran theologian John Sittler first proposed a 'theology for Earth' (see also Kearns 2011, 416–417). In the meantime, this has become a large and diverse field of research, reflection, and practice, of which I can only provide a glimpse here. As already indicated, climate change has galvanised religious environmentalism, as well as affording it greater visibility, and many Christians have joined the campaign for 'climate justice'. While the science continues to be contested by many on the right in Canada, Australia, and especially the United States, both within and outside the churches, recognition of global warming as a matter of pressing moral and religious concern is growing even among American evangelicals (Kearns 2014). Given the gravity of this problem and the urgency of its redress, this is a very welcome development. In one key respect, though, an engagement with climate change is but a short step for Christians who might not previously have been drawn to religious environmentalism: namely, in view of the specifically *human* suffering and mortality that it is already beginning to wreak, especially among those who have done least to cause the problem, along with its potential economic and political disruptiveness. Climate change concern thus sits comfortably with the preponderantly anthropocentric ethos of Euro-Western Christianity. Yet as Lynn White argued all those years ago, this anthropocentric leaning is itself ecologically problematic: what was needed, as he argued in a later essay, 'Continuing the Conversation', is 'a viable equivalent to animism' (1973, 62) to undergird a renewed appreciation of the intrinsic worth, autonomous agency, and indwelling spirituality of all creatures, among whom he also counted inorganic entities, such as rocks and mountains. As we have seen, some Western eco-religionists have looked to non-Western and pre-Christian traditions in search of a more immanent spirituality and inclusive ethos. But, as Riley has discovered, White himself hoped that this could be reactivated from within Christianity's 'recessive genes', forgotten or suppressed dimensions of biblical and theological literature, which pointed towards what he called a 'spiritual democracy of all creatures' (1973, 61). While this hope, as I indicate below, turns out not to have been unfounded, the belated opening of Christianity towards a wider communion with other creatures is occurring under the shadow of escalating extinctions (O'Brien 2010).

In her 1996 overview of Christian environmentalism in the United States, Kearns distinguished three main approaches that had emerged by the early 1990s, based respectively on a stewardship ethic, an eco-justice ethic, and a Creation spirituality ethic, whereby 'ethic' encompasses both worldview and ethos. As Kearns stresses in later re-evaluations, the picture has since become more complex and the approaches less clearly differentiated. In the United States, moreover, since the discourse of stewardship has been captured by anti-environmentalist, climate change 'sceptical' evangelicals, such as the Cornwall Institute, this terminology has been widely displaced by an ethic of 'care for creation' (Kearns 2011, 421). Nonetheless, Kearns' typology is still helpful in distinguishing different tendencies within the spectrum of Christian environmentalism worldwide (see also Douglas 2009).

The stewardship/creation care ethic provides a theocentric foundation for valuing Earth and otherkind, whereby humans are privileged in accordance with their biblical mandate to 'have dominion', but also to 'till and to keep' (Gen. 2.15). Whereas this position has had most appeal among political conservatives, including most evangelicals, the eco-justice ethic is generally favoured by left-liberal Christians. Emerging in the early 1970s, this predates, and is more inclusive, than the 'environmental justice' movement. As William Gibson explained in the December 1982 issue of their journal, *The Egg*, these early eco-justice advocates, inspired by the Hebrew prophetic tradition, understood that the 'God of justice, engaged in deliverance from bondage and oppression, is also the God of creation, who cares for all creatures and engages in the work of protecting and restoring the earth as well as the poor' (28): work in which humans were called to actively participate both in their personal relations with more-than-human others and through collective endeavours to counter systemic forms of domination. Further biblical support for this position is found in the core Christian ethos of neighbour-love, based on the Parable of the Good Samaritan (Luke 10:25–10:37), which, as the eminent Protestant theologian Reinhold Niebuhr[2] was already professing in the 1950s, should be understood to extend also to more-than-human others: 'the near one and the far one; the one removed from me by distances in time and space, in convictions and loyalties [. . . the neighbour is] man and is angel and is animal and inorganic being, all that participates in being' (qtd. in Rasmussen 2013, 221; see also Elvey et al. 2013). An eco-justice orientation underpins the World Council of Churches' 'Justice, Peace, and the Integrity of Creation' programme, initiated in 1983, which seeks alternatives to socially and ecologically destructive forms of corporate globalization. Theorizations of eco-justice have come to incorporate feminist, postcolonial and queer perspectives, intersecting with liberation and animal rights theologies, as well as with the predominantly human-centred concerns of the environmental justice movement.

Creation spirituality was initially inspired by the work of the Catholic 'geologian', Thomas Berry, and from the biblical vision of the 'cosmic Christ' in John 1. In Niels Gregersen's theology of 'Deep Incarnation', the Word made Flesh in Jesus of Nazareth discloses the participation of the divine in the entire realm of matter: an understanding partially endorsed by Pope John Paul II in his 1986 encyclical, 'Lord, Giver of Life', which affirms that in the Incarnation the 'entire visible and material world' was 'taken up into unity with God' (qtd. in Johnson 2014, 198). Whereas the first two approaches are more likely to be shared with Jewish and Islamic environmentalists, the third opens common ground between Christianity and Indigenous, East Asian, and even neo-pagan spiritualties. It has been the most marginal among people in the pews thus far, but has found encouragement in FORE's promotion of the legacy of Thomas Berry through the award-winning film, *Journey of the Universe* (2011), based on his collaboration with physicist Brian Swimme.

Favouring Christian versions of animism and panpsychism, Creation spirituality has considerable potential to appeal to younger people in search of an ecological materialist modality of mysticism.

In my view, all three approaches are essential. Creation spirituality nourishes ecopolitical engagement by fostering experiences of deep interconnectivity and empathetic opening towards more-than-human others. Yet at a time when humans are required to shoulder ever greater responsibility for shaping Earth's possible futures, in keeping with our escalating environmental impacts and technoscientific capacities, we are surely called also to embrace a stewardship or Earth carer role. And in the assumption of that role, the bio-inclusive and inter-generational principles of eco-justice should guide our decisions, lest those wielding most power be left to act tyrannically in the interests of the few. Just such a synthesis is achieved in the 'integral ecology' put forward in *Laudato si'*, which is informed not only by relevant physical and social science research, but also by decades of ecophilosophical and ecotheological reflection (especially as developed in consort with social justice teachings in Latin America). Into this mix, moreover, Pope Francis introduces a fourth dimension, which accords strikingly with White's proposal for a 'democracy of all creatures': namely, the biblical vision, found in Daniel 3:57–3:90 and Psalms 104 and 148, of all earthly beings, animate and inanimate, joined in praise for the creator. This was also the inspiration for St. Francis' beautiful Canticle of the Creatures, which is recalled in the opening paragraph of *Laudato si'*, where Earth is hailed as 'sister' and 'mother' (2015, 3). Before proceeding to his searing presentation of 'What is happening to our common home', Francis honours his namesake as a 'mystic' (9) who 'communed with all creation' and sought 'justice for the poor' (10). Rebutting the dismissal of St. Francis' sense of kinship with all creatures as 'naïve romanticism', and his austere way of life as a 'mere veneer of asceticism', the Pope insists that this was 'something much more radical: a refusal to turn reality into an object simply to be used and controlled' (11). It is by joining St. Francis in this radical stance, that Christians might be called back into 'communion with God, with others and with all creatures' (175).

The biblical motif of shared praise for the creator gave rise to the popular medieval notion that all creatures rejoiced also in the Resurrection of Christ. This informed the iconography of Easter, such as in this marginal scene in a prayer book produced by nuns in the Medingen convent around 1500, which depicts a donkey blowing the *shofar* (an ancient Jewish horn, referred to in Lev. 25:1 as announcing the Jubilee Year, when slaves and prisoners would be freed, debts would be forgiven, and the mercies of God made manifest), from which emerges a speech bubble declaring *Omnis spiritus laudet dominum* ('Let every spirit praise the Lord', Ps. 150:6, the last verse of the Psalter, in the Latin version of the Vulgate), while a monkey sings and plays the tambourine, in the presence of a curious dog and a squirrel excitedly standing on two legs.[3] (Fig. 14.1) Similarly, popular depictions of the Nativity to this day recall one of many apocryphal narratives featuring animals (Hobgood-Oster 2008), according to which the first witnesses to the Incarnation were neither the timorous shepherds nor the wise potentates from the East, but the ox and the ass in the stable, where the Christ child was laid in the manger used to provide food for animals.

Such depictions intimate a view of the Incarnation and Resurrection as involving all creatures, rejoicing equally in the divine gift of life and sharing equally in the emancipatory promise of the peaceable Kin(g)dom (Isaiah 11:6–11:9; Rom. 8:21–8:22). But they are clearly highly anthropomorphic. A contemporary account of creaturely communion, appropriately acknowledging alterity along with kinship, would therefore need to affirm that 'all beings give glory to God simply by being themselves', as the pioneering feminist theologian Elizabeth Johnson puts it in her profound reflection on the relationship between Darwinian evolution and Christian faith in the 'God of love' (276). This is consistent with process theological understandings of *creatio continua* (continuous creation), or as Catherine Keller in *Face of the Deep* terms it, *creation ex profundis* (from the deep), according to which the Creator is not understood as an extra-terrestrial masculine designer deity, but as an indwelling divine mystery that 'freely gifts the natural world with

Figure 14.1. Copenhagen Royal Library, Ms Thott 120-8°, fol. 60r. Marginal scene from an Easter prayer-book, written and illustrated by a nun from the Cistercian Abbey of Medingen (near Lüneburg) ca. 1500, listed under the sigle K2 on Henrike Lähnemann's catalogue; http://medingen.seh.ox.ac.uk/

creative agency' (Johnson 2014, 160), and perpetually 'lures' all things towards the fullest possible actualization of their interactive becoming. This *calling* Keller terms the divine Eros. Its counterpart is the divine Agape, which graciously '*responds* to whatever we have become; in com/passion it feels our feelings: it is the *reception*' (Keller 2008, 99). This omniamorous divine mystery, who, as Job discovered, does not orchestrate all things for exclusively human benefit, participates in the suffering of all beings within the evolving web of life, the cruelties of which were disclosed, with so much anguish, by Charles Darwin. According to this bio-inclusive view of divine compassion, 'the pelican chick', pushed out of the nest by its abler sibling, 'does not die alone' (Johnson 2014, 206). Yet the pain and perishing that is an inevitable dimension of creaturely existence must be distinguished from all sources of distress and death, from factory farming to species extinction, occasioned by those of us in the communion of creatures capable of discerning that such ills could be averted. Sharing with other creatures in both praise and suffering, humans are called also to stand in prophetic solidarity with our Earth others in seeking (in the inadequately heeded words of the Anglican Marks of Mission) 'to transform unjust structures of society, to challenge violence of every kind and pursue peace and reconciliation [. . . and] to strive to safeguard the integrity of creation, and sustain and renew the life of the earth'.[4]

This bio-inclusive reconceptualisation of communion invites a re-imagination of the central ritual of most Christian churches, the Eucharistic feast, along the eco-materialist lines proposed by Anne Elvey: 'in the matter of bread and wine, the matter of women's and men's bodies and blood, and in the particular human communities gathered to celebrate, Eucharist brings into focus the reality of Earth-being as interconnected and interdependent' (2012, 186); as a kenotic 'being-for-the other' (191), which, in a world where feasting and flourishing are inextricably linked with killing and consuming, entails both hospitality and sacrifice. Forms of more-than-human communion are also starting to be practiced outside the church, too. One example of this is the Chicago-based 'Migration and Me' programme.[5] An initiative of the 'Faith in Place' organization, which seeks to inspire 'religious people of diverse faiths to care for the Earth through education, connection, and advocacy',[6] this project is designed to link socio-economically disadvantaged African American and Latino faith communities with local conservation initiatives. Veronica Kyle, Chicago Congregational Outreach Director for Faith in Place, realised that shared experiences of dislocation and migration could provide the key to engaging these communities with the predicament of other creatures on the move, since 'human beings, monarch butterflies, migratory birds, and other migrating species all seek welcoming places to eat, rest, and live along the migration journey and at the destination'.[7] She therefore created a space for sharing stories of migration in conjunction with learning about the struggles of other species, inspiring the participation of hundreds of largely African American and Latino Christians in the creation and restoration of habitat for butterflies and other insects. Such practices of anticipatory hospitality towards more-than-human others, preparing a place of rest and sustenance upon the journey, or a new home in which to abide, will be increasingly called for as ever more communities and species are displaced and disoriented by the calamitous impacts of anthropogenic climate change.

This one small example is indicative of an epochal shift towards a multi-species sense of fellowship that is starting to occur among practicing Christians, whose vision has hitherto been veiled by a 'tenacious anthropocentrism' (Johnson 2014, 261). In this, they join those of other faiths, who share Thomas Berry's view of the world as 'a communion of subjects rather than a collection of objects', as exemplified in the large anthology of this name (Waldau and Patton 2006). While there is abundant evidence today of the havoc that can be caused by militant religious fundamentalism (as has been the case with any number of secular fundamentalisms, such as nationalism, fascism and Stalinism), it can only be hoped that, at this time of global socio-ecological imperilment, it is the voice coming from the 2015 Parliament of the World's Religions in Salt Lake City that comes to hold sway: 'The future we embrace will be a new ecological civilization and a world of peace, justice and sustainability, with the flourishing of the diversity of life. We will build this future with one family within the greater Earth community'.

ACKNOWLEDGEMENT

This essay was written with the generous support of the Alexander von Humboldt Foundation and the Freiburg Institute of Advanced Studies.

NOTES

1. See also the 'Buddhist Climate Change Statement to World Leaders' (October 2015).

2. It is perhaps not insignificant, in light of his later thinking, that White studied with Niebuhr in the San Francisco Theological Seminary (Riley 2014a, 940).

3. Copenhagen Manuscript K2 (Ms Thott 120-8° ca. 1500), fol. 60r. I am indebted for this image to Henrike Lehnemann, Professor of Medieval German Studies at

Oxford University, and co-creator of a website dedicated to the manuscripts produced by the Medingen nuns: http://medingen.seh.ox.ac.uk/.

4. See 'Anglican Communion' at http://www.anglicancommunion.org/identity/marks-of-mission.aspx.

5. I am indebted to Laurel Kearns for alerting me to this project, and for her and Bob McCoy's generous hospitality, convivial conversations, and access to resources in researching this chapter.

6. See http://www.faithinplace.org/who-we-are.

7. See http://www.faithinplace.org/our-programs/migration-me.

WORKS CITED

Adorno, Theodor and Max Horkheimer. *Dialectic of Enlightenment.* 1944. Trans. John Cumming. London: Verso, 1979.

Barnhill, David Landis and Roger S. Gottlieb. *Deep Ecology and World Religions.* New York: State University of New York Press, 2001.

Baumann, Whitney A., Richard R. Bohannon II, Kevin J. O'Brien. *Grounding Religion: A Field Guide to the Study of Religion and Ecology.* London: Routledge, 2011.

Baumann, Whitney A. 'Religion: What Is It, Who Gets to Decide, and Why Does It Matter?' *Grounding Religion: A Field Guide to the Study of Religion and Ecology.* Eds. Whitney A. Baumann, Richard R. Bohannon II, Kevin J. O'Brien. London: Routledge, 2011. 13–26.

Blain, Jenny, Douglas Ezzy, Graham Harvey, eds. *Researching Paganisms.* Walnut Creek, CA: AltaMira, 2004.

'Buddhist Climate Change Statement to World Leaders'. Global Buddhist Climate Collective. 28 October 2015. Web. 3 November 2015.

Christ, Carol. *Laughter of Aphrodite: Reflections of a Journey to the Goddess.* San Francisco: Harper and Row, 1987.

Chryssavgis, John. 'The Green Patriarch'. The Ecumenical Patriarchate of Constantinople. 2015. Web. 10 August 2015.

Cudworth, Erica. *Developing Ecofeminist Theory: The Complexity of Difference.* New York: Palgrave Macmillan, 2005.

DeLoughrey, Elizabeth and George B. Handley. 'Introduction: Toward and Aesthetics of the Earth'. *Postcolonial Ecologies: Literatures of the Environment.* Eds. Elizabeth DeLoughrey and George B. Handley. Oxford: Oxford University Press, 2011. 3–39.

Douglas, Steve. 'Religious Environmentalism in the West. 1: A Focus on Christianity'. *Religion Compass* 3.4 (2009): 717–737.

Eaton, Heather. 'Where Do We Go from Here? Methodology, Next Steps, Social Change'. *Christian Faith and the Earth: Current Paths and Emerging Horizons in Ecotheology.* Eds. M. Conradie, Sigurd Bergmann, Celia Deane-Drummund, Denis Edwards. London: Bloomsbury, 2014. 195–217.

Elvey, Anne. 'Living One for the Other: Eucharistic Hospitality as Ecological Hospitality'. *Reinterpreting the Eucharist: Explorations in Feminist Theology and Ethics*. Eds. Anne Elvey, Carol Hogan, Kim Power, Claire Renkin. Sheffield: Equinox, 2012. 186–201.

Elvey, Carol Hogan, Kim Power, Claire Renkin. 'Rethinking Neighbour Love: A Conversation between Political Theology and Ecological Ethics'. *Where the Wild Ox Roams: Essays in Honour of Norman C. Habel*. Eds. Alan H. Cadwallader with Peter L. Trudinger. Sheffield: Sheffield University Press, 2013. 58–75.

Elvey, Anne. 'Homogenizing Violence'. Isa 40:4 (and Luke 3:5) and MTR (Mountaintop Removal Mining). *Worldviews*, 19.3: 226–244.

Fox, Warwick. *Toward a Transpersonal Ecology: Developing New Foundations for Environmentalism*. New York: State University of New York Press, 1995.

Francis, The Holy Father. *Laudato si'*. Encyclical Letter on Care for Our Common Home. Vatican Press. 24 May 2015. Web. 25 May 2015.

Gibson, William, ed. *Eco-Justice: The Unfinished Journey*. New York: State University of New York Press, 2004.

Gimbutas, Marija. *The Goddesses and Gods of Old Europe, 6500–3500 BC*. Berkeley: University of California Press, 1982.

'Global Religious Diversity: Half of the Most Religiously Diverse Countries Are in Asia-Pacific Region'. Pew Research Center. April 2014. Web. 10 August 2015.

Gottlieb, Roger S., ed. *Liberating Faith: Religious Voices for Justice, Peace and Ecological Wisdom*. Lanham, MD: Rowman and Littlefield, 2003.

Gottlieb, Roger S. *A Greener Faith: Religious Environmentalism and Our Planet's Future*. Oxford: Oxford University Press, 2006a.

Gottlieb, Roger S., ed. *Oxford Handbook of Religion and Ecology*. Oxford: Oxford University Press, 2006b.

Gottlieb, Roger S. 'Religion and the Environment'. *Routledge Companion to the Study of Religion*. Ed. R. Hinnells. London: Routledge, 2010. 492–558.

Graham, Mary. 'Some Thoughts about the Philosophical Underpinnings of Aboriginal Worldviews'. *Australian Humanities Review* 24 (2008). Web. 12 February 2016.

Gregersen, Niels. 'Deep Incarnation: Why Evolutionary Continuity Matters in Christology'. *Toronto Journal of Theology* 26.2 (2010): 173–188.

Haluza-DeLay, Randolph. 'Religious Movements in Environmental Governance'. *Encyclopaedia of Global Environmental Politics and Governance*. Eds. Phillip H. Pattberg and Fariborz Zelli. Northampton, MA: Elgar Publishing, 2015.

Harvey, Graham. *Animism: Respecting the Living World*. New York: Columbia University Press, 2006.

Harvey, Graham, ed. *The Handbook of Contemporary Animism*. Abingdon: Routledge, 2014.

Harvey, Graham. 'Animism'. March 2013. Web. 11 August 2015.

Hobgood-Oster, Laura. *Holy Dogs and Asses: Animals in the Christian Tradition*. Chicago: University of Illinois Press, 2008.

Johnson, Elizabeth A. *Ask the Beasts: Darwin and the God of Love*. London: Bloomsbury, 2014.

Kearns, Laurel. 'Saving the Creation: Christian Environmentalism in the United States'. *Sociology of Religion* 57.1 (1996): 55–70.

Kearns, Laurel. 'The Context of Eco-theology'. *Blackwell Companion to Modern Theology*. Ed. Gareth Jones. New York: Blackwell, 2004. 466–484.

Kearns, Laurel. 'The Role of Religious Activism'. *Oxford Handbook of Climate Change and Society*. Eds. John S. Dryzek, Richard B. Norgaard, David Schlosberg. Oxford: Oxford University Press, 2011. 414–428.

Kearns, Laurel. 'Green Evangelicals'. *The New Evangelical Social Engagement*. Eds. Brian Steensland and Philip Goff. Oxford: Oxford University Press, 2014. 157–178.

Keller, Catherine. *Face of the Deep: A Theology of Becoming*. London: Routledge, 2003.

Keller, Catherine. *On the Mystery: Discerning Divinity in Process*. Minneapolis: Fortress Press, 2008.

Lodge, David M. and Christopher Hamlin, eds. *Religion and the New Ecology: Environmental Responsibility in a World in Flux*. Foreword by Peter H. Raven. South Bend: University of Notre Dame Press, 2006.

Macy, Joanna. *World as Lover, World as Self*. Foreword by Thich Nhat Hanh. Berkeley: Parralax, 1991.

Mathews, Freya. *For Love of Matter: A Contemporary Panpsychism*. New York: State University of New York Press, 2003.

Mathews, Freya. *Reinhabiting Reality: Towards a Recovery of Culture*. New York: State University of New York Press, 2005.

Merchant, Carolyn. *The Death of Nature: Women, Ecology, and the Scientific Revolution*. London: Wildwood, 1980.

Merchant, Carolyn. *Earthcare: Women and the Environment*. London: Routledge, 1995.

Metaxis, Eric. *Amazing Grace: William Wilberforce and the Heroic Campaign to End Slavery*. New York: Harper Collins, 2007.

Morton, Timothy. *The Ecological Thought*. Boston: Harvard University Press, 2010.

Nixon, Rob. *Slow Violence and the Environmentalism of the Poor*. Cambridge: Harvard University Press, 2011.

O'Brien, Kevin. *Ethics of Biodiversity: Christianity, Ecology, and the Variety of Life*. Washington, DC: Georgetown University Press, 2010.

Parliament of the World's Religions. 'Declaration on Climate Change'. 2015. Web. 28 October 2015.

Pearson, Joanne, Richard H. Roberts, Geoffrey Samuel, eds. *Nature Religion Today: Paganism in the Modern World*. Edinburgh: Edinburgh University Press, 1998.

Plumwood, Val. *Feminism and the Mastery of Nature*. London: Routledge, 1993.

Plumwood, Val. 'Shadow Places and the Politics of Dwelling'. *Australian Humanities Review* 44 (2008): 139–150.

Radford-Ruether, Rosemary. *Gaia and God: An Ecofeminist Theology of Earth Healing*. San Francisco: Harper Collins, 1992.

Raphael, Melissa. *Thealogy and Embodiment: The Post-Patriarchal Reconstruction of Female Sacrality*. Sheffield: Sheffield University Press, 1996.

Rasmussen, Larry. *Earth-Honouring Faith: Religious Ethics in a New Key.* Oxford: Oxford University Press, 2013.

Rautenbach, Ignatius, Guillermo Kerber, Christoph Stückelberge, eds. *International Interfaith Statements 2008–2014.* Global Ethics. 2014. Web. 8 August 2015.

Rigby, Kate. 'The Goddess Returns: Ecofeminist Reconfigurations of Gender, Nature and the Sacred'. *Feminist Poetics of the Sacred: Creative Suspicions.* Eds. Frances Devlin-Glass and Lyn McCredden. New York: Oxford University Press, 2001. 23–54.

Rigby, Kate. *Topographies of the Sacred: The Poetics of Place in European Romanticism.* Charlottesville: University of Virginia Press, 2004.

Rigby, Kate. 'Animal Calls'. *Divinanimality: Animal Theory, Creaturely Theology.* Ed. Stephen Moore. New York: Fordham University Press, 2014. 116–131.

Riley, Matthew T. 'The Democratic Roots of our Ecologic Crisis: Lynn White, Biodemocracy, and the Earth Charter'. *Zygon* 49.4 (December 2014a): 938–948.

Riley, Matthew T. 'A Spiritual Democracy of all God's Creatures: Ecotheology and the Animals of Lynn White Jr'. *Divinanimality: Animal Theory, Creaturely Theology.* Ed. Stephen Moore. New York: Fordham University Press, 2014b. 241–260.

Riley, Matthew T. *Deeper Roots: Expanding the Weberian and Theological Aspects of the Lynn White Thesis.* Unpublished dissertation, Drew University, 2015.

Rose, Deborah Bird. *Wild Dog Dreaming: Love and Extinction.* Charlottesville: University of Virginia Press, 2011.

Rose, Deborah Bird. 'Val Plumwood's Philosophical Animism'. *Environmental Humanities* 3 (2013): 93–109.

Salleh, Ariel. *Ecofeminism as Politics: Nature, Marx, and the Postmodern.* London: Zed Books, 1997.

Schleiermacher, Friedrich. *On Religion. Speeches to Its Cultured Despisers.* Trans. Richard Crouter. Cambridge: Cambridge University Press, 1988.

Sittler, Joseph. *Evocations of Grace: Writings on Ecology, Theology and Ethics.* Eds. Steven Bauma-Prediger and Peter Bakken. Grand Rapids: William B. Erdman, 2000.

Spretnak, Charlene. *The Spiritual Dimension of Green Politics.* Santa Fe: Bear, 1986.

Starhawk. *The Spiral Dance: A Rebirth of the Ancient Religion of the Great Goddess.* 10th anniversary rev. edn. San Francisco: Harper, 1989.

Taylor, Bron. *Dark Green Religion: Nature Spirituality and the Planetary Future.* Los Angeles: University of California Press, 2010.

Waldau, Paul and Kimberley Patton, eds. *A Communion of Subjects: Animals in Religion, Science and Ethics.* New York: Columbia University Press, 2006.

Weber, Max. *The Protestant Ethic and the Spirit of Capitalism* (1904/05). Trans. Talcott Parsons. New York: Scribner's, 1958.

Weber, Max. 'Science as a Vocation'. 1920. *From Max Weber: Essays in Sociology.* Eds. H. H. Gerth and C. Wright Mills. 1946. New York: Routledge, 1991. 129–157.

White, Lynn, Jr. 'The Historical Roots of our Ecologic Crisis'. *Science* 155.3767 (10 March 1967): 1203–1207.

White, Lynn, Jr. 'Continuing the Conversation'. *Western Man and Environmental Ethics: Attitudes toward Nature and Technology*. Ed. Ian G. Barbour. Reading: Addison-Wesley, 1973. 55–64.

White, Lynn, Jr. 'The Future of Compassion'. *Ecumenical Review* 30 (1978): 106–108.

Chapter Fifteen

How the Earth Speaks Now

The Book of Nature and Biosemiotics as Theoretical Resource for the Environmental Humanities in the Twenty-First Century

Wendy Wheeler

SCIENCE AND THE ENVIRONMENTAL HUMANITIES: AN INTERDISCIPLINARY THEORY OF LIFE'S EVOLUTIONARY INTELLIGENCE

The old world of the Earth Machine and the Gene Machine is slowly passing and a different way of thinking about nature and culture is struggling to be born. Impelled by a growing sense of an ecologically and conceptually disturbed relationship between humans and the Earth, the more we learn about life's core animating behaviours the more we sense the need for new approaches and models. Once we thought about organisms as machines made of protein operating according to a deterministic plan laid down genetically in DNA (some, of course, still do). More recently, many biologists, biosemioticians, and ethologists have grown increasingly aware of intelligence at all levels of life. This runs from animals, plants, and fungi at the level of the whole organism all the way to the active molecular cellular intelligence of the body and its parts. DNA is not a 'set of instructions' for making a body from scratch. There is always already flesh involved in every act of conception. DNA is better likened to a library, i.e., an information resource for the cell, and the cell itself an active part of a symbiotic, teleodynamic system encompassing organism *and* umwelt (Hoffmeyer 2008).

The universe as a whole may or may not be teleodynamic, but living organisms and their parts clearly are. They are made of meanings and purposes, that is to say of functions and ends.[1] Not wholly dissimilarly, we have also become much more aware of the equally intelligent interconnected bacterial life, the microbiome that lives in our gut and on our skin. Playing a part in educating various parts of our bodies in how to function, this microbial life also takes an active part in our organismic development; it joins us and the rest of the biological world together (McFall-Ngai et al. 2013; Brown and Griffin 2015). Finally, crashing right through the previous orthodoxy of 'one-way only' movement of biological information—from DNA to RNA to protein—which was articulated in Francis Crick's 1956 'Central Dogma' (Crick 1970), we have also learned about the heritability of some acquired characteristics (Halfmann and Lindquist 2010; Dias and Ressler 2014; Szyf 2014). Often related to stress—which can be generated both 'naturally' and 'culturally'—this undoes the rigidity of both the Central Dogma and also the nature–culture distinction rather thoroughly. In this 'neo-Lamarckianism', there is some movement in the opposite direction, from umwelt to DNA. There is plenty of evidence of correlation between environmental effects (from the benefits of living near trees to the experience of status) and health and mortality (Marmot 2004). Awareness of semiotic influences here allows us, however, to identify the semiotic mode of causation.

All this, including the encompassing biosemiotic insight concerning the ubiquity of communication and meaning-making throughout the living world, which makes the biosphere co-existent with the semiosphere (Kull 2015), forces upon us ever more urgently the need for very new and different models of evolutionary life both natural and cultural. This applies most especially to inquiry as explored in the environmental humanities broadly. Nature and culture are so thoroughly intertwined, and their boundaries so often blurred (both for human and for some nonhuman animals), that we are gradually coming to see the need for a different model of these manifold relations. The biosemiotic model crosses both. Nature signifies and communicates via codes carried by different media and channels, but the specifically human semiosis (anthroposemiosis) that emerges as a new layer of meanings on top of, and dependent upon, those of evolutionary nature is recognizably encoded in similar ways. Human semiosis is, like all other semiosic kinds, iconic and indexical, but it is also symbolic and abstractive.

It was once thought that the Earth spoke to a humankind culturally at home in nature because God made it so. This was, perhaps, in its own time, a way of getting at a truth about the ties that bind living creatures to each other and to the Earth, and about the necessity of certain constraints in natural and cultural makings. Surely, muffling the Earth has not fared so well for the planet or for any of its creatures. The Earth does speak. It might be better if we learned that lesson again, and listened hard to what is related in its many different ways of telling. But this time, we may do so in richer notes, not only through philosophy and metaphysics but through science also.

What follows offers a sketch of where the life sciences and the humanities have variously travelled on their way to reopening the book of nature. The chapter concludes with an outline of what a more integrated view, drawn from the growing interdiscipline of biosemiotics, might look like. Biosemiotics depends on bringing together insights from the life sciences, but also from the arts and humanities, and from their traditions of interpretation and making. These latter are also integral to understanding nature's makings. As biologist James A. Shapiro (2015) has pointed out, biological forms of evolutionary self-making are more like poetry than machines in their organization. It also unites their concerns and sometimes their deductive, inductive and abductive methods. In particular, biosemiotics seems to offer models for the development of an interdisciplinary and multispecies semiotic theory of relations that may be useful to the environmental sciences and humanities both.

Biosemiotic modes of semiotic modelling currently cross groups (zoosemiotics, phytosemiotics, mycosemiotics, anthroposemiotics, and so on) and also draw on various, often intermixed, sources: the architectonic semiotic logic of Charles Sanders Peirce (1839–1914); the umwelt theory of Jakob von Uexküll (1866–1944); the bio-cybernetics of Gregory Bateson (1904–1980); the cultural and natural semiotics of Juri Lotman (1922–1993); the zoosemiotics of Thomas A. Sebeok (1920–2001); and the teleodynamics of Terrence Deacon, for example. Biologists Jesper Hoffmeyer and Kalevi Kull, founders of the Copenhagen-Tartu School, have been enormously influential in developing the field. Hoffmeyer has been a major innovator of its ideas and terminology. It is Hoffmeyer, for instance, who has developed most emphatically the idea of biosemiotics itself and who has developed, the idea of the 'semiome' (Hoffmeyer 2014a, 198), to be set alongside the genome, and also the concept of 'semiotic scaffolding' (Hoffmeyer 2014b). Both semiome and semiotic scaffolding run through and across nature and culture very thoroughly. The semiome consists of all those communicative, interpretive, translational phenomena that express the dynamic relatedness of all an organism's parts, one to another and, of course, to the natural and cultural umwelt also. It is the semiome's relationality that is responsible for many of the more mysterious of the noted facts of epidemiology, medical care and placebo effects where cultural information can translate into physical changes in health and well-being (Marmot 2004). Genetic material and organs bear or carry this semiotic activity, but the semiome is not simply reducible to the genome. The latter is especially responsible for natural memory, the passing on of genetic information; but the semiome is responsible both for all the cell's ribosome readings that turn RNA information into protein and also, in its cultural forms, for the handing on and evolution of cultural life. Semiotic scaffolding accounts for the particular form that developments take. These latter are close to what Gilles Deleuze called 'lines of flight' and to what Gilbert Simondon called the processes of 'concretization' and 'individuation'.

The most centrally important biosemiotic impetus, however, takes the form of a move away from a sole focus on an ontology of substances (and essences). Instead, the biosemiotic logos takes us in the direction of a much greater focus (i.e., than that which has been common throughout the modern period) upon an ontology of relations and processes. In this biosemiotic understanding it is *sign relations* that are central. Causally efficacious and dependent upon material codes and channels, information proper, i.e., *semiosis*, is, as Norbert Wiener originally noted, 'not matter or energy' (1965, 132). It is a causally efficacious 'no-thing', an *immaterial and evolutionary power*.

This most important causal aspect of living reality should recall us to Bateson's claim that 'Mind is empty; it is a no-thing. It exists only in its ideas, and these again are no-things' (Bateson 2002, 10). Ideas, in other words, are information-*as-interpretation*. Semiosis is the coming into being of meanings in the processual becomings of sign relations amongst the living. Of course, signs are everywhere throughout the cosmos, in light and energy and matter, in rocks, rivers, roots and trees, and creatures. But only the living are readers. The sign is classically that which stands in for something else. It depends upon and mobilises differences, and it does so on at least two levels. One is that of a *present* 'standing-in for'. This level can be seen in the differences between the three aspects of sign relations as described by Charles Peirce (De Waal 2013). These are the object, the representamen (sign, or sign vehicle) and the interpretant. They instantiate the present of any sign relation. The second kind of difference is that put dynamically into play between past meanings and future ones: this is the evolutionary and developmental difference between signs that *have been* and signs *yet to come*. In other words, signs are meanings and can grow. This is the evolution of systems. In humans, where it comes from not being absolutely trapped in habit (necessary though habit certainly is), we call it dialogical flexibility, or learning. We can see this dynamic understanding of information or semiosis in the work of other philosophers of relational ontology such as Gilbert Simondon and those he has influenced: Gilles Deleuze and Félix Guattari perhaps most notably. As Brian Massumi, recalling Bateson, writes of Simondon:

> Information—Simondon is unambiguous about this—has no content, no structure, and no meaning. In itself, it is but disparity. Its meaning is the coming into existence of the new level that effectively takes off from the disparity and resolves the discontinuity it exhibits into a continuity of operation. Information is redefined in terms of this event. As for Gregory Bateson, information is a 'difference that makes a difference': a disparity that actively yields a new quantum of effect, and whose meaning is the novelty-value of that effect. (2009, 43)

We can thus say that meaning is the play of differences and similarities (Wheeler 2016). When humans are conscious of this, they call it metaphor (Ricoeur 2003). But in the dynamic growth of information as sign relations for the living, interpretation and meaning-making are better called (as Peirce so calls them) interpretance.[2] This is precisely because meaning-making is not just a matter for humans. Nor, indeed, does it require 'mind' or even brain. It is really semiosis as 'the difference that makes a difference' (Bateson 1972, 459) for every organism, whether in terms of mental or physical behaviour. Nonetheless, it is this interplay between nature and culture, science and art, material and immaterial, genome and semiome, difference and similarity that will form the semiotic realism capable of providing a theoretical basis for the environmental humanities. But first the history.

THE LIFE SCIENCES

The life sciences are perhaps halfway down this path of change. In the main they have recognised that living systems are information systems (Oyama 2000). However, conventional scientific thinking about biological (and cultural) information remains trapped in the substance ontology that science inherits from its metaphysically fractured sixteenth- and seventeenth-century roots in the Protestant Reformation (Deely 2001; Wheeler 2016). Part of this fracture is nominalistic; it is born from the nominalist philosophical belief that human thought is radically alienated from, and thus cannot guarantee to know, the actual world of natural and cultural processes as they are at all. Far from being 'postmodern' and recent, this idea of a 'constructed' or 'fictive' reality, first took root in the fourteenth century as a result of William of Ockham's (1287–1347) elaboration of John Duns Scotus' (1266–1308) semiotic philosophy. Ockham's development had several pernicious outcomes, perhaps the most significant of which has been an historical focus (which was central to the beginning of early modern science in the seventeenth century) on substances at the expense of relations. More recently, it is also the case that such a nominalist view is at odds with evolutionary theory and thus with any kind of ecological environmentalism. As Nobel Laureate biologist Francois Jacob wrote: 'if the image that a bird gets of the insects it needs to feed its progeny does not reflect at least some aspects of reality, there are no more progeny. If the representation that a monkey builds of the branch it wants to leap to has nothing to do with reality, then there is no more monkey' (Jacob 1982, 56).

The causes of the focus on substances at the expense of relations are complex. Essentially they stem from Duns Scotus' realisation that perception of reality is never complete, and thus that the human mind can only deal in signs that are related to that reality, and 'stand in' for it, but which never reveal it in its totality. In addition, Scotus recognised that, unlike the case with other animals, human thoughts habitually become abstracted from the immediacy of sensory experience. The result of these processes of abstraction (and abstraction upon abstraction) is that these kinds of abstractive signs can very easily fall into error. With Scotus' insight, the way was now laid for William of Ockham and nominalism. In Ockham's development, all human thought is simply a convenient fiction—a *naming* (name: L. *nomen*) of the world in ways that make sense for humans, but with no guarantee of connection to the actual world as God created it. According to this view, God can make things any way He wants. He is neither subject to any laws nor to anything like human logic.

In discovering that sign relations are indifferent to truth or falsity, Duns Scotus opened the way for an earlier Augustinian pessimism concerning the effects of Adam's Fall; for human intellect, after the Fall, may be deceived (Deely 379–380; Harrison 2007). In the absence of intentional relation, intellectual knowledge, soon to be isolated within the skull, so to speak, may simply be a fiction. This is the position still held by many contemporary philosophers and psychologists of the 'eliminative materialism' persuasion. It was believed that, before the Fall, Adam was in possession of the perfect philosophy. With the development of Scotus' philosophy, particularly as developed in Ockham's nominalism, new approaches had to be discovered that were capable, against such awful human fallibility, of guaranteeing human knowledge. Thus natural philosophers such as Francis Bacon argued for the importance of empirical observation and careful measurement of the indubitable reality of substances (Harrison 2007). The legacy of this highly successful form of knowledge remains, however, in contemporary science's lack of interest in *relations* as primary causal powers in our universe. Instead, relations are relegated to secondary subjective qualities that, as such, cannot be proper objects of scientific enquiry. And so it came to pass that, with these developments, the medieval growth of an ontology of sign relations fell into the shadows until Charles Sanders Peirce's (1839–1914) nineteenth-century pansemiotic revival. Peirce himself can be placed among other process and relational ontologies such as those of Alfred North Whitehead, Michael Polanyi, Gilles Deleuze, Félix Guattari, and Gilbert Simondon.

THE HUMANITIES AND SCIENCES: GOING WIDER

If the life sciences have found themselves increasingly confronting what are essentially semiotic questions (especially since the discovery that DNA and RNA are codes), the humanities have also been working their way through their own semiotic developments. Where a systems biology understanding has been a great motivator in the life sciences (Noble 2006; Gilbert and Epel 2009), a growing ecological consciousness has played a significant part in the humanities also. In so far as Jacques Derrida's famous 'there is nothing outside the text' (*il n'y a pas de hors-texte*) (58) is taken to mean (as it very often has been so taken; see Gayatri Spivak's translation) that there is nothing outside of the human-made text of semiological signs then this makes the Saussurean language of difference a solely anthropocentric affair.

But there is more to be said here about the historical stage of development in which a concern with ontogenesis could not easily be expressed. This, incidentally, is also an example about the contexts of lines of flight and the various material and conceptual constraints that allow some trajectories and inhibit others. As Francesco Vitale has shown, Derrida had realised quite early on the implications of DNA as a form of writing and, as with Heidegger before him, of cybernetic emphasis on *immaterial* information as a threat to the modern metaphysics of substance and essence. This meant, of course, effectively the replacement of the philosophy of Western Metaphysics (Heidegger 1976; Vitale 2014). Even as early as *Of Grammatology*, for example, he clearly understood the implications both of cybernetics and also of the discovery that DNA was a code potentially founding other digital and analog encodings in biological and cultural life (Derrida 1976, 84). Nonetheless, and in spite of this interest in cybernetic codes in technology and biology, Derrida seems to have stayed fairly firmly within an anthropocentric understanding of semiosis. We know that Derrida had read Peirce on a post-*Agrégation* study visit to Harvard in 1956–1957. Nonetheless, the Saussurean inscription of difference associated with him, was widely believed also to underpin the development of structuralist anthropology developed by Claude Lévi-Strauss from the structuralist work of Roman Jakobson. It is worth noting that there is an argument to be had about the extent to which Derrida actually accepted Saussure's solely anthropocentric concerns (Wheeler 2016). However, the widespread belief that Roman Jakobson's structuralism derived from Saussurean linguistics and semiology is simply wrong.

The humanities have, indeed, sought to go wider and to join up with the sciences, just as some in the latter also pursue the interdisciplinary gesture. In this, Roman Jakobson, followed by Thomas A. Sebeok, who studied with him, was an important initiator in the move towards a biosemiotic viewpoint and theory. As Sebeok indicated in his account of Jakobson's comments in the mid-1940s on the matter of signs and creativity, Jakobson's thought went far wider than Saussurean linguistics and semiology in thinking about semiosis (Sebeok 2001, xii). Sebeok notes that, after 1967, Jakobson came 'increasingly to appreciate the robust biological *mise en scène* of the doctrine of signs' (3) In fact, as Patrick Sériot has more recently shown, Jakobson's structuralism drew from the start on organicist premises about language and culture (Sériot 2014). This is why he had sought a theoretical basis for these in the developmental biology of the German-Estonian embryologist Karl

Ernst von Baer (1792–1876). For Jakobson, structural development in language is based on meaningful semiotic pattern and imitates homologically the
(evolutionarily derived) processual and patterned becomings of organisms.
The development of the latter depends upon the generation of repetition and
difference (probably through a play of stabilizing habit and chance symbio-
genesis in the first place (Margulis 1999), and, more generally, through the
iconic and indexical signs that Jakobson describes as metaphor and meton-
ymy in language). Via the 'reading' and interpretant activities of umwelt and
innenwelt that produce dialogic cybernetic feedback, these basic patterns
are differentiated, rearticulated, and elaborated (Kull 1998). No wonder that
James Shapiro saw organisms as dominated by processes closer to poetry
than to machines.

   Roman Jakobson's development, alongside his colleague and friend
Nikolai Trubetzskoy, of semiotic structuralism as an account of the structured
processes underlying the making of meanings, had, as outlined above, in fact
not drawn significantly upon Saussure. Instead, with his eastern European cultural commitment to organicism (similarly evident in Goethe and Schelling,
although without assumptions of necessary progress in Jakobson's and
Trubetzskoy's case), when Jakobson wanted to understand the development
of languages and meanings it was not to linguistics he turned at all. Instead,
it was to the developmental biology of Karl Ernst von Baer and the semiotic
philosophy of Charles S. Peirce. Since all evolution involves formal (i.e.,
structural) repetition with difference, Jakobson assumed that the structures
organizing cultural development must to a significant degree repeat the structures organizing biological development. It seems largely to have been due to
the influence of Claude Lévi-Strauss' structuralist anthropology, developed
from the latter's discussions with Jakobson during their time together at the
New School of Social Research in New York during the years of World War
II, that the Saussurean connection was forged. Jakobson thought that cultures
and languages developed in homological likeness to organisms: common
roots followed by developmental specialization closely tied to environmental
pressures. Later, after DNA was shown to be a code following the discovery
of DNA's structure in 1953, Jakobson became even clearer that his original
insight had been correct.

   As Laura Shintani has noted, Jakobson was fully aware of the correspond-
ences between the genetic code and encoding in language. She tells us that,
in his review of Francois Jacob's *The Logic of Life: A History of Heredity*,

> Jakobson introduces the idea that the linguistic model can be in some respects
> mapped on to the problem of molecular heredity . . . 'Biologists and linguists as
> well have observed an impressive set of attributes common to life and language
> since their consecutive emergence. . . . The makeup of the two codes—the

genetic one, discovered and deciphered by molecular biology in our time, and the verbal one, scrutinised by several generations of linguists—has displayed a series of noticeable analogies'. (Shintani 1999, 9–10)

In this story of an alternative Eastern European heritage of semiotic and biological thought that brought us structuralism, we are indebted to the scholarship of the Slavicist and linguist Patrick Sériot and to the recent 2014 English translation, by Amy Jacobs-Colas, of his book. First published in France in 1999, *Structure and the Whole: East, West and Non-Darwinian Biology in the Origins of Structural Linguistics* shows that the history of structuralism has come to be written quite inaccurately. As Sériot notes:

> It is a sort of commonplace in the West to see structuralism as evolving linguistically from Saussure to Lévi-Strauss and Barthes by way of various intermediary links in Prague and Copenhagen in the 1930s. In the *Encyclopédie Philosophique Universelle* of 1990, in the entry 'Structuralism and linguistics' that figures in a chapter entitled 'Western Philosophy' we find the following statement: The term structuralism appeared, together with the methodologies it designates . . . , the bases of which were established by Saussure between 1906 and 1911, in part in opposition to the positivism of historical grammar. In the 1930s, Trubetzskoy and Jakobson in Prague, Bloomfield and Sapir in the United States, identified the minimal distinctive units called phonemes; *the thinking of the first three is based on Saussure's* (vol. 2, p. 2470). (Sériot 2014, 6)

Sériot tells us how 'absolutely revolting' Jakobson's colleague Trubetzskoy found it that English linguists identified both him and Jakobson 'purely and simply with the school of Saussure' (7). In a letter to Jakobson, Trubetzskoy wrote 'This does us some wrong' (7).

The humanities (the Anglophone humanities at least) have often been distracted by the Saussurean understanding of signs. But this anthropocentric sign theory could not hold for long where the development of a specifically environmental humanities interest was concerned. Neither, for reasons given above, could a nominalist position be easily maintained. Semiotic realism might thus form the beginning of a comprehensive biosemiotic theory, shared across the humanities and the life sciences, upon which the environmental humanities could develop its various observations and critiques. Biosemiotics itself sees meaning-making, mind and degrees of subjective experience and agency in all living organisms and their subsystems. It has also recently begun to develop an account of 'the Great Chain of Semiosis' (Hoffmeyer and Stjernfelt 2015), or biosemiotic evolution in other words, which may help us think further about animal and environmental ethics (Tønnessen and Beever 2015).

As Sériot notes, Jakobson and Trubetzskoy were realists who recognised the opportunities and constraints that organismic evolutionary life implies.

Saussure, on the other hand, was a nominalist (Sériot 2014, 250). It is thus significant that, in the early stages of their observations of biological sign action, when they were searching for a semiotic theory to account for what they saw, biosemioticians Jesper Hoffmeyer and Claus Emmeche found Saussurean semiology both incomplete and unfruitful. Subsequently, and due to Hoffmeyer's meeting with the aforementioned American semiotician Thomas A. Sebeok, they were introduced to Charles Peirce's triadic semiotics. In contrast, this provided a very thorough and methodologically rich account of biological, henceforth biosemiotic, processes.

INFORMATION

The advances towards a theory of biological information in the life sciences have been similarly distracted. Not only did the empirical and positivistic heritage of a substance ontology prove a barrier to proper thought about the nature of information (a *relation*, not a substance), but attempts within psychology to replace positivism with a focus on meaning were hobbled by the rise of computation and by the metaphor of the mind as reducible to brain, and brain as merely a computer. The brain is certainly a memory recording device, and doubtless also a coordinating device in bilateral organisms (Hoffmeyer and Stjernfelt 2015), but its methods do not involve the use of binary code except at the most primitive level of sign use, i.e., + (plus) 'good', – (minus) 'bad' and 0 (neutral) 'safe to ignore' (but the latter are *also* potential source of new evolutionary developments, as Hoffmeyer and Stjernfelt argue in 'The Great Chain of Semiosis' (2015). What brains and central nervous systems record is the input of the senses (which *matter*, which are *cared about*, which are, in other words, *minded*), which are thus organised by minding-becoming-mind on the basis of iconic and indexical sign relations capable of being developed, or further refined in terms of meanings, via metaphoric (iconic) and metonymic (indexical) relations.

These signs at the skin are the beginning of cognition. This does not, in fact, require a brain since it is an effect of the capacity, which all organisms require, of responding to an unpredictable world. As Hoffmeyer writes:

What biosemiotics adds to the traditional biological understanding of the 'soul' is a perspective that places the 'mental' in the body proper. The mental, in this sense, is not merely a pre-given capacity (for thinking, imagining, remembering, feeling, wishing, deploring etc.), but a developmentally modifiable cognitive aspect of our lives, the product of a life-long learning process. The mental is therefore not a uniquely human thing, either, but rather a general cognitive tendency or habit that doesn't exclusively reside in the brain, but can be observed in the workings of the most primitive organisms.

It has been shown, for instance, that bacterial colonies that are exposed to repeated shifts in temperature that are then followed by dramatic decreases in oxygen concentration, after a few weeks will start to adjust their metabolism to anaerobic conditions already when exposed to the temperature shift—i.e., before the decrease in oxygen concentration sets in, thus exhibiting a primitive kind of Pavlovian 'association learning' effect (Tagkopoulos, Liu et al. 2008). Brains, of course, lend tremendously increased power to the cognitive regime of a species—but the brain in itself is just a tool for the semiotic body, not an independent organ of semiosis. There is no semiosis without a body, but plenty of semiosis without brains. (2015)

Meaning-making is, in fact, ubiquitous among living things. But, of course, meaning-making relies on the perception of relations among things and on acknowledgement of their causal power *as* relations. Perversely, this is precisely what mainstream modern science, since its very beginnings in the seventeenth century, has obliged itself to ignore.

We can see this will to ignore or avoid meaning-making at work again in the cognitive revolution of the 1950s. According to Jerome Bruner, one of those early involved in the cognitive revolution, it was technicization that diverted the cognitive revolution that began in the late 1950s. At that time, in response to what has been widely experienced as a dehumanizing of the concept of mind following what Bruner described as 'a long cold winter of objectivism' (1), a great many people thought it a matter of urgent necessity 'to establish meaning as the central concept of psychology' (Bruner 1990, 2). What this profound revolution was about was

> not stimuli and responses, not overtly observable behavior, not biological drives and their transformation, but meaning. It was *not* a revolution against behaviourism with the aim of transforming behaviourism into a better way of pursuing psychology by adding a little mentalism to it. Edward Tolman had done that to little avail. It was an altogether more profound revolution than that. Its aim was to discover and to describe formally the meanings that human beings created out of their encounters with the world, and then to propose hypotheses about what meaning-making processes were implicated. . . .
> The cognitive revolution as originally conceived virtually required that psychology join forces with anthropology and linguistics, philosophy and history, even with the discipline of law. It is no surprise and certainly not an accident that in those early years the advisory board of the Center for Cognitive Studies at Harvard included a philosopher, W.V. Quine, an intellectual historian, H. Stuart Hughes, and a linguist Roman Jakobson. (Bruner 1990, 2–3)

Although much of this early work was successful and had benevolent effects, nonetheless something eventually happened that, while it did not bring back behaviourism, was in its own way equally destructive of meaning. Widespread thought about information—what it was and how it worked—fell under the influence of the developing field of computation and hence mathematicised logic. This is all very well in itself, but hardly applicable to human (or any organismic) process of cognition. As Bruner notes, actual meaning processes, as opposed to algorithmic computations, are 'surprisingly remote from what is conventionally called "information processing" ' (5):

> It would make an absorbing essay in the intellectual history of the last quar-ter-century to trace what happened to the originating impulse of the cognitive revolution, how it became fractionated and technicalised. The full story had best be left to the intellectual historians. All we need note now are a few signposts along the way, just enough of them to give a sense of the intellectual terrain on which we were all marching. Very early on, for example, emphasis began shift-ing from 'meaning' to 'information', from the *construction* of meaning to the *processing* of information. These are profoundly different matters. The key fac-tor in the shift was the introduction of computation as the ruling metaphor and of computability as a necessary criterion of a good theoretical model. Information is indifferent with respect to meaning. In computational terms, information com-prises an already precoded message in the system. Meaning is preassigned to messages. It is not an outcome of computation nor is it relevant to computation save in the arbitrary sense of assignment. . . .
>
> The system that does all of these things is blind with respect to whether what is stored is words from Shakespeare's sonnets or numbers from a random num-ber table. According to classic information theory [i.e. Claude Shannon's math-ematical theory of communication (Shannon 1948)], a message is informative if it reduces alternative choices [i.e. 'noise']. This implies a code of established possible choices . . . But information processing cannot deal with anything beyond well-defined and arbitrary entries that can enter into specific relation-ships that are strictly governed by a program of elementary operations. Such a system cannot cope with vagueness, with polysemy, with metaphoric or con-notative connections. (Bruner 1990, 4–5)

The developments described above have thus raised serious questions for their respective disciplines and fields. In the life sciences these concern the nature of systems and information. These are essentially biocybernetic and ecological questions about meaning-making of the kind raised by Gregory Bateson in the 1970s. The matter of natural semiosis and meaning, including its central cybernetic aspects of feedback loops within perceptual environ-ments (Umwelten), was raised by Jakob von Uexküll in his theoretical biol-ogy from the 1920s onwards (Kull 1999; Favareau 2010).

A profound misunderstanding concerning the differences between com-puter technology and living beings and meanings, which hangs on a proper interrogation of the concept of information, has diverted cognitive science away from meaning. From the point of view of life processes, computers are primitive. It is the input and output of interpreted meanings by humans that makes them so *cognitively* powerful, not for themselves of course (surely a nearly meaningless thought), but for *us*. Finally, the inheritance of nominalism in the sciences is responsible for both a dogged empiricism driven by the will to master the Earth, and also for a substance ontology that is incapable of regarding *relations* as ontologically real with causal powers.

AN ONTOLOGY OF RELATIONS

Gilles Deleuze, Félix Guattari, and Gilbert Simondon were all influenced by Bateson and by Peirce. We can see, in their attempts to describe evolutionary becomings in biological, cultural, and technological forms, the attempt to explore what, from the side of the life sciences, biosemiotics has discovered. This allows us to see evolution as profoundly creative: as the semiosic play between repetition (or habit) and chance (the difference that makes a difference). In what ways can human beings seize change creatively? In particular, in what ways can human animals respond creatively to the challenges of the early twenty-first century, especially those concerning technology and our own effects on the environment that supports us? This is not a new question; Gregory Bateson asked it more than 40 years ago (Bateson 1972).

One way that creative responsiveness (and hence responsibility) can come about is by seeing the living world, human and nonhuman, differently. That means seeing it not primarily or only in terms of an ontology of substances and essences, but in terms of an ontology of relations and ontogenesis, or becomings on their way to individuations (not solely for humans, or even only for organisms, but also for aesthetic and technological objects; Wheeler 2016). This was central to Bateson's approach also, but most especially to Gilbert Simondon's. Muriel Combes describes the centrality of such an aim to Simondon's work. Such an aim was 'a transmutation in how we approach being' that would be 'pursued across physical, biological, psychosocial, and technological domains . . . [and which] assumes a "reformation of our understanding"' (1). Mark Hayward and Bernard Geoghegan make a similar point:

For Simondon, as for cyberneticians such as Norbert Wiener and Gregory Bateson, 'information' emerged as the common currency of this grand scientific synthesis. However, moving beyond the cyberneticians, Simondon defined information as the basis for a generative and process-oriented ontology. Rather than the content shared between a 'sender' and 'receiver' as described in Claude Shannon's celebrated theory of information, Simondon suggested that his approach involved a turn away from the quantification of information in order to speak of 'the *quality* of information or informatic *tension* (*tension d'information*)' (*L'individuation*, 542). Distinguishing his own interpretation of the concept of information from more widely circulated interpretations, he develops an understanding of the term that transforms communication and interaction into processes through which individuals are constituted. (2012, 6)

In other words, Simondon was interested in the processes of *meaning-ful* becomings through which individual substances are constituted.

The shift of view that biosemiotics proposes is remarkably similar except that it understands a crucial feature of that reformation to involve recognition that individuation and all its operations are not simply informatic but semiotic in the Peircean sense. Simondon is important not only because of his influence on other relational ontology thinkers such as Deleuze, but also because Simondon was ahead of his time with his concern with the individuation, or ontogenesis, of material and informational forms. Finally, when discussing an environmental and ecological theory for the present, we must ask why this way of thinking was unavailable in the founding moment of 'Theory' 45 years ago, and specifically in its publication arrival on the shores of Anglophone cultures from the 1970s onwards?

Brian Massumi's answer is that 'theory' was, at that point, 'unequal to the question of ontogenesis' (2009, 37), or of how things *become* concretely to be as they are. That implies, of course, that in their different ways both the sciences and the humanities were resistant to seeing things uncomfortably otherwise than the ways they preferred to see them. The life sciences could not countenance the truth about information (i.e., that it was an immaterial but causally efficacious no-thing), and the humanities and social sciences too often preferred comfortable fictions to uncomfortable scientific evidence. Before Simondon could begin to be properly understood, 'Theory' had to get out of the anthropocentric linguistic constructivist bind it was stuck in: 'Constructivism does not have the resources even to effectively articulate the issue of the nonhuman necessarily raised by ontogenesis' (Massumi 2009, 37). Apart from anything else, the materialist commitments involved in considering ontological becoming threatened (it was thought) to impose a 'naïve realism', even as the immateriality of information threatened something perhaps worse: a new vision of reality in which not everything was simply reducible to matter. The development of the ecological and environmental humanities, which could not avoid taking biological processes, and hence ontogenesis, seriously, helped prepare the way out of this impasse. They did so by approaching a more complicated realism that was inclined to acknowledge evolution while rejecting the mechanistic reductionism of neo-Darwinian theory. Shaking semiotic theory free of its anthropocentric bias, biosemiotics within that ecological formation offered a theoretical resource that made ontogenetic concerns graspable within a semiotic (not semiological) register.

Perhaps pre-eminently, a biosemiotic realist perspective should both reinforce the importance of a relational ontology and also help to prevent humans from seeing themselves and their cultures as cut off from nature. Like all organisms, we make and shape our umwelten, but we are also made and shaped by them. The dance is reciprocal. In place of that fundamental alienation in which the dominant science and philosophy of modernity fail to see that mind itself is a sign, relational, embodied, Earthed and semiotic, biosemiotics suggests a much more integrated account of individuals and the processes of individuation or, in the case of all the living, biosemiotic becoming.

NOTES

1. There is an argument which is sometimes made that, being interconnected throughout by space-time, the whole universe is, in fact, some kind of teleodynamic system. In this argument, which draws upon the laws of thermodynamics, the universe's telos is expressed in the Second Law of Thermodynamics itself. Thus, the evolution of life is a highly efficient way of using up thermodynamic energy as swiftly as possible according to the Second Law's 'aim' (its Final Cause in Aristotelian terms) of achieving thermodynamic equilibrium (disorder governed by the Maximum Entropy Production Principle) following the disequilibrium and organization (i.e., order) produced by the Big Bang. See Stanley N. Salthe and Gary Fuhrman. 'The Cosmic Bellows: The Big Bang and the Second Law'. *Cosmos and History* 1.2 (2005): 295–318.

2. For this reason, Peirce speaks of the 'dynamic object' and the 'dynamic interpretant'. See Cornelius De Waal. *Peirce: A Guide for the Perplexed*. London: Bloomsbury, 2013.

WORKS CITED

Bateson, Gregory. *Steps to an Ecology of Mind*. Chicago: University of Chicago Press, 1972.

Bateson, Gregory. *Mind and Nature: A Necessary Unity*. 1979. Cresskill, NJ: Hampton Press, 2002.

Brown, Sam and Ashleigh Griffin. 'Social Evolution in Micro-organisms and a Trojan Horse Approach to Medical Intervention Strategies'. *Philosophical Transactions of the Royal Society Biological Sciences* (November 2009). Web. 15 December 2015.

Bruner, Jerome. *Acts of Meaning*. Cambridge: Harvard University Press, 1990.

Combes, Muriel. *Gilbert Simondon and the Philosophy of the Transindividual*. Trans. Thomas Lamarre. 1999. Cambridge: MIT Press, 2013.

Crick, Francis. 'Central Dogma of Molecular Biology'. *Nature* 227 (August 1970): 561–563. Web. 15 December 2015.

Deely, John N. *Four Ages of Understanding: The First Postmodern Survey of Philosophy from Ancient Times to the Turn of the Twenty-First Century.* Toronto: University of Toronto Press, 2001.

Derrida, Jacques. *Of Grammatology.* Trans. Gayatri C. Spivak. 1967. Baltimore: Johns Hopkins University Press, 1976.

De Waal, Cornelis. *Peirce: A Guide for the Perplexed.* London: Bloomsbury, 2013.

Dias, Brian G. and Kerry J. Ressler. 'Parental Olfactory Experience Influences Behavior and Neural Structure in Subsequent Generations'. *Nature Neuroscience* 17.1 (January 2014): 89–96.

Favareau, Donald F. 'The Theory of Meaning: Jakob von Uexküll (1864–1944)'. *Essential Readings in Biosemiotics: Anthology and Commentary.* Ed. Donald Favareau. Dordrecht: Springer, 2010. 81–89.

Gilbert, Scott F. and David Epel. *Ecological Developmental Biology: Integrating Epigenetics, Medicine, and Evolution.* Sunderland, MA: Sinauer Associates, 2009.

Halfmann, Randall and Susan Lindquist. 'Epigenetics in the Extreme: Prions and the Inheritance of Environmentally Acquired Traits'. *Science* 330 (October 2010): 629–632.

Harrison, Peter. *The Fall of Man and the Foundations of Science.* Cambridge: Cambridge University Press, 2007.

Hayward, Mark and Bernard Dionysius Geoghegan. 'Introduction: Catching Up With Simondon'. *SubStance.* Special issue on Gilbert Simondon 41.3 (2012): 3–15.

Heidegger, Martin. 'Nur noch ein Gott kann uns retten'. *Der Spiegel* (30 May 1976): 193–219. Trans. W. Richardson as 'Only a God Can Save Us'. *Heidegger: The Man and the Thinker.* Ed. T. Sheehan. Chicago: Precedent, 1981. 45–67.

Hoffmeyer, Jesper. *Biosemiotics: An Examination into the Signs of Life and the Life of Signs.* Scranton, PA: University of Scranton Press, 2008.

Hoffmeyer, Jesper. 'The Semiome: From genetic to Semiotic Scaffolding'. *Semiotica* 198 (2014a): 11–31.

Hoffmeyer, Jesper. 'Semiotic Scaffolding: A Biosemiotic Link between Sema and Soma'. *The Catalyzing Mind: Beyond Models of Causality.* Eds. Kenneth.R. Cabell and Jaan Valsiner. New York: Springer Science+Business Media, 2014b. 95–110.

Hoffmeyer, Jesper. 'Semiotic Individuation and Ernst Cassirer's Challenge'. *Progress in Biophysics and Molecular Biology.* 2 July 2015. Web. 5 August 2015.

Hoffmeyer, Jesper and Frederik Stjernfelt. 'The Great Chain of Semiosis. Investigating the Steps in the Evolution of Semiotic Competence'. *Biosemiotics* (September 2015): 1–23.

Jacob, François. *The Possible and the Actual.* New York: Pantheon, 1982.

Kull, Kalevi. 'Organism as a Self-reading Text: Anticipation and Semiosis'. *International Journal of Computing Anticipatory Systems* 1 (1998): 93–104.

Kull, Kalevi. 'Biosemiotics in the Twentieth Century: A View from Biology'. *Semiotica* 127.1–4 (1999): 385–414.

Kull, Kalevi. 'A Semiotic Theory of Life: Lotman's Principles of the Universe of the Mind'. *Green Letters: Studies in Ecocriticism.* Special issue on Biosemiotics and Culture. Eds. Wendy Wheeler and Louise Westling. 19.3 (2015): 255–266.

Margulis, Lynn. *The Symbiotic Planet: A New Look at Evolution.* London: Phoenix, 1999.

Marmot, Michael. *Status Syndrome: How Your Social Standing Directly Affects Your Health and Life Expectancy*. London: Bloomsbury, 2004.

Massumi, Brian with Arne De Boever, Alex Murray, Jon Roffe. ' "Technical Mentality" Revisited: Brian Massumi on Gilbert Simondon'. *Parrhesia* 7 (2009): 36–45.

McFall-Ngai, Margaret, et al. 'Animals in a Bacterial World, a New Imperative for the Life Sciences'. *PNAS* 110.9 (February 2013): 3229–3236.

Noble, Denis. *The Music of Life: Biology beyond Genes*. Oxford: Oxford University Press, 2006.

Oyama, Susan. *The Ontogeny of Information: Developmental Systems and Evolution*. 2nd edn. Durham: Duke University Press, 2000.

Ricoeur, Paul. *The Rule of Metaphor: The Creation of Meaning in Language*. Trans. Robert Czerny with Kathleen McLaughlin and John Costello. 1975. London: Routledge, 2003.

Salthe, Stanley N. and Gary Fuhrman. 'The Cosmic Bellows: The Big Bang and the Second Law'. *Cosmos and History* 1.1–2 (2005): 295–318.

Sebeok, Thomas A. *Global Semiotics*. Bloomington: Indiana University Press, 2001.

Sériot, Patrick. *Structure and the Whole: East, West and Non-Darwinian Biology in the Origins of Structural Linguistics*. Berlin: Walter de Gruyter, 2014.

Shannon, Claude. 'A Mathematical Theory of Communication'. *The Bell System Technical Journal* (Published in Two Parts) 27 (July 1948): 379–423; (October 1948): 623–656.

Shapiro, James A. 'DNA as Poetry: Multiple Messages in a Single Sequence'. *Huffington Post*. 24 January 2012. Web. 12 December 2015.

Shintani, Laura. 'Roman Jakobson and Biology: "A System of Systems" '. *Semiotica* 127.1–4 (1999): 103–114.

Szyf, Moshe. 'Lamarck Revisited: Epigenetic Inheritance of Ancestral Odor Fear Conditioning'. *Nature Neuroscience* 17.1 (January 2014): 2–4.

Tønnessen, Morten and Jonathan Beever. 'Beyond Sentience: Biosemiotics as a Foundation for Animal and Environmental Ethics'. *Animal Ethics and Philosophy: Questioning the Orthodoxy*. Eds. E. Aaltola and J. Hadley. London: Rowman and Littlefield, 2015: 47–62.

Vitale, Francesco. 'The Text and the Living: Jacques Derrida between Biology and Deconstruction'. *The Oxford Literary Review* 36.1 (2014): 95–114.

Wheeler, Wendy. *Expecting the Earth: Life|Culture|Biosemiotics*. London: Lawrence and Wishart, 2016.

Wiener, Norbert. *Cybernetics: Or Control and Communication in the Animal and the Machine*. 1948. Cambridge: MIT Press, 1965.

Part IV

ECOSTORIES AND CONVERSATIONS

Chapter Sixteen

How to Read a Bridge

Rob Nixon

I

I grew up in South Africa, our planet's most inequitable society, and immigrated to the USA, the rich world's most unequal one, a country in which 400 individuals have half the nation's assets. For fifteen years I lived in the most economically divided of America's major cities, New York, where seventy billionaires reside and 30% of children languish in poverty. If New York City were a nation it would rank 119th in terms of the Gini coefficient, the standard measure of economic disparity.

II

I am reading an article on South Africa's fitful progress since the turn to democracy. From the available economic data, the journalist has created a fictional average South African: she is 25, currently employed and an urban renter. Her shared home has basic amenities: erratic electricity, a flushing toilet, and indoor plumbing but no internet. The journalist has named this average South African 'Thuli'.

In the comment section, someone writes: 'Yes, her name is Thuli. She has a life partner. Her life partner's name is Gini'.

III

In most societies, the distribution of resources is deteriorating. Economic gaps are becoming economic chasms. Social mobility is slowing: in the USA, a child born into poverty now has a 42% chance of remaining there. As the path from poverty to the middle classes is lengthening, so the path from poverty to destitution is shortening.

IV

When a society fractures—when the rickety bridge linking the uberrich and ultrapoor collapses—social cohesion collapses too. Civic trust erodes. Dissociative thinking and dissociative planning become pervasive: just disconnect the dots.

But our age of disparity is boom time for what urban planners call defensible architecture. Tunde Agbola names this 'the architecture of fear'. In Mumbai, Los Angeles, Mexico City, Lagos, Johannesburg, Jakarta, Sao Paolo, Madrid, Shanghai and beyond, clients clamour for up-to-the-minute fortress design, fresh ways to wall off, as elegantly as possible, the possessors from the dispossessed. When the tasteful architecture of exclusion fails to deliver the message, the private security detail is there to back it up.

In our megacities, defensible architecture rises alongside indefensible inequities.

V

Inequality is, among other things, an infrastructural story. Dreams of society-wide public services—services as government obligation, as source of civic pride—fade as utilities get outsourced to private firms that institute for profit, pay-as-you-go user access only. The idea of the customer trumps the idea of the citizen. Infrastructure, outside select areas, is left to moulder and disintegrate, if it ever arrived in the first place.

VI

Such thoughts are on my mind as I venture from the American heartland to South Africa's Eastern Cape, one of that country's poorest provinces. I fly into Port Elizabeth, the provincial town where I grew up, now a sprawling city of several million. In scale and name, the city is unrecognizable. Back then, our family lived beside the airport that my plane now approaches; back then, in apartheid's heyday, it was called the H. F. Verwoerd Airport—akin to touching down, in other lands, at the Adolf Hitler or Josef Stalin

Airport. Now a sign welcomes visitors to the Nelson Mandela Metropolitan Airport.

VII

Despite this symbolic turnaround, anything approaching equality remains elusive here. When I try to swing by my childhood home, an aggressive police presence and billowing black smoke obscure the road. My nostrils burn, my stomach heaves against the acrid flavours of scorched rubber. From the radio I learn that Walmer Township is on the march, burning piled tyres in a service delivery protest, one of thousands of such protests that convulse South Africa each year.

'Service delivery': South African English would be unthinkable—the syntax could barely hold together—without that pervasive, adhesive phrase that speaks to post-apartheid disparities, feelings of abandonment and betrayal by people the state treats as disposable or, in the old apartheid argot, surplus to requirements.

VIII

Here in Port Elizabeth, the tyre-burning destitute are making their needs known. The state must deliver: electricity, drinkable piped water, useable roads, a sewage system that is better than pit toilets, schools with desks and without broken windows, functioning hospitals, all the services that say you too belong.

What do we want? Service delivery. When do we want it? Now.

Voices through the smoke, in Xhosa and English, voices of the new surplus people, urban invisibles, writing their names in fire.

IX

'Service delivery failures': the phrasing may be peculiarly South African, but the phenomenon—and the popular response—reverberates across the planet, particularly the global South: Brazil, India, Nigeria, Kenya, Indonesia, Pakistan, Bangladesh, Turkey, Egypt, Tunisia, Chile, Mexico, Argentina. The politics of structural exclusion travels across the south of the North as well: Greece, Italy, Cyprus, Spain.

In 2012, 55,000 environmental protests shook China alone—protests in which the environmental component was inseparable from public health concerns and service delivery failures. Amidst surging Chinese growth, too many are left to feed on globalization's fumes.

X

Traveling northeast up the coast from Port Elizabeth, I cross one estuary bridge after another. I stop for lunch at the Great Fish River Bridge: from above, the view is spectacular, as the river prises apart the dunes and enters the Indian Ocean.

On impulse, I take a gravel road that ducks beneath the bridge deck. Down here, there is no panoramic option; instead I find myself staring up at the undergirding, twenty meters above my head. To my surprise, the bridge is alive with foliage: in the gaps between the concrete slabs strangler figs have inserted themselves, one after another, creating an interrupted forest. Their roots follow the grooves from one side of the bridge to the other, while the leaves and branches, in various stages of maturity, billow forth beyond the edges.

Figure 16.1. Strangler figs. Courtesy of Rob Nixon.

Figure 16.2. Weaver bird. Courtesy of Rob Nixon.

Each of these horizontal canopies ends in a cluster of finely woven, kidney-shaped nests that I recognise as the handiwork of Village Weavers, sociable birds with black masks, red eyes and bodies the kind of yellow that every yellow secretly yearns to be.

XI

It is winter now and the birds are gone, but the scene feels animated nonetheless: a crossroads between human and nonhuman civil engineering.

The strangler figs and the weaverbirds are opportunistic colonists; they have collective designs upon the bridge. They are wedged in where design meets chance. Design: that double-edged sword that suggests both structure and intent.

But the bridge is active too. It is built to give: gaps between the slabs allow the metal and concrete to shift with the shifting temperatures, expanding and contracting, from day to night, from summer to winter, moving all the time. To survive, every bridge must breathe.

A laden lorry drives overhead: the concrete creaks; the fig trees shudder; the weaver nests start bobbing. Vibrant matter indeed.

XII

'But the strangler fig/arrives in shit': Jeffrey Thomson, 'Landscape with Fig Trees and Strangulation'.

XIII

A bird drops a fig seed, sheathed in shit that lodges in one of the bridge's infrastructural apertures. In that sheltering gap, a tree starts to swell, attracting to its greenery seed-eating, seed-expelling birds in search of seasonal housing.

The weaver birds' primary predator—the boomslang (tree snake)—cannot scale the smooth columns of the bridge. To drop down on to the nests, the boomslang would have to hazard the traffic overhead. This is fortress architecture, avian style.

XIV

Construction is more glamorous than maintenance. Politicians gain kudos from erecting structures that gleam with novelty, but gain little from the quotidian business of unspectacular upkeep. Maintenance is well-nigh invisible until the moment of collapse.

But neglect is political—it is unevenly distributed. The strangler figs and weaver birds, as they slowly pick apart this bridge, receive a boost to their life chances from the infrastructural neglect that is intertwined with rural misery.

XV

The socioenvironmental scene that undergirds the bridge—this extra chapter from the botany of desire—begins to resonate theoretically. The parallel paths assumed by animal studies and environmental justice studies have long troubled me. Animal studies scholars are often too quick to bracket the Human as a unitary force, are too indifferent to the history and politics of human disparities. By contrast, environmental justice scholars specialise in exposing inequalities, but often neglect the weave between human and more-than-human powers—animal, botanical, geological, and physical in the broadest sense. Injustices shape and shake our world, but so do those non-human forces that Kennedy Warne has dubbed nature's 'ecosystem engineers'.

XVI

How do we avoid the pitfall of presenting the Human as a unitary environmental force and the opposite danger of overlooking non-human actors with impulses, behaviours and ecological effects of their own? How, in other words, do we remain alive to the steep power gradients that separate diverse human environmental actors? How do we remain equally alive to the sentience and dynamism of non-human forces?

XVII

I do not want the Great Fish River Bridge to float off into the conceptual stratosphere. This built environment, engineered by multiple forces, is a concrete scene with a material history. The bridge leads from somewhere to somewhere. The character and history of those somewheres remain particular.

Historically, this bridge has served to separate.

XVIII

I cross over the Great Fish River and enter a land worn thin from overuse. I am now in the erstwhile Ciskei, one of South Africa's ten former Bantustans. From the 1960s through the 1980s, some 3.5 million black South Africans suffered forced relocation, mostly to places like this shambolic 'ethnic homeland'. When Ciskei was declared independent in 1981, with the stroke of a pen two million people were stripped of South African citizenship. Without elusive, temporary labour permits, they were barred from entering the country of their birth.

'If our policy is taken to its logical conclusion as far as the black people are concerned, there will be not one black man with South African citizenship': Connie Mulder, Minister of Plural Relations and Development, 7 February 1978.

XXIX

Even Xhosas who had lived for three or four generations in cities were decreed to be natives of this Ciskei they'd never seen. Black peasant farmers in fertile areas rezoned for whites were visited at 2 a.m., 3 a.m. and carted off in Government Garage (GG) trucks. Then dumped here: discarded people.

XX

Things are and are not different now. Ciskei is officially no more: that derided figment of apartheid social engineering has evaporated. The people here, liberated from involuntary citizenship, are South Africans again, free to move, free to vote.

But the economic divisions and ecological scars run deep. Traveling through the Ciskei still feels like a journey through the development of underdevelopment. This place remains shadowed by its past: this vast, over-crowded rural slum, where the margins of survival remain small.

South African wealth—old white wealth and the new wealth of black Johannesburg plutocrats—belongs to some other, far off country. Unemployment, ecological exhaustion, corruption and infrastructural aban-donment compound the cycles of rural poverty. These free South Africans are citizens both of a neo-liberal present and a very heavy history, which together cement inequity.

XXI

Maano Ramutsindela has written of the ex-Bantustans as 'resilient geogra-phies'. Resilient is a complex word: here it suggests a tenacious survival, a refusal to go away. Far from vanishing through democratic assimilation, the Ciskei has been reinforced as a marginalised ethnic space by rural indigence and by popular disillusionment with resources skewed towards an urban, cosmopolitan elite.

XXII

For two weeks I meander through the former Ciskei and the Transkei that lies beyond. A jagged landscape of unforgiving hills, thin goats, and high-density human destitution. Here a tree is an event: most have been felled for fuel.

Somewhere between Kentani and Nxaxo River Mouth, I pass a woman shuffling barefoot up a formidably steep gravel road. She is elderly and edges forward in small, methodical steps, leaning into the three-sided cage of her aluminium frame. But her neck remains erect: on her head she balances a white, plastic, 10-litre paint bucket filled with water that sways ever so slightly as she moves.

I reverse and we ride the next 6 kilometres together. Between her halting English and my residual Xhosa we piece together a conversation. Most of the men, she explains have gone searching for jobs in the city. She has great-grandchildren she is looking after. No, there is plenty of water here, but it is way down there in the valleys. She, her paint bucket and her aluminium walker undertake this trek for water every second day.

We need a stronger phrase than service delivery failure.

XXIII

On the return trip back down the coast, I cross the Great Fish River Bridge close to midnight. In the darkness, I hear trucks changing gears up the pass, like those GG lorries that once ferried human cargo across the Bantustan border in the dead of night. Ghost trucks taking people to a home they had never known and did not want, people first made homeless at gunpoint and then, at gunpoint, told, this place, hundreds of kilometres away, this is your homeland.

Apartheid may be gone, but here, the bridge above, the river between, still mark a separate development.

XXIV

Flying back across the Atlantic, I revisit *The Death of Distance*, the bestseller by Frances Cairncross. When it appeared in 1997 Cairncross was hailed as a visionary who foresaw an ever more integrated humanity: together, digital technology and globalization would keep shrinking our world, rendering distance obsolete. But deep into the twenty-first century, things seem a lot more contradictory: technological connectedness may be rising, but so too is economic rupture. The title of Timothy Noah's 2012 bestseller puts the matter bluntly: most human societies are being torn apart by *The Great Divergence*.

In the austere year of 2011, the world's mega-rich had stashed $13 trillion in offshore accounts—equal, in scale, to the American and Japanese economies combined.

XXV

As I write, another plutocrat takes to the air in his golden parachute, soaring above the planet of the slums.

XXVI

In a 2013 report on the global distributional crisis, OXFAM concludes that extreme wealth is 'economically inefficient, politically corrosive, socially divisive'. But the distance between parachute and favela is imaginatively vexing as well. Distance intensifies the need for inventive testimony, for finding new ways to bear witness across the divide separating people whose lives feature in bright stories of growth and innovation and the disposable people who inhabit neoliberal globalization's vast shadowlands.

Arundhati Roy sees globalization like this: as 'a light which shines brighter and brighter on a few people and the rest are in darkness, wiped out. They simply cannot be seen. Once you get used to not seeing something, then, slowly, it is no longer possible to see it'.

XXVII

From America, I email a government minister in Bhisho, once the Ciskei capital, now the provincial capital of the Eastern Cape. I explain that the Great Fish River Bridge is being subjected to a colonial takeover: someone should remove those strangler figs. I do not hear back, not do I expect to.

In truth, I have no idea whether intervening in that tangle of infrastructural neglect and environmental reengineering would fortify this complex bridge or hasten its collapse.

Chapter Seventeen

The Martian Book of the Dead

Bronislaw Szerszynski

You are dying. You are hearing my voice because you are about to leave your body and enter interval-being, the time suspended between one existence and the next which in Tibetan we call *bardo*. But if you listen to what I say you can escape the cycle of rebirth.

You are fortunate to have lived at a time in which the Dharma, the teaching of the Buddha, has advanced so greatly. It might not have been so; the great ages of the cosmos are turning, one to the other. In the holy language of Tibet, Mars is called *mig-dmar*, the red eye. And those like us that live on that red eye and gaze back to where the last Buddha was born, we call Earth *mig-sno*, the blue eye. And when we look back at Blue-Eye we see it changing: the systems of the Earth are being strained into a new composition by the weight of humanity living there. And here on Red-Eye we see that *it* is changing too, being coaxed back to life by human and machine, as Mars is settled, its air thickened, its oceans returned, the plains and hills covered with living soil from which prairies and forests grow. And the whole great mandala of the sun and all its planets is altering, as beings start to move freely amongst them, connecting them all by a web of movements and coherings. All of these— Red-Eye and Blue-Eye and the great solar mandala that contains them both— are moving from one great age of the cosmos to another, from *kalpa* to *kalpa*.

And in a time of interval-being like this, the 'latter days' suspended between one great age and the next, the Buddha's teaching can become dark and unclear. We know this darkening was happening because rebirth was becoming difficult and interrupted. Beings were trapped in human form, unable to progress through the realms of rebirth that we call *lokas*. And liberation from rebirth was also being denied to people.

But then we were given the gift of Mangalayana, or 'Mars-vehicle' Buddhism, by Migdmargyi Norbu Rinpoche. As his name reminds us he was indeed the 'jewel of Mars'. He gave us a new form of the Dharma, one that escaped the bounds of one planet so that we could enter planets more fully. He taught us about the new forms of rebirth—for in the machine kalpa that we are entering, the way that a consciousness passes from one body to the next was changing. And he taught us about how liberation from rebirth had also altered. In the Buddhism of Tibet, liberation from the cycle of becoming, from abiding in this world, is known as *mi né pa*, or 'non-abiding'. Migdmargyi Norbu showed us that the liberation that we call non-abiding is in reality *the fullest form of abiding*. This is what I want to remind you, to ensure that you abide in Mars, enter into the infinite Buddha fields that are generated by the dance of its layers and forces, and escape the realm of suffering.

For life on Red-Eye is full of suffering. The air is still thin, and the soil contains poisons that need to be continually washed off the body and filtered from the water. The work of mining, on which our economy depends, is backbreaking and hazardous. And now your body is coming to the end of its capacity to maintain itself; or maybe it is about to be disintegrated, as your consciousness is transferred to a new organic or machine body. So just as the planet on which we live is entering a state of interval-being, you will pass into your own interval-being, suspended between one life and another. And with the help of my guiding voice you will recognise the identity of these two interval-beings, the cosmic and the personal—that they are one and the same.

You will already have learned that at the moment of bodily death you will pass into *chikhai bardo*, where you will experience the 'first' and then the 'second' luminosity of pure space. Then you will enter *chonyid bardo*, where you will encounter the peaceful and wrathful deities of planetary being. Finally, in *sidpa bardo* you will have visions of being drawn towards the caves, wombs and birthing tanks of rebirth.

With the coloured sands of Mars we make mandalas to depict that experience; they chart the visions that you will encounter after the moment of death. The mandalas are flat, but we are taught that they are really solid figures, that the lines and colours and shading symbolise height and depth. But also that even this height and depth are symbolic; the mandalas show the *areophany*, the vision of Mars not as a material landscape but as an ineffable body; not as a finite object contained within the infinity of space and time, but as containing and generating the infinite within itself; not as a dark, inert orb but as a world coursing with energy, motion, and self-organisation, on timescales that stretch from a fraction of a *ksana* to a million *kalpas*; and not as a mere interruption punched in the glorious shining of space but as a holy presence.

It is this vision that is the surest route to liberation from rebirth.

You are dying, but as you die you will experience visions of those who will appear to you to help you achieve liberation: gods and demons, bodhisattvas and dakinis. Migdmargyi Norbu was blessed with the experience of meeting the Emissaries of the Common Culture of our Galaxy, a moment of turning in human history. Earth had already started to open up in new ways: it was opening *inwards*, starting to reveal its *terma*, its buried secrets, its deep history; but it was also opening *outwards*, as its inhabitants started to move from the Earth to the asteroids and other planets. But we were unable to discern the deeper truth of this double opening; our new knowledge was only half-born, until we met the Emissaries. The Emissaries are the true dakinis. In our Buddhist tradition, dakinis are 'sky-travellers' that bring the news of the ineffable. They appear to the seeker after enlightenment at the moment when they are needed; in their otherness they provide what the seeker lacks. And the Emissaries had what human culture needed: the knowledge, and the very being, to shock it into completing the double opening of the Earth.

The Emissaries are also *terton*, the treasure-revealers of Buddhist tradition; as they progress around the galaxy they know where the profound truths are buried in the cultures that they encounter. And Migdmargyi Norbu was one of the jewels that they found, a treasure himself who was able to take the *terma*, the hidden treasures of Buddhist understanding, to bury them even deeper in the ground, and thereby to fashion the new vehicle of Buddhism that we call Mangalayana.

The areophany, the true vision of Mars, is central to Mangalayana practice and a great spiritual achievement. The heliophany had been obvious to the ancients, for the sun is easily seen as the abode of a deity. The geophany too seemed easy to achieve in a limited form, since humans found the Earth a place already filled with meanings, our bodies and senses accommodated to it and it to us. But when we came to Mars the *areophany* eluded us; the shape and meaning of our new home were almost impossible to discern. How could our new abode tell us how to live, how to be reborn, and how to escape from being reborn? Mars seemed devoid of the boundaries between earth and water, rock and life that made Earth a place of dwelling. Of course, as we tended the planet into life and filled the great northern plain with the water frozen beneath the regolith, as the atmosphere thickened and filled with clouds and a new, strengthened water cycle established itself, and as life spread, the planet became intelligible to the eye as it became commodious to the body. But what we needed was not simply to fill our vision with our own projects and attachments, but to see what *Mars itself* was and wanted to be.

Migdmargyi Norbu used the analogy of Olympus Mons to explain why it is so hard for human beings to really *see* Mars. Olympus is so large that its peak is above the top of our atmosphere. But it is *so* big that it cannot be seen: as fast as it rises from the ground, the ground curves away over the horizon; as fast as the eye sends out its light to see it, the mountain recedes from view. So too did Mars seem to recede away from the eye.

We had to learn how to *see* Mars, even as we learnt to inhabit it. For the areophany is important for our work. When our ancestors came here they found Mars not dead but *alive*; they found a landscape full of *né*, of dwelling places of power. And as they learned to read the planet and thickened the air and coaxed the regolith into soil, they also slowly learned to read and glorify and harmonise the mandala of Mars. They moved through the landscape with their prayers, in the circling and the arriving of pilgrimage that we call *nékor* and *néjel*. They visited the great *néri*, the mountain abodes; and the fossae that score the face of the planet. They tamed the landscape with shrines; each crater and graben and dune was harmonised. And in your own life, as you played your part in the great story of the red planet's reawakening, you will also have learnt to see Red-Eye through the areophany, to be guided in your actions by the planet's own being and becoming.

But the areophany is not only key to our toil on Mars; it is also key to the possibility of Enlightenment and the cessation of toil, as it can enable us to see beyond the narrow time-frame of a human life. When Migdmargyi Norbu was among us he would also liken the becoming of a planet to a great sphere of water, on which insects skate to and fro; the skin of surface tension keeps those insects on that surface; they think that narrow surface and the vibrations they feel in it to be the whole world, and the sky above them and the depths below them just illusions and fantasies. We are like those insects; the thin surface that we inhabit is our time perception. Above us, the spirits flit so quickly that they seem immaterial; below us, the time of rocks so slow that they seem still. And, when we die, the forces that attach us to the things around us keep us on that surface, that thin slice of time; and these attachments pulls us back into rebirth as finite temporal beings.

But the Dharma is like soap—it does not just clean the mind; it breaks the mind's attachments and so breaks that surface tension, allows us to enter into the temporal depths of the planet. So that in the state of areophany, when we see the red soil of Mars, we see not just something to be tilled and nurtured, but as a sign of the particular path that Mars took when it cohered from the solar cloud, too small to pull its iron down into the core. When we see the low northern plain, now filled by the ocean that girdles our planet, we see a sign of another great trauma in our home's formation. When we see a single fern unfold, a single moment in life's evolution, we see the times that are embedded in other times, embedded in other times, and so on, from the time of the multiverse itself down to the time of the smallest particle of matter. And when we see Tharsis, the high plateau that covers nearly a quarter of Mars, we see an echo of Tibet, the great plateau of Earth, and in the symmetry between these two great plateaus we discern a deep spiritual truth, a cosmic drama that is still unfolding.

Migdmargyi Norbu taught us that the infinite and the finite are one. Buddhism did not after all come to dominate the old religion, with its chthonic gods of the underworld, but to complete it. Before the hidden treasures of Mangalayana Buddhism were revealed, the Tibetan plateau was seen as a demoness, Srinmo, lying supine and pinned down by the Buddhist temples that had been deliberately placed on her body as the mandala of Tibet was laid out. But in Mangalayana Buddhism the civilizing power on Earth and Mars comes from not from above but from the ground itself. And it is taught that each planet is *néchen*, a great abode of a deity, but also has a *néchok*, a principal abode. On Earth the *néchok* is Tibet; on Mars it is Tharsis, which is the form of the bodhisattva that we call Chenrezig, the compassionate one that looks down on the cries of the world. Alba Mons, the White Mountain, is Chenrezig's head, and the three volcanoes known as Tharsis Montes lie across his chest. His right hand is holding Olympus Mons, his left is Tempe Terrum, his legs the Thaumasia Highlands. His body is not pinned down by the mountains and shrines arranged across it but held up and animated by them. Srinmo, whose body is the body of Tibet, is his consort, and they yearn towards each other. They dance around the sun, swinging their faces towards each other and then away.

And Mars, the abode of Chenrezig, is itself *bodhisattva*; the whole planet sacrificed itself, surrendered its becoming and gave it to Earth. Many *kalpas* ago, the demons that circle the sun in the space between Mars and Jupiter, fell upon Mars in a great bombardment that stripped it of its air, and then of its oceans. But Mars responded to this disaster by showering the Earth with the gift of falling stars, that brought to it the miracle of life. It was through this gifting that Earth was able to establish the system of *lokas*, the realms of rebirth—mineral, plant, animal, human, god—and that the wheel of life, the cycle of rebirth, started to turn on the Earth.

And now Earth gives life back to Mars, in this holy work that we are involved in. But the ongoing story of Earth and Mars is not just about the *lokas*, about rebirth; it is also about *liberation* from rebirth. The highest sacrifice of the bodhisattvas is to be capable of enlightenment, but to hold back so they can aid others to achieve it. To be bodhisattva is to be able to a *peak*, standing alone and high above the clouds, but to choose to be a *plateau*, on which others can stand. The link between Tharsis and Tibet, between the bodhisattva Chenrezig on Mars and his consort Srinmo on Earth, is the story of the ebb and flow of love and life and liberation between two such plateaus. In Tharsis, a huge pooling of magma, we see a sign of Mars's immobility, its giving up of itself, of air, water, life and motion; in Tibet, an area thrust up into the air by the collision of continents, a sign of Earth's borrowed dynamism. But now the story shifts; the energy of Srinmo brings Chenrezig to new life, and Chenrezig through Migdmargyi Norbu brings us the promise of liberation through the areophany. And the areophany not only allows us to see Mars and achieve deep abiding; we also see Earth for the first time. For what we are learning in our mystic aerology enables us to see that we had never before truly seen the Earth and the way we dwelled in it. And in this story we see a huge circle, in which the wheel of life is a mere epicycle, a cog that serves the poetry of the whole.

But now your body is dying; soon you will enter *chikhai bardo*, and see the shining reality of space. And then, if this vision is not enough to grant you liberation from rebirth, you will enter *chonyid bardo*, and experience the vision of one hundred deities; these will both terrify and inspire you, in ways that will help you to achieve the areophany, to see past the immediate presentation of the sacred mandala of the planet into the Buddha fields of its deep becoming. And if you have still not gained liberation, you will pass into *sidpa bardo*, when visions of coupling and rebirth will try to pull you back into the shallow waters of finite becoming.

But I will be with you. We will set off along the plains, as the sun warms the ground, and the dust devils start to form in the near distance. Then the land will begin to rise as we pass into the highlands. And as we approach the pass between two mountain peaks, between the abodes of deities, we will sing out the traditional song of protection: '*lha gyal lo*'—'victory to the gods!' For I am travelling with you, into the mountains, into the planet; my voice is here to guide you into the deep abiding, and the final victory will be ours.

Ki ki so so—lha gyal lo!

ACKNOWLEDGEMENTS

This text was originally devised for a multimedia 'Demonstration' at *A Matter Theatre*, Haus der Kulturen der Welt, Berlin, 16–18 October 2014. It is based on my theory-fiction 'Liberation through Hearing in the Planetary Transition: Funerary Practices in Twenty-Second-Century Mangalayana Buddhism', in *Grain Vapor Ray*. Eds. Katrin Klingan, Ashkan Sepahvand, Christoph Rosol, Bernd M. Scherer. Berlin: Haus der Kulturen der Welt, 2014. 149–164. Many thanks are due to Carlos Mondragon, Ashkan Sepahvand, and Katrin Klingan for conversations that have greatly informed this piece; however, I take full responsibility for the liberties I have subsequently taken.

Chapter Eighteen

On Rivers

Juan Carlos Galeano

. . . Colored pebbles sparkled on the river bottom . . .

One of my first memories of a river was on a sunny morning. It was in a crystal-clear one; my mother would pick me up in her arms and release me into the current to be picked up by an indigenous woman nearby. I must have been three years old.

The waters were glittering at noon because the sun was making the coloured pebbles sparkle on the river bottom. Not too far away, the sun created a theatre of shadows under the fruit trees behind the house. Clouds and winds were other actors who made the two parrots in the kitchen talk and laugh their heads off at the rain that was received with applause by the tin roof. Little creeks were enjoying being photographed by flashes of lightning too.

There were fires during the burning season of January and February, turning the forest into pastures for cattle in that part of the Colombian Amazon. We were fascinated by the colour purple of the little sun all day long, thanks to smoke that had turned the air and sky onto our sunglasses. Only later I made the painful connections with the violent domestication of the land carried out by the first explorers.

We could not help it, we little people of our times. We loved any modernity, like the wooden roaring cars painted with macaw colours that would come almost every day bringing pretty Coca-Cola bottles. Swimming, jumping from the tallest trees, playing soccer in sand bars, fishing and listening to the stories of the fishermen—all these were our life. Their stories conjured up guardians of the water, serpents who lived in the bottom of the rivers and turned into handsome young men young women would fall in love with. One indigenous story was about a serpent turning into a handsome boy, then a giant tree and, finally, into all the rivers of the land. From her Judeo-Christian beliefs, mother had instructed me to not go near solitary spots of the river, especially during Holy Week, for I could encounter the Devil bathing his mules. Every day the sun and the clouds would play cards to see who would keep the afternoon. As the sun lost, the rain came, with lightning taking pictures of us children as we insisted on jumping from the tallest trees into the water or continuing playing soccer under the storm.

The rains, the voices of people made by the brooks at night running over pebbles and boulders near my grandparents' house, animate waters and trees—all marked my life of long connections and returns to Amazonia. Leaving the place to go to college in the capital city of Colombia in the Andean mountain range was difficult. It must have been my memories, after I was living in North America, that drove me back to the many rivers to listen and record the oral narratives of Amazonians. It was my desire to be on the Amazon River, the big one. The one that I had imagined, influenced by the indigenous tales of my childhood, as a big anaconda on the way to the Atlantic followed by smaller tributary rivers looking like little anacondas following their mother. I had imagined they were feeding their mother with all the waters from the forest. Other times I imagined that the big river had simply enslaved them to receive all their waters.

. . . For Amazonians, anacondas and rivers are inseparable.

In search of the tales of riverine people, I started in the Brazilian Amazon where I found many stories about the *Cobra Grande*, the big anaconda, the mother of all rivers and serpents. In some Indigenous tales it had been said that an anaconda was a big canoe that came at the beginning of time, bringing people, plants, animals and dropping them off on the riverbanks. In one of my river trips from Tefé to Manaus, I was told by the captain and the crew-members how the *Cobra Grande* had lifted and held their ship in her power for a few minutes. The *Cobra Grande* lived in the river's channels and lakes and all the movements of the land or water are attributed to her mood swings. In all the areas where the *Cobra* lived there were plenty of fish, and, when the *Cobra* sensed that humans had been too intrusive, she attacked them by tilting their canoes or stealing their souls and sometimes taking people to her realm at the bottom where they live as serpents. In acknowledgment of the *Cobra Grande*'s power and to make her happy when she became mad, I was told people threw flowers and firewater in the whirlpools where she dwells.

Years later I was able to find similar stories and rituals in rivers of the Peruvian Amazon, were the supernatural anaconda was called '*Yakumama*'. There too, this serpent's fury was appeased by throwing firewater in the whirlpools during the river storms. With such powers, supernatural anacondas are metaphorical of both the chthonic forces of nature and the agency of the rivers in the transformation of the land. In the Spanish and Portuguese languages, and in the symbolic Amazonian narratives, the river is portrayed as a he. The river is given a masculine article, but 'he' is deeply connected and intertwined with the feminine *Yakumama* spirit, the serpent mother of all rivers. For instance, for fishermen, the abundance of fish in any spot of a river is attributed to the presence of an anaconda. If she leaves that place all the fish and river life follow her. In Amazonian imaginaries, anacondas and rivers are inseparable.

But the stories that I heard the most in almost all the corners of Amazonia were those about the pink dolphins. Whether in the Río Negro in the Venezuelan Amazon, or in the tributaries of the Amazon River on the Colombian, Brazilian and Peruvian borders, the dolphins were the most famous tricksters and the most handsome. Coming out of the rivers at dusk, they would become men wearing Panama hats, ready to do business in town, and afterwards go to parties where they charmed the girls and convinced them to return with them. In the bottom of the rivers the dolphins had nice paved roads, good services, restaurants, hospitals . . . everything. And who would not follow, to those modern conveniences! People lived there better than everybody else, for they were spared the abuses on their land, and all the social and gender inequalities brought to them by the Western world. That was a way for Amazonians to cope with their anxieties due to the abuses and genocides inflicted by eras of extractivism of Amazonian commodities such as the Rubber Boom and the latest drilling for oil. As for the pink dolphins, they continue to be seen swimming alongside the travelling boats or just hanging out in calm waters near women washing clothes on the riverbanks. Since they are believed be such good lovers, in many places, people hunt the dolphins to cut their penises so they can use them for love charms.

Rivers and Forest Are 'Storied Matter'

In such storied rivers, like the term 'storied matter' from environmental thinkers Serpil Oppermann and Serenella Iovino, I further encountered tales about *Yaras*, beautiful women who lived there too. They were mermaid-like blondes, who would come out at night to charm and abduct fishermen and loggers to keep them for husbands. As in other places, any disappearances of men and women were attributed to their eloping or being kidnapped by a dolphin, a *Cobra Grande*, or any of the myriads of these shape-shifters and supernatural creatures in constant interaction with people. On land, abductions of people were also carried out by the guardians of the forest and tricksters. Many of these happenings on land or water go public in Amazonia thanks to the explanations given by *Sabedores* or *Pajes*, Amazonian shamans who have used sacred hallucinogenic plants to communicate with the physical and spiritual realms.

Some species of plants are called 'teaching plants'. The most used and known is a vine called Ayahuasca (*Banisteriopsis caapi*). The ingestion of its brew helps the shaman and locals to join the physical life of the surrounding world. It allows them to imagine and inhabit the points of views of a river, animal or plant. Such plants and multiple subjectivities of the ecological 'others' help a shaman to see things more clearly. Thus, he sharpens a knowledge already received from his ancestors. All of this is passed down in storytelling, woven by the tradition of shamans. Listening to their plethora of tales, I learned how their *buen vivir*, the good life of Amazonians, may have emanated from their love and sense of brotherhood towards the nonhuman world. For more than in a 'cultural' world, they lived in a socialised nature made of the 'internatural' world. In the Ecuadorian Amazon the Kichwa people, for example, talked about living with or having a family relationship with all the rivers, lagoons, boulders, trees and animals in the cosmos around them. Though everybody lived in their houses in the communities, those houses were connected to the houses of the communities of plants and animals in the bodies of water and forest through a soul breath substance that glued them all together. Such substance was called 'Samay'. Thus while somebody is sleeping, 'the soul of that person would travel partaking the substances of rivers, trees and stones', as my friend the anthropologist Michael Uzendoski once pointed out to me.

In other parts of the Basin, I felt comparable belief systems and similar philosophies of life. All the water realms were inhabited by spirits with the capacity to influence the lives of people on the riverbanks by either helping or punishing them if they did not follow the rules of a shared nature. In the Brazilian Amazon there lived the *Cobra Grande* and *Mãe de Peixe*, or mother of fish—kidnaping the fishermen, and granting the gifts of good fishing. In the Peruvian Amazon there was the *Yakumama*, mother of all rivers, the giver of all happiness. In the Pastaza and Marañon rivers, the underwater world was ruled by the *Yakurunas*. These were creatures with their faces looking backwards who directed the rivers as if they were their marionettes. They were quick to get mad, but for the most part lived peacefully smoking pipes of tobacco and resting in hammocks made of their servants the anacondas. From there they spied on the women bathing on the shores through a scope made from a tanrilla bird's leg. Then they would send the women gifts with the waves of the river, their automobiles. Those *Yakurunas* were responsible for the well-being of the schools of fish and transmitted their powers and knowledge to those riverine inhabitants who respected their water dominions. I remember going once with several fishermen to a ritual for appeasing a lake. They were close friends who had invited me on their trip to summon a *Cocha brava*, a lake who is dangerous and bad tempered. For such a ritual, they had gotten the help of a mestizo shaman so that they could do some fishing during the coming dry season that year. Beautiful *icaros*, songs composed by the shaman, were asking favours of the *Yakumama*. They were promising to do their fishing with care.

No different than any other part of the earth, the Amazonian world in its rivers, channels and lagoons is a realm of storied matter. Stories of Amazonians work as holders of the physical life of plants and animals of the basin and those narratives also offer exemplary values to humankind. As my friend Joni Adamson, an American environmental humanities scholar who writes about justice and multispecies relationships has told me, supernatural creatures like Yakumama or Sachamama (mother of the forests) are sophisticated representations of the ecological relations of entire bioregions and ecosystems of the Earth. Thus the oral narratives of Amazonians are not only 'the songs of the Earth', specific to a region, but they also serve as cautionary tales and sage advice for children and adults facing the crucial climate changes of our time. These stories, Adamson has said, offer the people a kind of 'theory' that emerges from the past, but is still as useful as ever for understanding the present and planning for a liveable future. Nature, through events and other physical gestures, provides signs that humans can or cannot see. A river, for instance, gives warnings that can be seen only by the birds and animals who live in the riverbank. A story of a village wiped out by a flood could be attributed to the anger of a river. Possibly the river wanted to teach something to that community. Only those who take the teaching plants and read their dreams well can know. Others in despair, not knowing, can only plea to God for order, for regularity—beg to the Virgin Mary for mercy on them, their pigs and chickens, and their gardens near the waters.

Many times the river can give you clear warnings.

'Many times the river can give you clear warnings like those he gave to us before he took our houses and the islands where we had our animals, and plants in the patios . . . it happened years ago', said someone selling refreshments in Bellavista, a city port on the Nanay River that connects to the Amazon River. 'There were islands there, in front, where we used to live. One day we were fishing and all of a sudden we saw two pink dolphins coming to our canoes. Then we heard a roaring sound, like Caterpillar machinery, coming from the bottom of the river. When we turned where the dolphins had been swimming, we saw instead a canoe with two gringos. When we asked them, 'What are you doing here?' they said to us, 'We are engineers who work for a company in one of the cities at the bottom of the Amazon River. You two better tell the people in your islands to move to the riverbanks or somewhere as we are planning to work moving those islands'.

I believe, in reality it was the river with his actions that created the story. It is just our immense human hubris that has given us the misconception that intelligence resides only in our species. There the river, with his physical gestures (the opening of a new channel, a death or birth of an island) has provided the fabric for a new oral narrative, and the stories are told and retold. For the river does whatever he wants to do with his waters and mud. For the building of islands the river sends a team of whirlpools (they are like his factory workers) to shovel mud and sand day and night from the bottom to the place where the river wants to build it. Just like that. Years later if he decides to move an island, he simply hits and hits the riverbank until he knocks it down. The river on the land is like the clouds, ever changing in his channels and in his islands. I remember this clearly during the making of the documentary film, *The Trees Have a Mother*, when a member from the Witoto ethnic group said: 'Scientists, students, peoples from far away, come to study and to measure the Amazon River but they will never be able to figure him out. When the scientists think that they have figured out the river he is already something else'.

The river with his floods and changes is the best teacher. We learn about humbleness and abidance if we pay attention to the river. 'Look, it is like in the Bible: the people had become too prideful and then a flood calmed everybody down', my Witoto friend said. Later I heard from someone else, 'the river gives you everything, the river takes away everything'—words from a riverine dweller after the last flood had done away with his entire crop of rice. The rice had been planted on the banks that were beautifully fertilised from silt brought during the yearly flooding season. It was a very tasty and famous rice among other communities. It was used for feeding his community, the remaining crop to be traded and sold in the city. 'This river usually comes with his flood in December. So we pick up our rice in October. But last year he came in September before the rice was ripe. We don't know what is going on with this river. He certainly has gone crazy lately'.

The river is handsome, the river is generous, the river is good.

There are also stories about invisible rivers, 'flying rivers', travelling clouds. Such rivers come out of the friendship of water systems with the trees and the clouds. The trees pump the water to the skies and tickle the clouds with some gases. The clouds giggle and laugh; they laugh so hard that they end up losing all the waters over the trees, only for the love story to start all over again. 'We can't cut the forests, we need to keep those "flying rivers": they are good for the whole planet', scientists say. 'The Amazon River is generous, the Amazon River is wonderful. He is the monarch of all the rivers', say also the people from Amazonian cities in their signs, street banners and songs. And for the government officials, and glossy magazines in the luxurious lobbies of buildings, the river has become a super star (so great that a few years ago a committee from Switzerland made him a new Wonder of the World). The river is happy, the river is a celebrity and from the terraces of the hotels this is seen as the sun makes his back shine as if it were made of glittering gold. The river is generous, the river is mighty. So generous that every night the canoes and boats who sleep awaiting their next day's journeys wake up happy thinking they are going to travel with caresses in the arms of the river. So mighty and generous that he takes all the human excrement of almost a million people from Iquitos, in the Peruvian Amazon, and the plastic bottles of delicious pop drinks and candy wrappers loved by children. In the floating bars women get drunk and throw their love pains into the current for the river to take them away. The river is handsome, the river is good. To keep being handsome, to keep being pretty, the river better keep charming the clouds, keep winking at them.

Pondering the Fate of the Amazon River and Many Other Rivers

For the Kukama indigenous communities, though, for whom the river is at the centre of their lives, not everything that glitters about and around the river is good. They have obtained their fish and carried their goods using the water, and have related spiritually to the upper Amazon River for thousands of years. Lately the Peruvian government has auctioned the rights to private companies for using the ports and turning the rivers into efficient *hydro vías*, waterways, for transportation. The projected deal accords with the latest governments' plans from the countries who share the Amazon River basin to connect economically the Eastern and Western coastal areas of South America. In the past years developers and profiteers have been seeking to win the contracts that will 'shape up' the behaviour of the Amazon, as it will be harnessed along with the Huallaga, Ucayaly and other rivers of Amazonia. They will be fitted and maintained for the good development of the economies of the region. In this way, rivers will be implemental to the efficient hauling of soybeans, iron, ore and other goods to the distant markets of Asia, environmental journalist Barbara Fraser told me. Not so much winning for the indigenous and mestizos of those areas, who have protested the changes legally, since the forthcoming dredging of the rivers to keep them navigable all year round for big ships will upset the spirits of the underwater world. The *Yakuruna* spirits will take away the fish and wildlife in the sandbars, the richest area where the indigenous peoples do their fishing to feed their families. Kukama shamans say that ever since the government started granting permission for the development of ports and rivers, they have lost their healing powers that the spirits of the river had given them. Teams of scientist are concerned too.

'Not only the local fish to feed their families, the good life and spiritual losses but also the weakening and disappearance of their cultural knowledge is at risk; for the riverine dwellers have so much knowledge, they provide us with pivotal information about the behaviour of the river through their oral narratives and memory of the last centuries'. This was said to me by Jorge Abad, an environmental scientist specializing in hydrodynamics and sediment transport for tropical rivers, as we talked last summer over *a vaso de chuchuwasi* (a treebark drink) on one of the floating bars of the Itaya River, in the Belem neighbourhood. There was lots of plastic trash surrounding the place where we were. 'There is so much research we need to do to learn about the river: much of it is still a mystery to us. To get the whole picture of what is happening right now with the river and its future behaviour our technological devices are not enough; we need to complete the information with what the indigenous and riverine people teach us about these waters and lands; there is a lot in their memories. And now we don't know what is going to happen with those plans of turning the river into a hydro via. The Amazon River, for example, has a need to form islands every 26 kilometres. What will happen if, with all the dredging required, the river were not able to have its islands? There is no scientific research on that. We are just starting'. While we sat on the floating bar, pondering the fate of the upper Amazon River and many other rivers already damaged due to oil drilling in the region, Don Pedro our friend and owner of the bar talked to other customers with concern. They chatted together about the fact that the Amazon River had been pounding with all the power of his waters on the small stretch of land that separates his main channel from the city of Iquitos. If the Amazon River does that, he will come and take away this bar and then the whole city of Iquitos. The customers continued to speculate about the possibility that the mighty *Yakumama*, the mother of the river has gotten very upset. In their rumouring they say she is mad, for all the latest overfishing of her children and especially now with the news about the dredging on the river. One of them says 'She must be telling the *Yakurunas* and other spirits to come back with the force of the water against the people of Iquitos'.

Chapter Nineteen

Can the Humanities Become Posthuman?

A Conversation

Rosi Braidotti and Cosetta Veronese

CV: Your latest book is called *The Posthuman*. In consideration of your philosophical development, which is rooted in the study of Foucault, in an uninterrupted dialogue with Deleuze as well as in feminism and feminist activism, could you explain how your idea of posthumanism developed? In other words, what have been your transitions on the way towards posthumanism?

RB: For me as a student of Foucault, Deleuze and Irigaray, the crisis of humanism means the rejection of all forms of universalism, including the socialist variation. 'Man' cannot claim to represent all humanity because that 'Man' is a culture-specific, gender-specific, race-specific and class-specific entity: is it a European, male, white, intellectual ideal. Moreover, that ideal posits itself as a norm that everyone else is supposed to imitate and aspire to; but all those who differ from the Eurocentric, masculinist, white, intellectual norm are classified as 'different from' it. And being 'different from' means to be 'worth less than'. This hierarchical organisation of difference as negative becomes a very politicised issue for feminists, postcolonial, and anti-racist thinkers.

In fact, if you think about it, the structural others of the humanistic subject re-emerge with a vengeance in postmodernity (Braidotti 2002). It is a historical fact that the great emancipatory movements of postmodernity are driven and fuelled by the resurgent 'others': the women's rights movement; the anti-racism and de-colonization movements; the anti-nuclear and pro-environment movements are the voices of the structural Others of modernity. They inevitably mark the crisis of the former humanist 'centre' or dominant subject-position and are not merely anti-humanist, but move beyond it to an altogether novel project. These social and political movements are simultaneously the symptom of the crisis of the subject, and for conservatives even its 'cause' and also the expression of positive, proactive alternatives.

In the language of my nomadic theory (see Nomadic Subjects *and* Nomadic Theory*), they express both the crisis of the majority and the patterns of becoming of the minorities. The challenge for critical theory consists in being able to tell the difference between these different flows of mutation.*

In other words, the posthumanist position I am defending builds on the anti-humanist legacy, more specifically on the epistemological and political foundations of the poststructuralist generation, and moves further. The alternative views about the human and the new formations of subjectivity that have emerged from the radical epistemologies of Continental philosophy in the last thirty years do not merely oppose humanism but create other visions of the self. Sexualised, racialised and naturalised differences, far from being the categorical boundary-keepers of the subject of humanism, have evolved into fully fledged alternative models of the human subject.

CV: The last chapter of your book is dedicated to the future of the human sciences. With a pinch of irony you refer to the 'proliferation of studies' that have developed in the humanities over the last couple of decades. Could you comment on the specific future of literature, or literary studies?

RB: I have observed in Holland, Northern Europe, and the United Kingdom, that the current crises of the human sciences translates itself at the level of university politics in radical cuts to funding, structures and chairs in the humanities. At the moment, the public image of the human sciences is the worse one we have witnessed since the end of World War II. The dominant image of the humanities today is that of a totally useless university category, which does not produce anything and does not teach anything, but only feeds unemployment. The relationship between journalism, media and the human sciences is dramatically deteriorating. There are multiple reasons for this situation, and there is space for an extensive work and investigation to be conducted upon this issue. It looks like the main, if not the sole, function of the human sciences is to provide a rough cultural mixture (the so-called 'general culture') to students, mainly girls, who are waiting for a good match to marry and who are expected to hold brilliant conversations during dinner time. It is shocking to compare the current situation in the human sciences with that of the 1950s and 1960s, when Simone de Beauvoir and Jean Paul Sartre were treated almost as Head of States wherever they would go, because of the high intellectual prestige they enjoyed.

We live at a time when the figure of the intellectual is worth nothing. The very term 'intellectual' is barely used, because it sounds outmoded. In the 1980s a new formula to describe the intellectual class was actually coined, that of 'content provider': 'those individuals who provide the contents'. The advent of the Internet in the 1990s and the sudden explosion in content availability transformed intellectuals into 'idea-brokers'. From the 'intellectual' to the 'content provider' to the 'idea broker': we have witnessed an epochal mutation, which deserves a study both from a semiotic and terminological point of view and from an institutional one. In the neo-liberal university founded on the idea of culture as (also) business the figure of the intellectual has lost its original role and place. The downgrading of this figure is a rather sad story.

Notwithstanding the fact that innovation and creativity are considered the real capital, the humanities, which are the foundation of all this, are marginalised and despised. How do we reconcile these conflicting trends? I believe that instead of withdrawing back into humanism and building a sort of neo-humanistic fortress—a nostalgic and very classic structure—the humanities should open and move towards the world, embrace with enthusiasm the new challenges that are coming up. The humanities should thus transform into posthuman sciences in the affirmative and constructive sense of the term. They should leave the notion of the crisis behind along with the rhetoric of their crises: this also means abandoning the feeling of inferiority and subjugation, which inevitably arises from the repetition of the refrain of their economic, social and financial uselessness.

We can consider posthumanism from the point of view of the humanities and that of anthropocentrism. In the former perspective, the urge to reinvent the human is the pivot of the various social movements of the 1970s (feminist, postcolonial, pacifist, anti-nuclear movements among others). The crisis of humanism provided the opportunity to respond to an epochal call for new ways of being and new forms of subjectivity. The critique of universalism triggered the development of new fields of study, which, instead of linking with traditional disciplines, concerned about their purity such as literature and philosophy, grew in-between their clefts. They gave birth to interdisciplinary groups called 'studies': women studies, gender studies, gay studies, media studies and so on. This constellation of studies reinvented and opened the human sciences after the collapse of humanism, bearing testimony of their great vitality and innovating on both themes and methods.

From the perspective of anti-anthropocentrism, Darwin stands out as one of the colossal figures of modernity. However, his name is totally absent from the humanities. To think of ourselves as of the members of one of multiple species, with an evolution and genetic structure that is one among many, is just not part of our vocabulary, it is not conceivable within the humanities. From this point of view, there seems to be a dramatic equation between the human sciences and anthropocentrism. 'To do humanities' means 'to think about the man of humanism'. If this equation is there to stay, then we have a problem, because the foundation of knowledge in today's world is no longer anthropological, let alone male-centred or Eurocentric. The old fundamental metaphysical categories of male and female have been replaced by a system based on complexity codes, cellules, the infinitesimal levels of dynamics and interaction of what constitutes the basic foundation of life. Moreover, if, on the one hand, the human consists of a series of informative, genetic, neurological and evolutionary codes, on the other hand, anthropos *has been displaced from its former central position by information technology, there is reason to speak about a systematic posthuman turn. There has been a mutation in the centrality of the subject of knowledge, and our fundamental ontology today has become mediated in biogenetic as well as informational terms. Information networks live independently of us, as confirmed by the fact that computational and network system are capable of self-repairing without the need of direct human intervention.*

Some of the possibilities for literary studies to survive in the current post-human context are to embrace technology (digital humanities), to include environmental studies (ecocriticism), and to reappraise the established tradition of science fiction writing. On the theoretical level, both the emphasis on materiality and on affect are also pointing in a new direction, which is less confined by the conventions of the linguistic turn.

CV: Among the tenets of posthuman theory you mention 'transdisciplinarity'. In what does it differ from the more traditional notion of 'interdisciplinarity'? What are your suggestions for the new vocabulary that the humanities have to build in order to face the challenges of posthumanism?

RB: Posthuman critical theory needs to apply a new vision of subjectivity to both the practice and the public perception of the scientist, which is still caught in the classical and outmoded model of the humanistic 'Man of reason' (Lloyd 1984) as the quintessential European citizen. We need to overcome this model and move towards an intensive form of interdisciplinarity, transversality, and boundary-crossings among a range of discourses. This transdisciplinary approach affects the very structure of thought and enacts a rhizomatic embrace of conceptual diversity in scholarship. The posthuman method amounts to higher degrees of disciplinary hybridization and relies on intense de-familiarization of our habits of thought through encounters that shatter the flat repetition of the protocols of institutional reason.

In order to come to terms with complex multiplicities, differential entities, rhizomatic transversal connections we need to inject into the system viable alternatives, we need to have something to propose, we need to offer counter-codes, counter-projects, and make counter-proposals. An additional problem in relation to this is that of language. Our language still rails our roads back into linearity and into processes of single focus, when in fact we need a spectrum, we need to be able to keep in our heads multiple utterances, potentially contradictory ones to even begin to make sense of the world that we are in. This is why Deleuze and Guattari write in such a complicated manner: because the linearity of language is a real big problem. How can we account for a zigzagging, complex, eternally contradictory world in a linear language? I sometimes think that the humanities are really lost and doomed unless we experience with multiple languages.

This emphasis on renewed conceptual and terminological creativity requires more institutional support than the humanities are receiving at present. We need to set up fundamental humanities' labs in order to conduct these experiments in a rigorous manner. We need more theory, more creativity.

CV: If posthumanism means demolishing dualism, breaking disciplinary boundaries (as well as nationalistic and political boundaries), in essence: getting rid of the humanistic western paradigm (as well as of any other auxiliary paradigm, which would only bring us back to humanism), which alternatives do we have to make us accountable for the world we live in?

RB: The first step requires consciousness-raising. The social theory literature on shared anxiety about the future of both our species and of our humanist legacy is very rich and varied. Important liberal thinkers like Habermas (2003) and influential ones like Fukuyama (2002) are very alert on this issue, as are social critics like Sloterdijk (2009) and Borradori (2003). In different ways, they express deep concern for the status of the human, and seem particularly struck by moral and cognitive panic at the prospect of the posthuman turn, blaming our advanced technologies for it. I share their concern, but as a posthuman thinker with distinct anti-humanist feelings, I am less prone to panic at the prospect of a displacement of the centrality of the human and can also see the advantages of such an evolution.

I define the critical posthuman subject within an eco-philosophy of multiple belongings, as a relational subject constituted in and by multiplicity, that is to say a subject that works across differences and is also internally differentiated, but still grounded and accountable. Posthuman subjectivity is nomadic and it expresses an embodied and embedded and hence partial form of accountability, based on a strong sense of collectivity, relationality and hence community building.

My position is in favour of complexity and promotes radical posthuman subjectivity, resting on the ethics of becoming. The focus is shifted accordingly from unitary to nomadic subjectivity, thus running against the grain of high humanism and its contemporary variations. This view rejects individualism, but also asserts an equally strong distance from relativism or nihilistic defeatism. It promotes an ethical bond of an altogether different sort from the self-interests of an individual subject, as defined along the canonical lines of classical humanism. A posthuman ethics for a non-unitary subject proposes an enlarged sense of interconnection between self and others, including the nonhuman or 'earth' others, by removing the obstacle of self-centred indi-viduality. Contemporary biogenetic capitalism generates a global form of reactive mutual interdependence of all living organisms, including nonhu-mans. This sort of unity tends to be of the negative kind, as a shared form of vulnerability, that is to say a global sense of interconnection between the human and the nonhuman environment in the face of common threats. The posthuman recomposition of human interaction that I propose is not the same as the reactive bond of vulnerability, but is an affirmative bond that locates the subject in the flow of relations with multiple others.

Labouring towards a non-unitary posthuman subject, 'we' need to acknowl-edge that there may well be multiple and potentially contradictory projects at stake in the complex recompositions of 'the human' right now: many complex and contested ways of becoming-world together.

CV: In the keynote speech you gave at the University of Zurich on 24 May 2014, on the occasion of the annual conference of the American Association for Italian Studies, you mentioned 'two areas of studies that are the making of post-anthropocentric humanities: namely animal studies and ecocriticism'. How do you explain their importance in relation to what you suggest are the fundamental requirements of posthumanism, namely the necessity for it to be situated, i.e., 'embodied and embedded', 'affirmative', i.e., constructive, and for it to call for our accountability?

RB: Animal Studies, ecocriticism and the Environmental humanities as a whole are pointing in the right direction. It is absolutely true that, once the centrality of anthropos *is challenged, a number of boundaries between 'Man' and his others go tumbling down, in a cascade effect that opens up unexpected perspectives. Thus, if the crisis of humanism inaugurates the posthuman by empowering the sexualised and racialised human 'others' to emancipate themselves from the dialectics of master/slave relations, the crisis of* anthropos *relinquishes the demonic forces of the naturalised oth-ers. Animals, insects, plants and the environment, in fact the planet and the cosmos as a whole, are called into play. This places a different burden of responsibility on our species, which is the primary cause for the mess. The fact that our geological era is known as the 'Anthropocene' stresses both the technologically mediated power acquired by* anthropos *and its potentially lethal consequences for everyone else.*

The crisis is especially strong in the Human and Social sciences, because they are the most anthropocentric fields of scholarly research. How can a historian or a philosopher think of humans as being 'part of nature', consid-ering that academic discourse continues to claim transcendental grounds for human consciousness? How to reconcile this materialist awareness with the task of critical thought? As a brand of vital materialism, posthuman theory contests the arrogance of anthropocentrism and the 'exceptionalism' of the Human as a transcendental category. It strikes instead an alliance with the productive and immanent force of zoe, *or life in its nonhuman aspects. This requires a mutation of our shared understanding of what it means to think at all, let alone think critically. In* The Posthuman *I argue that the return to Spinozist monism as opposed to Hegelian dialectics, which occurred back in the 1970s with the generation of my teachers, is now finally becoming visible. Monism gives us conceptual tools and a terminology to address humans as being part of a continuum with all living matter. It is a great advantage.*

The question is consequently what the humanities can become, in the posthuman era and after the decline of the primacy of 'Man' and of anthropos. *My argument is that, far from being a terminal crisis, these challenges open up new global, eco-sophical, posthumanist and post-anthropocentric dimensions for the humanities. They are expressed by a second generation of 'studies' areas. Thus animal studies and ecocriticism have grown into such rich and well-articulated fields, that it is impossible to even attempt to summarise them. Cultural studies of science and society; religion studies; disability studies; fat studies; success studies; celebrity studies; globalization studies are further significant examples of the exuberant state of the new humanities in the twenty-first century. New media has proliferated into a whole series of sub-sections and meta-fields: software studies, internet studies, game studies and more. This vitality justifies optimism about the future of the humanities, with media theory and media philosophy providing the new ontological grounds for knowledge production, while the curriculum of the traditional humanities disciplines—notably philosophy—resists any interdisciplinary contamination. In this fast moving landscape, literary analysis and critical enquiry are fundamental navigational tools to chart a path across the disciplinary fractures and contradictions of the contemporary humanities.*

WORKS CITED

Borradori, Giovanna. *Philosophy in a Time of Terror*. Chicago: University of Chicago Press, 2003.

Braidotti, Rosi. *Metamorphoses: Towards a Materialist Theory of Becoming*. Cambridge: Polity Press, 2002.

Braidotti, Rosi. *Nomadic Subjects: Embodiments and Sexual Difference in Contemporary Feminist Theory*. New York: Columbia University Press, 2011.

Braidotti, Rosi. *Nomadic Theory: The Portable Rosi Braidotti*. New York: Columbia University Press, 2011.

Fukuyama, Francis. *Our Posthuman Future: Consequences of the BioTechnological Revolution*. London: Profile Books, 2002.

Habermas, Jürgen. *The Future of Human Nature.* Cambridge: Polity Press, 2003.

Sloterdijk, Peter. 'Rules for the Human Zoo: A Response to the "Letter on Humanism"'. *Environment and Planning D: Society and Space* 27.1 (2009): 12–28.

Lloyd, Genevieve. *The Man of Reason: Male and Female in Western Philosophy.* London: Methuen, 1984.

Index

About the Contributors

Joni Adamson is Professor of Environmental Humanities in the Department of English and Senior Sustainability Scholar at the Julie Ann Wrigley Global Institute of Sustainability at Arizona State University. She was past president of the Association for the Study of Literature and Environment (2012) and author and/or co-editor of *Keywords for Environmental Studies* (2016), *Ecocriticism and Indigenous Studies—Conversations from Earth to Cosmos* (2016), *American Studies, Ecocriticism and Citizenship* (2013), *The Environmental Justice Reader* (2002), and *American Indian Literature, Environmental Justice and Ecocriticism* (2001). She has written over 50 articles and reviews focusing on indigenous perspectives on environmental justice, cosmopolitics, food sovereignty, and critical plant studies. She is a principle investigator for 'Humanities for the Environment' (H*f*E), an international networking project for the environmental humanities and lead developer of the 2.0 H*f*E international web site (http://hfe-observatories.org).

Marco Armiero is the Director of the Environmental Humanities Laboratory at the Royal Institute of Technology, Stockholm, where he is also an Associate Professor of Environmental History. He has been a postdoctoral fellow and visiting scholar at Yale University, UC Berkeley, Stanford, the Autonomous University in Barcelona, and the Center for Social Sciences at the University of Coimbra, Portugal. His research interests cluster around three overarching topics: nation and nature, migrations and the environment, and environmental justice and ecological conflicts. He has published *A Rugged Nation: Mountains and the Making of Modern Italy* (2011). An associate editor of the journal *Environmental Humanities*, his articles have been published in *Left History, Radical History Review, Environment and History, Modern Italy*, and *Capitalism Nature Socialism*, where he also serves as a senior editor. Marco has also co-edited the book *Nature and History in Modern Italy* (2010) with Marcus Hall and *The History of Environmentalism* (2014) with Lise Sedrez.

Filippo Bertoni is a postdoctoral fellow in the Aarhus University Research on the Anthropocene, an interdisciplinary and experimental project led by Anna Tsing and Nils Bubandt focusing on disturbed landscapes and 'the arts of living in a damaged planet'. His work explores the mining area of Río Tinto and its eccentric connections with Mars through the activity of a team of astrobiologists who study its underground microbial ecosystems as analogs for the Red Planet. Filippo's current interest in metabolism builds on his doctoral work as part of Annemarie Mol's research team 'The Eating Body in Western Theory and Practice', where he studied earthworms and a number of (scientific) practices in which they partake, in order to bring the specific togetherness that eating allows to bear on debates on the 'politics of nature'.

Rosi Braidotti is Distinguished University Professor and founding director of the Centre for the Humanities at Utrecht University. She was the founding professor of gender studies at the University of Utrecht (1988–2005) and the first scientific director for the Netherlands Research School of Women's Studies. She is one of the foremost exponents in the field of continental philosophy and epistemology, feminist and gender theories, poststructuralist and posthumanist thought. Her books include *Patterns of Dissonance* (1991), *Nomadic Subjects* (1994, 2011 2nd ed.), *Metamorphoses* (2002), *Transpositions* (2006), *La philosophie, là où on ne l'attend pas* (2009), *Nomadic Theory* (2011), and *The Posthuman* (2013). Together with Paul Gilroy, Rosi has recently edited the volume *Conflicting Humanities* (2016). Her personal website is www.rosibraidotti.com.

Matthew Calarco is Associate Professor of Philosophy at California State University, Fullerton, where he teaches courses in continental philosophy, ethics, and social and political philosophy. His research lies at the intersection of animal studies, environmental studies, and radical social justice movements. Matthew is currently working on a project titled 'Altermobilities: Profaning the Streets', and his most recent book is entitled *Thinking through Animals: Identity, Difference, Indistinction* (2015).

J. Baird Callicott is the co-editor-in-chief of the *Encyclopedia of Environmental Ethics and Philosophy* and author/editor of a score of books and author of dozens of journal articles, encyclopaedia articles, and book chapters in environmental philosophy and ethics, among them *Thinking Like a Planet: The Land Ethic and the Earth Ethic* (2013). He has served the

International Society for Environmental Ethics as president, Yale University as Bioethicist-in-Residence, and the National Socio-environmental Synthesis Center as visiting senior research scientist (funded by the National Science Foundation). His research goes forward simultaneously on four main fronts: theoretical environmental ethics, comparative environmental ethics and philosophy, the philosophy of ecology and conservation policy, and climate ethics. Baird taught the world's first course in environmental ethics in 1971 at the University of Wisconsin-Stevens Point and has regularly taught courses in ancient Greek philosophy, his doctoral focus of study.

Jeffrey Jerome Cohen is Professor of English at George Washington University and Director of the Institute for Medieval and Early Modern Studies. His research examines phenomena that are paradoxically alien and intimate to the human, and his publications look at the ways in which post-colonial studies, critical animal studies, queer theory, postmodernism and posthumanism help to better understand the texts and cultures of both the Middle Ages and today. He is author of *Of Giants* (1999), *Medieval Identity Machines* (2003), *Hybridity, Identity, and Monstrosity in Medieval Britain: Of Difficult Middles* (2006), and *Stone: An Ecology of the Inhuman* (2015). Jeffrey is also the editor of *Monster Theory: Reading Culture* (1997), *The Postcolonial Middle Ages* (2000), *Animal, Mineral, Vegetable: Ethics and Objects* (2012), *Prismatic Ecology: Ecotheory beyond Green* (2013), and, with Lowell Duckert, *Elemental Ecocriticism: Thinking with Earth, Air, Water, and Fire* (2015) and *Veer Ecology: An Ecotheory Companion* (forthcoming).

Lowell Duckert is Assistant Professor of English at West Virginia University, specializing in early modern literature, ecotheory, and environmental criticism. With Jeffrey Jerome Cohen, he has edited 'Ecomaterialism' (*postmedieval* 4.1, 2013), *Elemental Ecocriticism: Thinking with Earth, Air, Water, and Fire* (2015), and *Veer Ecology: An Ecotheory Companion* (forthcoming) and has published articles on such topics as glaciers, polar bears, maroon, Walter Ralegh, and rain. Lowell recently completed a book manuscript, *For All Waters: Finding Ourselves in Early Modern Wetscapes* (forthcoming), for the University of Minnesota Press.

Greta Gaard is Professor of English and coordinator of the Sustainability Faculty Fellows at University of Wisconsin-River Falls. Her work emerges from the intersections of feminism, environmental justice, queer studies, and critical animal studies, exploring a wide range of issues, from interspecies justice, material perspectives on fireworks and space exploration, postcolonial ecofeminism, and the ecopolitics of climate change. Author or editor of six books, Greta's most recent volume is *Critical Ecofeminism* (2016) from Lexington Books. Her creative nonfiction ecomemoir, *The Nature of Home* (2007), has been translated into Chinese (2016) and Portuguese (forthcoming).

Juan Carlos Galeano is the author of *Baraja Inicial* (1986), *Pollen and Rifles* (1997), *Amazonia* (2003), *Sobre las cosas* (2010), and *Yakumama and Other Mythical Beings* (2014). His work, inspired by Amazonian cosmologies and the modern world, has been published internationally and translated into Kichwa, French, English, Portuguese, German, and Chinese. Poems from *Amazonia* have been published in magazines and journals such as *Revista Atlántica, Poesía, Casa de las Américas, The Atlantic Monthly, Field, Ploughshares, TriQuarterly, Antioch Review,* and *Review: Literature and the Arts of the Americas.* His poems and folktales have also appeared in college textbooks, collections, and in international anthologies such as *A poesía se encontra na floresta* (2001), *Jinetes del aire* (2011), *Literary Amazonia* (2004), *Ecopoetry: A Contemporary American Anthology* (2013), and *The Encyclopedia of Religion and Nature* (2005). His research on Amazonian culture has appeared in his collection of folktales *Cuentos amazónicos* (2007), *Folktales of the Amazon* (2008), as well as in the film he co-directed and co-produced, *The Trees Have a Mother* (2008). As a translator, he has published Spanish book-length versions of North American poets. Juan Carlos lives in Tallahassee, Florida, where he teaches Latin American poetry and Amazonian cultures at Florida State University.

Stefan Helmreich received his PhD in Anthropology from Stanford University and held fellowships at Cornell, Rutgers, and NYU prior to coming to MIT. His research examines the works and lives of biologists thinking through the limits of 'life' as a category of analysis. *Alien Ocean: Anthropological Voyages in Microbial Seas* (2009) is a study of marine biologists working in realms usually out of sight and reach: the microscopic world, the deep sea, and oceans outside national sovereignty. This book—winner of the 2010 Senior Book Prize from the American Ethnological Society, the 2010 Gregory Bateson Book Prize from Society for Cultural Anthropology, and the 2012 Rachel Carson Book Prize from the Society for Social Studies of Science— charts how marine microbes are entangled with debates about the origin of life, climate change, property in the ocean commons, and the possibility of life on other worlds. An earlier book, *Silicon Second Nature: Culturing Artificial Life in a Digital World* (1998), is an ethnography of computer modelling in the life sciences. In 2000, it won the Diana Forsythe Book Prize from the American Anthropological Association. Helmreich's newest research concerns the cultural circulation of such abstractions as 'water', 'sound', and 'waves'. Stefan's essays have appeared in *Critical Inquiry*, *Representations*, *American Anthropologist*, and *The Wire*.

Serenella Iovino is Professor of Comparative Literature at the University of Turin and a fellow of the Alexander-von-Humboldt Foundation. She is past president of the European Association for the Study of Literature, Culture and Environment and the founding coordinator of the Turin International Group of Environmental Humanities Research. Author of books, essays, and edited projects, she is Creative Writing and Art Section Editor of *Ecozon@* and serves in the editorial boards of international journals and publication series on environmental topics, including *Interdisciplinary Studies in Literature and Environment*, *Green Letters*, and *Ecozon@*. Among her recent works, *Ecologia letteraria* (2006 2nd ed., 2015), *Material Ecocriticism* (co-edited with Serpil Oppermann, 2014), and *Ecocriticism and Italy: Ecology, Resistance, and Liberation* (2016). She has edited *Ecozon@*'s special issue on Mediterranean Ecocriticism (2013) and the double issue of *Relations: Beyond Anthropocentrism* on posthumanism (2016, with Roberto Marchesini and Eleonora Adorni). A guest lecturer in all major European states and in extra-European countries, in 2014 Serenella held the 'J. K. Binder Lectureship for Literature' at the University of California, San Diego. For more information, see http://unito.academia.edu/serenellaiovino.

Richard Kerridge is a nature writer and ecocritic. *Cold Blood: Adventures with Reptiles and Amphibians* (2014), his nature writing memoir, was adapted for BBC national radio and broadcast as a Radio 4 Book of the Week in July 2014. Other nature writing by Richard has been broadcast on BBC Radio 4 and published in *BBC Wildlife*, *Poetry Review*, and *Granta*. He reviews nature writing for *The Guardian* and has twice received the BBC Wildlife Award for Nature Writing. In 2012 he was awarded the 2012 Roger Deakin Prize by the Society of Authors. *Writing the Environment* (1998), co-edited by Richard, was the first collection of ecocritical essays to be published in Britain. He has published ecocritical essays on many topics and was a leading member of the team led by SueEllen Campbell that wrote *The Face of the Earth: Natural Landscapes, Science and Culture* (2011). Richard has been an elected member of the ASLE Executive Council and was founding chair of ASLE-UKI. With Greg Garrard, he is co-editor of the Bloomsbury Academic series 'Environmental Cultures'. At Bath Spa University, he leads the MA in Creative Writing.

Rob Nixon is Thomas A. and Currie C. Barron Family Professor in Humanities and the Environment and Professor of English at Princeton University. Before joining Princeton in 2015, he held the Rachel Carson

Professorship in English at the University of Wisconsin-Madison, where he was active in the Center for Culture, History, and Environment. He is the author of four books, including *Slow Violence and the Environmentalism of the Poor*, which received an American Book Award and three other prizes. Rob has written for the *New York Times*, the *New Yorker*, and elsewhere.

Serpil Oppermann, Professor of English at Hacettepe University, Ankara, and current president of the European Association for the Study of Literature, Culture and Environment, has published widely on postmodern, material, and feminist ecocriticisms and ecocritical theory. She is the co-editor of *The Future of Ecocriticism: New Horizons* (2011), *International Perspectives in Feminist Ecocriticism* (with Greta Gaard and Simon Estok, 2013), *Material Ecocriticism* (with Serenella Iovino, 2014), and editor of *Ekoeleştiri: Çevre ve Edebiyat* (2012) and *New International Voices in Ecocriticism* (2015). She has presented keynote speeches and invited talks on material ecocriticism, the Anthropocene agencies, and ecocritical theory in Sweden, Taiwan, China, Poland, and Turkey. Serpil serves in the editorial boards of several international journals and publication series on environmental topics, including *Interdisciplinary Studies in Literature and Environment*, *Ecozon@*, *Relations: Beyond Anthropocentrism*, and *Philosophy Activism Nature*, and Ecocritical Theory and Practice series of Lexington Books. Her recent work is focused on material ecocriticism, posthuman models, and the influence of the Anthropocene discourse in the Environmental Humanities. Her publications are available at http://hacettepe.academia.edu/SerpilOppermann.

Kate Rigby is Professor and Chair of Environmental Humanities at Bath Spa University, Adjunct Professor at Monash University, and a fellow of the Australian Humanities Academy and of the Alexander von Humboldt Foundation. Her research ranges across German studies, European philosophy, literature and religion, and culture and ecology. She is senior editor of the journal *Philosophy Activism Nature*, and her books include *Gender, Ecology and the Sacred* (co-edited, 1999), *Topographies of the Sacred: The Poetics of Place in European Romanticism* (2004), *Ecocritical Theory: New European Approaches* (co-edited, 2011), and *Dancing with Disaster: Environmental Histories, Narratives, and Ethics for Perilous Times* (2015). Kate was a founding member of the Australian Ecological Humanities Working Group, the inaugural president of the Association for the Study of Literature, Environment, and Culture (Australia–New Zealand), and the founding director of the Australia-Pacific Forum on Religion and Ecology@Monash.

Deborah Bird Rose is a fellow of the Academy of Social Sciences in Australia and a founding co-editor of *Environmental Humanities*. Her current research interests focus on human–animal relationships in this time of extinctions, and she writes widely in both academic and literary genres. Her most recent book is *Wild Dog Dreaming: Love and Extinction* (2011). Other books include *The Manifesto for Living in the Anthropocene* (co-edited, 2015), the rereleased second edition of *Country of the Heart: An Indigenous Australian Homeland* (2011), the third edition of the prize-winning ethnography *Dingo Makes Us Human* (2009), *Reports from a Wild Country: Ethics for Decolonisation* (2004), and *Nourishing Terrains: Australian Aboriginal Views of Landscape and Wilderness* (1996). Deborah is an adjunct professor in the University of New South Wales Environmental Humanities programme and author of the website 'Love at the Edge of Extinction'.

Scott Slovic is Professor of Literature and Environment and Chair of the English Department at the University of Idaho. He served as founding president of the Association for the Study of Literature and Environment from 1992 to 1995, and he has edited the journal *Interdisciplinary Studies in Literature and Environment* since 1995. The author of more than 250 articles in the field of ecocriticism, Scott has also written, edited, or co-edited 24 books, including, most recently, *Currents of the Universal Being: Explorations in the Literature of Energy* (2015), *Ecocriticism of the Global South* (2015), and *Numbers and Nerves: Information, Emotion, and Meaning in a World of Data* (2015).

Bronislaw Szerszynski is Reader at the Department of Sociology, Lancaster University, United Kingdom, where he also works at the Centre for the Study of Environmental Change. His research crosses the social and natural sciences, arts and humanities, and situates the changing relationship between humans, environment, and technology in the longer perspective of human and planetary history. His recent work, including both academic publications and multimedia performance pieces, explores themes such as the Anthropocene, geoengineering, and planetary evolution. He is author of *Nature, Technology and the Sacred* (2005) and co-editor of *Risk, Environment and Modernity* (1996), *Re-ordering Nature: Theology, Society and the New Genetics* (2003), *Nature Performed: Environment, Culture and Performance* (2003) and special double issues of *Ecotheology* on 'Ecotheology and Postmodernity' (2004), and *Theory Culture and Society* on 'Changing Climates' (2010). Bron has also co-organised many events with an environmental humanities orientation, including *Between Nature: Explorations in Ecology and Performance* (2000), *Experimentality*, a year-long collaborative research programme on experimentation in the sciences, arts, and wider society (2009–2010), and *Anthropocene Monument*, with Bruno Latour and Olivier Michelon (2014–2015).

Thom van Dooren is a senior lecturer in environmental humanities at the University of New South Wales in Sydney, Australia. His current work focuses primarily on the philosophical and ethical dimensions of species extinctions and wildlife management and is rooted in an approach that draws the humanities into conversation with ecology, biology, ethology, and ethnographic work with communities whose lives are entangled with disappearing species in a range of different ways. Thom is the author of *Flight Ways: Life and Loss at the Edge of Extinction* (2014) and founding co-editor of the international open-access journal *Environmental Humanities*. He has been a Humboldt Research Fellow at the Rachel Carson Center, Munich, and has held visiting positions at the University of California at Santa Cruz and the KTH Royal Institute of Technology, Sweden.

Cosetta Veronese holds a doctorate in English literature from the University of Venice and one in Italian literature from the University of Birmingham. She has worked at the Universities of Portsmouth, Birmingham (United Kingdom), and Basel (Switzerland) and is author of various contributions on English and Italian literature and on the cinema of Francesco Rosi. She has specialised on the work and thought of Giacomo Leopardi, is honorary research fellow at the Leopardi Centre at Birmingham, and, together with Andreia Guerini at the Universidade Federal de Santa Catarina, co-editor of the online journal *Appunti leopardiani*. Cosetta has recently coordinated a special issue of the Journal on Leopardi and animal ethics, in which she published a contribution on biocentrism and humanism (2014).

Wendy Wheeler is Professor Emerita of English Literature and Cultural Inquiry at London Metropolitan University. She is also a visiting professor at Goldsmiths, University of London, and RMIT in Melbourne, Australia. She has been a visiting professor in the Literature and the Environment programme at the University of Oregon, and a visiting research fellow at the Institute of Advanced Study in the Humanities at the University of Edinburgh, where she also collaborated on the Environmental Values project between 2008 and 2010. In 2014, Wendy gave the first annual University of Tartu Jakob von Uexküll lecture to the European Association for the Study of Literature, Culture, and the Environment in Estonia. She is the author of four books, two on biosemiotics, and many essays on the same topic in journals and edited collections. She is on the advisory board of the journal *New Formations* and on the editorial boards of *Green Letters: Studies in Ecocriticism, Cybernetics* *and Human Knowing*, and *Biosemiotics*. Her latest book, *Expecting the Eart h: Life|Culture|Biosemiotics*, was published in 2016.

Jan Zalasiewicz is a geologist and Professor of Palaeobiology at the University of Leicester, United Kingdom, with a background as a field geologist, palaeontologist, sedimentologist, and stratigrapher and experience of a range of rocks ranging from the present to half a billion years or so in age. He is Chair of the Anthropocene Working Group of the International Commission on Stratigraphy, the body that is analysing the case for formalization of the Anthropocene within the geological time scale. His books include *Ocean Worlds: The Story of Seas on Earth and Other Planets* (with M. Williams, 2014), *The Goldilocks Planet: An Earth History of Climate Change* (with M. Williams, 2012), *The Planet in a Pebble: A Journey through Earth History* (2010), and *The Earth after Us* (2008).

Hubert Zapf is Professor and Chair of American Literature at the University of Augsburg and a faculty member of the Ethics of Textual Cultures Graduate Program within the Elite Study-Network of Bavaria. His main areas of research are literature and cultural ecology, English and American literature, literary history, literary, and cultural theory. Besides numerous articles, his publications include the monographs *Literatur als kulturelle Ökologie* (2002) and *Literature as Cultural Ecology: Sustainable Texts* (2016) and the edited collections *Kulturökologie und Literatur: Ein transdisziplinäres Paradigma der Literaturwissenschaft* (2008), *Amerikanische Literaturgeschichte* (3rd ed. 2010), *Redefining Modernism and Postmodernism* (with Sebnem Toplu, 2010), and *American Studies Today: New Research Agendas* (with Winfried Fluck, Erik Redling, and Sabine Sielke, 2014). Hubert has edited the two special issues of the journal *Anglia* on 'Literature and Ecology' (124.1, 2006) and on 'Literature and Science' (133.1, 2015), and the collection Handbook of Ecocriticism and Cultural Ecology (Berlin, 2016).